Praise for *The Politics of Congressional Elections, Eleventh Edition*

"Carson and Jacobson offer the most up-to-dat' treatment of congressional elections available. I interesting to specialists and accessible to nonsp key developments and puts them in historical c(not just what has changed in congressional elec national politics and policy."

D0705885

— Frances E. Lee, Princeton University

"*The Politics of Congressional Elections* has long been a valuable resource for scholars, students, and anyone else interested in elections. This edition is no exception as Carson and Jacobson provide thorough, thoughtful, and accessible analyses and discussions on a wide range of topics."

— Ryan Williamson, University of Wyoming

"Carson and Jacobson provide the definitive account of congressional elections and how they influence the larger American political system. The authors have done a commendable job of balancing both rigor and approachability such that the text can be of value to both researchers and students alike. The updates to this most recent edition ensure that Carson and Jacobson will be required reading for anyone who wants to understand the contemporary Congress and its electoral politics."

— Joel Sievert, Texas Tech University

"*The Politics of Congressional Elections* once again provides simple, straightforward, yet detailed, analysis of a complex and ever-changing electoral environment. This book continues to be a must-read for anyone interested in congressional elections and their influence on all facets of American politics."

— Sarah Treul, University of North Carolina at Chapel Hill

"Carson and Jacobson's *The Politics of Congressional Elections* remains the gold standard in texts about legislative elections and their implications. This edition, updated to include the 2022 midterm cycle, offers important insight into the increasing nationalization of elections and the effects of these dynamics on how Congress does (and does not) work. It is a must-read for students and scholars alike."

— Tracy Sulkin, University of Illinois

THE POLITICS OF
CONGRESSIONAL ELECTIONS

ELEVENTH EDITION

JAMIE L. CARSON

UNIVERSITY OF GEORGIA

GARY C. JACOBSON

UNIVERSITY OF CALIFORNIA SAN DIEGO

ROWMAN & LITTLEFIELD

Lanham · Boulder · New York · London

Executive Acquisitions Editor: Michael Kerns
Assistant Editor: Elizabeth Von Buhr
Sales and Marketing Inquiries: textbooks@rowman.com

Credits and acknowledgments for material borrowed from other sources,
and reproduced with permission, appear on the appropriate pages within the text.

Published by Rowman & Littlefield
An imprint of The Rowman & Littlefield Publishing Group, Inc.
4501 Forbes Boulevard, Suite 200, Lanham, Maryland 20706
www.rowman.com

86-90 Paul Street, London EC2A 4NE

British Library Cataloguing in Publication Information Available

Library of Congress Cataloging-in-Publication Data

Names: Carson, Jamie L., author. | Jacobson, Gary C., author.
Title: The politics of congressional elections / Jamie L. Carson, Gary C. Jacobson.
Description: Eleventh editon. | Lanham, Maryland : Rowman & Littlefield, 2024. |
  Includes bibliographical references and index.
Identifiers: LCCN 2023030233 (print) | LCCN 2023030234 (ebook) |
  ISBN 9781538176733 (paperback) | ISBN 9781538176740 (epub)
Subjects: LCSH: United States. Congress—Elections.
Classification: LCC JK1976 .J27 2024 (print) | LCC JK1976 (ebook) |
  DDC 324.973—dc23
LC record available at https://lccn.loc.gov/2023030233
LC ebook record available at https://lccn.loc.gov/2023030234

For Marty and Karen

For Tammy

Contents

★　★　★

List of Figures

★ ★ ★

List of Tables

★ ★ ★

Preface

★ ★ ★

FOR THIS ELEVENTH EDITION OF *The Politics of Congressional Elections*, we extend the ongoing analysis of congressional elections initiated with the first edition published back in 1983. This new edition includes:

- Updated coverage through the 2022 elections, including analysis of key 2022 House races that contributed to changes in partisan control of the chamber;
- Thorough examination of the increasing nationalization of electoral politics that has produced more president- and party-centered congressional elections and a striking decline in the incumbency advantage;
- Expanded and updated analysis of campaign finance in light of record candidate spending and analysis of voter turnout, which was again incredibly high for a midterm election;
- Enhanced analysis of congressional elections data extending back to the pre–Civil War era.

The eleventh edition is also available in a full-color e-book, and instructors will have access to PowerPoint presentations of all tables and figures.

Like the previous ten editions, this book is about congressional election politics, broadly understood. In writing it, we have kept in mind that elections are means, not ends in themselves. What happens during campaigns or on election days is, of course, fascinating and important, and the authors do not neglect congressional candidates, campaigns, and voters. But campaigns and elections are more than curious rituals only because they reflect deeper structural patterns and currents in American political life and help determine how—and how well—we are governed. Part of the book is therefore devoted to tracing the connections between the electoral politics of Congress and other important political phenomena. Examining congressional election politics in this way inevitably raises fundamental questions about representation and responsibility, and these are the central normative concerns of the book. The intent here, then, is to offer a systematic account of what goes on in congressional elections and to show how electoral politics reflect and shape other basic components of the political system, with profound consequences for representative government.

Research on congressional elections continues to thrive, and it will quickly become clear to the reader how much the authors have learned from the work and ideas of other scholars. Information on congressional voters, candidates, and campaign finances becomes richer with each passing election as well. The American National Election Studies time series continues, but only for presidential election years. When the National Science Foundation declined to finance midterm election studies over a decade ago, other academic research teams picked up the slack, most notably with the Cooperative Election Study (formerly the Cooperative Congressional Election Study), which now delivers data on samples large enough to support inferences about state and district electorates. Innovative large-scale data collections on campaign advertising and campaign contributors have now been added to the mix as well. These developments, along with the remarkable upheavals produced by the congressional elections of the early 1990s and the rapid shifts in party fortunes recorded between 2006 and 2022, continue to make thinking and writing about congressional elections an intellectual pleasure.

Jacobson remains deeply indebted to the many friends and colleagues who have guided and stimulated his thinking about congressional election politics. The genesis of this book was his work as a member of the Committee on Congressional Election Research of the Board of Overseers of National Election Studies, which designed the congressional component included in American National Election Studies since 1978. Everyone he worked with on the committee contributed to it in some way: Alan Abramowitz, David Brady, Heinz Eulau, Richard Fenno, John Ferejohn, Morris Fiorina, Barbara Hinckley, Malcolm Jewell, Jack Katosh, James Kuklinski, Thomas Mann, David Mayhew, Warren Miller, Glenn Parker, Barbara Sinclair, Michael Traugott, Raymond Wolfinger, and Gerald Wright.

Subsequently, continuing association with the National Election Studies Board helped keep him in touch with other scholars who contributed in various ways to his understanding of congressional elections and politics: Larry Barrels, Richard Brody, Stanley Feldman, William Flanigan, Charles Franklin, Edie Goldenberg, Mary Jackman, Stanley

Kelley, Rod Kiewiet, Donald Kinder, David Leege, Douglas Rivers, Steven Rosenstone, Gina Sapiro, Merrill Shanks, Walter Stone, Mark Westlye, and John Zaller. More recently, Steve Ansolabehere deserves special thanks for making Jacobson's involvement in the Cooperative Election Study project so productive.

Jacobson is also grateful to past and present colleagues at the University of California, San Diego, for providing an environment wonderfully conducive to scholarly work. Samuel Kernell read and commented on several chapters and has shared some of the research reported in the book. Jacobson also enjoyed instructive and stimulating conversations with Nathaniel Beck, Amy Bridges, Peter Cowhey, Gary Cox, Scott Desposato, Elizabeth Gerber, Seth Hill, Thad Kousser, Richard Kronick, David Laitin, Skip Lupia, Mathew McCubbins, John Mendeloff, Keith Poole, and Samuel Popkin. Mo Fiorina, Herbert Jacob, Burdett Loomis, Tom Mann, and Steve Rosenstone read the entire manuscript of the first edition, and their service continues to register down the years. John Bertalan, Jon Bond, Matthew Childers, Garrett Glasgow, Jason MacDonald, Franco Mattei, Timothy Nokken, Lynda Powell, David W. Romero, Priscilla Southwell, Wayne Steger, Michael Tofias, Darrell West, and many anonymous scholars reviewed previous editions; this new one benefited from the reviews of Matthew C. Dempsey, Reed Welch, Ryan D. Williamson, and Simon Zschirnt. The book is better for their suggestions and probably the worse for the authors' not having heeded more of them.

Jacobson is obliged to Denise Gimlin, Edward Lazarus, Del Powell, and David Wilsford for helping to gather some of the data analyzed in Chapter 6. Greg Bovitz, Mike Dimock, Tommy Kim, and Jeff Lazarus helped with earlier revisions in various important ways (whether they know it or not). He is grateful, too, to colleagues who have generously shared data with him: James E. Campbell, George W. Edwards III, Michael Malbin, Nolan McCarty, Norman J. Ornstein, Keith T. Poole, and Howard Rosenthal.

Carson is thankful for conversations with a number of his current and former colleagues at the University of Georgia about various aspects of this book, including Ryan Bakker, Alexa Bankert, Michael Lynch, Anthony Madonna, Steve Nicholson, and Geoff Sheagley. He also would like to thank Jason Byers, Spencer Hardin, Aaron Hitefield, Mark Owens, Stephen Pettigrew, Ridge Powelson, Jason Roberts, Joel Sievert, Ryan Williamson, and Stewart Ulrich for assistance with data collection and help with creating figures in Stata.

Part of the research reported here was supported by a grant from the National Science Foundation (SES-80-7577), for which Jacobson is most grateful. Some of the data used in this book were made available by the Inter-university Consortium for Political and Social Research.

The data for the 1978–2008 American National Election Studies and the 1988–1992 Senate Election Study were originally collected by the Center for Political Studies of the Institute for Social Research, University of Michigan, under grants from the National Science Foundation. Neither the original collectors of the data nor the consortium bears any responsibility for the analyses and interpretations presented here, and the same, of course, holds for anyone else the authors have mentioned.

Finally, we want to thank the folks at Rowman & Littlefield—Michael Kerns, Elizabeth Von Buhr, Jehanne Schweitzer, Alden Perkins, and Ami Reitmeir—for their assistance in pulling together the eleventh edition of this book. They have been great to work with, and we appreciate their ideas and inspiration along the way. We also wish to thank Anu Sivakolundhu, the Project Manager at Integra Software Services, who oversaw production of this latest edition of the book.

1

Introduction

★ ★ ★

ELECTIONS STAND AT THE CORE of American political life. They provide ritual expression of the myth that makes political authority legitimate: We are governed, albeit indirectly, by our own consent. Elections are also the focus of thoroughly practical politics. They determine who will hold positions of real power in the political system and, by establishing a framework in which power is pursued, profoundly affect the behavior of people holding or seeking power. The mythical and practical components of elections meet at the point where electoral constraints are supposed to make leaders responsive and responsible to the public. How comfortably they fit together has deep consequences for the entire political system. Almost any important development in American political life will be intertwined with the electoral process.

Congressional elections in particular are intimately linked to many basic phenomena of American politics. In countless ways, obvious and subtle, they affect the performance of Congress and, through it, the entire government. At the same time, they reflect the changing political landscape, revealing as well as shaping its fundamental contours.

The basic questions to be asked about congressional elections are straightforward: Who gets elected to Congress and how? Why do people vote the way they do in congressional elections? How do electoral politics affect the way Congress works and the kinds of policies it produces? What kind of representation do congressional elections really provide? Every answer has further implications for the workings of American politics, and we must trace many of these out in order to grasp the deeper role of congressional elections in the political process.

This book aims to explain what goes on in congressional elections and to provide an understanding of how they connect in myriad ways with other aspects of American political life. It also has a more pointed intention: to use a careful examination of the complex, multifaceted business of electing Congress to help elucidate why politicians in Washington find it so difficult to fashion measured solutions to pressing national problems.

A central theme in earlier editions of this book was that Congress's institutional performance suffered from an electoral process that gave senators and representatives every reason to be individually responsive but little reason to be collectively responsible. Since the third edition was published, the chickens of collective irresponsibility have come home to roost. First, the 1992 elections brought the highest turnover of House seats in fifty years. Then the 1994 elections put Republicans in control of both houses of Congress for the first time in forty years. Republicans maintained power by narrow margins (though losing the Senate for a time in the 107th Congress because of a party switcher) until the 2006 election, when public dissatisfaction with the Republican regime put Democrats back in control. The brief period of unified government after the 2008 election ended dramatically in 2010, when unhappiness with a Democratic president and Congress gave Republicans their largest House majority since 1946. That majority became even larger after 2014, when Republicans also regained control of the Senate. Despite winning the presidency in 2016, Republicans lost seats in both the House and Senate but not enough to create divided government. Following the referendum on President Trump in 2018, Democrats gained control of the House while Republicans shored up control of the Senate. In 2022, the Republicans narrowly gained control of the House but actually lost a seat in the Senate despite relatively low levels of popularity for President Biden, ensuring divided government for the foreseeable future.

Meanwhile, party loyalty and ideological polarization in Congress have grown apace, and imposing collective responsibility on its members has become far more feasible. But the consequence of stronger, more unified parties has been not responsible party government but rather legislative stalemate and partisan gridlock. These developments have raised many new questions and opened many new possibilities for analysis, and we spend a good deal of time in this edition examining their electoral bases.

Congressional elections are complex, multifaceted events. This is evident in the number of different perspectives from which we can examine congressional elections. Consider the alternative ways to answer the question, "How's the congressional election going?" A candidate or campaign manager would immediately begin talking about what was going on in the district or state, who was ahead, what groups were supporting which candidate, how much money was coming in, what issues were emerging, what the campaign ads were saying, and so on. A national party leader—the president, for example—would respond in terms of how many seats the party might gain or lose in the House and Senate and what that might mean for the administration's programs. A private citizen might grumble about the hot air, mudslinging, and general perfidy of politicians—or be scarcely aware that an election was taking place.

Similarly, political scientists and other people who study congressional elections do so from a variety of research orientations. Some study voters: Why do people vote the way they do? Why do they vote at all? Others study candidates and campaigns: Who runs for Congress and why? What goes on in campaigns? How is money raised and spent—and what difference does it make? How do national parties and independent spending groups affect campaigns? Or they explore the aggregate results of congressional elections: What accounts for the changes in the distribution of House and Senate seats between the two parties? Still others are interested in representation: How are the performance of Congress as an institution and the activities of its members connected with what goes on in elections? These and other questions deserve individual attention. But it is no less essential to understand how they all interrelate.

People involved in congressional elections are at least implicitly aware of the connections between the different levels of analysis. Voters were once interested primarily in the candidates and campaigns in their state or district, but many are now conscious of the broader political context and may, for example, adapt their congressional voting decision to their feelings about presidential candidates or presidents. Presidents worried about the overall makeup of the Congress are by no means indifferent to individual races and sometimes involve themselves in local campaigns. Candidates and other congressional activists are mindful of national as well as local political conditions that they believe influence election outcomes, and of course they spend a great deal of time trying to figure out how to appeal effectively to individual voters.

Scholars, too, are fully aware that, although research strategies dictate that the congressional election terrain be subdivided into workable plots, no aspect of congressional elections can be understood in isolation. It is essential to integrate various streams of investigation to obtain a clear account of what is going on. This is no simple task. One difficulty is quite familiar to students of the social sciences: how to connect the accounts of individual behavior to large-scale social phenomena. The problem is one of coordinating the micro- and macro-level accounts of political behavior (there are middle levels, too, of course). But it turns out to be a most fruitful problem. Its solution is a rich source of insight into congressional election processes and their consequences.

This book examines congressional elections from several perspectives while attending throughout to the interconnections among them.

Chapter 2 sets out the legal and institutional context in which congressional elections take place. This formal context is easily taken for granted and overlooked, but it is, on reflection, fundamental. The very existence of congressional elections depends on this structure, which shapes them in a great many important ways. Chapter 2 also surveys briefly the rich variety of social, economic, and ethnic mixes found among states and congressional districts, for this diversity underlies many distinctive aspects of congressional election politics.

Chapters 3 and 4 examine, respectively, congressional candidates and campaigns. The pervasive if variable and, at present, declining effects of incumbency inject a theme common to both of these chapters. The resources, strategies, and tactics of candidates vary sharply, depending on whether a candidate is an incumbent, a challenger to an incumbent, or running for an open seat where neither candidate is an incumbent. They also differ between House and Senate candidates in each of these categories. These chapters explore the strategies of candidates in different electoral situations and the consequences of diverse strategies, as well as the influences of campaign money, organization, campaign activities and tactics, the national parties, outside advocacy groups, and the local political context. Campaigns both reflect and work to reinforce candidates' assumptions about the electorate, and they are also closely linked to the behavior in office of those elected.

Chapter 5 deals with voting in congressional elections. Information about who votes and what influences the voting decision is valuable in its own right, but such knowledge is even more important as a means of understanding what congressional elections mean—what they can and cannot accomplish. The way voters react is tied closely to the behavior of candidates and the design and operation of campaigns—and to what members of Congress do in office.

Chapter 6 examines congressional elections as aggregate phenomena. When all the individual contests are summed up over an election year, the collective outcome determines which party controls each chamber and with how large a majority. It also strongly influences the kinds of national policies that emerge; it is at this level that the American people impose, or fail to impose, collective responsibility on their national legislature. Congressional elections clearly respond to aggregate political conditions. But aggregate outcomes are no more than the summation of individual voting decisions in the districts to election results across all districts. The path that leads from aggregate political conditions to individual voting decisions to aggregate congressional election outcomes is surprisingly complicated; candidates' strategies turn out to provide a critical connecting link. Reviews of each biennial election from 1992 through 2022 illustrate the points in this chapter.

Finally, of course, congressional elections are important for how they influence the behavior of elected leaders and therefore the success or failure of politics. In fact, the knowledge that they are elected officials is the key to understanding why members of Congress do what they do in office. It matters not only that they are elected but how. How candidates mount campaigns and how voters choose between them has a crucial effect on what members of Congress do with their time and other resources and with the quality, quantity, and direction of their legislative work. Electoral necessities enhance or restrict in predictable ways the influence of individuals, groups, parties, congressional leaders, and presidents. And all these things affect the performance of Congress as a policy-making institution. Chapter 7 argues these points and explores the electoral basis of the record levels of partisan polarization observable in both chambers, considers proposed congressional reform, and speculates about the elections of 2024 and beyond.

2

The Context

★ ★ ★

SINCE THE EARLY 1990S, the growing influence of national partisan forces has challenged the ascendant importance of individual candidates and campaigns that characterized the electoral politics of Congress from the 1960s through the 1980s. Elections during the past two decades have, as we shall see, set new records for partisan electoral coherence across states, districts, and federal offices. Nonetheless, congressional campaigns themselves continue to be largely candidate- rather than party-focused affairs. Even as national forces have come to exert a powerful influence on the results, their effects continue to vary according to how they are exploited locally. National party organizations have greatly expanded their efforts to recruit and finance candidates, but their ability to produce victories still depends to an important extent on the decisions of politicians operating as individual political entrepreneurs. Despite the strong financial support that the most promising congressional aspirants can now expect from national parties and independent organizations, individual candidates still absorb the balance of the risks, pains, and rewards of mounting a campaign. Most instigate their own candidacies, raise the bulk of their own resources (at least the crucial early money that signals a viable candidacy), and put together their own campaign organizations. Their skills, resources, and strategies continue to have an important effect on election outcomes. Although voters exhibit growing partisan loyalty, ideological consistency, and attentiveness to national issues and leaders, their assessments of the particular candidates running in their states and districts continue to influence their decisions strongly.

This chapter reviews some of the features of American electoral institutions that encouraged and facilitated candidate-centered electoral politics during the twentieth century and continue to contribute an irreducible local component to congressional elections, even in an era of strongly partisan and nationalized electoral politics. It examines the constitutional, legal, and political contexts in which elections take place—for these are fundamental sources of the electoral habits and practices that characterize the uniquely American process for electing a national legislature, and it cannot be understood apart from them.

THE CONSTITUTIONAL FRAMEWORK

Whether to have an elected legislature was never a question during the Constitutional Convention that met in Philadelphia in 1787. The influence of British parliamentary tradition and colonial experience was decisive—all thirteen colonies had legislatures with at least one popularly elected house. Beyond question, the new government would have one. But not much else about it was certain. Delegates disagreed about how the legislative branch would be organized, what its powers would be, and how its members would be selected.

The matter of selection involved several important issues. The most crucial was the basis of representation: How were seats in the legislature to be apportioned? Delegates from large states naturally preferred representation according to population; otherwise, their constituents would be underrepresented. Those from smaller states were convinced that their interests would be in jeopardy if only numbers counted, so they proposed equal representation for each state. The controversy coincided with another unsettled and unsettling issue: Was the government to be a national one representing a national citizenry or a federal one representing sovereign states?[1]

A quintessential political deal resolved the conflict. General sentiment strongly favored a bicameral legislature,[2] and this made a solution easier. Each side got what it wanted. Seats in one chamber, the House of Representatives, would be apportioned by population; each state's representation would be determined by its share of the population as measured in a decennial census (Article I, Section 2 of the US Constitution). In the other chamber, the Senate, states would enjoy equal representation, each choosing two senators (Article I, Section 3).

This "great compromise," as it has been called, opened the way for resolving another dispute. At issue was the extent of popular participation in electing officials in the new government. Most delegates were skeptical of democracy as they conceived it, but to varying degrees. A bicameral legislature allowed different levels of popular involvement in

---

[1]See James Madison, Alexander Hamilton, and John Jay, *The Federalist*, ed. Edward Meade Earle (New York: Modern Library, 1937), nos. 37 and 39.

[2]Ten of the thirteen colonies and, of course, Britain had bicameral legislatures.

choosing members of Congress. Representatives were to be "popularly"[3] chosen in frequent elections. Biennial elections were the compromise choice between the annual elections proposed by many delegates and the three-year term advocated by James Madison.[4] Broad suffrage and short terms were meant to ensure that one branch of government, the House, remained as close as possible to the people.

The framers designed the Senate, in contrast, to be much more insulated from momentary shifts in the public mood. They set the term of office at six years (another compromise, as terms of three, four, five, six, seven, and nine years had been proposed).[5] Election of one-third of the Senate's membership every two years enhanced continuity. Furthermore, state legislatures rather than voters chose the senators. The Senate could thus act as a stable and dispassionate counterweight to the more popular and radical House, protecting the new government from the volatility thought to be characteristic of democracies. Its structure could also embody the elements of state sovereignty that remained.[6]

The opposition to popular democracy embodied in the indirect election of senators diminished during the nineteenth century. Restrictions on suffrage were gradually lifted, and more and more offices came to be filled by popular election. The Civil War effectively settled the issue of national sovereignty. By the beginning of the twentieth century, most Americans had come to view the constitutional method of choosing senators as undemocratic and corrupt; the Seventeenth Amendment (ratified in 1913) replaced it with popular election. Members of both houses of Congress are now chosen in elections in which nearly every citizen eighteen years and older is eligible to vote.[7]

CONGRESSIONAL DISTRICTS

The Constitution itself apportioned seats among states for the first Congress (Article I, Section 3). Following the initial census in 1790, membership of the House was set at 105, with each state given one seat for every 33,000 inhabitants. From that point on, until 1911, the House grew as

---

[3]The Constitution specifies, "Electors in each State shall have the Qualifications requisite for the Electors of the most numerous Branch of the State Legislature" (art. 1, § 2). Property and other qualifications were, in fact, common in the early years of the nation; universal suffrage was a long time in arriving.

[4]*Electing Congress* (Washington, DC: Congressional Quarterly Press, 1978), 135.

[5]*Electing Congress*, 135.

[6]Madison, Hamilton, and Jay, *The Federalist*, No. 62.

[7]The exceptions are people in penal and other institutions and, in many states, former felons. Senate seats vacated because of retirement, death, or resignation before the end of the term may be filled by special gubernatorial appointment until the next regular general election; vacated House seats are filled by special elections.

the population increased and new states joined the nation. Congress added seats after each decennial census to limit the politically painful reductions in representation faced by states suffering unfavorable population shifts. Eventually, however, its leaders concluded that further growth could seriously impair the House's efficiency. Membership was set at 435 after the 1910 census, and there developed a strong opposition to any further increase.

A crisis thus arrived with the 1920 census results. Large population shifts between 1910 and 1920 and a fixed House membership would mean that many states—and members of Congress—would lose seats. Adding to the turmoil was the census's revelation that, for the first time, a majority of Americans lived in urban rather than rural areas. Reapportionment was certain to increase the political weight of city dwellers and reduce that of farmers. The result was an acrimonious stalemate that was not resolved until 1929, with passage of a law establishing a permanent system for reapportioning the 435 House seats after each census; it would be carried out, if necessary, without additional legislation.[8]

The new system took effect after the 1930 census. Because twenty years had passed since the last apportionment, unusually large shifts occurred, with twenty-seven seats redistributed from slower- to faster-growing states; the big winner was California, which went from eleven to twenty districts. Subsequent shifts have not been so dramatic, but the beginning of each decade still ushers in a period of heightened uncertainty and anxiety among congressional incumbents.

This anxiety is not misplaced. In 2022, redistricting gave forty members the choice of retiring or facing another incumbent in the primary or general election. Thirty-two retired; eight ended up losing contests to other incumbents. As in past decades, the new distribution of House seats following the 2020 census reflected population shifts since the previous census, redistributing power among states and regions. States in the East and Midwest lost a total of six seats to states in the South and West. Texas gained two seats; Colorado, Florida, Montana, North Carolina, and Oregon, one each. California, Illinois, Michigan, New York, Ohio, Pennsylvania, and West Virginia each lost one seat. Table 2.1 displays the distribution of House seats after the 2020 census resulting from these changes.

At first, federal law fixed only the number of representatives each state could elect; other important aspects of districting were left to the states. Until 1842, single-member districts were not required by law, and a number of states used multimember or at-large districts. Thereafter, apportionment legislation usually required that states establish

---

[8]*Congressional Quarterly's Guide to U.S. Elections* (Washington, DC: Congressional Quarterly Press, 1976), 530–34.

Table 2.1 The Apportionment of House Seats after the 2020 Census

State	2020 Seats	Change from 2010	State	2020 Seats	Change from 2010
California	52	−1	Louisiana	6	0
Texas	38	2	Oregon	6	1
Florida	28	1	Connecticut	5	0
New York	26	−1	Oklahoma	5	0
Illinois	17	−1	Arkansas	4	0
Pennsylvania	17	−1	Iowa	4	0
Ohio	15	−1	Kansas	4	0
Georgia	14	0	Mississippi	4	0
Michigan	13	−1	Nevada	4	0
North Carolina	14	1	Utah	4	0
New Jersey	12	0	Nebraska	3	0
Virginia	11	0	New Mexico	3	0
Washington	10	0	West Virginia	2	−1
Arizona	9	0	Hawaii	2	0
Indiana	9	0	Idaho	2	0
Massachusetts	9	0	Maine	2	0
Tennessee	9	0	New Hampshire	2	0
Maryland	8	0	Rhode Island	2	0
Minnesota	8	0	Montana	2	1
Missouri	8	0	Alaska	1	0
Wisconsin	8	0	Delaware	1	0
Colorado	8	1	North Dakota	1	0
Alabama	7	0	South Dakota	1	0
South Carolina	7	0	Vermont	1	0
Kentucky	6	0	Wyoming	1	0

Source: US Bureau of the Census, https://www.census.gov/library/visualizations/2021/dec/2020-apportionment-map.html.

contiguous single-member districts, and in some years it required that they be of roughly equal populations and even "compact" in shape. Such requirements were never (when ignored by mapmakers) successfully enforced. Single-member districts became the overwhelming norm by the 1870s, but districts composed of "contiguous and compact territory … containing as nearly as practicable an equal number of inhabitants," in the words of the 1901 Reapportionment Act, did not.[9]

Many states continued to draw districts with widely differing populations. In 1930, for example, New York's largest district (766,425) contained nearly nine times as many people as its smallest (90,671).

---

[9]*Congressional Quarterly's Guide to U.S. Elections*, 528.

As recently as 1962, the most populous district in Michigan (802,994) had 4.5 times the inhabitants of its least populous (177,431).[10] Rural populations were usually overrepresented at the expense of people living in cities and suburbs. The Supreme Court's 1964 ruling in *Wesberry v. Sanders*,[11] however, applied the principle of one person, one vote to congressional districts, and since then malapportioned districts have, under the watchful eye of the courts, become extinct. Surprisingly, however, the question of which persons should count for redistricting purposes remained unresolved until recently. Conservative activists—who want only eligible voters, not the entire population, to be included in the calculations—have challenged the common use of whole populations for years. They aim to produce a larger share of Republican-dominated districts by eliminating noncitizens, most of them Latino, from the count.

After years of avoiding the issue, the Supreme Court took up the question and in 2016 decided unanimously that the entire population was to be counted.[12] In 2018, the Trump administration took another crack at diminishing the political strength of regions with an abundance of noncitizens by proposing that the 2020 census ask about individuals' citizenship status, a step that would lead many of the ten million or so undocumented US residents to avoid the census and thus be left out of the count. In late June of 2019, the Supreme Court halted the move toward including a question about citizenship on the 2020 census on the grounds that the administration's justification for doing so had been disingenuous; a firm deadline for printing the census forms left no time for another justification to be prepared and reviewed in court, compelling the administration to abandon the effort. The onset of the coronavirus pandemic just as the 2020 census was getting underway raised new and related concerns about undercounting voters as a result of widespread disruptions around the country.[13]

Partisan Gerrymandering

The requirement of equal district populations encouraged another old political custom: gerrymandering. District boundaries are not politically neutral. Parties controlling state governments are naturally tempted to draw district lines to maximize the number of seats they can win, given the number and distribution of their usual voters. The idea is to concentrate

---

[10]*Congressional Quarterly's Guide to U.S. Elections*, 528.

[11]U.S. 1 (1964).

[12]*Evenwel v. Abbott*, 578 U.S. ___ (2016).

[13]D'Vera Cohn and Jeffrey S. Passel, "Key Facts about the Quality of the 2020 Census," *Pew Research Center*, June 8, 2022, https://www.pewresearch.org/fact-tank/2022/06/08/key-facts-about-the-quality-of-the-2020-census/

the opposing party's voters in a small number of districts that it can win by wide margins, thus "wasting" many of its votes, and to create as many districts as possible where the controlling party has a secure, though not overwhelming, majority.[14] Forced by the Court's strict standard of equality to ignore community boundaries in drawing districts, legislators are freer to pursue naked partisan advantage. Modern computer technology allows precise integration of partisan with egalitarian objectives.[15]

Partisan gerrymanders are easier to calculate than to carry out, however. Arrangements that might add to a party's share of seats often conflict with other political necessities, particularly the protection of incumbents unwilling to increase their own electoral risks to improve their party's collective welfare.[16] Voters more attuned to candidates than to parties have sometimes frustrated partisan schemes.[17] But given the opportunity, state legislators routinely try to draw lines favoring their party's House candidates—and they often succeed. The redistricting activity that followed the 2020 census offers an example of how effective partisan gerrymandering can be.

The Republicans' victories in 2020 statewide legislative races provided ample opportunities for subsequent gerrymandering. They controlled the redistricting process in nineteen states, with a total of 177 House seats, including four states in which the allocation of seats changed (two lost seats; two gained seats). Democrats controlled the process in only seven states, with a total of forty-nine seats; only two had a change in seat allocation. (In one of the remaining states, the parties shared control; nine were redistricted by commissions, eight were determined by courts, and six were single-district states.) Republicans exploited this opportunity to shore up some of their marginal districts, adding Republican voters where their seats were most vulnerable.[18] This is clear from an analysis of Charlie Cook's Partisan Voting Index (PVI), computed for 2022 as the difference between the average district-level presidential vote in 2016 and 2020 and the national presidential vote averages

[14]Bruce E. Cain, *The Reapportionment Puzzle* (Berkeley: University of California Press, 1984), 148–50.

[15]David Cottrell, "Using Computer Simulations to Measure the Effect of Gerrymandering on Electoral Competition in the U.S. Congress," *Legislative Studies Quarterly* 44 (2019): 487–514.

[16]Cain, *Reapportionment*, 151–57.

[17]Richard Born, "Partisan Intentions and Election Day Realities in the Congressional Redistricting Process," *American Political Science Review* 79 (1985): 317.

[18]Chris Leaverton, "Who Controlled Redistricting in Every State," *Brennan Center*, October 5, 2022, https://www.brennancenter.org/our-work/research-reports/who-controlled-redistricting-every-state, accessed February 21, 2023.

Table 2.2 Control of Redistricting and Changes in the District Partisan Balance, 2020–2022

Control of Redistricting		District Partisan Advantage (from Cook PVI)		
		Democrat >2	Balanced	Republican >2
All districts	2020	189	34	212
	2022	187	31	217
	Change	−2	−3	+5
Republican control	2020	45	13	127
	2022	40	5	133
	Change	−5	−8	+6
Other control	2020	144	21	85
	2022	147	26	84
	Change	+3	+5	−1

Source: David Wasserman, "Introducing the 2022 Cook Political Report Partisan Vote Index," *Cook Political Report*, July 13, 2022, https://www.cookpolitical.com/cook-pvi/2022-partisan-voting-index/introducing-2022-cook-partisan-voting-index (accessed March 1, 2023).

for these elections.[19] For example, with the national average of the Democratic presidential vote in these two elections at 51.7 percent, a district in which the average was 53.7 percent would have a PVI of +2, whereas a district in which the average was 49.7 percent would have a PVI of −2.

As the data in table 2.2 reveal, the Republicans already enjoyed a major advantage by this measure before the 2022 redistricting, with 212 Republican-leaning districts (defined here as having a PVI less than −2), compared with 189 Democratic-leaning districts (PVI greater than 2); the remaining thirty-four districts were balanced with PVIs between −2 and +2. After the 2022 redistricting, there were five more Republican-leaning districts, two fewer Democratic-leaning districts, and three fewer balanced districts. This result was obviously intended; where Republicans controlled redistricting, the party gained six favorable districts, the Democrats lost five, and balanced districts were reduced by eight. Where Republicans did not control the process, Democrats gained three favorable districts, Republicans lost one, and the number of balanced districts increased by five.

Once the votes were counted, House election results matched district leanings as measured by the PVI with great consistency (table 2.3). Only eight Democrats won Republican-leaning districts in 2022, and five Republicans won in a Democratic-leaning district. The balanced districts favored Democrats by a nearly three to one advantage, despite

---

[19]"2022 Cook PVI^SM: District Map and List," *Cook Political Report*, July 11, 2022, https://www.cookpolitical.com/cook-pvi/2022-partisan-voting-index/district-map-and-list, accessed February 22, 2023.

Table 2.3 District Partisanship and House Election Results, 2022

Cook PVI Advantage	Won by Democrat	Won by Republican	Number of Districts
2022			
Democrat >2	182	5	187
Republican >2	8	209	217
Balanced	23	8	31
Total	213	222	435

Note: The Cook PVI Advantage is described in the text; it is based on the 2016 and 2020 presidential votes for 2022.
Source: Compiled by the authors.

the Democrats only winning 47.8 percent of the national vote share in 2022. These results underline the powerful effect of district partisanship in determining election results in the most recent election, a point we reiterate throughout this book.

Partisan gerrymanders were litigated for several decades before the Supreme Court finally determined in 2019 that "partisan gerrymandering claims present political questions beyond the reach of the federal courts."[20] An earlier Court had declared in 1986 (*Davis v. Bandemer*[21]) that a sufficiently egregious partisan gerrymander could be unconstitutional, but it set no standard for determining what would qualify. In 2004, the Court rejected a challenge to the 2002 Republican gerrymander in Pennsylvania in a 5–4 decision (*Vieth v. Jubelirer*[22]), with four justices concluding that partisan gerrymandering could never be subject to court challenge on the grounds that no coherent standard could be drawn to establish its constitutional limits. A fifth, Justice Anthony Kennedy, left open the possibility of finding a standard while rejecting the challenge in the Pennsylvania case. Each of the four dissenters proposed a different set of criteria, underlining the problem that led the first four to throw up their hands. With Kennedy's departure and replacement by Brent Kavanaugh in 2019, the dissenting view became the opinion of the Court. Free of federal court supervision, the states' partisan configurations and redistricting procedures are free to determine the extent of partisan gerrymandering after the 2020 census.

Redistricting between Censuses

The issue of partisan gerrymandering arose in another guise when Colorado's Republican government, newly elected in 2002, redrew the state's new court-imposed House districts to make two formerly competitive

---

[20]*Rucho v. Common Cause*, No. 18-422, 588 U.S. (2019).
[21]U.S. 109 (1986).
[22]U.S. 267 (2004).

seats safely Republican, aiming to solidify the party's 5–2 majority in the delegation. However, the state's supreme court voided the move on the grounds that the Colorado constitution specified that redistricting take place only once every decade.

Texas Republicans were more successful. They won full control of the Texas state government in the 2002 elections and, at the behest of House Majority Leader Tom DeLay, proposed new district lines that would thoroughly dismantle several House Democrats' districts. The effect would be to give these Democrats largely unfamiliar, more conservative constituencies; to force them to move by placing them in districts with other Democratic incumbents; or, in two cases, to pit them against incumbent Republicans in new, overwhelmingly Republican districts. With nothing in federal or Texas law standing in the Republicans' way, Democrats in the state legislature twice tried to thwart the remap by fleeing the state en masse (once to Oklahoma, once to New Mexico) to prevent action by denying legislative quorums while avoiding arrest under a Texas statute aimed at preventing just this tactic.[23] It took five months and two special legislative sessions before the Democrats capitulated.

The Texas lawmakers did not overestimate the stakes. Prior to the 2003 redistricting, Republicans held fifteen of Texas's thirty-two House seats. After enactment of the new map, one House Democrat (Ralph T. Hall) defected to the Republican Party, another retired, another was defeated in a primary, and four lost in the general election. Only one targeted Democrat, Chet Edwards, managed to survive; he dodged defeat until 2010. After the 2004 election, Republicans held twenty-one of Texas's seats, a gain of six. The Texas gerrymander survived US Supreme Court review in 2006 (*League of United Latin American Citizens v. Perry*[24]); the Court ruled that states were free to redistrict as often as they liked, but it did require Texas to adjust several district boundaries because one district was found to discriminate against Latinos in violation of the Voting Rights Act. Substantively, the new Texas map could hardly be tagged unfair, for it actually reversed a court-drawn plan that had amounted to a pro-Democratic gerrymander; in 2002, Democrats had won 53 percent of the Texas seats with 45 percent of the vote in a state where Al Gore had won 41 percent in 2000.

In redrawing new gerrymandered districts between censuses, Texas was actually reviving a practice once common in many states. For example, Ohio redrew its district map seven times between 1878 and 1892 as

---

[23]DeLay sought help from federal agencies to track the missing Democrats, a move that earned him a formal admonishment from the House Ethics Committee.
[24]U.S. 399 (2006).

control of its government switched back and forth between the parties.[25] This practice coincided with a period, not unlike the present, of heated partisan competition for control of Congress. But obstacles, such as the state constitutional barrier that thwarted the new Colorado gerrymander, make widespread imitation of Texas's example unlikely.

Racial Gerrymandering

In a 1986 decision (*Thornburg v. Gingles*[26]), the Supreme Court construed the Voting Rights Act to require that legislative district lines not discriminate, even unintentionally, against racial minorities. The decision was widely interpreted as requiring mapmakers to design districts in which racial or ethnic minorities comprised a majority of voters wherever residence patterns made this feasible. Assiduous pursuit of this goal, backed by modern computer technology, produced some of the strangest-looking districts on record.

Gerrymandering often produces bizarrely shaped districts; the term itself comes from a cartoon depicting an odd, salamander-like creature suggested by a district drawn under the administration of Elbridge Gerry, an early governor of Massachusetts. Perhaps the most audacious modern example of partisan gerrymandering was Philip Burton's redrawing of the 6th District of California for his brother, John (who surprised everyone by retiring from Congress before he could enjoy it). The district comprised three sections connected only by the waters of San Francisco Bay; just a narrow strip of land underlying some railroad yards linked two parts of one section.

Racial gerrymandering after 1990 inspired some equally creative artwork; the 12th District of North Carolina, for example, stitched together African American communities in several of the state's larger cities, using Interstate 85 (northbound lanes in one county, southbound lanes in another) as the thread. Racial gerrymandering was typically far more effective than partisan gerrymandering: The 1992 elections raised African American representation in the House from twenty-five to thirty-eight and Hispanic representation from ten to seventeen. In 1993, however, a more conservative Court ruled (in *Shaw v. Reno*[27]) that bizarrely shaped districts designed to concentrate minority voters might violate the constitutional rights of white voters. The Court went further in 1995 (*Miller v. Johnson*[28]), striking down Georgia's districting on the grounds that any

---

[25]Erik J. Engstrom and Samuel Kernell, "Manufactured Responsiveness: The Impact of State Electoral Laws on Unified Party Control of the Presidency and House of Representatives, 1840–1940," *American Journal of Political Science* 49 (July 2005): 535–37.

[26]U.S. 30 (1976).

[27]U.S. 630 (1993).

[28]U.S. 900 (1995).

mapping in which race was the "predominant factor" violated the Constitution's guarantee of equal protection.[29] Subsequent court decisions forced the modification of racially gerrymandered districts in Florida, Georgia, Louisiana, New York, Texas, and Virginia, but every minority incumbent running in a redrawn district won. The only casualty was Cleo Fields, who did not seek reelection after his Louisiana district fell from 55 to 28 percent black.[30]

Shaw v. Reno did not overturn Thornburg v. Gingles, and the Court decreed in Hunt v. Cromartie[31] that race could be considered in drawing districts if the primary motive was to achieve a partisan rather than racial concentration.[32] The Court's restrictions on racial gerrymandering work to the disadvantage of Republicans, because most minority voters are Democrats. The careful creation of minority-majority districts after the 1990 census had helped Republican candidates elsewhere; racial gerrymandering was responsible for as many as ten of the seats Republicans gained in the South in 1992 and 1994.[33]

During the past decade, courts have required adjustments to districts judged to be impermissible racial gerrymanders in Virginia, North Carolina, and Texas. The Republican-controlled legislature in North Carolina responded to an adverse 2017 Supreme Court ruling by recasting its racial gerrymander as a partisan gerrymander—easy to do because African Americans in North Carolina vote overwhelmingly for Democrats. As its legislative designer put it, "I think electing Republicans is better than electing Democrats. So I drew this map to help foster what I think is better for the country."[34] The recasting worked. A panel of federal judges disagreed

---

[29]Holly Idelson, "Court Takes a Harder Line on Minority Voting Blocs," *Congressional Quarterly Weekly Report*, July 1, 1995, 1944–46.

[30]Michael Barone and Grant Ujifusa, *The Almanac of American Politics 2000* (Washington, DC: National Journal, 1999), 697.

[31]U.S. 541 (1999).

[32]Caroline E. Brown, "High Court Upholds Minority Districts," *Congressional Quarterly Weekly Report*, May 22, 1999, 1202.

[33]Kevin A. Hill, "Does the Creation of Majority Black Districts Aid Republicans? An Analysis of the 1992 Congressional Elections in Eight Southern States," *Journal of Politics* 57 (1995): 384–401. Professor Hill kindly provided the 1994 update (personal communication). John W. Petrocik and Scott W. Desposato argue that the damage to Democrats from racial gerrymandering was largely indirect (forcing incumbent Democrats to run in new districts with many new constituents) and contingent on the strong pro-Republican tide among white southerners in 1992 and 1994; see John W. Petrocik and Scott W. Desposato, "The Partisan Consequences of Majority-Minority Redistricting in the South, 1992 and 1994," *Journal of Politics* 60 (1998): 613–33.

[34]Armand Emamdjomeh, Ann Gerhart, and Tim Meko, "Why North Carolina's House District Lines Have Been Upended—Again," *Washington Post*, August 31, 2018, at https://www.washingtonpost.com/graphics/2018/politics/north-carolina-redistricting/?noredirect=on&utm_term=.3ae9c6a5a1f4.

and ruled on August 27, 2018, that the districts violated First and Four-teenth Amendments rights (although later deciding that it was too late to redraw the lines before the 2018 election, as the primary had been in May). The Supreme Court's 2019 decision rejected the lower court's constitutional arguments, letting the Republican gerrymander stand.

In January 2022, a three-judge district court ruled that an Alabama redistricting plan adopted after the 2020 census likely violated Section 2 of the Voting Rights Act, which bans racial discrimination with respect to voting practices in the states. Alabama's legislative plan allowed for the creation of one majority-Black district, but critics claimed that it should have drawn two, given the number of black voters living in the state. After the lower court's ruling was appealed by the state, the Supreme Court in a 5-4 decision froze the district court's order while it appealed, setting oral arguments for later in the fall. In June 2023, the Supreme Court ruled in *Allen v. Michigan* that Alabama's congressional district map diluted the votes of Black voters in violation of the Voting Rights Act.[35]

Bipartisan Gerrymanders

States sometimes draw district lines to favor incumbents of both parties, a practice that depresses competition by giving both parties safer seats. The most egregious recent example is from California, where a redistricting scheme for 2002 to 2010 endorsed by both parties left not a single one of the state's fifty-three House districts truly competitive. In the 265 House contests held in California from 2002 through 2010, for instance, only one of these seats changed party hands: Republican Richard Pombo, beset by personal scandal and a modest increase in Democratic registration in his 11th District, was defeated in 2006. This stasis inspired a ballot initiative, adopted by California voters in 2008, that handed congressional redistricting chores to a citizens' commission chosen by a comically Byzantine process meant to insulate it from political considerations.[36] Among other restrictions, the commission was forbidden to consider party registration figures, voting patterns, or incumbency in drawing the new lines for 2012. The commission's work did produce a number of potentially competitive seats, but because the California electorate had become increasingly Democratic over the decade, the number of districts with Democratic registration exceeding 56 percent, thirty-three, was the

[35]Amy Howe, "Conservative Justices Seem Poised to Uphold Alabama's Redistricting Plan in Voting Rights Act Challenge," *Scotusblog*, October 4, 2022, https://www.scotusblog.com/2022/10/conservative-justices-seem-poised-to-uphold-alabamas-redistricting-plan-in-voting-rights-act-challenge/

[36]For a description of the process, see the California Citizens' Redistricting Commission website (http://wedrawthelines.ca.gov).

same before and after redistricting. The increase in competitive districts was thus almost entirely at the expense of Republicans who had backed the reform out of fear that Democratic legislative majorities would draw an even more unfavorable map.

Since 2012, every district has become more Democratic in registration and, through 2018, all of the seats that changed parties went to Democrats. After their rout in the 2018 midterm, Republicans held only seven seats in California, all in what had been the most solidly Republican districts. Nonpartisan redistricting turned out to be no defense against Donald Trump's extreme unpopularity in the state; Democrats took all forty-six districts Hillary Clinton had won in 2016, while Republicans held onto the seven won by Trump.[37] Republicans managed to pick up five additional House seats in California during the 2022 midterms following the 2020 census (which resulted in the loss of a California seat for the first time ever), all of which President Biden won in the 2020 election.

Districting commissions are popular among reformers but not necessarily in partisan legislatures. Republican legislators in Arizona, eager to use their large majorities to draw districts more favorable to their candidates, challenged the constitutionality of that state's independent redistricting commission, adopted by voters in 2000, on the grounds that its creation by ballot initiative was illegitimate. They argued that the Constitution gives state legislatures authority to determine the "times, places, and manner of holding elections for senators and representatives" (Article I, Section 4), which includes drawing district lines. The Supreme Court disagreed and upheld the commission in a 5–4 decision that disappointed Arizona Republicans but no doubt inspired a sigh of relief among their California counterparts.

THE REPUBLICAN ADVANTAGE IN HOUSE DISTRICTS

As the data in table 2.2 displaying the distribution of Democratic- and Republican-leaning districts reveal, Republicans enjoy a major structural advantage in the competition for House seats. This advantage arises because their regular voters are distributed more efficiently across House districts than are regular Democratic voters. Although Republican gerrymanders reinforced this advantage through redistricting after the 2000, 2010, and 2020 censuses, it is nothing new—for its roots are demographic. Democrats win a disproportionate share of minority, single, young, secular, highly educated, and LBGTQ voters, who are concentrated in urban districts that deliver lopsided Democratic majorities.

---

[37]See previous editions for graphical evidence of these districting trends in California over time.

Figure 2.1 District Partisan Advantage, 1952–2022

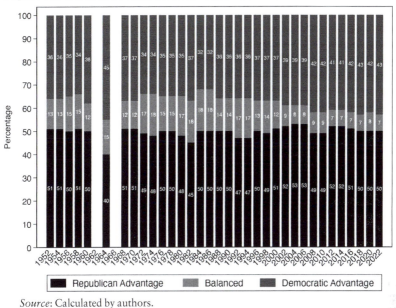

Source: Calculated by authors.

Republican voters are spread more evenly across suburbs, smaller cities, and rural areas, so that fewer Republican votes are "wasted" in highly skewed districts. Figure 2.1 illustrates the consequences. During the past five decades, a substantially larger proportion of House seats have leaned Republican than have leaned Democratic (with "leaning" estimated as having the district vote for their party's presidential candidate at least two points above the national average for that year or, for midterms, for the previous presidential election).

As later chapters will show, the Republicans' structural advantage has grown more consequential over time with the increase in party-line and straight-ticket voting among district electorates. The consequences were apparent in 2016 and 2020. In 2016, although the Democratic presidential candidate, Hillary Clinton, won 51.1 percent of the major-party vote and 2.86 million more votes than Republican candidate Donald Trump, Trump nonetheless outpolled Clinton in 228 of the 435 House districts, while Clinton ran ahead in only 207. In 2020, Joseph Biden won over 7 million more votes than Trump, but Trump won the most votes in 217 districts and Biden in 184 districts. There are currently 217 districts where Trump ran at least two percentage points ahead of his national major-party share (47.7 percent) and only 187 where Biden ran more than two points ahead of his national share; the thirty-one remaining districts fall in between. This means that even if Democrats win all of

Figure 2.2 Winning against the Partisan Grain, by Decade

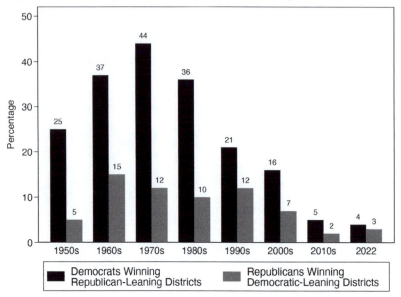

Note: Leaning districts are defined as those in which the district-level presidential vote was at least 2 percentage points higher than the national average for that election; decades are defined by the reapportionment cycle (e.g., 2010s is 2012–2020).

Source: Compiled by authors.

the Democratic-leaning districts and all of the balanced districts (by this measure), they will barely win a majority (218).

In past decades, Democrats were able to win a substantial proportion of Republican-leaning districts—as high as 44 percent in the 1970s (see figure 2.2). For reasons examined in chapters 5 and 6, their ability to win such seats has dropped dramatically since the 1980s. Republicans have never done particularly well in Democratic territory and remain less successful than Democrats in this regard, but this is not a problem for them at present because their structural advantage can deliver Republican House majorities, even if they win none of the balanced or Democratic-leaning districts. Figure 2.1 also shows that the proportion of closely balanced districts (delivering presidential results within two percentage points of the national vote) has shrunk by nearly two-thirds since the 1980s and after 2022 was down to 7 percent; thus very few representatives now serve districts without a clear partisan tilt. Although critics blame partisan gerrymandering for the trend, it stems mainly from changes in the behavior of voters, discussed in detail in later chapters.[38]

---

[38]Gary C. Jacobson, "Competition in U.S. Congressional Elections," in *The Marketplace of Democracy: Electoral Competition and American Politics*, eds. Michael P. McDonald and John Samples (Washington, DC: Brookings Institution, 2006), 34–38.

States as Electoral Units

For the Senate, "districts" are fixed by state boundaries, and the question of reapportionment never arises. It is easy to find examples of state boundaries that, like House district lines, cut across natural economic units—greater New York City, with suburbs in Connecticut and New Jersey, forms such a unit—and of states that are sharply divided into distinct and conflicting political regions (Tennessee, for example). But this matters less than for House districts because states are, after all, important political units for purposes other than Senate elections. Indeed, this is an important basis for some of the differences, spelled out in later chapters, between House and Senate elections.

States form an odd set of electoral units for another, quite obvious, reason: their great diversity in population. A senator from California represents nearly sixty-eight times as many people as a senator from Wyoming. The nine largest states are home to 51 percent of the population but elect only 18 percent of the Senate; the smallest twenty-six states control 52 percent of the Senate but hold only 18 percent of the population. The "great compromise" endowed citizens of small states with a perpetual political advantage—equal weight in one chamber, superior weight in the other.

Research into the potential electoral bias introduced by unequal state population suggests that it has varied over time. During the post–Civil War era, it favored Republicans.[39] Since the advent of popular election of senators, the bias has generally favored whichever party is in the minority nationally: the Democrats between 1914 and 1930, and the Republicans during the New Deal realignment and from 1956 through the present. It also currently produces a bias against ideological liberals and racial minorities.[40]

By allowing the minority party to win a share of seats significantly larger than its share of votes, Senate malapportionment makes it harder for popular majorities to rule, just as the framers of the Constitution intended.[41] Indeed, without it, Republicans would not have held the Senate in the early 1980s; they won majority control by taking

[39]An exception may be the years 1876 to 1892, when Republicans were able to win the Senate more consistently than the House or the White House by winning a disproportionate share of newly admitted, less populous states in the West. See Charles H. Stewart III, "Lessons from the Post–Civil War Era," in *The Politics of Divided Government*, eds. Gary Cox and Samuel Kernell (Boulder, CO: Westview Press, 1991), 203–38.

[40]John D. Griffin, "Senate Apportionment as a Source of Political Inequality," *Legislative Studies Quarterly* 31 (2006): 405–32; David Wasserman, "The Congressional Map Has a Record-Setting Bias against Democrats," *FiveThirtyEight*, August 7, 2017, at https://fivethirtyeight.com/features/the-congressional-map-is-historically-biased-toward-the-gop/.

[41]Frances E. Lee and Bruce I. Oppenheimer, "Senate Apportionment: Competitiveness and Partisan Advantage," *Legislative Studies Quarterly* 22 (1997): 3–24.

a disproportionate share of the smaller states, winning twenty-two of thirty-four Senate contests in 1980 while winning less than a majority of Senate votes cast nationwide.[42] Today, with the two parties nearly even in popular support nationally, the Republicans enjoy the same sort of structural advantage in Senate as in House elections. In 2012, Obama, with five million more votes than Romney, won barely more than half the states (twenty-six); in 2016, Clinton won 51 percent of the vote but only twenty of the fifty states. Biden won seven million more votes than Trump in the 2020 election, but only managed to win a bare majority (twenty-six) of the states.

ELECTION LAWS

The diversity that once characterized state election laws has gradually given way to substantially greater uniformity, but important differences remain. Congress was given the constitutional power to regulate all federal elections (Article I, Section 4) but was in no hurry to do so. Initially, states were allowed to go entirely their own way. For example, at one time many states elected members of Congress in odd years; the practice did not entirely end until 1880. The date of federal elections was not fixed as the first Tuesday after the first Monday in November until 1845, and states could still hold elections on different dates if their constitutions so required. For a time, some states required the winner of a congressional election to receive a majority of all votes cast; now all states except Louisiana permit election by plurality, at least in general elections. (Louisiana requires a runoff if no candidate receives an absolute majority.)

Restrictions on suffrage once varied from state to state; constitutional amendments, court decisions, and federal laws have now eliminated almost every restriction on suffrage for citizens who have passed their eighteenth birthday and have not been convicted of felonies.[43] Partisan politics naturally permeated the historical battles over extensions of the right to vote, for alterations in the makeup of the electorate tend to favor one party over the other. Laws enacted since 2006 by Republican legislatures requiring people to show picture identification before being permitted to vote are a contemporary example. Those citizens without driver's licenses, passports, or other acceptable forms of identification are

---

[42]John T. Pothier, "The Partisan Bias in Senate Elections," *American Politics Quarterly* 12 (1984): 89–100.

[43]Felons are denied the right to vote temporarily in most states and permanently in some. In 2018, Florida voters passed a referendum re-enfranchising more than one million former felons who had completed their sentences. Because they were disproportionately African American, the effect will be to boost the proportion of Democratic voters in this closely balanced state, although by how much remains to be seen.

more likely to be poor, minority, and elderly, and thus Democrats, and insofar as these requirements discourage participation by raising the cost (in the form of the fees, time, and effort needed to acquire picture IDs from state bureaucracies), they are expected to have a disproportionate depressive effect on the Democratic vote. That is, of course, their purpose; the Republican proponents of ID requirements have produced very little evidence that the problem they are supposed to address, voter fraud by impersonation, is other than extremely rare.[44] The ID requirements in several states have been set aside by courts because of their disproportionate effect on minorities; their actual effectiveness in discouraging voting fraud has yet to be determined.[45]

The trend toward more uniform election laws is not merely of historical interest. A single date for all federal elections encourages national campaigns, party tickets, and coattail effects. Each election is more than an isolated, idiosyncratic event, or at least voters can treat it as such. The removal of formal and informal barriers to voting has substantially altered the political complexion of some areas, notably in the Deep South, where formerly excluded black voters are now an important political force. Lowering the voting age to eighteen has made the student vote a key factor in districts encompassing large university towns, such as Ann Arbor, Michigan, and Madison, Wisconsin.

The process of voting itself has undergone important changes. Prior to the 1890s, each local party produced its own ballots listing only its own candidates, which were handed to voters outside the polling place. The party ballots were readily distinguishable; voting was thus a public act. Because local parties printed the ballots, internal party rivalries were sometimes fought with multiple or competing party ballots, frustrating state party leaders' pursuit of electoral unity and control.[46] The system invited voter intimidation and other forms of corruption, and it

---

[44]Mike Turzai, majority leader of the Pennsylvania House of Representatives, was candid about the goal of the state's new law, boasting (inaccurately, as it turned out) at a state Republican event in 2012, "Voter ID … is gonna allow Governor Romney to win the state of Pennsylvania." See Suevon Lee, "Everything You Ever Wanted to Know about Voter ID Laws," *ProPublica*, November 5, 2012, http://www.propublica.org/article/everything-youve-ever-wanted-to-know-about-voter-id-laws, accessed February 24, 2015.

[45]The evidence is mixed; the Government Accountability Office (GAO) review reported that of ten studies, four found a significant negative effect of voter ID requirements on turnout, five found no effect, and one found a positive effect. See GAO, "Elections: Issues Related to State Identification Laws," September 2014, http://www.gao.gov/assets/670/665966.pdf, accessed February 24, 2015. For scholarly evidence on the debate, see Zoltan Hajnal, Nazita Lajevardi, and Lindsay Nielson, "Voter Identification Laws and the Suppression of Minority Votes," *The Journal of Politics* 79 (January 2017): 363–379.

[46]Lisa A. Reynolds, "Reassessing the Impact of Progressive Era Ballot Reform" (PhD diss., University of California, San Diego, 1995), 23–27.

was expensive for the parties to administer. A remarkable burst of reform between 1888 and 1896 led to about 90 percent of the states adopting what was called the Australian ballot (after the country of its origin). An Australian or secret ballot is produced by the government, lists candidates from all parties, and is marked in the privacy of a voting booth.

Although the Australian ballot has been blamed for weakening party loyalty by making it easier for voters to vote for different parties' candidates for different offices,[47] in some forms it increased partisan loyalty, at least initially. In states that adopted the *party-column* ballot, which lists candidates by party, ticket splitting diminished. Beyond using the party-column format, the ballot could foster straight-ticket voting by allowing voters to mark a single spot (or pull a single lever on a voting machine) to vote for all a party's candidates. On the other hand, where states adopted the *office-bloc* ballot, which lists candidates by office, ticket splitting was facilitated. The search for partisan advantage led some states to switch back and forth between the two forms, depending on which party or faction was in power.[48] Differences among ballot types and their consequences persist to this day, although fewer than ten states still use party-column ballots.[49] The technology of voting continues to evolve to varying degrees across states and sometimes with considerable controversy as we saw following the 2020 election. Absentee and early balloting have grown increasingly common; Oregon now conducts all elections exclusively by mail, and the debate over the security and accuracy of computerized touch-screen voting—as well as of older rival balloting systems—has yet to be resolved.

Again, variations in formal procedures can be politically consequential. The effects of ballot formats that make ticket splitting easier run counter to those of uniform election dates. Easier ticket splitting weakens coattails and other partisan links between candidates by making it easier to focus the election on candidates rather than on parties.[50] Early and absentee balloting stretch the crucial part of the campaign period when voters are making their final decision, favoring candidates with

---

[47]Jerrold G. Rusk, "The Effects of the Australian Ballot Reform on Split Ticket Voting: 1876–1908," in *Controversies in Voting Behavior*, eds. Richard G. Niemi and Herbert F. Weisberg (San Francisco: W. H. Freeman, 1976), 485–86.

[48]Reynolds, "Progressive Era Ballot Reform," 77–106.

[49]Rusk, "Australian Ballot Reform," 493–509; Angus Campbell et al., *The American Voter* (New York: John Wiley, 1960), 276; Erik J. Engstrom and Jason M. Roberts, *The Politics of Ballot Design: How States Shape American Democracy* (New York: Cambridge University Press, 2020).

[50]Rusk, "Australian Ballot Reform," 1232; Jason M. Roberts, "Bicameralism, Ballot Type, and Split Ticket Voting" (manuscript, University of North Carolina, Chapel Hill, October 16, 2009).

enough resources to spread their campaign advertising over a longer period; in 2022, over 40 percent of voters cast ballots before the official election day.[51]

POLITICAL PARTIES

Without question, the most important additions to the institutional framework established by the Constitution have been political parties. The parties, along with the system of presidential elections that inspired their development, are the formal institutions that contribute most to making congressional elections something other than purely local festivals and politicians something other than purely independent political entrepreneurs. The long-term atrophy of party organizations and the weakening of partisan ties from the 1950s through the 1970s thus contributed to the detachment of congressional elections from national political forces and to the rise of candidate-centered campaigns. For the same reason, the emergence of more vigorous national party organizations in recent decades has contributed to a complete reversal of these trends over the past twenty years (see chapter 4 for more on this topic).

The decline of parties stemmed from a variety of causes; several of the most important ones are discussed later. A fundamental factor, however, was clearly institutional: the rise and spread of primary elections as the method for choosing party nominees for the general election. Nineteenth-century parties nominated candidates in caucuses and, later, conventions. Often dominated by self-elected party elites, these came under increasing criticism when the United States entered into a period of sectional one-party dominance following the election of 1896. Parties faced with serious competition found it prudent to nominate attractive candidates; without this constraint—with the assurance of victory because of an overwhelming local majority—they could freely nominate incompetent hacks or worse. With the nomination tantamount to election in so many places, the general election, and therefore the voter, seemed increasingly irrelevant.

The direct primary election was introduced as a way to weaken party bosses by transferring the right to choose the party's nominees to the party's voters and to allow people to cast meaningful votes despite meaningless general elections. It was also an effective method for settling

---

[51]Jeffery M. Jones, "Early Voting Higher Than in Past U.S. Midterms," Gallup, November 2, 2022, https://news.gallup.com/poll/404558/early-voting-higher-past-midterms.aspx. The 2022 general election turnout was approximately 107.7 million; see Drew Desilver, "Turnout in 2022 House Midterms Declined from 2018 High, Final Official Returns Show," Pew Research Center, March 10, 2023, https://www.pewresearch.org/fact-tank/2023/03/10/turnout-in-2022-house-midterms-declined-from-2018-high-final-official-returns-show/

disputes over who the party's official candidate was, which became necessary when states adopted the Australian ballot. In the South, where one-party dominance was most pronounced, most states eventually established a second, runoff primary between the two candidates receiving the most votes when neither won a majority on the first ballot. Today, election laws in every state provide for primary elections for House and Senate nominations—although the rules governing them vary from state to state—and party leaders are able to control the nomination in very few places. They and their interest-group allies can, however, help direct the flow of campaign money to favored candidates, providing an edge if not always a victory. A few states still hold nominating conventions that exercise some control—usually incomplete—over access to the ballot. In 2010, for example, the Utah Republican convention denied renomination to third-term senator Robert F. Bennett by giving two other Republican candidates, Mike Lee and Tim Bridgewater, more delegate votes than Bennett. (Under Utah's rules, only the top two convention vote-getters make the primary ballot.) Although a solid conservative, Bennett had offended the conservative Republican base by voting for the 2008 bailout of the financial industry and Obama's 2009 economic stimulus package; Lee, a Tea Party favorite, won the nomination and election.[52]

Scattered modern instances of party-machine control over congressional nominations can still be found. When the congressman who represented the 5th District of Illinois (in Chicago) died in 1975, State Representative John Fary "was called into Mayor Richard J. Daley's office. At 65, Fary had been a faithful servant of the machine; and he thought the Mayor was going to tell him it was time to retire. Instead, he was told he was going to Congress."[53] He did, declaring on the night of his special-election victory, "I will go to Washington to help represent Mayor Daley. For twenty-one years I represented the Mayor in the legislature, and he was always right."[54] When, in 1982, Fary ignored the party's request that he retire, he was crushed in the primary. More recently, veteran Illinois congressman William Lipinski announced he would not seek reelection only days before the August 26, 2004, deadline for a party to replace any candidate who had withdrawn. Among the local political leaders who gathered to pick his replacement were Lipinski himself, John Daley, son of the late Mayor Daley and brother of the then current

---

[52]Michael Barone and Chuck McCutcheon, *The Almanac of American Politics 2012* (Chicago: University of Chicago Press, 2011), 1627.

[53]Michael Barone, Grant Ujifusa, and Douglas Matthews, *The Almanac of American Politics 1980* (New York: E. P. Dutton, 1979), 246.

[54]Alan Ehrenhalt, ed., *Politics in America: Members of Congress in Washington and at Home* (Washington, DC: Congressional Quarterly Press, 1981), 333.

Mayor Daley, and a number of long-standing stalwarts of Chicago's legendary Democratic organization. To no one's surprise, their unanimous choice was Lipinski's son, Daniel, a political scientist on the faculty of the University of Tennessee who had not lived in Illinois for fifteen years.[55] Lipinski, one of the most socially conservative Democrats in Congress, represented his Illinois district in the House until 2020 when he was defeated in the Democratic primary by Marie Newman—who went on to lose her primary two years later as a result of changes to her district stemming from redistricting.[56]

Fary's tale and Lipinski's sudden ascent from seminar room to Capitol Hill are noteworthy because they are so atypical. The local party organization's influence on congressional nominations varies but is typically feeble. Few congressional candidates find opposition from the local party leaders to be a significant handicap; neither is their support very helpful. National party leaders control much greater resources and hence potential influence. In the past, the parties used their resources sparingly in primaries and were often thwarted when they did so. In 2010, for example, several Republican Senate candidates associated with the party's radically conservative Tea Party faction upset candidates favored by the party's conventionally conservative establishment. Three of them then went on to lose potentially winnable seats in the general election.[57] Similar problems probably cost Republicans another two Senate seats in 2012.[58] Absorbing the lesson, Republican Senate leader Mitch McConnell and his financial allies took vigorous preemptive action in 2014 against Tea Party challenges to him and two other Republican senators. McConnell's predication that "we are going to crush them everywhere"[59] turned out to be accurate. In 2018, both national parties intervened in the 2018 West Virginia Republican primary to choose Democratic senator Joe Manchin's challenger—Republicans to prevent the nomination of a coal executive who had served time in prison for his role in a deadly mine disaster, and Democrats to prevent the nomination of a congressman they

[55]Michael Barone with Richard E. Cohen, *The Almanac of American Politics 2006* (Washington, DC: National Journal, 2005), 567–68.

[56]Kate Ackley, "Democrats Back Casten over Newman in Illinois' 6th District," *Roll Call*, June 28, 2022, https://rollcall.com/2022/06/28/democrats-back-casten-over-newman-in-illinois-6th-district/

[57]Gary C. Jacobson, "The Republican Resurgence in 2010," *Political Science Quarterly* 126 (Spring 2011): 39.

[58]Gary C. Jacobson, "How the Economy and Partisanship Shaped the 2012 Presidential and Congressional Elections," *Political Science Quarterly* 128 (Spring 2013): 30–31.

[59]Carl Hulse, "Leading Republicans Move to Stamp Out Challenges from Right," *New York Times*, March 8, 2014, http://www.nytimes.com/2014/03/09/us/politics/leading-republicans-move-to-stamp-out-challenges-from-right.html, accessed February 24, 2015.

thought would be Manchin's strongest opponent. Both succeeded; Manchin held onto the seat by a narrow margin in November.[60] Republicans again expressed frustration with disappointing outcomes in two key Senate races in 2022—Georgia and Pennsylvania—where candidates handpicked and endorsed by former President Trump underperformed in the midterm and likely cost Republicans control of the chamber.[61]

The introduction of primary elections deprived local parties of a crucial source of influence over elected officials: control of access to the ballot and therefore to political office. And if the party cannot determine who runs under its label, it cannot control what the label represents. Although attempts by national party organizations to influence nominations in competitive states and districts are now common and often successful, party leaders do not threaten primary challenges to keep their current legislators in line for fear of losing seats to the opposition following divisive intraparty battles.[62] For example, even Lincoln Chaffee of Rhode Island, the least loyal Republican in the Senate, got full national-party backing when challenged in the 2006 primary. (Chaffee won the primary 54–46 but lost his seat to a Democrat in the general election—just the result the party had sought to avoid.) Thus the primary system has long been an important barrier to strong party discipline in Congress. American parties lack a crucial sanction available to some of their European counterparts—namely, the ability to deny renomination to uncooperative members. Hence House Speaker Paul Ryan, Republican leader in the 115th Congress (2017–18), had great difficulty keeping his disruptive Freedom Caucus faction in line in part because he could not credibly threaten electoral damage to members who ignored his wishes. Current House Speaker Kevin McCarthy will likely experience similar difficulties in the 118th Congress (2023–24), given the narrow majority that Republicans control and the demands of the outspoken members of the Freedom Caucus.[63]

The primary election system also complicates the pursuit of a congressional career. Candidates must be prepared to face two distinct, if overlapping, electorates. Primary electorates are more partisan and prone to ideological extremity than general election voters, and the need

[60]Alexander Burns and Jonathan Martin, "6 Takeaways from Tuesday's Primary Elections," *New York Times*, May 9, 2018, https://www.nytimes.com/2018/05/09/us/politics/primary-results-west-virginia-ohio.html.

[61]Gary C. Jacobson, "The 2022 Elections: A Test of Democracy's Resilience and the Referendum Theory of Midterms," *Political Science Quarterly*, 138 (Spring 2023): 1–22.

[62]Hans J. G. Hassell, *The Party's Primary: Control of Congressional Nominations* (New York: Cambridge University Press, 2017).

[63]Sarah A. Binder, "McCarthy Paid a Steep Price for his Speakership—Now What?" *Brookings Institution*, January 10, 2023, https://www.brookings.edu/blog/fixgov/2023/01/10/mccarthy-paid-a-steep-price-for-his-speakership-now-what/

to please them is one force behind party polarization in Congress (see chapter 7). Indeed, the main threat to renomination today comes not from party leaders punishing disloyalty but from outside groups bent on imposing ideological purity. In addition to Utah's Bennett, another Senate victim was Richard Lugar of Indiana, a moderately conservative Republican senator who lost to an immoderately conservative Tea Party challenger in his 2012 primary. And an even sharper example was the surprise primary defeat in 2014 of Republican majority leader Eric Cantor by a Tea Party–aligned economics professor in Virginia's 7th District.

Differences in primary election laws underlie much of the diversity among congressional election processes across states. The date of the general election may be fixed, but primaries are held at any time from February through September. The runoff primary used in ten states (nine of them in the South) has already been mentioned; now that two-party competition has become the norm, candidates must occasionally win three serious contests to gain office. Washington and California recently joined Louisiana in adopting a "top-two" or "jungle" primary system, in which all candidates regardless of party compete in the same primary; if no candidate receives an absolute majority of votes, the top two vote-getters compete in the general election—even if they are from the same party.[64]

Rules governing access to the ballot also differ. Some states require only a small fee and allow virtually anyone to run; others require a larger fee or some minimum number of signatures on a petition. Challenges to incumbents, as well as third-party or independent candidacies, are thus encouraged or discouraged to differing degrees; top-two primaries in particular make it almost impossible for other than major-party candidates to get on the general election ballot.

This discussion of the legal and institutional framework of congressional elections has necessarily been brief; filling in all the details would demand volumes. But it is sufficient to point out some of the important ways in which the formal context shapes the activities of candidates, voters, and other participants in congressional elections.

It is important to remember that the formal context does not arrive mysteriously from somewhere outside the political system. Politically active people consciously create and shape rules and institutions to help them achieve their goals. Rules that allow members of Congress to pursue their aims independently of their party evolve when politicians thrive on independence; when loyal partisanship becomes more conducive to political success, rules are altered to encourage party cohesion. Although

---

[64]Louisiana treats the November election as the jungle primary, with the top two candidates facing off in a December runoff if no candidate wins more than 50 percent of the November vote.

in the short view it seems that the formal framework establishes a set of independent parameters to which political actors must adapt, it does not. Rather, the framework itself reflects the values and preferences prevalent among politically active citizens, and it changes as those values and preferences change.

SOCIAL AND POLITICAL CONTEXTS

The rules and customs that control districting and primary elections may contribute to the idiosyncratic component of congressional elections, but the contribution is hardly decisive. Idiosyncrasy is deeply rooted in the cultural, economic, and geographical heterogeneity of the United States. A few short examples will suggest the astonishing variety of electoral conditions that would-be candidates must be prepared to face. States and districts vary in geography, population, economic base, income, communications, ethnicity, age, and political habits.

- *Geography*: Simple geography is an abundant source of variation. Current House districts are as small as New York's 10-square-mile 13th District and as large as Alaska's 586,000 square miles, in which campaigning by airplane is essential and occasionally fatal.[65] Even Michigan has a district that is more than 450 miles from end to end (the 1st). The range in geographical size among states is smaller but still enormous. The purely physical problems of campaigning in or representing constituencies differ greatly and can be quite severe.
- *Population*: Obviously, states vary widely in population, and both districts and states also vary in population density. Imagine the problems faced by California's senators, who are expected to represent over 39 million people living more than 2,500 miles from Washington, DC. Alaska's senators serve only 733,500 people, but they are even farther from the US capital and are scattered over a far larger area. Rhode Island, in contrast, is a "tiny little city state,"[66] compact, with slightly more than 1 million inhabitants.
- *Economic base*: The high-tech companies of Silicon Valley dominate the economic life of California's new 16th District; 80,000 workers in and around Washington's 2nd District get their paychecks from Boeing; Wyoming's prosperity rises and falls with that of the energy and mining sectors; West Virginia's largest

---

[65]House Majority Leader Hale Boggs and Alaska congressman Nick Begich were killed in a plane crash while campaigning in that state in 1972.
[66]Barone and Ujifusa, *Almanac of American Politics 2000*, 2410.

private employer is Walmart; Maryland's 3rd District includes more than 160,000 federal workers and retirees.[67] Delaware is the home of DuPont, which has far greater revenues than the state government. At the other extreme are states and districts with thoroughly heterogeneous local economies.

- *Income*: Kentucky's 5th District is the second poorest in the nation; its median family income in 2022 was $44,200. The wealthiest is Virginia's 11th, with a median family income of $140,800. The Kentucky district gave Donald Trump 80 percent of its votes in 2020 and is represented in the House by a Republican; the Virginia district gave Joseph Biden 71 percent and is represented by a Democrat. After the 2022 election, Democrats held half of the ten wealthiest districts and a substantial majority of the top fifty.[68]

- *Communications*: Districts such as Missouri's 1st (St. Louis) and Oklahoma's 5th (Oklahoma City) coincide with media markets and are covered efficiently by newspapers and television and radio stations. Compare them with any of the thirty-five or so districts that fall in the New York City media market or to a state such as Wyoming, with multiple media markets. Or consider New Jersey, a state of nearly nine million people, all of whom live in media markets centered outside the state in neighboring metropolitan areas (specifically, New York and Philadelphia). Campaigning and representing are largely based on communication. It is easy to see how the media-market structure determines which tactical options are available to candidates and how easily they can attract public attention.[69] But subtler influences operate in the mix as well. In some districts, for example, a member of Congress is a newsworthy politician; in others, he or she is lost in the crowd.

- *Ethnicity*: Some districts are overwhelmingly of one racial or ethnic group; for example, 66 percent of the residents of Mississippi's 2nd District are African American; for years, 88 percent in California's 40th District were Hispanic. Twenty-two current US districts have African American majorities, eighteen California districts

[67] Rich Cohen, Charlie Cook and Michael Barone, *The Almanac of American Politics 2022*, Washington, DC: Rowman & Littlefield.

[68] August Benzow, "Mapping the Economic Well-Being of the Nation's New Redistricted Congressional Districts," Economic Innovation Group, November 3, 2022, https://eig.org/economic-wellbeing-of-congressional-districts/

[69] Richard G. Niemi, Lynda W. Powell, and Patricia L. Bicknell, "The Effects of Congruity between Community and District on the Salience of U.S. House Candidates," *Legislative Studies Quarterly* 11 (1986): 190–98; Dena Levy and Peverill Squire, "Television Markets and the Competitiveness of U.S. House Elections," *Legislative Studies Quarterly* 25 (May 2000): 313–25.

have Hispanic majorities, and two districts are majority Asian. Non-Hispanic white majorities are found in nearly 70 percent of the districts (302), with Kentucky's 5th District being the whitest (94 percent).[70] States, too, have very different ethnic mixes: The politically important Jews in New York, Irish in Massachusetts, and Hispanics in New Mexico are familiar examples.

- *Age*: The median age in Florida's 13th District is fifty-six; 33 percent of the eligible voters are older than sixty-five. Compare this with a district such as Utah's 3rd, where the median age is thirty, or with Ohio's 3rd, which includes sixty-six thousand university students. Imagine how the dominant political concerns differ among the three.

- *Political habits*: Some areas have historic traditions of strong loyalty to the candidates of one party or the other; intense two-party competition characterizes others. Still others undergo rapid political flux through demographic shifts created by a restless, mobile population. Voter turnout in recent House elections in which both major parties fielded candidates has ranged from below 10 to above 80 percent; for Senate elections, the range is narrower—from 28 to 74 percent—but still striking.

CONCLUSION

These categories and examples do not begin to exhaust the possibilities, but they are sufficient to make the point that politically relevant conditions vary enormously across states and districts and are a potent source of localism and idiosyncrasy in the electoral politics of Congress. The problem for each congressional aspirant is to devise a strategy to win and maintain the support of voters in a particular state or district, and it is not surprising that no common formula has been discovered. Nor is it surprising that candidates often try to nurture an image of independence. Recognition of the heterogeneity among states and districts cannot, however, explain why electoral fragmentation increased sharply during the 1960s and 1970s and makes it even more difficult to explain why this trend has reversed sharply since then. Indeed, the wonder is that in the most recent elections, these diverse constituencies have responded to national forces with remarkable uniformity.

---

[70]Data from: https://www.census.gov/mycd/

3

Congressional Candidates

★ ★ ★

EACH STATE OR CONGRESSIONAL DISTRICT is a unique electoral arena. Diversity among constituencies underlies the astonishing variety of political forces operating in congressional politics. When we shift attention to particular states or districts, however, as when we examine congressional candidates and campaigns—the subjects of this chapter and the next—the local context becomes a constant rather than a variable factor. Its elements are fixed, at least for the short run. Electoral variation originates elsewhere, in changing political conditions and issues and in the skills, resources, and strategies of candidates, parties, and other participants in electoral politics.

THE INCUMBENCY FACTOR

From the 1950s through the 1980s, the electoral importance of individual candidates and campaigns expanded, while that of party labels and national issues diminished. The emergence of a more candidate-centered electoral process helped one class of congressional candidates to prosper: the incumbent officeholders. Indeed, the electoral advantage enjoyed by incumbents, at least as measured by electoral margins, increased so notably after the mid-1960s that it became the main focus of congressional elections research for a generation. This research left little doubt that incumbency conferred major electoral benefits, but it also revealed that those benefits were neither automatic, nor certain, nor constant across electoral contexts. Even during the 1970s and 1980s, when House incumbents were riding their highest, impressive reelection rates and expanded electoral margins seemed ever more dearly bought. The pursuit of reelection absorbed a great deal of time, energy, and money, reflecting

35

members' enduring sense of electoral uncertainty and risk. The electoral upheavals in elections since then, particularly in 1994, 2006, 2010, and 2018, show that their worry was not misplaced; the advantages of incumbency proved to be far more contingent than the surface evidence might have suggested.

Incumbents still invest a great deal of time and effort in pursuing reelection, but the payoffs are not as impressive as they once were. The value of incumbency, measured in vote shares, has declined steadily since the 1980s. Once worth as much as ten or twelve percentage points, the incumbency bonus has diminished to such an extent that it now averages only two or three points. What accounts for this striking trend? As we document in detail in later chapters, growing party loyalty and the nationalization of elections has made it increasingly difficult for incumbents to attract voters across party lines and thus to win in districts or states that lean in the opposite partisan direction. Incumbents still win reelection at high rates, but mainly because the vast majority of them represent districts where any candidate of their party would be favored.

Even with the recent decline in the measurable incumbency advantage, incumbency remains a conspicuous factor in congressional elections from almost any perspective. Most obviously, incumbency is a dominant consideration because incumbents who seek reelection are consistently successful—and everyone involved in politics knows it. At a deeper level, whether the candidate is already an incumbent, is challenging an incumbent, or is pursuing an open seat previously held by an incumbent still strongly influences nearly everything pertaining to candidates and campaigns for Congress.

The basic picture seems clear enough. The data in table 3.1 show just how thoroughly incumbents have dominated postwar House elections. Typically, more than 90 percent of the races have included incumbents, and more than 90 percent of those incumbents have won. From 1946 to 2022, only 1.7 percent of officeholders seeking reelection have been defeated in primary elections, and only 5.8 percent have lost general elections. Even in years very unfavorable to one of the parties, a large majority of its House incumbents return. In 2010, the Democrats' worst year since 1946, 78 percent of the House Democrats who sought reelection won. In 2018, a bad year for Republicans, 85 percent of the Republican incumbents who ran were returned to office.

The story is somewhat different for Senate incumbents. Although the odds still favor them, senators have not been as consistently successful in winning reelection as have representatives. Since the end of World War II, 80.9 percent have won reelection, 4.1 percent have lost primaries, and 15.2 percent have lost general elections. Moreover, their electoral fortunes have fluctuated much more widely from year to year. In 1980,

Table 3.1 Reelection Rates of House and Senate Incumbents, 1946–2022

Year	Number Seeking Reelection	Number Defeated in Primaries	Number Defeated in General Elections	Percentage Reelected
House				
1946	398	18	52	82
1948	400	15	68	79
1950	400	6	32	91
1952	389	9	26	91
1954	407	6	22	93
1956	411	6	16	95
1958	396	3	37	90
1960	405	5	25	93
1962	402	12	22	92
1964	397	8	45	87
1966	411	8	41	88
1968	409	4	9	97
1970	401	10	12	95
1972	390	12	13	94
1974	391	8	40	88
1976	384	3	13	96
1978	382	5	19	94
1980	398	6	31	91
1982	393	10	29	90
1984	409	3	16	95
1986	393	2	6	98
1988	408	1	6	98
1990	406	1	15	96
1992	368	19	24	88
1994	387	4	34	90
1996	384	2	21	94
1998	402	1	6	99
2000	403	3	6	98
2002	398	8	8	96
2004	402	2	7	98
2006	398	3	22	94
2008	403	4	19	95
2010	396	4	54	85
2012	392	13	27	93
2014	395	5	13	95
2016	393	6	8	97
2018	378	4	30	91
2020	391	8	12	95
2022	381	15	9	94

(continues)

Table 3.1 Cont.

Year	Number Seeking Reelection	Number Defeated in Primaries	Number Defeated in General Elections	Percentage Reelected
Senate				
1946	30	6	7	57
1948	25	2	8	60
1950	32	5	5	69
1952	31	2	9	65
1954	32	2	6	75
1956	29	0	4	86
1958	28	0	10	64
1960	29	0	1	97
1962	35	1	5	83
1964	33	1	4	85
1966	32	3	1	88
1968	28	4	4	71
1970	31	1	6	77
1972	27	2	5	74
1974	27	2	2	85
1976	25	0	9	64
1978	25	3	7	60
1980	29	4	9	55
1982	30	0	2	93
1984	29	0	3	90
1986	28	0	7	75
1988	27	0	4	85
1990	32	0	1	97
1992	28	1	4	82
1994	26	0	2	92
1996	21	1	1	91
1998	29	0	3	90
2000	29	0	6	79
2002	27	1	3	85
2004	26	0	1	96
2006	29	1[a]	6	79
2008	30	0	5	83
2010	25	3[b]	2	84
2012	23	1	1	96
2014	28	0	5	82
2016	29	0	2	93
2018	32	0	5	84
2020	32	0	5	85
2022	28	0	0	100

Note: [a]Senator Joseph Lieberman lost the Connecticut Democratic primary but won reelection as an independent.

[b]Senator Lisa Murkowski lost the Republican primary in Alaska but won reelection as a write-in candidate.

Sources: Norman J. Ornstein, Thomas E. Mann, and Michael J. Malbin, *Vital Statistics on Congress, 2001–2002* (Washington, DC: American Enterprise Institute, 2002), tables 2–7 and 2–8; data for 2002 to 2022 compiled by the authors.

Figure 3.1 Success Rates of House and Senate Incumbents Seeking Reelection, 1946–2022

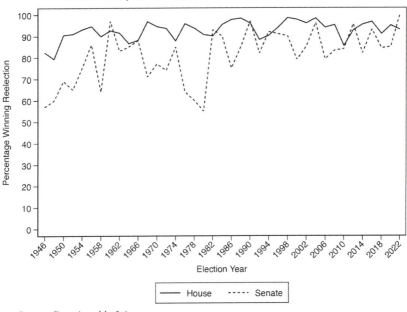

Source: Data in table 3.1.

for example, only 55 percent of incumbent Senate candidates pursuing reelection succeeded. In 1986, more incumbent senators than representatives lost, even though fourteen times as many of the latter ran. Yet in 1982, 1990, 1994, 2012, and 2022, Senate incumbents were more difficult to defeat than House incumbents. This is only the first of many instances of greater variability among Senate elections.

Figure 3.1 graphs the fluctuations in the success rates of House and Senate incumbents running in elections from 1946 through 2022. In both chambers, the percentage winning reelection gradually increased over time. Nevertheless, the sharp swings in the fortunes of Senate incumbents are clearly visible. House incumbents were much more vulnerable in 1946 and 1948 than in later elections; after 1948, their fortunes have varied, with notably high rates of success sustained in elections from 1984 through 1990 and again from 1998 through 2004. House reelection rates slipped slightly in 2018 but were back up around 95 percent in 2020, with only a one-point decline to 94 percent in 2022.

Measuring the Value of Incumbency

Figure 3.2 displays the most straightforward measure of the incumbency advantage: the average percentage of the two-party vote won by incumbent House candidates in contested elections. We analyzed this aspect

Figure 3.2 Average Percentage of the Major-Party Vote Won by House Incumbents in Contested Elections, 1840–2022

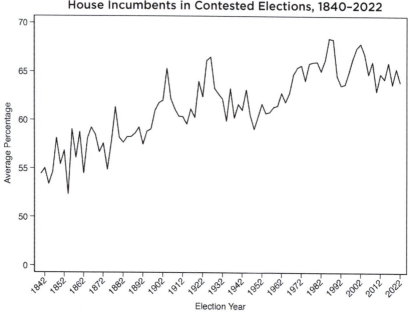

Source: Compiled by authors.

of incumbency from 1840 to 2022 to get a better historical perspective on how the average incumbent's vote percentage has changed over time. As the figure clearly shows, incumbents have won by much larger margins in the modern era than they did in the past. Despite minor fluctuations across election years, the average incumbent vote share has increased steadily since the late antebellum era. Two of the largest spikes occurred in the early part of the twentieth century—during the 1904 and 1926 elections—arguably attributable to changing patterns of candidate competition arising from the adoption of primary elections by the states.[1] After a modest decline prior to World War II, the average incumbent's vote share rose quite steadily from the late 1940s to the late 1980s, from about 60 to about 68 percent. After its peak in 1986 and 1988, it dropped back below 65 percent for the next four elections, before rising again between 1998 and 2004; the trend has since been downward, reaching a four-decade low of 63 percent in 2010, with only a slight resurgence between 2012 and 2020, before again dipping to 64 percent in 2022.

---

[1]On this point, see Jamie L. Carson and Jason M. Roberts, *Ambition, Competition, and Electoral Reform: The Politics of Congressional Elections across Time* (Ann Arbor: University of Michigan Press, 2013).

Despite the clear pattern observed in figure 3.2, the average incumbent's vote share is in reality an ambiguous measure of the incumbency advantage. Some proportion of it reflects the partisan makeup of the district, votes that would go to any candidate with the same party label; conceivably, all of an incumbent's votes could fall into this category.[2] The incumbency advantage is therefore more appropriately gauged by how much better candidates do running as incumbents than they would do running as nonincumbents. Scholars have taken several approaches to estimating this difference, but all of them support the same conclusion: the electoral value of incumbency, measured in votes, increased sharply during the 1960s but has, in the most recent elections, fallen to pre-1960 levels.

The simplest approach is to look at what happens to the district vote in adjacent elections with and without the incumbent. Scholars initially estimated the incumbency advantage by calculating the *sophomore surge* (the average gain in vote share won by candidates running as incumbents for the first time compared to their vote share in the initial election) and the *retirement slump* (the average drop in the party's vote from the previous election when the incumbent departs and the seat becomes open).[3] Averaged together into a single index, they form the *slurge*.[4] More elaborate approaches have sought to refine estimates by eliminating selection bias and other sources of error in the components of the slurge.[5] Although complete consensus has yet to emerge on which technique is most appropriate, the choice makes little practical difference. All the indices tell the same basic story.

Figure 3.3 displays the postwar trends in three measures: the slurge, Gelman and King's index, and a modified version of their index that

---

[2] John R. Alford and David W. Brady, "Personal and Partisan Advantage in U.S. Congressional Elections, 1846–1990," in *Congress Reconsidered*, ed. Lawrence C. Dodd and Bruce I. Oppenheimer, 5th ed. (Washington, DC: Congressional Quarterly Press, 1993), 146–47.

[3] Albert D. Cover and David R. Mayhew, "Congressional Dynamics and the Decline of Competitive Congressional Elections," in *Congress Reconsidered*, ed. Lawrence C. Dodd and Bruce I. Oppenheimer, 2nd ed. (Washington, DC: Congressional Quarterly Press, 1981), 70; see also Robert S. Erikson, "Malapportionment, Gerrymandering, and Party Fortunes in Congressional Elections," *American Political Science Review* 66 (1972): 1240.

[4] David W. Brady, Brian Gaines, and Douglas Rivers, "The Incumbency Advantage in the House and Senate: A Comparative Institutional Analysis" (manuscript, Stanford University, 1994).

[5] Andrew Gelman and Gary King, "Estimating Incumbency Advantage without Bias," *American Journal of Political Science* 34 (1990): 1142–64; Michael Krashinsky and William J. Milne, "The Effects of Incumbency in U.S. Congressional Elections, 1950–1988," *Legislative Studies Quarterly* 18 (1993): 321–44; Brady, Gaines, and Rivers, "Incumbency Advantage."

Figure 3.3 Incumbency Advantage in House Elections, 1952–2022

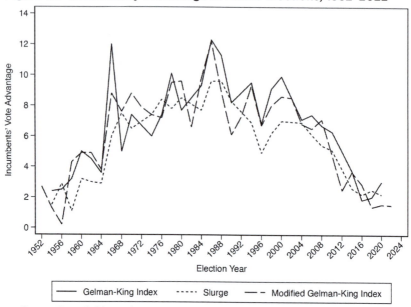

Source: Compiled by authors.

allows inclusion of years ending in 2.[6] All three show the growing value, in votes, of holding a House seat from the 1950s to the mid-1980s; all show a particularly sharp increase in the mid-1960s; and all show an irregular decline in the incumbency advantage, so measured, since the late 1980s. According to the slurge, the average value of incumbency, in vote percentage, jumped from an average of 1.6 percent in the 1946–64 period to 7.2 percent for 1966–84 and to 8.5 percent for 1986–90; according to Gelman and King's index, it jumped from 2.2 to 8.2 percent and then to 10.6 percent over the same time spans. Since the beginning of this century, however, the estimated vote value of incumbency has declined steeply; for 2020 and 2022, the estimates are all at or below 3 percent.

The value, in votes, of Senate incumbency also increased during the 1960s. Trends in Senate elections are more difficult to detect than trends

---

[6]Gelman and King compute the incumbency advantage by regressing the Democrat's share of the two-party vote on the Democrat's vote in the previous election, the party holding the seat, and incumbency (which takes a value of 1 if the Democratic candidate is an incumbent, –1 if the Republican is an incumbent, and 0 if the seat is open). The coefficient on the incumbency variable estimates the value (in percentage of votes) of incumbency for each election year. The index cannot be calculated for elections in years ending in 2 because of redistricting. The modified version substitutes the district-level presidential vote for the lagged House vote, allowing years following redistricting—most importantly, 2022—to be included. See Gary C. Jacobson, "It's Nothing Personal: The Decline of the Incumbency Advantage in U.S. House Elections," *Journal of Politics* 77, no. 3 (July 2015): 861–73.

in House elections because the number of contests is much smaller (thirty-three or thirty-four in most election years), and only one-third of the Senate's seats are automatically up for election in any election year. Still, careful analysis suggests that Senate incumbency, worth a little more than 2 percent of the vote in elections from 1914 (when senators first became subject to popular election) to 1960, rose to 7 percent for the 1962–92 period.[7] One study indicates that it peaked in the 1980s at about 9 percent but has fallen to below 6 percent in the 2010, 2012, and 2014 elections.[8] In more recent elections, the value of Senate incumbency was essentially zero.

The Vanishing Marginals

David Mayhew identified and named one effect of the augmented House incumbency advantage observed during the 1960s: the "vanishing marginals."[9] Increased vote shares meant that fewer incumbents held *marginal seats*, those taken with narrow margins of victory and therefore thought to be at heightened risk for future losses. Conventionally, seats won with less than some specified share of the two-party vote are designated marginal; 60 percent is the most common threshold used. Figure 3.4 shows how the proportion of incumbents and open-seat winners whose vote lifted them out of the marginal range (60 percent or less) has varied since 1840. Prior to the mid-twentieth century, the two series coincided; approximately the same percentage of incumbents and open-seat victors won with 60 percent or more of the major-party vote during this period, with a noticeable uptick for both around the turn of the twentieth century.

Shortly after World War II, the patterns for incumbents and open-seat winners began to diverge, most conspicuously after 1954. From 1946 through 1966, an average of 61 percent of House incumbents won in excess of 60 percent of the vote; the proportion jumped to 73 percent for the 1968–82 period (the jump that caught Mayhew's eye) and higher still, to 83 percent, for 1984–88. For the 1990–98 period, it dropped back down to 71 percent, then rose to an all-time high of nearly 88 percent in 2002, before falling back below 70 percent in 2010. After increasing to about 77 percent in 2014 and 2016, it dropped back to 68 percent in 2022. As Mayhew also pointed out (and figure 3.4 shows), most contests for open seats have remained in the marginal range during the postwar

[7] Brady, Gaines, and Rivers, "Incumbency Advantage," table 3.

[8] Gary C. Jacobson, "It's Nothing Personal: The Decline of the Incumbency Advantage in Congressional Elections," *Journal of Politics* 77, no. 3 (July 2015): 861–73.

[9] David R. Mayhew, "Congressional Elections: The Case of the Vanishing Marginals," *Polity* 6 (1974): 295–317.

Figure 3.4 House Candidates Receiving More Than 60 Percent of the Major-Party Vote, 1840–2022

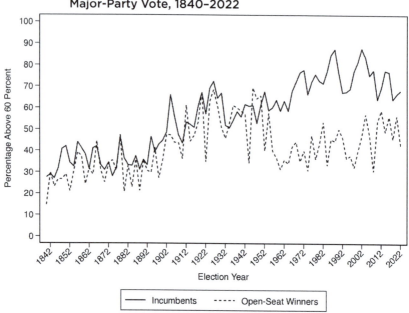

Source: Compiled by authors.

period (2016 and 2020 are two recent exceptions), so the vanishing marginals were not simply the effect of a more general decline in the proportion of closely contested elections. Incumbency itself had something to do with it.

Scholars who first noticed the rise in the value of incumbency according to these measures understandably took it to signify a decline in electoral competition. With wider margins of safety, fewer incumbents should lose, turnover should decline, and therefore so should the *swing ratio*, the percentage of seats changing hands for a given percentage swing in the national partisan vote.[10] Remarkably, none of these things occurred until more than a decade after they were anticipated, and they arose not for the reasons initially proffered. House incumbents were not significantly less likely to lose

---

[10]To calculate the swing ratio, simply divide the change in the percentage of seats a party wins by the change in the percentage of votes it wins; for example, if one party's share of seats rises from 45 percent to 55 percent when its share of the vote rises from 47 percent to 52 percent, the swing ratio is 2.0 [(55–45) / (52–47) = 2.0]; see Erikson, "Malapportionment," 1240–41; Edward R. Tufte, "The Relationship between Seats and Votes in Two-Party Systems," *American Political Science Review* 67 (1973): 540–54; Mayhew, "Vanishing Marginals," 312–14; Cover and Mayhew, "Congressional Dynamics," 78; Morris P. Fiorina, "The Case of the Vanishing Marginals: The Bureaucracy Did It," *American Political Science Review* 71 (1977): 177.

in the 1970s than they were in the 1950s. Neither, if marginality is defined correctly, did the number of marginal House seats decline over this period. And seat swings remained nearly as sensitive to vote swings as before.

Measures of marginality are, in essence, estimates of vulnerability. Members of Congress who win with less than some specified share of votes supposedly have a higher risk of defeat in the next election because they are more exposed to contrary national tides and are more likely to attract strong challengers. Such thresholds are arbitrary, however, and make sense only if they are, in fact, stable indicators of vulnerability. As we showed in previous editions of this text, they are not.[11] As the "marginal" incumbents (by the customary 60 percent standard) became safer, nonmarginal incumbents became more vulnerable. Indeed, an incumbent elected in the 1970s with between 60 and 65 percent of the vote was more likely to lose in the next election than an incumbent in the 1950s who had been elected with 55 to 60 percent of the vote (8.0 percent compared with 6.9 percent). Although the mean incumbent's vote increased by about five percentage points during the 1960s, incumbents added almost nothing to their electoral security in the 1970s because they were little safer with a 65 percent margin than they had been in the 1950s with a 60 percent margin; their comparative risk at higher margins (above 65 percent) was also greater. Because incumbent defeats did not diminish, and marginal seats—correctly defined—did not dwindle, there was no reason to expect the swing ratio to be significantly lower during this time, and it was not.[12]

How could vote margins increase without adding to House incumbents' security, diminishing competition, or dampening swings? The answer lies in another crucial change, first noticed by Thomas E. Mann: an attendant increase in the heterogeneity of interelection vote swings among districts. As the average incumbent's vote margin grew from the 1950s through the 1970s, so did the heterogeneity of interelection vote swings. In the 1940s and 1950s, the standard deviation of the swing averaged 5.4; in the 1970s, it averaged 8.6. Vote margins could increase without making incumbents significantly safer because electorates became more volatile and electoral change more idiosyncratic across districts.[13]

---

[11] Gary C. Jacobson and Jamie L. Carson, *The Politics of Congressional Elections*, 9th ed. (Lanham, MD: Rowman & Littlefield), 44–46.

[12] John A. Ferejohn and Randall L. Calvert, "Presidential Coattails in Historical Perspective," *American Journal of Political Science* 28 (1984): 131; Gary C. Jacobson, "The Marginals Never Vanished: Incumbency and Competition in Elections to the U.S. House of Representatives, 1952–1982," *American Journal of Political Science* 31 (1987): 126–41.

[13] The increase in volatility remains when effects of changes in the sophomore surge and retirement slump are removed; see Gary C. Jacobson, *The Electoral Origins of Divided Government: Competition in U.S. House Elections, 1946–1988* (Boulder, CO: Westview Press, 1990), 17–18.

Table 3.2 Incumbents Defeated in General Elections to the US House of Representatives, by Previous Vote Margin and Decade (Percentages)

Decade	Vote Margin in Previous Election			Standard Deviation of Vote Swing	Loser's Mean Vote in Prior Election	Losers Who Were Not Marginal
	50.0–59.9%	60.0–64.9%	>65%			
1940s	27.7	4.2	1.2	5.1	54.5	7.8
1950s	13.4	1.9	0.8	5.6	54.1	10.5
1960s	13.3	3.3	1.5	6.1	55.6	17.9
1970s	12.6	8.0	2.7	8.6	58.0	35.7
1980s	8.0	2.4	0.6	8.3	56.2	28.9
1990s	10.7	4.2	0.2	5.3	55.0	18.1
2000s	19.4	7.2	0.1	5.4	56.7	32.5
2010s	12.2	2.4	1.9	5.0	58.5	8.9

Note: Includes only incumbents who faced major-party opponents in stable (non-redistricted) districts. Decades are defined by reapportionment cycles; for example, the 1950s include 1952 through 1960; the exception is the 1940s, which includes 1946 through 1950.

Source: Compiled by the authors.

In the late 1980s, some of the effects anticipated from the vanishing marginals finally came to pass. Incumbents were reelected at record rates in 1986 and 1988. The swing ratio finally underwent a statistically significant decrease (of about 25 percent).[14] Critics proclaimed the end of electoral competition; President Ronald Reagan, among others, made the invidious observation that there was "less turnover in Congress than in the Supreme Soviet."[15] Incumbency, it seems, had finally overwhelmed all other electoral forces. In retrospect, however, the elections of the late 1980s did not establish a new norm for congressional elections; all the relevant figures and tables in this chapter show a sharp revival of electoral competition for incumbent-held seats in the mid-1990s. This broad historical arc raises a number of questions. Why did House incumbents' vote margins increase sharply in the mid-1960s? Why did competition revive so vigorously after the early 1990s? Why has it continued to vary from election to election? Why did district electorates become first more and then much less volatile in their voting patterns across the past six decades? The answers involve a complicated, interlocking set of institutional, behavioral, and contextual elements that we begin to examine in this chapter but that will take the rest of the book to explicate fully.

[14]Jacobson, *The Electoral Origins of Divided Government*, 82–93.

[15]Judy Mann, "Eyes Turn to Hill's Fortress of Incumbency," *Washington Post*, May 24, 1989, B3.

SOURCES OF THE INCUMBENCY ADVANTAGE

The Institutional Characteristics of Congress

The search for an explanation for the sharp rise in the incumbency advantage during the 1960s proceeded on several fronts. One major focus was the institutional characteristics of Congress. David Mayhew, summarizing the results of his close examination of Congress as of the early 1970s, put it succinctly: "If a group of planners sat down and tried to design a pair of American national assemblies with the goal of serving members' reelection needs year in and year out, they would be hard pressed to improve on what exists."[16]

The congressional system that Mayhew described permitted the widest individual latitude for pursuing reelection strategies. For example, a highly decentralized committee and subcommittee structure allowed members to specialize in legislative areas where they could best serve local interests. It also provided most members with a solid piece of legislative turf. The operative norm for writing legislation was similar: something for everyone. Positive-sum distributive politics, represented by pork barrel legislation and the Christmas tree bill (one with separate little "gifts" for a variety of special-interest groups), were much more prevalent than the zero-sum competition for scarce resources. Members deferred to each other's requests for particular benefits for their states or districts in return for deference to their own.

The parties also bowed to the varied electoral needs of members. Party discipline within Congress was lightly applied. In the face of controversial and divisive issues, Mayhew noted, "the best service a party can supply to its congressmen is a negative one: It can leave them alone. And this is in general what the congressional parties do."[17] Party leaders, taking the position that the first duty is to get reelected, encouraged members to vote the district first; members happily complied.

The system allowed legislators to take the "right" positions, make pleasing statements, and bring home the bacon while avoiding responsibility for the collective performance of Congress. It provided a setting for emphasizing individual achievements while insulating members from blame for the general failures and inadequacies of the institution, which were at least in part a consequence of the patterns of individual behavior encouraged by the system itself. This is important because the public's assessment of the performance of Congress was often strongly negative.

---

[16]David R. Mayhew, *Congress: The Electoral Connection* (New Haven, CT: Yale University Press, 1974), 81–82.

[17]Mayhew, *Congress*, 99–100.

Ratings of Congress actually declined while House incumbents were increasing their vote margins in the late 1960s and early 1970s. Disdain for Congress did not extend to its individual members; people generally rated their representatives far higher than they did their Congress.[18]

Members of Congress also voted themselves an astonishing array of official resources that they could use to pursue reelection. These include salary, travel, office, staff, and communication allowances now amounting to an average of nearly $1.83 million per year for each House member and up to several times that much for senators (whose allowances vary by state population).[19] All these perquisites were augmented dramatically in the 1960s and 1970s, with trends flattening out in the 1980s. Personal staffs of House and Senate members also increased sharply, growing by more than 300 percent between the 1950s and the late 1970s.[20] The value to members of personal staff was underlined in 1994 when the new Republican House majority voted to slash committee staff by one-third but rejected a proposal to reduce personal staff from eighteen to sixteen.[21] Travel allowances grew in comparable fashion before being included as part of a lump-sum benefit starting in 1978.[22]

The growth of other official resources kept pace. The most important congressional perquisite is the franking privilege, which allows members to use the mail free of charge for "official business," which is broadly interpreted to include most kinds of communications to constituents. Franked mail grew by more than an order of magnitude between the 1950s and 1980s. Public criticism led both houses to tighten up the rules governing franked mail in 1990, so the volume fell substantially from its peak in 1984.[23] Republican reformers proposed even tighter rules in 1994, but newly elected members representing large Western districts successfully opposed reforms.[24] It is easy to understand members' reluctance to deny themselves such a serviceable tool. Other media have been adopted as technology has advanced. Facilities for preparing radio and television

---

[18]Glenn R. Parker and Roger H. Davidson, "Why Do Americans Love Their Congressmen So Much More Than Their Congress?" *Legislative Studies Quarterly* 4 (1979): 53–61.

[19]Ida A. Brudnick, "Congressional Salaries and Allowances: In Brief," Congressional Research Service, updated December 16, 2022, https://sgp.fas.org/crs/misc/RL30064.pdf.

[20]Norman J. Ornstein, Thomas E. Mann, and Michael J. Malbin, *Vital Statistics on Congress, 2012* (Washington, DC: Brookings Institution, 2013), tables 5.1 and 5.5.

[21]"GOP's House-Cleaning Sweep Changes Rules, Cuts Groups," *Congressional Quarterly Weekly Report*, December 10, 1994, 3487.

[22]Gary C. Jacobson, *The Politics of Congressional Elections*, 8th ed. (Boston: Pearson, 2013), table 3.3.

[23]Jacobson, *The Politics of Congressional Elections*, figure 3.6.

[24]"GOP's House-Cleaning Sweep Changes Rules, Cuts Groups."

tapes and films have long been available to members free of charge. In 1977, members voted themselves unlimited wide-area telephone service for long-distance calls. Members' offices are now linked to the Internet, and nearly all of them maintain professionally designed websites. As of February 2023, more than 97 percent of members regularly use social media such as Facebook or Twitter to keep in touch with constituents.[25]

Changes in Voting Behavior

Obviously, one major advantage of incumbency is control of extensive official resources for reaching and serving constituents. The remarkable expansion of these resources during the 1960s thus offered a ready explanation for larger incumbent vote margins: more vigorous exploitation of ever-expanding communications resources.[26] The accepted ideas about voting behavior in congressional elections lent support to this view. Voters were known to favor candidates with whom they were familiar (that is, whose names they could recall when asked), so more extensive self-advertising by members could be expected to have direct electoral payoffs, assuming it made them more familiar to voters. Apparently, it did not. John Ferejohn showed that the proportion of voters who could recall incumbents' names did not increase between 1958 and 1970; nor did incumbents' familiarity advantage over their challengers grow. He proposed that a change in voting behavior was behind the enlarged incumbency advantage. Voters had become substantially less loyal to political parties during the 1960s and early 1970s. Perhaps they were merely substituting one simple voting cue, incumbency, for another, party.[27]

This explanation reflected a conception of voters as remarkably uninformed and superficial in their approach to voting decisions. As chapter 5 will report in greater detail, later research challenged this view of congressional voters. If the congressional electorate is at least modestly more sophisticated and better informed than was once commonly thought, voters' preference for incumbents must arise from something more than the simple fact of incumbency.

Constituency Service

Morris P. Fiorina argued that members of Congress enhanced their own electoral fortunes not simply by advertising themselves more extensively but also by changing the focus of their activities and thus

---

[25]"Members on Twitter," https://twitter.com/i/lists/34179516?lang=en, accessed February 9, 2023.

[26]Mayhew, *Congress*, 311.

[27]John A. Ferejohn, "On the Decline of Competition in Congressional Elections," *American Political Science Review* 71 (1977): 174.

the content of the message they sent to voters. Essentially, they created needs and then reaped the rewards of spending more time and energy catering to them. In the three decades following World War II, Congress enacted legislation that greatly increased the size and scope of the federal government. Government growth generated an increasing volume of demands from citizens for help in coping with bureaucratic mazes or taking advantage of federal programs. Members responded to the demand by continually adding to their capacity to deliver assistance, including the previously mentioned growth of personal staffs. The placement of new staff was equally significant; the largest share went into augmenting members' capacity to provide services to constituents. In 1972, 13 percent of personal Senate staff and 23 percent of personal House staff worked in district or state offices; by 2016, the proportions had grown to 43 and 47 percent before declining slightly in 2020 to 41 and 46 percent, respectively.[28]

The greater demand for services and the greater resources for providing them created more opportunities to build credit with constituents. For electoral purposes, Fiorina noted, "the nice thing about casework is that it is mostly profit; one makes many more friends than enemies."[29] Casework is also nonpartisan. The party affiliation of the member delivering assistance or of the constituent receiving it is irrelevant. What counts is the member's ability to deliver services, which increases with tenure in Washington and consequent seniority and familiarity with the administrative apparatus. It is therefore perfectly reasonable for voters to prefer candidates on the basis of their incumbency rather than their party label or policy positions. And it is equally reasonable for members to concentrate on providing services rather than on making national policy as a strategy for staying in office.

The evidence regarding Fiorina's thesis has been equivocal. The amount of time spent in the district appears to have little effect on the incumbent's vote margin, for example.[30] The value of pork barrel legislation has also been called into doubt, although some research suggests

[28]Congressional Research Service, "Senate Staff Levels in Member, Committee, Leadership, and Other Offices, 1977–2020," table 2, https://sgp.fas.org/crs/misc/R43946.pdf; Congressional Research Service, "House of Representatives Staff Levels in Member, Committee, Leadership, and Other Offices, 1977–2021," table 2, https://crsreports.congress.gov/product/pdf/R/R43947.

[29]Fiorina, "The Bureaucracy Did It," 180.

[30]Glenn R. Parker and Suzanne L. Parker, "Correlates and Effects of Attention to District by U.S. House Members," *Legislative Studies Quarterly* 10 (1985): 239; R. Michael Alvarez and Jason L. Saving, "Deficits, Democrats, and Distributive Benefits: Congressional Elections and Pork Barrel Politics in the 1980s," *Political Research Quarterly* 50 (1997): 809–31.

that Democrats, at least, benefited from delivering local projects.[31] Nor is it fully established that personal and district services persuade voters to prefer incumbents, although, again, some research, including some clever experimental studies, indicates that they do.[32] Part of the analytical problem is that if members work the district harder the more insecure they are, then harder work may be associated with narrower electoral margins, even if it is what keeps the member in office.[33]

As originally proposed, none of these explanations took note of the fact that, despite wider reelection margins, House incumbents kept losing at about the same rate as before until the late 1980s. Once this is recognized, the evidence marshaled on their behalf takes on a rather different cast. For example, it is striking that the steep increase in staff, travel, and communications allowances during the 1960s and 1970s failed to produce any net improvement in incumbents' reelection prospects at the time they were occurring. Not until the late 1980s—well after the growth in official resources had flattened out—did the average incumbent's probability of reelection actually grow, and that change was reversed in the early 1990s and has continued to decline ever since. Considered in this

---

[31]Patrick Sellers, "Fiscal Consistency and Federal District Spending in Congressional Elections," *American Journal of Political Science* 41 (1997): 1024–41; Alvarez and Saving, "Deficits, Democrats, and Distributive Benefits"; Kenneth N. Bickers and Robert M. Stein, "The Electoral Dynamics of the Federal Pork Barrel," *American Journal of Political Science* 40 (November 1996): 1300–26; Justin Grimmer, Solomon Messing, and Sean J. Westwood, "How Words and Money Cultivate a Personal Vote: The Effect of Legislator Credit Claiming on Constituent Credit Allocation," *American Political Science Review* 106 (2012): 703–19; Justin Grimmer, "Appropriators Not Position Takers: The Distorting Effects of Electoral Incentives on Congressional Representation," *American Journal of Political Science* 57 (2013): 624–42; Austin C. Clemens, Michael H. Crespin, and Charles J. Finocchiaro, "The Political Geography of Distributive Politics," *Legislative Studies Quarterly* 40(2015): 111–36.

[32]See John R. Johannes and John C. McAdams, "The Congressional Incumbency Effect: Is It Casework, Policy Compatibility, or Something Else?"; Morris P. Fiorina, "Some Problems in Studying the Effects of Resource Allocation in Congressional Elections"; Diana Evans Yiannakis, "The Grateful Electorate: Casework and Congressional Elections"; and John C. McAdams and John R. Johannes, "Does Casework Matter? A Reply to Professor Fiorina," all in *American Journal of Political Science* 25 (1981): 512–604. See also John R. Johannes and John C. McAdams, "Congressmen, Perquisites, and Elections," *Journal of Politics* 50 (1988): 412–39; Albert D. Cover and Bruce S. Brumberg, "Baby Books and Ballots: The Impact of Congressional Mail on Constituent Opinion," *American Political Science Review* 76 (1982): 347–59; Morris P. Fiorina and Douglas Rivers, "Constituency Service, Reputation, and the Incumbency Advantage," in *Members of Congress at Home and in Washington*, ed. Morris P. Fiorina and David Rohde (Ann Arbor: University of Michigan Press, 1989); David W. Romero, "The Case of the Missing Reciprocal Influence: Incumbent Reputation and the Vote," *Journal of Politics* 58 (November 1996): 1198–207.

[33]Morris P. Fiorina, *Congress: Keystone of the Washington Establishment*, 2nd ed. (New Haven, CT: Yale University Press, 1989), 94–97; Fiorina, "Resource Allocation in Congressional Elections," 545–50; Bickers and Stein, "The Electoral Dynamics of the Federal Pork Barrel."

light, it appears that incumbents have had to run ever harder just to stay in the same place.

Similarly, the idea that incumbents prospered by exploiting the decline of partisanship among voters requires amendment. The basic argument is that a less partisan, more candidate-oriented electorate favors incumbents. Diminished partisanship means fewer automatic votes against an incumbent, so personal cultivation of the district can pay off in a wider vote margin—but it also means fewer automatic votes for an incumbent and thus larger potential vote losses, should local electoral circumstances change.[34] A less partisan electorate is more fickle, the vote is less stable from one election to the next, and a wide margin in one election is a weaker guarantee of success in the next.[35]

Although it, too, was proposed as part of an explanation for greater incumbent security, Fiorina's main point—that incumbents' increased emphasis on nonpartisan district services has altered the meaning of the electoral choice—is not necessarily blunted if incumbents' security has been exaggerated. Attention to constituency service plainly does command a large share of the time of members and their staffs.[36] Fiorina's thesis thus helps explain why first-term House members, once much more vulnerable than more senior incumbents, became considerably more difficult to defeat.

Prior to the changes of the 1960s, new members were often swept into the House on a partisan tide and then swept out again two years later as it receded. Between 1946 and 1966, for example, 20.4 percent of all new House members lost their first reelection bids, a rate of defeat nearly quadruple that of members who had served two or more terms (5.2 percent). For the next three decades, first-termers held on to newly won seats much more consistently; only 7.0 percent lost, compared to 3.2 percent of more senior incumbents. After 2004, however, the greater vulnerability of new members returned; in elections from 2006 through 2022, 11.2 percent of first-termers lost, compared with only 4.3 percent of senior members.

The greater insulation from outside forces in the latter decades of the past century did not reduce uncertainty or risk. The locus of competition merely shifted to the district, and incumbents assumed a larger burden of responsibility for winning reelection. Before the 1970s, House members who lost could put much of the blame on forces beyond their control.

---

[34]Morris P. Fiorina, "The Incumbency Factor," *Public Opinion Quarterly* (September/October 1978): 42–44.

[35]Jacobson, *The Electoral Origins of Divided Government*, 15–19, 56–57.

[36]Parker and Parker, "Attention to District by U.S. House Members," 229; see also Glenn R. Parker, *Homeward Bound: Explaining Changes in Congressional Behavior* (Pittsburgh, PA: University of Pittsburgh Press, 1986).

On average, their interelection vote swing was only 3.7 percentage points worse than their party's mean swing. In the 1970s and 1980s, the average loser's vote swing was 7.9 points worse than the party mean. In the most recent decade, however, the gap has fallen back to 4.4 points, indicating that forces beyond the incumbent's control have again become relatively more important in shaping their electoral fates.

The Variability of the Incumbency Advantage

All of the existing explanations for the growth in the incumbency advantage are contingent upon the decline of party-line voting in the electorate and the disassociation of congressional from presidential voting. Both trends initially contributed to the emergence of a more candidate-centered electoral system that greatly advantaged incumbents. During the past three decades, however, party loyalty within the electorate has risen steadily, the link between congressional and presidential elections has tightened, and electoral politics have grown increasingly nationalized. In short, the erosion of partisanship in the 1960s and 1970s provided the opportunity for incumbents to improve their electoral security, while increased resources, constituency services, and pork barrel projects provided the means (the motive, as Mayhew suggested in his classic work, remained constant). As these trends have reversed, House incumbency status has lost a considerable portion of its electoral value.[37]

As we shall see in chapter 5, partisan loyalty in the electorate has grown steadily since the early 1990s—which is one reason that electoral volatility (table 3.2) and the incumbency advantage have diminished (figure 3.3) from their peaks in the 1980s. Incumbency remains an advantage, to be sure. But its electoral value clearly varies across both election years and districts. It depends in part on what the incumbent does with the resources available and on how hard and shrewdly he or she works to build and maintain support in the district. And this varies among members, although the degree of variation declined during the 1970s and 1980s as members less inclined to endless pursuit of reelection quit or were weeded out.

Its value depends even more on the kind of opposition the incumbent faces; as we shall see, differences in the skills and resources of challengers are a primary source of variation over time in incumbents' electoral fortunes. And it depends on what competing considerations—notably, national issues and leaders—shape voters' judgments, as the 1994, 2006, 2010, 2014, and 2018 midterms made clear.[38] It is safe to assume that

---

[37] Jacobson, "Decline of the Incumbency Advantage in Congressional Elections."

[38] For an analysis of the varying effects of incumbency based on American National Election Study survey data, see John R. Petrocik and Scott W. Desposato, "Incumbency and Short-Term Influences on Voters," *Political Research Quarterly* 57 (2004): 363–73.

incumbents who seek reelection want to stay in Congress. Why do some exploit the resources of office less vigorously than others to this end? The principal reason is that they have other important things to do with their time, energy, and staff. Single-minded pursuit of reelection detracts from work in Washington and therefore from a member's power and influence in Congress and impact on public policy. Reelection is an instrumental, not ultimate, goal. Sometimes a member must forgo opportunities to build support back in the district in order to share in governing the country. And the longer a member is in office, the more opportunities he or she has to influence policy and to gain the respect of others in government. Members very soon find that they have to balance their desire for electoral security with their desire for a successful career in Washington.

One reelection strategy might diminish this trade-off. For incumbents who stake their electoral futures on their party's performance, cultivating the district could lose some of its urgency. Many of the Republicans taking office for the first time in 1994 initially wedded their fortunes to the party's "Contract with America," dedicating their energies to dismantling welfare and regulatory programs and balancing the budget. Pledged to limiting their stay in Congress, they claimed to want careers that were, in the words of one of them, Steve Largent of Oklahoma, "brilliant but brief."[39] But even members far more interested in revolutionizing government than in lengthy congressional careers do not necessarily pay less attention to their districts. Losing would jeopardize the revolution. Insofar as supporting fundamental change forces members to cast politically dangerous votes, members have all the more reason to please constituents in every other way they can. The Republican insurgents elected in 1994 and 2010 promising radical and controversial changes in federal policy thus continued to provide constituents with the services they had come to expect from their representatives and to work energetically to maintain a strong district presence. The Republicans newly elected to the House in 2022 can be expected to do the same.

DISCOURAGING THE OPPOSITION

Doing casework, making trips back to the district, sending newsletters and tweets, and all the other activities legislators engage in to promote reelection are not aimed merely at winning votes in the next election. They are also meant to influence the perceptions formed by politically active people of the member's hold on the district. The electoral value of

---

[39] "Freshmen: New Powerful Voice," *Congressional Quarterly Weekly Report*, October 28, 1995, 3251.

incumbency lies not only in what it provides to the incumbent but also in how it affects the thinking of potential opponents and their potential supporters. Many incumbents win easily by wide margins because they face inexperienced, sometimes reluctant challengers who lack the financial and organizational backing to mount a serious campaign for Congress. An incumbent who can convince potentially formidable opponents and people who control campaign resources that he or she is invincible is very likely to avoid a serious challenge and so will be invincible—as long as the impression holds.

This is so because politically skilled and ambitious nonincumbents follow rational career strategies, people who control campaign resources make strategically rational decisions about deploying them, and the volume of campaign resources at the disposal of a nonincumbent candidate has a great deal to do with how well he or she does at the polls. Other things being equal, the strongest congressional candidates are those for whom politics is a career. They have the most powerful motive and the greatest opportunity to master the craft of electoral politics. They are most likely to have experience in running campaigns and in holding elective office. They have the incentive and opportunity to cultivate other politically active and influential people and to put them under some obligation. Ambitious career politicians also have the greatest incentive to follow a rational strategy for moving up the informal but quite real hierarchy of elective offices in the American political system. An experienced politician will have acquired valuable political assets—most typically, a lower elective office—that increase the probability of moving to a higher office. However, these assets are at risk and may be lost if the attempt to advance fails. Thus the potentially strongest congressional aspirants will also make the most considered and cautious judgments about when to try for a congressional seat.[40]

Incumbency is central to their strategic calculations. Politically knowledgeable people are fully aware of the advantages of incumbency and of the long odds that challengers normally face, and they adjust their behavior accordingly. Hence, for example, typically more than half of

---

[40]Gary C. Jacobson and Samuel Kernell, *Strategy and Choice in Congressional Elections*, 2nd ed. (New Haven, CT: Yale University Press, 1983), chapter 3; Thomas A. Kazee, "Ambition and Candidacy: Running as a Strategic Calculation," in *Who Runs for Congress? Ambition, Context, and Candidate Emergence*, ed. Thomas A. Kazee (Washington, DC: Congressional Quarterly Press, 1994), 171–77; L. Sandy Maisel and Walter P. Stone, "Determinants of Candidate Emergence in U.S. House Elections: An Exploratory Study," *Legislative Studies Quarterly* 22 (February 1997): 79–96; Jamie L. Carson et al., "Constituency Congruency and Candidate Competition in U.S. House Elections," *Legislative Studies Quarterly* 36 (2011): 461–82; Matthew Buttice and Walter Stone, "Candidates Matter: Policy and Quality Differences in Congressional Elections," *Journal of Politics* 74 (2012): 870–87.

Table 3.3 The Probability of Victory and the Quality of Nonincumbent Candidates for the US House of Representatives, 1946–2022

Type of Race	Number of Cases	Winners (%)	Former Officeholders (%)
Open Seats			
No general election opponent	114	100.0	72.8
Held by candidate's party	1,530	76.9	68.4
Held by neither party	323	50.0	54.2
Held by opposite party	1,530	25.2	35.6
Total	3,497	52.9	52.9
Challenges to Incumbents			
Incumbent's vote in last election (%)			
50.0–54.9	1,902	20.5	48.6
55.0–59.9	1,914	8.6	26.8
60.0–64.9	1,941	4.0	16.5
65.0–69.9	1,720	2.0	13.8
70.0 or more	2,430	0.5	7.0
Unopposed	1,748	0.9	4.4
Total	11,655	3.4	19.2

Note: Data for incumbents excludes districts that were redrawn between elections.
Source: Compiled by the authors.

the candidates for open House seats have previously held elective offices, whereas such experienced candidates comprise fewer than one-fifth of the candidates challenging incumbents. Within this larger pattern, experienced challengers are more likely to run against incumbents who had closer contests in the last election. Table 3.3 presents the evidence for these points and shows the close association between the prospects for victory and the presence of experienced House candidates.[41]

This has not always been the case, however, as figure 3.5 demonstrates. Throughout much of the nineteenth century, House incumbents were much more likely than their modern-day counterparts to face experienced challengers because of that era's vigorous party machines. Party bosses could induce experienced candidates to run by offering them "insurance" in the form of patronage jobs or other forms of employment in the event they lost. This promoted greater electoral competition than is commonly observed today. Following the Progressive movement's successful attack on party machines at the end of the century, the percentage of incumbents facing strong challengers declined precipitously.

---

[41]The entries in the second and third columns are correlated at 0.94.

Figure 3.5 Percentage of Incumbents Facing Quality Challengers, 1840-2022

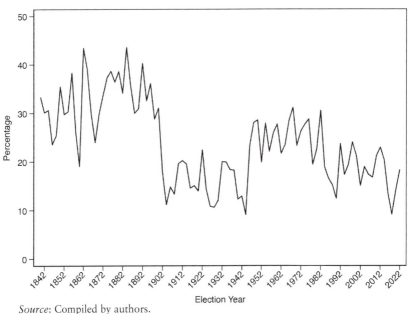

Source: Compiled by authors.

The reforms deliberately enfeebled the party machines, depriving them of the resources to recruit and underwrite the campaigns of experienced challengers. This, in turn, helped contribute to the growing careerism in Congress because high-quality challengers were less willing to risk taking on incumbents without the safety net provided by strong local party organizations.

Although the post–World War II era did see a resurgence in the percentage of incumbents facing experienced challengers, the effect was short-lived, and the proportion has continued to decline during the past few decades.[42] Indeed, the 2018 midterm witnessed the lowest percentage of experienced challengers running against incumbents (9 percent) in any election since 1944. Republican officeholders reacted as expected in a difficult year, and only 5 percent of Democratic incumbents faced experienced challengers, a record low for the party. But the proportion of Republicans facing experienced Democratic challengers (13 percent) was also below average and far below the last election in which Democrats picked up as many seats, 1974 (42 percent).

The 2020 and 2022 elections did observe an increase in the percentage of incumbents facing experienced challengers—14 and 18 percent

---

[42]Carson and Roberts, *Ambition, Competition, and Electoral Reform*.

respectively—but this is somewhat lower than one might expect given the opportunities to run that are routinely available. Indeed, the pattern of candidate emergence in the most recent elections suggests that electoral experience is no longer a necessary indicator of challenger quality and that electoral prospects need not be the most important consideration. In a more nationalized electoral context, candidate quality matters far less than it once did relative to one's party label. This was especially true in the 2022 midterms where numerous Republican candidates with prior elective experience opted not to run and were instead represented in their primaries by political amateurs who embraced former President Trump's rhetoric about the 2020 election being stolen—several of which went on to win.[43]

The strategies of individuals and groups that control campaign resources complement and reinforce the career strategies of potential congressional candidates. The most important of these resources is money, although other forms of assistance can also be valuable. People and groups contribute to congressional campaigns for reasons ranging from selfless idealism to pure venality. Regardless of the purpose, however, most contribute more readily to nonincumbent candidates in campaigns expected to be close.[44] So do political parties.[45] Resources are limited, and most contributors deploy them where they have the greatest chance of affecting the outcome; donors naturally try to avoid wasting money on hopeless candidates. Figure 3.6 displays one consequence of this tendency. Candidates for open seats typically have substantially more money to spend than those challenging incumbents, and their average spending exceeds that of incumbents in some election years. The data also show how these elections have grown rather steadily more expensive since the 1970s, when accurate spending totals first became available. (These and later spending totals are adjusted for inflation, 2022 = 1.00.)

According to figure 3.6, average spending by incumbents has risen faster than spending by challengers, widening their typical financial advantage over time—until, that is, 2018, when the average spent by challengers increased dramatically, more than doubling the recent averages and sharply reducing the gap. This achievement was short-lived, however, as challenger spending declined in both 2020 and 2022 compared

[43]See Jamie L. Carson and Aaron A. Hitefield, "A Red Wave or a Ripple? Nationalized Politics and the 2022 Midterms," *The Forum* 21 (2023): https://doi.org/10.1515/for-2023-2002.

[44]Gary C. Jacobson, *Money in Congressional Elections* (New Haven, CT: Yale University Press, 1980), 72–101.

[45]Gary J. Jacobson, "A Collective Dilemma Solved: The Distribution of Party Campaign Resources in the 2006 and 2008 Congressional Elections," *Election Law Journal* 9 (2010): 381–97.

Figure 3.6 Average Campaign Spending in House Elections, 1972-2022

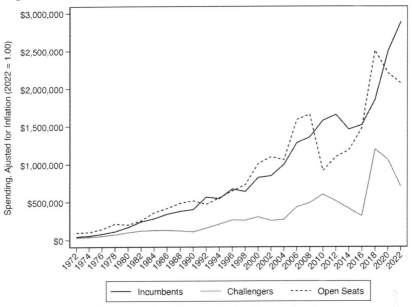

Source: Compiled by authors from Federal Election Commission data.

to incumbent spending across both election years. In 2022, incumbent spending approached $3 million, whereas average challenger spending barely exceeded $700,000, representing the widest gap between the two types of candidates to date.

Even before 2018, however, these data masked a crucial difference among districts, revealed by figure 3.7. House incumbents representing districts with a favorable partisan advantage have faced poorly funded challengers all along, with very little change from the early 1970s—until 2018. Those incumbents competing in more balanced districts or where challengers enjoy a favorable partisan climate, in contrast, faced increasingly well-funded opponents.[46] The upward trend over the past decade was impressive, but the 2018 totals were rather historic. Although incumbents were not at a financial disadvantage in the years between 2006 and 2016—they outspent the challenger in 79 percent of these districts and by an average of $940,000 (that is, by 42 percent)—it became more difficult for them to prevail. During these years, 30 percent of incumbents running in districts favoring the challenger lost, compared to 16 percent in balanced districts and less than 2 percent in districts favoring the incumbent; the comparable figures for 1972–2004 had been 10 percent, 6 percent, and 2 percent, respectively.

---

[46]Again, this district balance is defined by whether the party's presidential vote was at least two points above its national average in the current or, for midterms, most recent prior election year.

Figure 3.7 Campaign Spending by Challengers, by District Partisan Leanings, 1972–2022

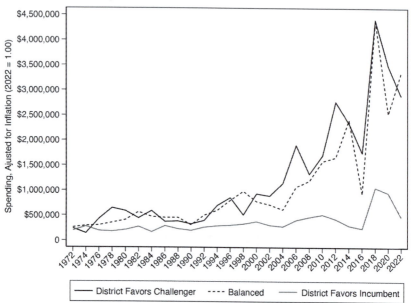

Note: Amounts are in millions of dollars, adjusted for inflation, 2022 = 1.00.
Source: Compiled by authors from Federal Election Commission data.

The spending data for 2018 are of another dimension altogether, a spike produced entirely by Democratic challengers. However, this record surge appears to be short-lived as revealed by spending patterns in both 2020 and 2022. As evident in figure 3.8, Democrats challenging Republican incumbents in balanced or Democratic-leaning districts spent an average of $7 million in 2018, more than three times as much as in any previous election year. Republican incumbents also jacked up their spending in these districts, but they were still outspent by 60 percent of the challengers and by an average of $1.75 million. Even in Republican-leaning districts, Democratic challengers spent an average of $1.7 million in 2018, two and a half times as much as spent in any previous election by challengers in this category. By contrast, spending by Democratic challengers in 2020 and 2022 declined rather significantly relative to Republican incumbents, returning to pre-2018 levels.

As party loyalty among voters has grown over the past three decades, largely reversing its earlier decline (see chapter 5), the partisan makeup of a district has become an increasingly important indicator of electoral prospects and, thus, a strategic consideration for potential candidates and contributors. In contests involving incumbents, an additional consideration governs prospects: the availability of issues—personal, local, and national—that the challenger's campaign might use effectively to

Figure 3.8 Average Campaign Spending by Republican Incumbents and Democratic Challengers, by Competitiveness of the District, 1972–2022

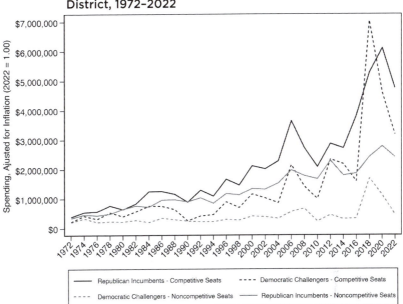

Note: Amounts are in millions of dollars, adjusted for inflation, 2022 = 1.00.
Source: Compiled by authors from Federal Election Commission data.

undermine the support that the incumbent has enjoyed in past elections. Expectations about the likelihood of electoral success clearly influence the decisions of potential candidates and campaign contributors. The better the electoral odds, the more likely the race is to attract a strong challenger and the more money will be contributed to his or her campaign. Furthermore, strong candidates themselves attract campaign money, and the availability of campaign money attracts strong candidates. A system of mutually reinforcing decisions and expectations thus links nonincumbent candidates and contributors with each other and with perceived electoral prospects.

The strategies pursued by potential congressional candidates and their prospective backers mattered a great deal in a candidate-centered election process because the quality and experience of challengers, as well as the campaign resources made available to them, had a powerful effect on election results. As elections have grown more nationalized and less candidate-centered in recent decades, the partisanship of the constituency has weighed more heavily in strategic career decisions. We present a variety of evidence for this conclusion in the following pages. For now, the relevant point is that variations in the quality and resources of challengers offered an alternative explanation for increased vote margins enjoyed by incumbents between the 1960s and 1990s.

Gary Cox and Jonathan Katz, for example, parsed the House incumbency advantage into direct, scare-off, and quality effects. *Direct effects* derive from the expansion of resources and district activities we have already discussed. *Scare-off effects* contribute to the incumbency advantage when strong challenges are successfully discouraged. *Quality effects* measure the difference that candidate experience makes. (All incumbents are, by assumption, high-quality candidates; nonincumbents, many of whom have never before held elective office, supply the variation.) Cox and Katz concluded that the most important source of growth in the incumbency advantage was an increase in the electoral effect of quality differences. The value of incumbency grew not because of greater resources or more effective deterrence of quality challengers but because the difference in electoral performance between experienced and inexperienced candidates grew. Cox and Katz attributed this change to the weakening of party ties and the consequent growth of candidate-centered electoral politics.[47] One attraction of this explanation is its consistency with evidence that the incumbency advantage also increased in elections for state legislature, governor, and other statewide offices during the same period.[48]

David Brady, Brian Gaines, and Douglas Rivers's analysis, using somewhat different methods, reached a similar conclusion. Moreover, they found that the effect of the challenger's quality on the incumbent's vote had grown by about the same amount in Senate and House elections. Senators did not become more secure, however; unlike House districts, states became more competitive—that is, more evenly balanced in a partisan sense—over the same time span, offsetting the growing incumbency advantage.[49] This research suggests that the incumbency advantage depends not so much on what incumbents do as on what potential opponents do and that it grew because the impact of the opposition's level of mobilization grew.[50]

---

[47]Gary W. Cox and Jonathan Katz, "Why Did the Incumbency Advantage in U.S. House Elections Grow?" *American Journal of Political Science* 40 (1996): 478–97.

[48]Stephen Ansolabehere and James M. Snyder Jr., "The Incumbency Advantage in U.S. Elections: An Analysis of State and Federal Offices, 1942–2000," *Election Law Journal* 1 (2002): 315–38.

[49]Brady, Gaines, and Rivers, "Incumbency Advantage," 14.

[50]Marcus Prior has offered an alternative explanation for the rise of the incumbency advantage—the spread of television—but other research has not supported his hypothesis. See Marcus Prior, "The Incumbent in the Living Room: The Rise of Television and the Incumbency Advantage in U.S. House Elections," *Journal of Politics* 68 (2006): 657–73; Stephen Ansolabehere, Erik C. Snowberg, and James M. Snyder Jr., "Television and the Incumbency Advantage in U.S. Elections," *Legislative Studies Quarterly* 31 (2006): 469–90. For historical evidence on the incumbency advantage, see Jamie L. Carson, Erik J. Engstrom, and Jason M. Roberts, "Candidate Quality, the Personal Vote, and the Incumbency Advantage in Congress," *American Political Science Review* 101 (2007): 289–301.

Figure 3.9 The Vote Value of Prior Office to House Challengers, 1952–2022

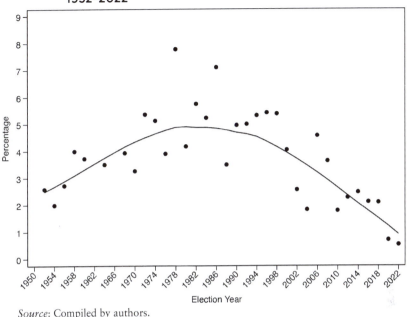

Source: Compiled by authors.

Like the value of incumbency, the effects of challenger quality (as measured by prior elective office) has fallen sharply in the past decade. This is evident from figure 3.9, which reports estimates regressing the challenger's vote on prior elective office, controlling for district partisanship and the challenger's party.[51] Although somewhat noisy, the smoothed trajectory of quality effects matches that of the incumbency advantage quite closely. From the 1970s through the 1990s, it averaged 5.2 percentage points; over the seven elections since 2010, the average is 1.7 percentage points. The evidence, then, is that the effects of candidate quality have varied historically along with the effects of incumbency and for the same reason. Candidate quality appears to matter substantially less when party matters more (except, to a degree, during the late nineteenth century when strong party machines were able to boost competition by recruiting stronger challengers).[52] In twenty-first-century elections, challengers are still strategic about when they decide to run, but they now

---

[51]District partisanship is measured by the vote for the challenger's party's presidential candidate in the contemporary or, for midterms, prior presidential election; party is controlled to account for national trends in each election year; experience is a categorical variable that takes values of 1 if the challenger has held prior elective office, 0 otherwise.

[52]Carson and Roberts, *Ambition, Competition, and Electoral Reform*, 2013.

appear to be riding the electoral tide rather than contributing much to it.[53] We will have more to say about strategic challengers and electoral tides in chapter 6.

MONEY IN CONGRESSIONAL ELECTIONS

Mobilization requires money. Congressional aspirants are wise, indeed, to worry about the availability of money for a campaign. How well non-incumbent candidates do at the polls is directly related to how much campaign money they raise and spend. The precise relationship between campaign spending and election results is difficult to pin down, however, because most candidates and contributors act strategically. Potential donors try to avoid wasting their money on hopeless causes. The better a candidate's prospects, the more contributors of all kinds are willing to invest in the campaign. The connection for nonincumbents between spending and votes is therefore at least potentially reciprocal: Money may help win votes, but the expectation that a candidate can win votes also brings in money. To the degree that (expected) votes influence spending, ordinary measures will exaggerate the effects of spending on votes.

Spending by incumbents is also reciprocally related to the vote, but in a rather different way: The higher the incumbent's expected vote, the *less* money flows into the campaign. This is not because secure incumbents have trouble raising money; quite the contrary. Many interest groups contribute to campaigns not so much to influence the outcome as to gain influence with, or at least access to, people who are likely to be in a position to help or hurt them. They waste no money on sure losers but have no qualms about giving money to sure winners, even when it is not really needed. Whether incumbents tap this source of funds depends on whether they think they need the money (or may sometime in the foreseeable future).

Most members of Congress do not particularly enjoy asking for money and tend to limit their fund-raising efforts if they do not see a pressing need for additional campaign cash (given the strength of the opposition they are facing), although in recent elections their party leaders have encouraged them to raise funds to pass along to the party's needier candidates. If they feel threatened, though, incumbents have sources that are not nearly so readily available to challengers. In addition to groups seeking access, party committees and ideological interest groups rally to support threatened incumbents of the preferred party or

---

[53]Gary C. Jacobson, "Partisanship, Money, and Competition: Elections and the Transformation of Congress since the 1970s," in *Congress Reconsidered*, ed. Lawrence C. Dodd and Bruce I. Oppenheimer, 10th ed. (Washington, DC: Congressional Quarterly Press, 2013), 138.

ideology on the grounds that it is easier to hold on to a seat than to take one from the opposition. Incumbents, then, can generally raise as much campaign money as they think they need. Again, the anticipated vote affects spending—but for incumbents, the relationship is negative: the larger their expected vote, the less they raise and spend. To the degree that (expected) votes influence spending, ordinary measures will underestimate the effects of incumbent spending on votes.

To measure the effect of campaign spending on votes or victories, then, it is necessary to subtract the reciprocal effect of (expected) votes or victories on spending. Although theoretically feasible, this turns out to be extremely difficult in practice, and after over forty years of research, the appropriate solution remains elusive. We simply do not know the extent to which analyses that ignore the problem overestimate the effects of challenger spending or underestimate the effects of incumbent spending—if at all.

The Connection between Money and Success

Nonetheless, certain things are clear. First, congressional challengers rarely win if they do not spend a substantial amount of money, and the more they spend, the more likely they are to win. Figures 3.10 and 3.11

Figure 3.10 Challengers' Expenditures and Victories in House Elections, 1972–2022

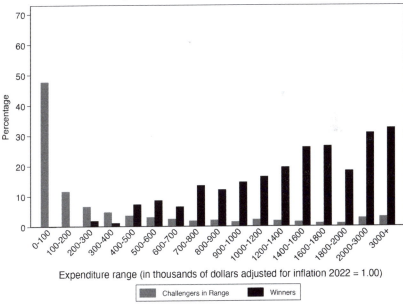

Source: Compiled by authors from Federal Election Commission data.

Figure 3.11 Winning House Challengers, by Level of Campaign Spending, 1972–2022

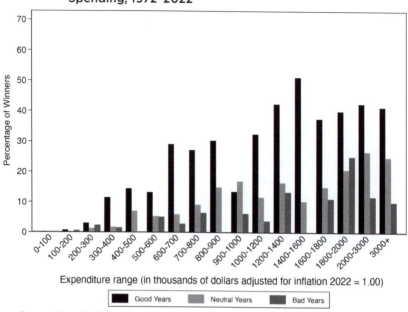

Expenditure range (in thousands of dollars adjusted for inflation 2022 = 1.00)

Source: Compiled by authors.

leave no doubt on this point. Figure 3.10 displays the percentage of winning challengers in House elections from 1972 through 2022 at ascending levels of campaign spending (adjusted for inflation, 2022 = 1.00). It also displays the proportion of challengers at each level of spending. The odds against challengers who spent less than $100,000 were long indeed; only one of 4,097 was successful. Nearly a majority (48 percent) of all House challengers fell into that category. Chances were only slightly better for challengers who spent between $100,000 and $200,000 (1 of 1000 won); they and the first group include nearly 60 percent of all challengers. Prospects improved with increased spending. Nearly 26 percent of challengers spending $1.2 million or more won, as did 33 percent of challengers spending at least $3 million.

Of course, not all election years are alike. Some elections feature national political tides—driven by recessions, scandals, unpopular wars, presidential politics, and the like—that strongly favor one party's candidates. Conditions in other years seem nearly neutral between parties. Intuitively, a House challenger's chances of winning should vary with the strength and direction of national partisan tides. Figure 3.11 shows that challengers favored by national conditions—Democrats in 1974, 1982, 1996, 2006, 2018, and Republicans in 1980, 1984, 1994, 2010, 2014— won more frequently at every level of campaign spending. Anything over

$300,000 was enough to make a race of it; 35 percent of those spending more than $600,000 won their contests, and those spending more than $1 million won 44 percent of the time. In addition, challengers were able to spend more money in good election years compared with neutral or bad years. This is further evidence of strategic behavior on the part of contributors.

In the absence of strong partisan tides, challengers have a much harder time winning and need to spend more than $800,000 to enjoy better than a one-in-ten chance of winning. Against contrary partisan tides, challengers raise the least amount of money and find it very difficult to win no matter what they spend; even those spending more than $1.2 million have won only 10 percent of the time.

What do these data tell us about the cost of a minimally competitive challenge? Obviously, the amount varies from district to district and from state to state, depending on the structure and cost of mass media advertising, the vigor of local parties and other politically active organizations, and local campaign styles. It also varies with national partisan tides and has certainly grown over time (even taking inflation into account). Still, if we set an arbitrary but reasonable standard for a competitive campaign as one giving the challenger at least a 15 percent chance of winning, $800,000 (in 2022 dollars) is a plausible estimate of the threshold for the entire period. Only 18 percent of all House challengers crossed this threshold; a large majority spent far too little to make a contest of it. If we confine our analysis to more recent elections, the minimum price tag for a competitive House campaign under average conditions is probably more than $1 million; 200 of the 245 challengers who defeated incumbents in this century exceeded this threshold.

Defeating a House incumbent is clearly expensive (and a serious Senate campaign can cost more than ten times as much in a large state such as California, New York, or Texas); relatively few challengers have been able to raise enough funds to be serious threats. Challengers who do acquire sufficient resources can make incumbents feel anything but safe. For incumbents, spending a great deal of money on a campaign is a sign of weakness rather than strength. In fact, the more money they spend on the campaign, the worse they do at the polls. That is, the relationship between the incumbent's level of spending and share of votes or likelihood of victory is negative. Spending money does not cost them votes, to be sure; rather, incumbents raise and spend more money the more strongly they feel themselves challenged. The more their opponents spend, the more they spend. Challengers evidently get more bang for their buck; therefore, the more spent by both the challenger and the incumbent, the greater the challenger's share of the vote, and the more likely the challenger is to win the election.[54]

Table 3.4 Campaign Spending and Challenger Victories, 1992–2022 (Percentages)

Incumbents' Spending ($1,000s)	Challengers' Spending ($1,000s)							
	<200	200–400	400–600	600–800	800–1,000	1,000–2,000	>2,000	Row Average
<200	0.0	0.0	0.0	0.0	0.0	0.0	0.0	0.0
200–400	0.0	0.0	0.0	0.0	0.0	0.0	0.0	0.0
400–600	0.0	3.9	0.0	0.0	0.0	0.0	0.0	0.9
600–800	0.0	2.3	8.0	16.7	0.0	0.0	40.0	1.7
800–1,000	0.0	0	0.0	0.0	12.5	20.0	12.0	1.6
1,000–2,000	0.08	0.4	3.2	3.1	8.0	23.5	51.4	3.3
>2,000	0.3	1.1	6.3	0.0	8.3	16.9	41.7	17.0
Column Average	0.07	0.8	4.0	2.3	8.5	19.0	44.5	6.5

Number of Cases	<200	200–400	400–600	600–800	800–1,000	1,000–2,000	>2,000	Row Total
<200	19	0	1	0	1	3	1	25
200–400	123	5	2	1	0	1	0	132
400–600	299	26	10	5	0	5	0	345
600–800	400	44	25	6	8	1	1	485
800–1,000	441	62	24	11	8	10	5	561
1,000–2,000	1282	280	157	98	88	145	35	2,085
>2,000	371	90	79	50	72	308	403	1,373
Column Total	2,935	507	298	171	177	473	445	5,006

Note: Spending is adjusted for inflation, 2022 = 1.00.
Source: Compiled by the authors.

Table 3.4 displays these relationships, in a simplified manner. It lists the percentage of winning challengers at different combinations of incumbent and challenger spending in elections since 1992. The column average shows that the more challengers spent, the more likely they were to win. Only one of the 2,935 who spent less than $200,000 won, while 19 percent of those spending more than $1 million, and 44 percent spending more than $2 million, replaced the incumbent.

[54]Jacobson, *Money in Congressional Elections*, 136–45; Gary C. Jacobson, "Money and Votes Reconsidered: Congressional Elections, 1972–1982," *Public Choice* 47 (1985): 16–40; Gary C. Jacobson, "Enough Is Too Much: Money and Competition in House Elections, 1972–1984," in *Elections in America*, ed. Kay L. Schlozman (New York: Allen & Unwin, 1987), 173–95; Gary C. Jacobson, "The Effects of Campaign Spending in House Elections: New Evidence for Old Arguments," *American Journal of Political Science* 34, no. 2 (1990): 334–62. For the contrary argument that incumbent spending has powerful effects, see Donald P. Green and Jonathan S. Krasno, "Salvation for the Spendthrift Incumbent: Reestimating the Effects of Campaign Spending in House Elections," *American Journal of Political Science* 32 (1988): 884–907; Donald P. Green and Jonathan S. Krasno, "Rebuttal to Jacobson's 'New Evidence for Old Arguments,'" *American Journal of Political Science* 34 (1990): 363–72.

The row average shows that the more incumbents spent, the more likely they were to lose. None in the lowest category, and less than 2 percent who spent less than $1 million, failed to win reelection; 17 percent in the highest spending category did so. At any given level of incumbent spending, challengers do better the more they spend; at any given level of challenger spending, the incumbent's spending makes little apparent difference in the outcome. The variation across every row (except the first three that have only a handful of observations in the higher spending categories) is statistically significant at p < .001; the variation down every column is insignificant.

More elaborate multivariate models that analyze votes or victories as a function of campaign spending and other variables (e.g., national tides, district partisanship) tell the same story.[55] This pattern appears in Senate elections as well.[56] Unfortunately, the problem of reciprocal causation renders all such results suspect. Because challengers raise more money the better they are expected to do, this kind of analysis exaggerates the effects of their campaign spending. Because incumbents raise less money the better they are expected to do (remember, their spending is reactive), the analysis underestimates the effects of their spending. What we do not know is by how much.

Scholars have designed a variety of models to take reciprocal causation into account, but the findings vary widely. At one extreme, results simply reinforce the original findings; at the other, they suggest that marginal returns on spending are as high for incumbents as for challengers. Most often, however, they suggest that the marginal returns on spending are indeed greater for challengers than for incumbents, but to a lesser degree than the original findings would indicate. Also, at least two studies have found that the returns on spending by first-term incumbents are about as large as the returns on spending by their opponents—and much larger than the returns on spending by more senior members.[57]

---

[55]Jacobson, *Money in Congressional Elections*, 136–46; Alan I. Abramowitz, "Incumbency, Campaign Spending, and the Decline of Competition in U.S. House Elections," *Journal of Politics* 53 (1991): 34–56; Stephen Ansolabehere and Alan Gerber, "The Mismeasure of Campaign Spending: Evidence from the 1990 U.S. House Elections," *Journal of Politics* 56 (1994): 1106–18. Ansolabehere and Gerber show that the result holds if only the money spent directly on campaign communications is measured as spending, although the coefficient on communications spending is naturally larger than the coefficient on total spending in their model.

[56]Alan I. Abramowitz, "Explaining Senate Election Outcomes," *American Political Science Review* 82 (1988): 385–403; Jacobson, *Money in Congressional Elections*, 152–55.

[57]Robert S. Erikson and Thomas R. Palfrey, "Campaign Spending and Incumbency: An Alternative Simultaneous Equations Approach," *Journal of Politics* 60 (1998): 355–73; Christopher Kenny and Michael McBurnett, "An Individual-Level Multi-equation Model of Expenditure Effects in Contested House Elections," *American Political Science Review* 88 (1994): 669–707; Larry Bartels, "Instrumental and 'Quasi-instrumental' Variables," *American Journal of Political Science* 35 (1991): 777–800.

The results from an alternative approach to the problem—using panel or multiple-wave surveys to measure the effects of spending on changes over time in popular support for candidates—are considerably more consistent in finding that the marginal returns on spending are substantially higher for challengers than for incumbents.[58]

Despite the uncertainties that remain, several things are abundantly clear. Challengers (and candidates for open seats who face well-financed opponents) rarely win without spending a great deal of money. Even rarer is a losing incumbent who might plausibly blame defeat on a shortage of funds.[59] Moreover, there are solid reasons challengers should get a larger return than incumbents on their spending. However, there are also good reasons for believing that, under some circumstances, the incumbent's spending should affect the outcome as well.

Why Campaign Money Is More Important to Challengers Than to Incumbents

Campaign spending is subject to diminishing returns; the more dollars spent, the less gained by each additional dollar. Congressional incumbents usually exploit their official resources for reaching constituents so thoroughly that the additional increment of information about their virtues put forth during the campaign adds comparatively little to what is already known and felt about them.[60] As we shall see in chapter 5, the extent to which voters know and like incumbents is unrelated to how much is spent on the campaign. The situation is quite different for nonincumbents. Most are largely unknown before the campaign, and the extent to which they penetrate the awareness of voters—which is crucial to winning votes—is directly related to how extensively they campaign. The money spent on nonincumbents' campaigns buys the attention and recognition that incumbents already enjoy at the outset of the campaign.

If this is true, we would expect spending by both candidates to affect the outcomes of contests for open seats, and indeed it does. Table 3.5

---

[58]Gary C. Jacobson, "Campaign Spending Effects in U.S. Senate Elections: Evidence from the National Annenberg Election Survey," *Electoral Studies* 25 (June 2006): 195–226; Gary C. Jacobson, "Measuring Campaign Spending Effects in U.S. House Elections," in *Capturing Campaign Effects*, ed. Henry E. Brady and Richard Johnston (Ann Arbor: University of Michigan Press, 2006), 199–220; Jacobson, "New Evidence," 334–62.

[59]Between 1992 and 2022, losing House incumbents spent an average of nearly $3.5 million in inflation-adjusted dollars (2022 = 1.00); 94 percent spent more than $1 million; 63 percent outspent their victorious challengers, with an average spending advantage of more than $650,000.

[60]See Henry Kim and Brad Leveck, "Money, Reputation, and Incumbency in U.S. House Elections, or Why Marginals Have Become More Expensive," *American Political Science Review* 57 (2013): 492–504, for evidence that incumbent spending has skyrocketed in marginal compared to safe House districts.

Table 3.5 Campaign Spending and Democratic Victories in Open House Seats, 1992–2022 (Percentages)

Republicans' Spending ($1,000s)	Democrats' Spending ($1,000s)							
	<200	200–400	400–600	600–800	800–1,000	1,000–2,000	>2,000	Row Average
<200	66.7	100	100	100	100	100	100	98.0
200–400	0	0	100	66.7	100	94.4	100	89.7
400–600	0	0	100	66.7	60	75	20	48.1
600–800	0	0	33.3	33.3	50	72.7	66.7	39.5
800–1,000	0	0	40	12.5	50	46.2	85.7	29.3
1,000–2,000	2.1	0	6.7	0	4.2	34.2	64.5	26.8
>2,000	0	12.5	25	33.3	50	24.4	41.6	33.7
Column Average	4.4	6.3	43.2	41.5	46.7	54.2	53.8	42.9

Number of Cases	<200	200–400	400–600	600–800	800–1,000	1,000–2,000	>2,000	Row Total
<200	6	1	10	14	11	37	22	101
200–400	1	1	2	3	6	18	8	39
400–600	5	0	1	3	5	8	5	27
600–800	11	3	3	3	6	11	6	43
800–1,000	18	3	5	8	4	13	7	58
1,000–2,000	48	16	15	16	24	73	62	254
>2,000	25	8	8	6	4	41	178	270
Column Total	114	32	44	53	60	201	288	792

Note: Spending is adjusted for inflation, 2022 = 1.00.
Source: Compiled by the authors.

displays the relationships in their most elementary form: Democrats do better the more they spend, and Republicans do better the more they spend. Democrats thrive in the combinations appearing in the upper-right section of the matrix (winning 79 percent of the time); Republicans thrive in the lower-left section below the diagonal (winning 88 percent of the time). Along the diagonal, results are split (Democrats win 46.5 percent overall). Multivariate analyses recapitulate these results.[61]

In general, then, spending should matter more to nonincumbent candidates than to incumbents because they have yet to get their message out, and getting a message out costs money. Spending may also matter to incumbents if they have to get out a *new* message. That is, when an incumbent is in trouble for some reason (personal, such as involvement in the House Bank scandal in 1992, or political, as with Democrats facing the Republican tide in 1994, Republicans saddled with an unpopular

---

[61]Jacobson, "Money and Votes Reconsidered," 28–30.

president and war in 2006, Democrats facing popular discontent about the economy and Barack Obama's policies in 2010, Republicans weighed down by Donald Trump's unpopularity in 2018, or Democrats worried about high rates of inflation in 2022) and needs to counter with a new pitch, campaign money is essential. It comes down to this: Regardless of their potential, if challengers cannot raise lots of money, they can forget about winning. If incumbents are strongly challenged, raising and spending lots of money may not help them much, although there is no reason to think it hurts. Even if the marginal return on spending by incumbents is very small, spending a great deal of money is probably a rational strategy because even a small number of votes may make the difference between winning and losing.

Plainly, though, spending huge sums of money does not ensure reelection. The amount spent by the challenger (and how qualified and skillful he or she is) matters much more. This means that the incumbent's most effective electoral strategy is to discourage serious opposition. He or she can do this most effectively by avoiding showing signs of electoral vulnerability. Even the most implacable political enemies will not mobilize their full range of resources against an incumbent if they see no prospect of success. Maintaining an active presence in the district is designed to discourage the opposition.[62] So is working to maintain the electoral coalition that put the member into office in the first place. Because elections are the most pertinent source of information on a member's electoral strength, it is particularly important to avoid slippage at the polls. An unexpectedly weak showing in one election inspires even stronger opposition in the next. As one incumbent put it, "It is important for me to keep the young state representatives and city councilmen away. If they have the feeling that I'm invincible, they won't try. That reputation is very intangible. [But] your vote margin is part of it."[63] With the emergence of national parties and outside groups looking for any signs of electoral weakness (discussed more fully in chapter 4), more strongly partisan electorates, and the increasing nationalization of campaigns, the strategy of discouraging strong opposition has become much harder to execute for incumbents not blessed with a favorable partisan environment, but they still try.

---

[62]Or so politicians think. One empirical study found that district attention, variously measured, had no discernible effect on the quality of the challenger or the money spent against the incumbent; see Jon R. Bond, Cary Covington, and Richard Fleisher, "Explaining Challenger Quality in Congressional Elections," *Journal of Politics* 47 (1985): 523. However, this study is subject to the same doubts raised about negative findings in other studies on the effects of district attention, discussed earlier.

[63]Quoted in Richard F. Fenno Jr., *Home Style: House Members in Their Districts* (Boston: Little, Brown, 1978), 13.

Incumbents may also try to diminish the intensity of opposition in the district. No one can please everyone, and nothing is to be gained by alienating one's supporters, but occasional friendly gestures to potentially hostile political interests may dampen their enthusiasm for organizing an all-out campaign against the member. From an incumbent's perspective, then, elections are not merely discrete hurdles to be cleared at regular two-year intervals. They are, as Richard F. Fenno Jr.'s unique research showed, a series of connected events that form part of a "career in the district," which parallels the career in Washington.[64] Winning is always crucial, of course, but winning in a way that minimizes future opposition is just as desirable in the long run.

THE CAREER IN THE DISTRICT

Other important insights into congressional election processes emerge from thinking in terms of congressional careers rather than single elections. Fenno's observations in the 1970s led him to conclude that House members' careers in the district passed through identifiable stages. In the first, the *expansionist phase*, members devoted a great deal of time and energy to building up their base of regular supporters. Beginning with a core of solid backers, they worked to reach additional individuals and groups in the district that they hoped to incorporate into their electoral coalitions. The expansionist phase began before the first election and continued for at least a few more. The capacity of first-term members to increase their electoral margins, even in the face of strongly contrary electoral tides, was a sign of this effort and its efficacy.

Fenno observed that at some point, after a few elections, members typically entered into a *protectionist phase*, during which they worked to maintain the support they had built up over the years but no longer attempted to add to it. By this time, they had often discouraged serious opposition through a show of growing electoral strength and had been in Washington long enough to have acquired some influence and responsibility. Working the district became a less attractive alternative to making policy and exercising legislative skills. At this stage, members risked "losing touch with the district," to use the politicians' cliché. If they did, they could become vulnerable at the polls. But their vulnerability might not become apparent at all until it was tested.

The stages of congressional career development may no longer be so clear-cut for most legislators, as many now show little sign of diminishing attention to district matters as their seniority grows.[65] Still, the pattern

---

[64]Fenno, *Home Style*, chapter 6.
[65]Richard F. Fenno Jr., *The Challenge of Congressional Representation* (Cambridge, MA: Harvard University Press, 2013).

influences the strategies pursued by nonincumbents seeking congressional seats. The best opportunity arises when the incumbent dies or retires, and it is not uncommon to find ambitious young politicians biding their time until a seat becomes open, after which a lively scramble ensues among them for the nomination and election.[66] First-term members also attract unusually vigorous opposition; their challengers are twice as likely to have held elective public office and spend, on average, more than twice as much money as challengers to more senior incumbents. The strategic assumption is that newly elected members do not have as firm a hold on their districts as they will later develop, so it is better to go after them now rather than later.[67] Politicians who use electoral margins as evidence of electoral vulnerability will focus on these new incumbents because so many of them initially win office in close elections.

Incumbents who survive the first bid for reelection should be most vulnerable in the protectionist stage of their careers. Electoral support is not won once and for all. It requires continual renewal and reinforcement. Members who work merely to maintain their base of support may actually let it slip, especially if they enjoy a few elections with feeble opposition that disguises any weakening of their hold on the district.[68] A challenger who, through luck or cleverness, puts together a serious campaign against a member whose hold on the district has imperceptibly atrophied may surprise everyone, including the incumbent and the challenger.

One example is Duncan Hunter, who defeated Democratic incumbent Lionel Van Deerlin in the 1980 contest for the 42nd District of California. Van Deerlin had not been seriously challenged in years; he was unaware of his own electoral weakness and of the progress his challenger was making until it was too late to do anything about it. Hunter had decided to run only at the last minute and then on the theory that, although he was likely to lose, he would be in a stronger position to take the seat in 1982, especially if, as many anticipated, Van Deerlin retired. Hunter's hesitation did not prevent a vigorous and well-financed campaign, and

---

[66]Robeck, "State Legislator Candidates," 511; Harvey L. Schantz, "Contested and Uncontested Primaries for the U.S. House," *Legislative Studies Quarterly* 5 (1980): 550; Jamie L. Carson et al., "Constituency Congruency and Candidate Competition in Primary Elections for the U.S. House," *State Politics & Policy Quarterly* 12 (2012): 127–45; Robert G. Boatright, *Getting Primaried: The Changing Politics of Congressional Primary Challengers* (Ann Arbor: University of Michigan Press, 2014).

[67]For example, here is Martin Franks, then executive director of the Democratic Congressional Campaign Committee, on why first-termers head the Democrats' target list: "The best chance of getting them is now. Every day they are here they become harder to unseat." Quoted in David Kaplan, "Freshmen Find It Easier to Run as Incumbents," *Congressional Quarterly Weekly Report*, November 2, 1985, 2225.

[68]Arjun Wilkins, "Electoral Security of Members of the U.S. House, 1900–2006," *Legislative Studies Quarterly* 37 (2012): 277–304.

he wound up with 53 percent of the vote, compared with the 24 percent won by the token Republican challenger in 1978—a shift of twenty-nine percentage points between the two elections.

Van Deerlin was only the most surprised of a number of senior House Democrats in 1980. Republican challengers defeated fourteen incumbents who had served at least five terms and eight who had served at least nine terms. The 1992, 1994, 2006, 2010, 2014, and 2018 elections also proved disastrous for some entrenched members, in the first instance largely because of the House Bank scandal and in the others because of powerful partisan tides. Among the victims (all Democrats) in 1994 were Tom Foley of Washington, Speaker of the House (fifteen terms); Jack Brooks of Texas, chairman of the Judiciary Committee (twenty-one terms); Neal Smith of Iowa, Appropriations Subcommittee chairman (eighteen terms); and Dan Glickman of Kansas, chairman of the Intelligence Committee (nine terms). Twelve of the twenty-two Republican incumbents defeated in 2006 had served six or more terms, and four had served ten or more terms. Most of the fifty-two Democratic incumbents defeated in 2010 were recent electees (thirty-six had first taken office in 2006 or 2008), but eleven had served seven or more terms. The 2014 election marked the end of an era as well; Republican Rick Allen's defeat of Georgia's five-term incumbent John Barrow eliminated the remaining conservative white Democrat from the Deep South.[69] About two-thirds of the Republican incumbents defeated in 2018 were in their first or second terms, but several veterans also lost, including Dana Rorabacher (fifteen terms), Pete Sessions (eleven terms), and John Culberson (nine terms). Incumbents are also sometimes surprised in primary elections. During the 2018 congressional primaries, twenty-eight-year old Alexandria Ocasio-Cortez defeated ten-term incumbent Joseph Crowley, fourth ranking Democrat in the House of Representatives and a potential successor to Nancy Pelosi.[70] And in 2014 the Republican House Majority leader Eric Cantor lost his primary to Tea-Party upstart David Brat.

These elections offer a powerful illustration of how fickle district electorates can be. A member's personal relationship with constituents can keep the district safely in his or her hands—but only through a continuing high level of personal attention and only if potent new issues detrimental

[69]Deirdre Walsh, "Last White Democrat from Deep South Loses Congressional Seat," CNN, November 5, 2014, http://www.cnn.com/2014/11/05/politics/last-southern-white-democrat-in-congress. In the Senate, Susan Collins (R-ME) is the last of a dying breed, as she is one of the few remaining moderate Republicans in the upper chamber.

[70]Shane Goldmacher and Jonathan Martin, "Alexandria Ocasio-Cortez Defeats Joseph Crowley in Major Democratic House Upset," *The New York Times*, June 26, 2018, https://www.nytimes.com/2018/06/26/nyregion/joseph-crowley-ocasio-cortez-democratic-primary.html.

to the incumbent do not intrude. Mayhew noted that to say, "Congress-man Smith is unbeatable," means only that he "is unbeatable as long as he continues to do the things he is doing."[71] After the 1994 and four of the five most recent midterms, we should add, "And only as long as what he is doing is what voters care about when deciding how to vote." Only unrelenting entrepreneurial effort will maintain a wide reelection margin; allow for a letup or a slipup that attracts and is exploited by a formidable opponent wielding a potent issue, and it can evaporate quickly. Personal ties to the district pay electoral dividends, but only as long as members are willing to invest the time and energy required to maintain them. Even then, there are no guarantees that personal ties will prevail in the face of troublesome new issues or a contrary partisan tide. This has proven espe-cially true in recent decades as increasing electoral nationalization has diminished the relative weight of local or regional factors.[72]

MOTIVATING CHALLENGERS

Most senators and representatives are willing to pay the price to remain members of Congress, at least for a time; retirement or defeat awaits those who refuse.[73] Because most incumbents work hard to remain in office and are therefore extremely difficult to defeat, it is not absurd to ask why, under most circumstances, anyone challenges them at all. Part of the answer is that a fair proportion of incumbents are not challenged at all. In 2002, for exam-ple, seventy-nine House incumbents had no major-party opponent in the general election, and almost all of them were spared primary opposition as well. More recently, the number of unopposed incumbents has varied from a low of twenty-six in 2010 to a high of sixty-four in 2014; the number for 2022 was also relatively low at twenty-nine. Not surprisingly, the partisan balance of unopposed incumbents varies strongly with national conditions that shape strategic decisions regarding candidacies; in 2010, a very good Republican year, only four Democratic incumbents were unopposed in the general election; in 2022, what initially looked like a strong Republican year, only six Democrats were similarly blessed. Still, most incumbents attract challengers even when they appear to be unbeatable. Why?

One reason suggested by several early studies of congressio-nal challengers is naïveté. As David Leuthold noted in his study of

---

[71]Mayhew, *Congress*, 37.

[72]Dan Hopkins, *The Increasingly United States: How and Why American Political Behavior Nationalized* (Chicago: University of Chicago Press, 2018).

[73]See, for example, the story of how Fred Eckert, a first-term incumbent Republican, man-aged to lose a Republican district in upstate New York, in Linda L. Fowler and Robert D. McClure, *Political Ambition: Who Decides to Run for Congress* (New Haven, CT: Yale University Press, 1989).

San Francisco–area congressional campaigns, "Inexperienced candidates often did not realize that they had no chance of winning."[74] Most challengers recognize that the odds are against them, of course, but the inherent uncertainties of electoral politics and a large dose of self-deception may buoy their hopes. Writing from personal experience—he is a political scientist who ran for Congress but did not get past the primary—Sandy Maisel pointed out that "politicians tend to have an incredible ability to delude themselves" about their electoral prospects.[75]

Maisel's report of his own and other congressional primaries in 1978 provides several additional insights into the question. Many congressional candidates had planned for years to run for Congress—someday. The only question was when. Then, when circumstances seemed only a little bit more favorable than usual, their thinking was, "If not now, when?" or, more desperately, "It's now or never."[76] This is also consistent with more recent work that argues that the decision for many candidates is not about *whether* to run, but *when* to run.[77]

Candidates can delude themselves all the more easily when they lack the resources to discover just how difficult their task is; impoverished candidates cannot afford top-quality polls to gauge their status with the electorate. They most often rely instead on their own political intuition and, to less degree, on the opinions of local political activists.[78] Both sources are inclined to tell them what they want to hear, so it is not difficult to see why they might overestimate their chances.

Other scholars, though, discern rationality rather than naïveté when inexperienced candidates challenge incumbents. Jeffrey Banks and D. Roderick Kiewiet argue that inexperienced challengers choose to run when their prospect of defeating the incumbent appears dim because this nonetheless maximizes their probability of getting elected to Congress. Because the long odds deter ambitious career politicians, political neophytes are much more likely to win the nomination than they would be if conditions were more promising (had, for example, the incumbent retired). Their much greater chance of winning the nomination more than offsets the smaller chance of knocking off the incumbent in the general election.

---

[74]David A. Leuthold, *Electioneering in a Democracy: Campaigns for Congress* (New York: John Wiley, 1968), 22.

[75]Louis Sandy Maisel, *From Obscurity to Oblivion: Running in the Congressional Primary* (Knoxville: University of Tennessee Press, 1982), 23.

[76]Maisel, *From Obscurity to Oblivion*, 17.

[77]Cherie D. Maestas, Sarah A. Fulton, L. Sandy Maisel, and Walter J. Stone. "When to Risk It? Institutions, Ambitions, and the Decision to Run for the U.S. House." *American Political Science Review* 100 (2006): 195–208.

[78]Maisel, *From Obscurity to Oblivion*, table 2.2; see also Fowler and McClure, *Political Ambition*, 68.

In the event that the incumbent finds him- or herself embroiled in a political scandal, political amateurs may on occasion find themselves in the right place at the right time. The odds may be very long, but they are still the best an inexperienced amateur can envision.[79]

At least a few such candidates are rewarded with unanticipated success, and that no doubt encourages others to take the plunge. In 1988, for instance, Ronald Matchley, a political novice, was nominated unopposed (the expected nominee, a former state party chair, inexplicably failed to meet the filing deadline) to face Democratic representative Fernand J. St Germain, the powerful chairman of the Committee on Banking, Finance, and Urban Affairs. Matchley was able to exploit St Germain's ethical problems to achieve, "the most improbable triumph in recent Rhode Island history."[80] In 1990, first-time candidates managed to defeat Douglas Walgren of Pennsylvania and Robert Kastenmeier of Wisconsin, despite little prior indication that these veteran House incumbents were vulnerable.

Moreover, elections such as 1992, 1994, 2006, 2010, 2014, and 2018 show that boldness is sometimes rewarded across the board. Challengers who had put themselves in a position to exploit the House Bank scandal, popular disgust with President Bill Clinton and gridlock, discontent with George W. Bush and the Iraq War, high unemployment and unhappiness with the Obama administration, or frustration with the Trump presidency ended up with a great shot at the brass ring. No doubt many Republican newcomers elected in 1994 and 2010 were surprised to find themselves in the House, let alone in the majority, as were some of the Democratic challengers in 2006. The success of so many Democratic women who took the field in 2018 to take a stand against Trump's actions and behavior again showed the potential rewards for taking a chance regardless of initial prospects.[81] "Wave" elections and the occasional demise of seemingly entrenched incumbents serve as seductive object lessons for prospective challengers, who may imagine that they, too, might find themselves in the right place at the right time to beat the long odds against defeating an incumbent.

Even candidates who are certain they will not win find motives for running. The most common reason given is to provide some opposition, to make sure the party is represented on the ballot, or "to demonstrate

---

[79] Jeffrey S. Banks and D. Roderick Kiewiet, "Explaining Patterns of Candidate Competition in Congressional Elections," *American Journal of Political Science* 33 (1989): 997–1015; Boatright, *Getting Primaried.* For a contrary view, see David T. Canon, "Sacrificial Lambs or Strategic Politicians? Political Amateurs in U.S. House Elections," *American Journal of Political Science* 37 (1993): 1119–41.

[80] "Rhode Island—1st District," *Congressional Quarterly Weekly Report*, December 31, 1988, 3618.

[81] Thomsen, Danielle, and Aaron King, "Women's Representation and the Gendered Pipeline to Power," *American Political Science Review* 114 (2020): 989–1000.

that the party [has] a spark of life in the district."[82] Local party leaders may run themselves when they are unable to find anyone else willing to face a drubbing.[83] Some run to build for their own or the party's future, as did many southern Republicans in the 1950s and early 1960s. Others run to promote strongly held ideological beliefs.[84] Opponents of abortion and other religious conservatives have swelled the ranks of Republican challengers in recent years. Still others evidently run to advertise themselves in their professions; this reason is not often volunteered, and with the profession of politics in such low repute, it may no longer be very common. But for much of the postwar period, a remarkable proportion of young attorneys, insurance agents, and real estate brokers turned up as challengers in districts where they had little hope of winning.

In the past, some people apparently found the process of running itself reward enough.[85] This motive has no doubt become rarer as campaigns have become more grueling, with their incessant fund-raising, scurrilous personal attacks, and a heavy toll on family life. Such costs may contribute to the ideological polarization of candidates (discussed in the next chapter) and thus of Congress (discussed in chapter 7) if only ideological zealots now find it sufficiently rewarding to run in the absence of very good prospects of victory.[86] Danielle Thompson found evidence that ideological moderates have indeed been reluctant to run for or stay in Congress in recent years, leaving the field to more extreme candidates, which is consistent with candidate trends observed in both 2020 and 2022.[87] Nevertheless, the Democrats pursuing House seats in 2018 showed that passions transcending ideology can also inspire candidacies, and the Democratic caucus that served in the 116th Congress included as many moderate centrists as insurgent progressives.[88]

---

[82]Robert J. Huckshorn and Robert C. Spencer, *The Politics of Defeat* (Amherst: University of Massachusetts Press, 1971), 75.

[83]John F. Bibby, "The Case of the Young Old Pro: The Sixth District of Wisconsin," in *The Making of Congressmen: Seven Campaigns of 1974*, ed. Alan L. Clem (North Scituate, MA: Duxbury Press, 1976), 216.

[84]Robert G. Boatright, *Expressive Politics: Issue Strategies of Congressional Challengers* (Columbus: Ohio State University Press, 2004), 123–41.

[85]David T. Canon, *Actors, Athletes, and Astronauts: Political Amateurs in the United States Congress* (Chicago: University of Chicago Press, 1990), 38–39.

[86]Eric McGhee et al., "A Primary Cause of Partisanship? Nomination Systems and Legislator Ideology," *American Journal of Political Science* 58 (2014): 337–51.

[87]Danielle Thompson, *Opting Out of Congress: Partisan Polarization and the Decline of Moderate Candidates* (New York: Cambridge University Press, 2018).

[88]Geoffrey Skelley, "The House Will Have Just as Many Moderate Democrats as Progressives Next Year," *FiveThirtyEight*, December, 20, 2018, https://fivethirtyeight.com/features/the-house-will-have-just-as-many-moderate-democrats-as-progressives-next-year/, accessed February 22, 2019.

Regardless of the factors motivating candidates to run today, the increased nationalization of elections and the subsequent decline in the incumbency advantage in recent years make elections far less predictable than they used to be just a few decades ago. Congressional incumbents face much greater uncertainty in the electoral process, given the prominence of various groups such as political action committees, national party campaign committees, independent spenders, and polling agencies that have learned to adapt their strategies to changing political circumstances. This has been further compounded by the dramatic surge in campaign spending witnessed in recent elections, which is unlikely to diminish any time soon. The next chapter explores how these factors have affected campaign politics.

4

Congressional Campaigns

★ ★ ★

IT SHOULD BE APPARENT BY NOW that much of the action in congressional election politics takes place outside of the formal campaigns and election periods. This in no way implies that campaigns are inconsequential. The bottom line is that candidates must seek votes, and the most concentrated work to win them takes place through the campaign. The formal campaign is, of course, crucial to those candidates, including most nonincumbents, who have not been able to match the more-or-less incessant campaigning now typical of congressional incumbents.

Despite the increasing nationalization of congressional elections documented in the preceding chapters and the dramatically expanded involvement of national organizations in recent years, congressional election campaigns have not lost their predominantly candidate-centered focus. To be sure, party committees, political action committees (PACs), and independent spending organizations have become major players, but mainly by learning to operate effectively in an electoral system where candidates rather than parties are usually the center of attention. Credit belongs to parties, PACs, and other outside groups, along with independent professional campaign consultants, for the continuing stream of innovations in campaign technology and strategy that have transformed congressional campaigning in recent years. They also, consequently, share responsibility for higher costs, harsher rhetoric, greater partisan polarization, and the effects that all of these things have had on how members of Congress do their job.

Election campaigns have a simple dominant goal: to win at least a plurality of the votes cast and thus the election. Little else is simple about them, however. Campaigns present candidates with difficult problems of analysis and execution, which, even in the best of circumstances, they master only imperfectly.

The variety of campaign contexts set forth in chapter 2 suggests the analytical work required for an effective congressional campaign. States and districts are not homogeneous lumps; voters do not form an undifferentiated mass. They are divided by boundaries of community, interest, class, race, generation, ideology, moral values, and geography. Candidates (and those who help them put campaigns together) need to recognize these myriad boundaries and understand their implications for building winning electoral coalitions. Often, those without political experience do not understand these intricacies—and this in itself guarantees failure.[1]

The basic questions are straightforward: Which constituents are likely to become solid supporters? Who might be persuaded? Which groups are best written off as hopeless, and how can they be discouraged from voting? How can potential supporters be reached? How can they be induced to vote? What kinds of appeals are likely to attract their support? All these questions must be answered twice, and in different ways, if there is a primary contest. They cannot be addressed at all without some cognitive handle on the constituency: Campaigners are necessarily theorists.

Successful campaigners recognize this, at least implicitly. Members of the House develop highly differentiated images of their constituencies. A coherent diagnosis of district components and forces guides their behavior. Knowledge is grounded in experience; they learn at least as much about their constituents from campaigning and from visiting the district between elections as their constituents learn about them. This kind of learning takes time, and its necessity is another reason for viewing House elections from a time perspective longer than a campaign period or a two-year term.[2] It is also one source of the incumbency advantage and helps explain why politically experienced nonincumbents typically make superior House candidates.

The analytic tasks facing Senate candidates are, in most states, substantially more formidable than those facing House candidates. Senate candidates normally deal with larger and more diverse constituencies, scattered over much wider areas. Incumbents as well as challengers usually suffer far more uncertainty about how to combine constituent groups into winning coalitions. Few have the opportunity to know their states as intimately as House candidates may know their districts.

In earlier times, candidates could sometimes get a feel for unfamiliar neighborhoods and communities from local party activists who were a part of them. Now they are more likely to rely on professional

---

[1]See Ronald Keith Gaddie, *Born to Run: Origins of the Political Career* (Lanham, MD: Rowman & Littlefield, 2004).

[2]Richard F. Fenno Jr., *Home Style: House Members in Their Districts* (Boston: Little, Brown, 1978), 171–72.

research—if, of course, they can afford it. Commercial vendors offer detailed voter lists, complete with information on family incomes, demographics, consumption patterns, group memberships, voting histories, addresses, and phone numbers. Professionally conducted polls probe the opinions and attitudes of district residents. Focus groups—small groups of ordinary citizens brought together to mull over candidates, issues, and campaign themes under the guidance and observation of experienced researchers—provide a sense of what lies behind the polling results. Intelligence gathering, like every other aspect of campaigning, can now be farmed out to specialists if a campaign has enough money to hire them.[3]

The deepest understanding of the political texture of a state or district will not, by itself, win elections. Effective campaigns require a strategy for gathering at least a plurality of votes and the means to carry out that strategy. The central problem is communication. As chapter 5 shows, what voters know about candidates has a strong effect on how they decide to vote. Voters who have no information about a candidate are much less likely to vote for him or her than those who do. The content of the information is equally consequential, to be sure, but no matter how impressive the candidate or persuasive the message, neither will help if potential voters remain unaware of them.

Two resources are necessary to communicate with voters: money and organization. They may be combined in different ways, but overcoming serious opposition requires adequate supplies of both. Money is crucial because it buys access to the media of communication: radio, television, newspapers, direct mail, pamphlets, videos, billboards, bumper stickers, bullhorns, websites, and so on. Organization is necessary to design and execute campaign strategy, to raise money, to schedule the candidate's use of personal time devoted to cultivating voters and contributors, and to help get out the vote on election day or, increasingly, during the absentee and early-voting period leading up to election day.

CAMPAIGN MONEY

Raising money is, by consensus, the most unpleasant part of a campaign. Many candidates find it demeaning to ask people for money and are uncomfortable with the implications of accepting it.[4] Most do it, however, because they cannot get elected without it. The trick, neophyte

---

[3]See any edition of *Campaigns & Elections* for the ads of vendors of these and all other campaign services.

[4]Gary C. Jacobson, *Money in Congressional Elections* (New Haven, CT: Yale University Press, 1980), 170–71; Martin Schram, *Speaking Freely: Former Members of Congress Talk about Money in Politics* (Washington, DC: Center for Responsive Politics, 1995), 71–76.

campaigners are advised, is to "learn how to beg, and do it in a way that leaves you with some dignity."[5] Fund-raising is also enormously and, to most candidates, distressingly time-consuming, especially for Senate candidates from large states.[6]

The Federal Election Campaign Act (FECA) of 1972 and its amendments, enforced by the Federal Election Commission (FEC), are supposed to regulate congressional campaign finances. The law requires full disclosure of the sources of campaign contributions and restricts the amount of money that parties, groups, and individuals may give to congressional candidates.[7] The FECA was originally intended to limit campaign costs and reduce the influence of wealthy contributors in electoral politics. The opposite occurred, partly because the Supreme Court declared limits on campaign spending to be an unconstitutional violation of the First Amendment[8] and partly because the act itself, by establishing a clear legal framework for campaign finance activities, invited parties and PACs to flourish.[9]

In response to concerns that party contribution limits were choking off traditional local party activity in federal elections, Congress liberalized the FECA in 1979 to allow unrestricted spending for state and local party-building and get-out-the-vote activities. In 1996, a Supreme Court decision freed parties to engage in unfettered independent spending for their candidates.[10] Funds for these activities were commonly called "soft money," as distinguished from the "hard money" raised and spent under

---

[5]Diane Granat, "Parties' Schools for Politicians Grooming Troops for Election," *Congressional Quarterly Weekly Report*, May 5, 1984, 1036.

[6]Schram, *Speaking Freely*, 37–46.

[7]Before the passage of the Bipartisan Campaign Reform Act (BCRA) of 2002, individuals could give no more than $1,000 per candidate per campaign (primary and general election campaigns are considered separate campaigns), up to a total of $20,000 in an election year; nonparty PACs could give no more than $5,000 per candidate per campaign (other party contribution limits are discussed later in this chapter). Under BCRA, individual contributions limits were raised to $2,000, to be adjusted for inflation after 2002; for the 2022 elections, the limit was $2,900 (see "2022 Campaign Contribution Limits," OpenSecrets .org, https://www.opensecrets.org/elections-overview/contribution-limits, accessed February 10, 2023). As of April 2, 2014, following the Supreme Court's decision in *McCutcheon v. FEC*, 134 S. Ct. 41 (2014), individual donors are allowed to give to as many candidates and committees as they want, assuming they abide by the per-candidate, PAC, and party committee limits. The PAC limits were not changed or indexed.

[8]*Buckley v. Valeo*, 96 S. Ct. 612 (1976).

[9]Gary C. Jacobson, "Parties and PACs in Congressional Elections," in *Congress Reconsidered*, eds. Lawrence C. Dodd and Bruce I. Oppenheimer, 4th ed. (Washington, DC: Congressional Quarterly Press, 1988), 117–21. For a balanced and thorough account of all aspects of campaign finance in the 1980s, see Frank J. Sorauf, *Money in American Elections* (Glenview, IL: Scott, Foresman, 1988).

[10]*Colorado Republican Federal Campaign Committee v. Federal Election Commission*, 518 U.S. 604 (1996).

the FECA's limitations. Other groups may also finance independent campaigns either explicitly (in which case they must report their spending to the Federal Election Commission) or under the guise of "issue advocacy" or "voter education" (which they need not report, as long as the campaign does not explicitly urge a vote for or against a particular candidate). Organizations taking the latter route are called "527" or "501(c)" groups, after the sections in the tax code regulating them. The details of a group's organization determine the section under which it falls; 527s are purely political organizations, whereas 501(c) groups include social welfare organizations, labor unions, and business associations.

Unrestricted raising and spending of soft money, along with unregulated issue advocacy and voter-education campaigns, effectively destroyed the limits on campaign money in federal elections. The Bipartisan Campaign Reform Act (BCRA), enacted in 2002, attempted to put the lid back on by banning soft money and regulating independent spending on issue advocacy and voter education. But the explosive growth of campaigning by 527 groups beginning in 2004 and of independent party spending beginning in 2006, discussed as follows, shows that while BCRA may have affected the sources of money spent outside the candidates' official campaigns, it could not prevent the injection of massive, essentially unregulated sums into election politics.[11] The Supreme Court put the final touches on an unfettered system in 2010, in *Citizens United v. Federal Election Commission*,[12] by overturning a ban on campaigns financed directly from corporate and union treasuries on the grounds that organizations enjoy the same First Amendment rights as individuals. The decision inspired a liberal public relations firm, Murray Hill Inc., to announce that, because "corporations were people too," it would file to run for Maryland's 8th District.[13]

Following the Court's decision in *Citizens United*, enormous sums of money poured into presidential and congressional elections. Spending by the candidates, party committees, and independent groups in 2020 produced the most expensive presidential and congressional elections

---

[11]Robert G. Boatright et al., "Interest Group and Advocacy Organizations after BCRA," in *The Election after Reform: Money, Politics and the Bipartisan Campaign Reform Act*, ed. Michael J. Malbin (New York: Rowman & Littlefield, 2006), 137–38.

[12]S. Ct. 876 (2010).

[13]"Until now," Murray Hill Inc. said in a statement, "corporate interests had to rely on campaign contributions and influence peddling to achieve their goals in Washington. But thanks to an enlightened Supreme Court, now we can eliminate the middle-man and run for office ourselves"; see Catherine Rampell, "Corporation Says It Will Run for Congress," *New York Times*, February 2, 2010, http://economix.blogs.nytimes.com/2010/02/02/corporation-says-it-will-run-for-congress. Murray Hill Inc. never made it to the ballot; its attempt to register to vote was rejected by the Maryland State Board of Elections because it was "not human." See "Next Step after 'Citizens United': Corporate Candidates," *Politico*, October 29, 2010, http://www.politico.com/news/stories/1010/44388_Page2.html.

in history at a cost of $14.4 billion.[14] The 2022 elections were also lavishly financed, with candidates for the House spending approximately $1.91 billion and candidates for the Senate spending over $1.75 billion. Candidate, PAC, party, and outside spending in 2022, combined, came to approximately $8.9 billion.[15] We will have more to say about the distribution of these expenditures later in the chapter.

Contributions to Candidates

Table 4.1 presents, in aggregate, figures on the amounts and sources of money contributed to House and Senate campaigns from 1972 through 2022. Average campaign receipts have grown steadily, although the growth rate is considerably less impressive than these nominal dollar figures would suggest if inflation is taken into account. In real dollars, contributions to House candidates have grown an average of 8 percent and those to Senate candidates have risen an average of 12 percent, from election year to election year, over this period.

Private individuals contribute the greatest share of campaign money; Senate candidates are especially dependent on individual donations. PACs are the second most important source of campaign funds. Their share grew rather steadily until the early 1990s, peaking at 44 percent for House candidates (1990) and 26 percent for Senate candidates (1988) before falling back in the 2000–20 elections to averages, respectively, of 35 and 15 percent. In 2020 the PAC share dropped noticeably for both sets of candidates, to 23 percent and 10 percent—not because PACs cut back their donations, but because individuals increased theirs. The PAC category includes the various committees organized by unions, corporations, trade and professional associations, ideological and issue-oriented groups of many kinds, and political leaders.

PACs

There is a simple explanation for the growth and then modest decline in the financial importance of PACs. As campaign costs increased and the real value of the dollar declined (losing more than 86 percent of its value between 1972 and 2022), candidates, constrained by the FECA's fixed contribution limits, naturally put more effort into soliciting funds from sources that may legally contribute up to $10,000—the PACs—and

---

[14]Karl Evers-Hillstrom, "Most Expensive Ever: 2020 Election Cost $14.4 Billion," *Open Secrets*, February 11, 2021, https://www.opensecrets.org/news/2021/02/2020-cycle-cost-14p4-billion-doubling-16/.

[15]Taylor Giorno and Pete Quist, "Total Cost of 2022 State and Federal Elections Projected to Exceed $16.7 Billion," *Open Secrets*, November 3, 2022, https://www.opensecrets.org/news/2022/11/total-cost-of-2022-state-and-federal-elections-projected-to-exceed-16–7-billion/.

Table 4.1 Sources of Campaign Contributions to House and Senate Candidates, 1972–2022

Year	Average Contributions ($)	Percentage of Contributions from				
		Individuals	Parties	PACs	Candidates[a]	Unknown
House						
1972	51,752[b]	60[c]	27	14	—	9
1974	61,084	73	4	17	6	—
1976	79,421	59	8	23	9	—
1978	111,232	61	5	25	9	—
1980	148,268	67[c]	4	29	—	—
1982	222,260	63[c]	6	31	—	—
1984	240,722	51	3	39	6	—
1986	280,260	52	2	39	7	—
1988	282,949	49	2	43	6	—
1990	291,246	48	1	44	7	—
1992	358,925	50	1	39	10	—
1994	414,812	54	1	37	8	—
1996	510,997	55	1	34	7	3
1998	544,349	53	1	36	6	4
2000	661,472	53	1	35	7	4
2002	699,736	50	1	37	9	3
2004	766,752	57	.6	36	4	3
2006	953,044	54	1	35	5	5
2008	1,031,148	54	.02	34	7	5
2010	1,160,870	58	.2	34	6	2
2012	1,178,004	56	1	35	5	3
2014	1,093,405	53	1	37	5	3
2016	1,111,729	53	1	39	2	5
2018	1,575,272	62	1	28	2	7
2020	1,842,923	64	1	30	1	4
2022	1,831,950	67	1	23	2	7
Senate						
1972	353,933[b]	67	14	12	.4	8
1974	455,515	76	6	11	1	6
1976	624,094	69	4	15	12	—
1978	951,390	70	6	13	8	—
1980	1,079,346	78[c]	2	21	—	—
1982	1,771,167	81[c]	1	18	—	—
1984	2,273,635	68	1	20	11	—
1986	2,721,793	69	1	25	6	—
1988	2,649,492	68	1	26	6	—
1990	2,166,031	70	1	24	5	—
1992	2,638,964	68	1	25	6	—
1994	3,659,650	61	1	17	22	—

(continues)

Table 4.1 Cont.

Year	Average Contributions ($)	Percentage of Contributions from				
		Individuals	Parties	PACs	Candidates[a]	Unknown
1996	3,274,940	63	1	19	13	4
1998	3,530,099	62	1	19	12	6
2000	5,305,051	55	.2	14	25	6
2002	4,013,845	68	.9	20	8	3
2004	5,418,860	76	.6	17	4	2
2006	7,943,400	68	.3	13	13	5
2008	5,698,551	64	.02	20	5	11
2010	7,555,000	64	.3	14	14	8
2012	9,325,906	67	3	13	13	4
2014	7,827,052	71	4	13	6	6
2016	4,546,879	74	4	18	1	3
2018	9,134,324	70	3	9	13	5
2020	15,131,286	83	3	9	2	3
2022	13,148,805	84	3	10	0	3

Note: [a]Includes candidates' loans unrepaid at the time of filing.
[b]Some contributions before April 7, 1972, may have gone unrecorded.
[c]Includes candidates' contributions to their own campaigns.
Source: Compiled by the authors from data supplied by Common Cause (1972 and 1974), the Center for Responsive Politics (https://www.opensecrets.org/elections-overview?; https://www.opensecrets.org/elections-overview/where-the-money-came-from?), and the Federal Election Commission (1976–2022).

less into soliciting private individuals, who were limited to contributions only one-fifth as large. As figures 4.1 and 4.2 indicate, the number of PACs available for solicitation also grew dramatically during the first decade under the FECA, as did the amount of money at their disposal. This growth flattened out in the mid-1980s while campaigns continued to raise larger sums, eventually reducing the PACs' share of the total. After BCRA raised the ceiling on individual contributions but not on PAC donations in 2002 (from $1,000 to $2,000 per campaign, effectively $2,000 and $4,000 when the primary is included) and allowed the ceiling to rise with inflation (hence a limit of $2,900 for 2022), the relative efficiency of soliciting PACs rather than individuals declined. Still, the number of PACs and their total contributions increased again in the past decade, reflecting the fierce fights for control of the House and Senate in recent elections.

Business-oriented PACs have grown the most in both numbers and total contributions to congressional candidates under the FECA. The number of corporate PACs rose from 89 to 1,972 between 1974 and 1992 before falling off somewhat, ending up at 1,634 in 2022; corporate

Figure 4.1 Political Action Committees, 1974–2022

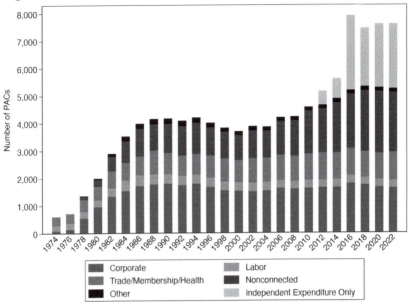

Source: Federal Election Commission.

Figure 4.2 Contributions by Political Action Committees, 1974–2022

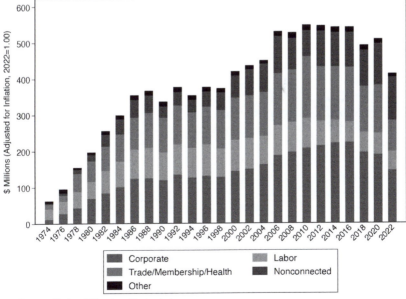

Source: Federal Election Commission.

PAC contributions have multiplied more than twelvefold in real (infla-
tion-adjusted) dollars since 1974, although they have declined since 2016.
Corporate PAC contributions surpassed those of labor PACs in 1980, and
because business associations dominate in the trade/membership/health
category, labor's importance relative to business as a source of campaign
funds has steadily declined.

This development created a potential problem for Democrats. Organized labor has traditionally been the Democrats' principal source of PAC
funds, and only labor PACs have shown much inclination to supply the
venture capital so important to the party's nonincumbent candidates.[16]
The growing financial strength of corporate and trade association PACs
during the first decade after passage of the FECA was expected to benefit
Republicans, and this expectation was borne out in 1978 and 1980.[17]
Republican challengers in both House and Senate contests were treated
generously (compared to other election years) by business-oriented PACs
in those elections.

After 1980, however, business PACs became more even-
handed—49 percent of corporate and 54 percent of trade association
PAC dollars went to Democrats in 1994, for example—but only because
so many of them pursued a dual strategy. They were generous to incumbents of either party who were in positions to help or hurt their interests
and were likely to remain there. As long as Democrats controlled Congress, business-oriented PACs sought to keep doors open and to avoid
antagonizing Democratic members who looked unbeatable—hence, their
generosity with incumbent Democrats and stinginess with Republican
challengers. They were, however, also willing to support promising nonincumbent Republicans—insofar as they could find any—as part of a
long-term strategy aimed at electing a more Republican, hence more
ideologically congenial, Congress. They gave nonincumbent Democrats
very short shrift.

Because PACs contribute strategically, the pattern of PAC contributions varies with electoral expectations. Business-oriented PACs give
more to nonincumbent Republicans when Republican prospects look
bright, particularly in Senate elections (e.g., 1980, 1994, 2010, 2014, and
2018), and more to Republican incumbents when the opportunities for
taking seats from Democrats look dim and they face strong Democratic
challenges, as in the 1982, 2006, 2008, and 2018 House elections.[18]

---

[16]See figures 4.3a and 4.3b in earlier editions for evidence of these trends across time.

[17]See figures 4.4a, 4.4b, 4.5a, and 4.5b in earlier editions for evidence of these trends in the
1970s and early 1980s.

[18]Theodore J. Eismeier and Philip H. Pollack III, *Business, Money, and the Rise of Corporate
PACs in American Elections* (New York: Quantum Books, 1988), 79–94.

Labor does the same thing from the opposite side, investing relatively more in Democratic challenges when conditions favor Democrats (e.g., 1982, 1996, 2006, and 2018) and relatively less when they do not. Because it matters a great deal how much challengers raise and spend, strategic contributions by PACs and other donors reinforce national partisan trends, with important consequences (discussed at length in chapter 6). Both business and labor PACs tend to give lavishly to candidates for open seats of their preferred party; the absence of an incumbent makes for a more competitive election and the best opportunity to take a seat from the other party.

PACs and the Pivotal 1994 Election

The 1994 election dramatically changed the pattern in PAC giving. Even before election day, the Republican surge caught the eye of PAC officials, who began opening their coffers to competitive nonincumbents. Some were no doubt responding to prospective Speaker Newt Gingrich's October threat that those who did not join the Republican cause could expect "the two coldest years in Washington" after the election.[19] Following the election, pragmatic business PACs scrambled to atone for years of supporting incumbent Democrats by helping newly elected Republicans retire their campaign debts and prepare for 1996. Willing to make a marriage of convenience with Democrats as long as Democrats were running the show, the PACs were now free to pursue a love match with the ideologically more compatible Republicans, who no longer talked of banning PACs.[20] Without their majority status and committee power to attract PAC contributions from business interests, the balance of PAC campaign resources shifted against the Democrats.

From 1988 to 1994, corporate PACs gave an average of 53 percent of their money to House Democrats and 49 percent to Democratic incumbents. For the six elections following the Republicans' takeover of Congress in 1994, the comparable figures were 34 and 31 percent, respectively. A nearly identical shift occurred in the pattern of trade association PAC donations. Of course, some of this change reflected the increase in the relative number of Republican incumbents, but a more detailed analysis, taking this and other relevant factors into account, found that loss of majority status cost Democratic incumbents an average of roughly $36,000 in corporate and trade association PAC

---

[19]"Momentum Helps GOP Collect Record Amount from PACs," *Congressional Quarterly Weekly Report*, December 3, 1994, 3457.

[20]"To the '94 Victors Go the Fundraising Spoils," *Congressional Quarterly Weekly Report*, April 15, 1995, 1055–59.

contributions, a reduction of about 19 percent in money from these sources.[21] After the Democrats retook control of Congress in 2006, corporate and trade association PACs immediately reverted to their pre-1994 patterns, giving more than half their contributions to Democrats (nearly all of it to incumbents) in 2008 and 2010. Beginning in 2012, the pattern began to swing sharply back to the Republicans, until after the 2018 elections when Democrats resumed control of the House. Incumbent Republicans, back in control of the House after 2022, can anticipate a bigger take from business-oriented PACs in 2024.

PAC contributions to Senate candidates are also influenced by majority status, although contribution patterns are a good deal more variable across election years, reflecting variations in the incidence of competitive campaigns and in the set of states holding Senate elections. Since the late 1970s, Democrats running for reelection to the Senate got an average of 32 percent of corporate and 27 percent of trade association PAC contributions when Democrats controlled the Senate, compared with 25 and 21 percent, respectively, when they did not. Again, a more detailed analysis indicates that, all else being equal, Senate majority status is worth an average of about $51,000 in corporate and trade association PAC contributions.[22] These groups have been most generous with incumbent Republican senators facing contrary national tides (2006, 2008, and 2018).

The "nonconnected" category largely consists of PACs with clear ideological or issue agendas, many of which therefore care more about influencing the makeup of Congress than about having access to officeholders. They thus comprise the only set with any inclination to be more generous to nonincumbents than to incumbents, and their numbers have been growing over the past decade. As with many of the other types of PACs, collectively these PACs started out with a pro-Republican bias that gradually shifted to a pro-Democratic bias before shifting back to the Republicans in recent elections.[23] Many of these groups raise their money through direct-mail appeals, which are most effective when they invoke threats that make people fearful or angry enough to send a check or donate money online, which is easier to do in opposition than in power. Conservative PACs thus flourished in the late 1970s, when all bad things could be blamed on Democratic leaders such as Jimmy Carter, Tip O'Neill, and Teddy Kennedy. Later, liberal PACs found gold in the Ronald Reagan administration, which, along with policies that threatened liberal values, offered such serviceable villains as James Watt (a secretary

---

[21]Gary W. Cox and Eric Magar, "How Much Is Majority Status in the U.S. Congress Worth?" *American Political Science Review* 93 (June 1999): 302–3.

[22]*Ibid*, 304–6.

[23] See figures 4.6a and 4.6b in earlier editions for evidence of these trends across time.

of the interior openly hostile to the environmental movement) and Edwin Meese (an uncompromisingly conservative attorney general). Conservative ideological PACs began to revive once Bill Clinton became available as a bogeyman, and in 1994 nonincumbent Republicans running for the House got more money than Democrats from nonconnected PACs for the first time since 1984. Groups in this category continued to favor Republicans until 2008 and from 2012 through 2018 (and will likely again in the post-2022 midterm environment), indicating that they, like corporate PACS, consider majority status in allocating their funds.

Party Money

Judging by the evidence presented in table 4.1, the political parties appear to be an unimportant and diminishing source of campaign money. They now account for only a tiny share of direct contributions received by House and Senate candidates. However, these data vastly understate the amount of help, financial and otherwise, congressional candidates receive from party sources. In close elections, the party may spend more in total for a candidate than the candidate's own campaign.

Direct party contributions are limited to $5,000 per candidate per election for House candidates. This means that any party committee can give, at most, $10,000 to a candidate in an election year ($15,000 if there is a primary runoff). Both the national committees and the congressional campaign committees of each party can contribute this amount, so direct national party contributions can amount to $20,000 in House campaigns, a small fraction of what it costs to run a minimally serious campaign. The maximum allowable contribution to Senate candidates from all national party sources is only $51,200. Parties cannot be a major source of direct campaign contributions because the FECA will not allow it.

The FECA contains a special provision allowing party committees to spend money on behalf of congressional candidates, however. This *coordinated spending* is also limited, but the limits are higher and, unlike contribution limits, rise with inflation. The original limit of $10,000 set in 1974 for House campaigns had grown to $55,000 by 2022. The ceiling on coordinated party spending for Senate candidates varies with the state's population; in 2022, it ranged from $109,900 in the seven least populous states to $3,348,500 in California. The Senate limit applies to House candidates in any state with a single House seat.[24] State party committees are permitted to spend the same amount as national party committees on coordinated campaign activities but rarely have the

---

[24]"Coordinated Party Expenditure Limits Adjusted for 2022," Federal Election Commission, https://www.fec.gov/updates/coordinated-party-expenditure-limits-adjusted-for-2022/, accessed February 10, 2023.

money to do so. The parties have solved this problem by making the national party committee the state party's agent for raising and spending the money. In practice, this loophole doubles the amount the national party may spend on its candidates.

National party committees can play an important part in financing candidates' congressional campaigns. In 2022, for example, national party sources could give as much as $140,000 worth of assistance to a House candidate (direct donations of $5,000 in both the primary and general elections from the party's national committee, the congressional campaign committee, and the state party committee, plus twice $55,000 in coordinated expenditures). For Senate candidates, the total varied from about $219,800 to $6.7 million, depending on the state's voting-age population. Although significant, these sums still amount to no more than 20 percent of what it typically costs to mount a competitive campaign.

Of course, national party committees can spend money for candidates only after they have raised it. Following the FECA's enactment, Republican committees quickly outstripped their Democratic counterparts in raising funds. Between 1976 and 1984, total receipts for the National Republican Congressional Committee (NRCC) and National Republican Senatorial Committee (NRSC) grew from $14 million to $140 million. Over the same period, total receipts of the Democratic Congressional Campaign Committee (DCCC) and Democratic Senatorial Campaign Committee (DSCC) increased only from $195,000 to $19 million. Subsequently, Democratic fund-raising picked up, but Republican committees enjoyed a large fund-raising advantage in every election cycle until 2005–6, when the parties' Hill committee fund-raising was nearly even ($260 million for the DCCC and DSCC; $268 million for the NRCC and NRSC).

Republican superiority in fund-raising initially gave the party's congressional candidates a considerable advantage in party contributions and coordinated spending, but the Democrats closed some of the gap in the 1990s. Both parties now raise enough money to support all of their competitive candidates to the legal limit in direct contributions and coordinated spending. Between them, the Hill committees spent $1.2 billion in coordinated spending on behalf of House and Senate candidates in 2022.[25]

Coordinated party expenditures can be made for almost any campaign activity. The only condition is that the party, as well as the candidate, must have some control over how the money is spent. The party committees typically foot the bill for conducting polls, producing campaign ads, and

---

[25]Based on authors' analysis of data supplied by the Center for Responsive Politics at https://www.opensecrets.org/political-parties/national-republican-congressional-cmte/ NRCC/2022/summary and https://www.opensecrets.org/political-parties/democratic-congressional-campaign-cmte/DCCC/2022/summary, accessed February 10, 2023.

buying broadcast media time—major expenses in areas where technical expertise is essential. Coordinated spending does not begin to exhaust the services now performed by the Hill committees; indeed, it comprises a decreasing portion of their assistance to candidates. They run programs to train candidates and campaign managers in all aspects of campaigning: fund-raising, personnel management, legal compliance, advertising, press relations, and so on. For example, prior to the 1996 elections, the Republican National Committee (RNC) held training seminars in forty-one states, involving six thousand Republican candidates and activists; the NRCC conducted three four-day candidate schools; and the NRSC offered seminars on fund-raising and campaign techniques attended by representatives of twenty-two Senate campaigns. The Democratic National Committee organized training sessions for three thousand campaign operatives, and the DCCC and DSCC conducted training seminars for nonincumbent candidates and their campaign staffs.[26] Especially on the House side, the Hill committees have become trade schools of modern electoral politics.

The Hill committees have also assumed a central role in helping candidates raise money from PACs and other contributors. In addition to advising on fund-raising techniques and targets, they serve as matchmakers between potential contributors and promising but needy candidates. PACs use party cues in making strategic investment choices, so getting onto their party's watch list of competitive races has become crucial to the prospects of nonincumbent candidates. The Hill committees also arrange to have safe incumbents use their fund-raising prowess to help their party's other candidates (see the next section). Hill committee staffs also help candidates find suitable managers, consultants, pollsters, media specialists, direct-mail outfits, and other campaign professionals.

Beginning in 1996, the national party committees began exploiting the soft money option more intensely, and by 2002 transfers of both soft and hard money to state parties to be used to promote the election of House and Senate candidates had come to dwarf all other party assistance. Figures 4.3 and 4.4 display the trends in soft and hard money expenditures from 1988 through 2022. After BCRA banned the transfer of soft money to state parties for federal campaign activities following the 2002 elections, the parties adapted by ratcheting up their hard money fund-raising. The totals have continued to grow, with a particularly dramatic increase in funding for all of the congressional committees in 2020 and, to less extent, in 2022. They also redirected their efforts into independent campaigns, which since 2004 have absorbed by far the largest share of Hill party resources (figures 4.5 and 4.6). This avenue had been neglected

---

[26]Paul S. Herrnson, *Congressional Elections: Campaigning at Home and in Washington* (Washington, DC: Congressional Quarterly Press, 1995), 86.

Figure 4.3 Hard and Soft Money Raised by House Campaign Committees, 1988–2022

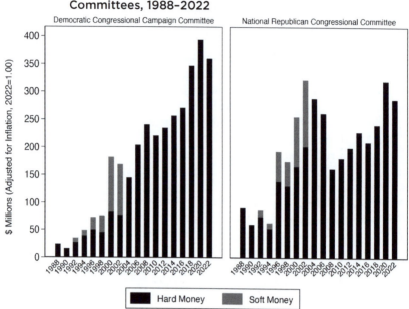

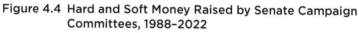

Source: Compiled by authors from Federal Election Commission Data.

Figure 4.4 Hard and Soft Money Raised by Senate Campaign Committees, 1988–2022

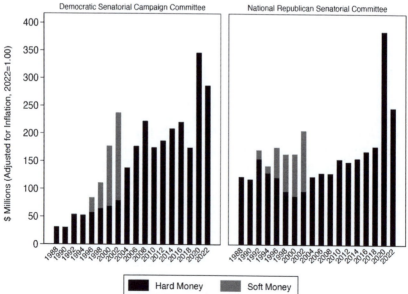

Source: Compiled by authors from Federal Election Commission Data.

Figure 4.5 House Party Committee Campaign Activity, 1990–2022

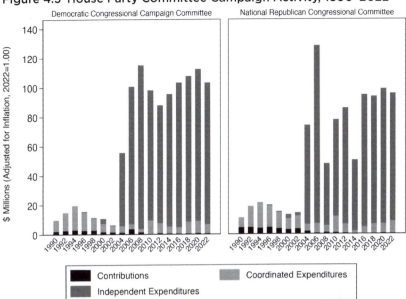

Source: Compiled by authors from Federal Election Commission Data.

Figure 4.6 Senate Party Committee Campaign Activity, 1990–2022

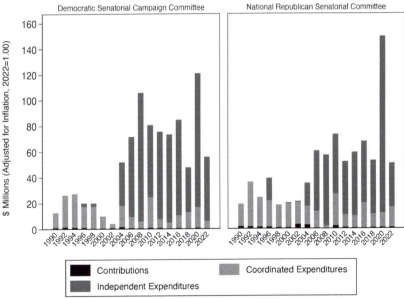

Source: Compiled by authors from Federal Election Commission Data.

while the soft money spigot was still open (note the low sums for 1990 to 2002) but was exploited with a vengeance once it was closed off.

With the addition of independent spending, party committees have become responsible for a substantial share of the funds spent on serious congressional campaigns. Party committees, like other donors and independent groups (discussed in more detail later), concentrate their efforts in competitive races, and in recent elections nearly every potentially competitive candidate has enjoyed adequate funding from one source or another. Indeed, over 90 percent of these funds are typically directed toward the most competitive House and Senate races in an election year.[27] The party committees have contributed to the ever-growing concentration of funds in the most competitive races, because, like other strategic participants in congressional campaign finance, they invest most heavily in what they anticipate to be close campaigns.

Party money does not come without strings. For example, in the extremely tight race for Colorado's 7th District in 2002, NRCC officials funneled about $2.4 million into the campaign of Republican Bob Beauprez, eventual victor by a mere 121 votes. Along with the money came continuing NRCC oversight of Beauprez's campaign; as his annoyed campaign manager put it, "They crawl up our ass on a daily basis."[28] The state party's executive director reported that the NRCC instructed how the money was to be spent "down to the dollar."[29] The national party used its clout to shape the content of the campaign—and the results were not always pretty. One direct-mail piece featured "side-by-side photographs of a cigar-chomping lobbyist and a rabid dog. The oversized postcard inveighed, 'what do you get when you cross this [cigar-chomping lobbyist] with this [rabid dog]? You get Mike Feeley [Beauprez's opponent]. And he wants to be your congressman.'"[30]

The Beauprez–Feeley race was not unique in this regard. National parties invest millions in congressional campaigns with the sole purpose of winning, and their inclination is to do whatever it takes to come out ahead. In doing so, they may even ignore their own candidate's preferences or reelection strategies. When Republican representative Jim Leach of Iowa was running for reelection in 2002, he publicly asked the party to stop running TV ads against his opponent because he thought them distorted and unfair. Leach also sought to position himself as a moderate

---

[27]See figures 4.7, 4.8, 4.9, and 4.10 in the ninth and tenth editions for evidence of these trends in prior election years.

[28]Daniel A. Smith, "Strings Attached: Outside Money in Colorado's Seventh District," in *The Last Hurrah? Soft Money and Issue Advocacy in the 2002 Congressional Election*, eds. David B. Magleby and J. Quin Monson (Provo, UT: Brigham Young University, Center for the Study of Elections and Democracy, 2003), 194.

[29]Smith, "Strings Attached," 196.

[30]Smith, "Strings Attached," 198.

(his district had given Al Gore 56 percent of its votes in 2000), but some national-party-driven Republican ads extolled his support of "Iowa's conservative values." Despite Leach's protest, the party committees kept on broadcasting ads, spending $1.5 million in the process. The national party may have made Leach the winner in spite of himself; one close observer of this contest concluded that "it is doubtful that he would have won without" its unwanted help.[31] In 2006, Republican committees spent only $21,000 for Leach and none against his opponent, and he lost the seat.

Contributions from Other Members of Congress

In an era of very narrow legislative majorities, when control of both the House and Senate is up for grabs every two years, members have a strong interest in helping fellow partisans win elections. Many of them also aspire to leadership positions in their party. Because in any given election most members face little electoral risk themselves, they can use their fund-raising prowess as incumbents to help their party and themselves by funneling money into the campaigns of colleagues in competitive races. They may form their own "leadership" PACs to pass out funds, contribute directly from their own campaign committees, or help attract contributors to other candidates' fund-raising events.[32] When successful, the strategy increases their party's representation and puts some of the winners in their debt. For example, Susan Davis, Adam Schiff, and Jane Harman, three California Democrats who defeated Republican incumbents in 2000, received $130,000, $170,000, and $130,000, respectively, from members' PACs and campaign committees. It is far from coincidence that Nancy Pelosi was elected minority leader in 2003, on her way to becoming Speaker of the House in 2007, after having contributed more than any other Democrat, about $1.9 million, to other House candidates over the previous two election cycles.[33] In 2022, eighteen members and former President Donald Trump passed more than $500,000 on to their party's other candidates; six of them, all senior leaders, donated more than $1 million.[34]

As figure 4.7 shows, members' donations to other candidates grew steeply at the beginning of the twenty-first century and remained at a high level until dropping off slightly in 2022; in the six previous elections, safe

---

[31]David Redlawsk, "The 2002 Iowa Senate and Congressional Elections," in *The Last Hurrah?*, 74, 84, 85.

[32]For a general analysis of these practices, see Eric S. Heberlig and Bruce A. Larson, "Redistributing Campaign Funds by U.S. House Members: The Spiraling Costs of the Permanent Campaign," *Legislative Studies Quarterly* 30 (2005): 597–624.

[33]Anne Bedlington and Michael J. Malbin, "The Party as Extended Network: Members Giving to Each Other and to Their Parties," in *Life after Reform: When the Bipartisan Campaign Reform Act Meets Politics*, ed. Michael J. Malbin (Lanham, MD: Rowman & Littlefield, 2003), 179.

[34]"Candidate to Candidate Giving," OpenSecrets.org, https://www.opensecrets.org/elections-overview/candidate-to-candidate, accessed February 10, 2023.

Figure 4.7 Contributions of Members' Campaign Committees and PACs to House and Senate Candidates, 1978–2022

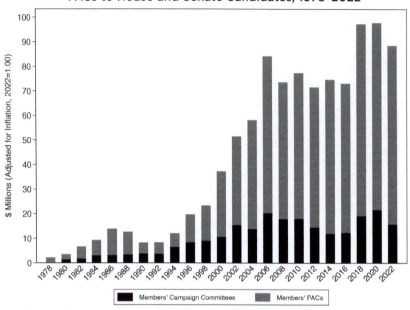

Sources: 1978–2002: Anne Bedlington and Michael J. Malbin, "The Party as Extended Network: Members Giving to Each Other and to Their Parties," in Life after Reform: When the Bipartisan Campaign Reform Act Meets Politics, ed. Michael J. Malbin (Lanham, MD: Roman & Littlefield, 2003), figure 7.1; 2004–2022: Center for Responsive Politics, OpenSecrets.org, (accessed January 30, 2023).

incumbents contributed an average of about $68 million to colleagues' campaigns.[35] Both parties have participated in the trend, although Republicans have done so a bit more than Democrats, except during the years when Democrats controlled Congress (figure 4.8). At the same time, in response to pressure from congressional leaders, members have also been transferring increasing sums to their party's campaign committees (figure 4.9); Democrats are typically more generous in this way than Republicans.[36] All modes of sharing the wealth with one's own side declined in 2022. Evidently, these avenues for investing in campaigns became less important as funds from other sources—particularly individual contributions and, in House elections, independent spending—surged dramatically.

---

[35] Figures are adjusted for inflation; 2022 = 1.00.

[36] Data collected from Center for Responsive Politics, https://www.opensecrets.org/elections-overview, accessed March 1, 2023. For an analysis of the sources of member giving to the Hill committees, see Bruce A. Larson, "Incumbent Contributions to the Congressional Campaign Committees, 1990–2000," *Political Research Quarterly* 57 (2004): 155–61; for broader accounts of party contribution patterns, see Marian Currinder, *Money in the House: Campaign Funds and Congressional Party Politics* (Boulder, CO: Westview Press, 2009); Damon Cann, *Sharing the Wealth: Member Contributions and the Exchange Theory of Party Influence in the U.S. House of Representatives* (Albany: State University of New York Press, 2008).

Figure 4.8 House and Senate Members' Contributions to Other Candidates' Campaigns, 1990–2022

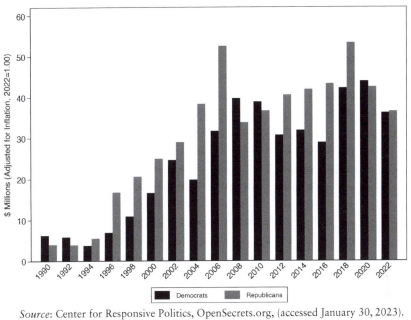

Source: Center for Responsive Politics, OpenSecrets.org, (accessed January 30, 2023).

Figure 4.9 House and Senate Members' Contributions to Congressional Campaign Committees, 1990–2022

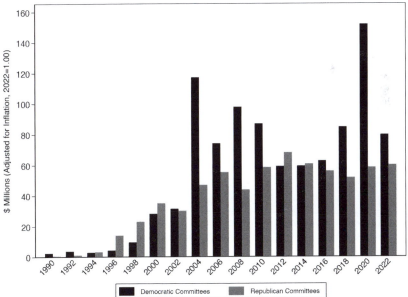

Source: Center for Responsive Politics, OpenSecrets.org, (accessed January 30, 2023).

Plainly, the increasing nationalization of elections and the growing awareness of the stakes involved in the party's collective electoral performance have led to a steep increase in national party involvement in congressional campaigns. However, this activity has not necessarily shifted the focus of electoral politics away from individual candidates and back to parties. Rather, most of the parties' activities are explicitly designed to produce candidates who are more competitive in the candidate-centric system as it currently operates. Republicans in particular set a high priority on recruiting and training candidates because their farm team—candidates holding the lower elective offices that serve as stepping stones to Congress—was, at least prior to the 1990s, much thinner than that of the Democrats. During the 1980s, national-level Republican committees even invested in state legislative races not only to elect more Republicans to the bodies that draw congressional district lines but also to expand their pool of seasoned candidates. (State legislatures are the single most important source of future representatives; approximately 45 percent of the House have served in them.) Newt Gingrich, while serving as House minority leader, formed a PAC (referred to as the GOPAC) to recruit, train, and finance candidates for state legislatures; Republicans whose initial forays into state politics were sponsored by Gingrich's GOPAC swelled the ranks of the majority that elected him Speaker in 1995.[37]

Today, both parties are heavily involved in candidate recruitment, again with a focus on potentially competitive seats; one important source of the Democrats' success in 2006 and 2008 lay in finding and nurturing House candidates who were sufficiently conservative to win some Republican-leaning districts (if not, as it turned out in most cases, sufficiently conservative to survive the anti-Democratic waves in 2010 and 2014). In 2018, Democratic leaders actively recruited women—not difficult, given the special antipathy Trump aroused among them—and connected them with female donors, a major source of their extraordinarily successful fundraising.[38] Republicans followed suit in seeking to attract more female candidates to run in 2020 and 2022, although their level of success was not as high compared to the Democrats.[39]

The flowering of national party activity in congressional election politics represents a sharp departure from past congressional campaign practices.

---

[37]John F. Persinos, "The GOP Farm Team," *Campaigns & Elections* 8 (March 1995): 20.

[38]Grace Haley, "Democratic Women Outraise Men among Female Donors—Another Record-Breaking First," Center for Responsive Politics, October 30, 2018, https://www.opensecrets.org/news/2018/10/democratic-women-outraise-men-among-female-donors-another-record-breaking-first/.

[39]Jamie L. Carson and Aaron A. Hitefield, "A Red Wave or a Ripple? Nationalized Politics and the 2022 Midterms," *The Forum* 21 (2023): https://doi.org/10.1515/for-2023-2002 (see table 3).

Formerly, parties were most active in congressional campaigns at the state and local levels. The declining vigor of these party units and their separation from congressional campaigns helped foster the system of personal, independent campaigning typical of congressional candidates from the 1960s through the 1980s. Parties at the national level focused on presidential elections, making only the most limited forays into other federal elections.

The steep increase in national party activity since then has altered this pattern radically. From the outset, national party activities have had the potential to reduce diversity and independence in the conduct of campaigns; the mere existence of a centralized source of advice on campaign management, strategy, and tactics imposes some uniformity on campaigns. Yet party officials are more concerned with winning elections than with restructuring electoral politics and so adapt their activities to current political habits. Not until the 1990s did the political environment offer campaign themes that resonated across numerous districts and states, and not until 1994 did these themes have a strong partisan thrust. However, once conditions were right, the Republicans' national party infrastructure helped candidates take full advantage of their extraordinary opportunity, and the party enjoyed a historic victory. In 2006, 2008, and 2018, it was the Democrats' turn, and they, too, proved organizationally capable of exploiting national issues locally to great effect, as did the Republicans again in 2010, 2014, and to a lesser extent in 2022.

Self-Financing by Candidates

Individuals, PACs, and parties aside, candidates can also obtain campaign money from their own pockets. The Supreme Court's 1976 decision in *Buckley v. Valeo* overturned limits on how much of their own money candidates may spend to get elected, conferring a significant advantage on wealthy candidates. They can finance as lavish a campaign as the family fortune allows without the aggravation that fund-raising entails, while their opponents must spend time hustling limited donations from a large number of individuals and groups. The earliest and most notorious example is Jon Corzine, who made a fortune in investment banking and spent a fair chunk of it—$60.2 million—to win a New Jersey Senate seat in 2000. A more recent example is Rick Scott, who spent $63.5 million of his own money in narrowly defeating Democratic incumbent Bill Nelson in a 2018 race for a Florida Senate seat. During the 2022 midterm elections, Mehmet Oz, Republican US Senate candidate in Pennsylvania, sank $26.8 million of his own money into his failed bid against Lieutenant Governor John Fetterman.[40]

---

[40]Brent D. Griffiths, "22 Candidates Have Together Pumped Nearly $433 (and counting) of Their Own Money into 2022 Midterm Races," *Business Insider*, November 14, 2022, https://www.businessinsider.com/dr-oz-jb-pritzker-wealthy-senate-house-congress-elections-2022-11.

Tapping the family fortune does not guarantee victory, to be sure; in 2010, Republican Linda McMahon, former CEO of World Wrestling Entertainment, spent $50 million in pursuit of a Connecticut Senate seat but won only 44 percent of the vote. McMahon ran again in 2012, spent $48 million the second time, and lost again by the exact same margin as in 2010. Pursuing Pennsylvania's 1st District, Democrat Scott Wallace spent $12.8 million of his own money in 2018, but he lost to Republican incumbent Brian Fitzpatrick, whose total campaign spending was less than one-fourth as much. In fact, wealthy self-financed candidates lose far more often than they win, according to research conducted by Jennifer Steen.[41] Of the 156 House candidates spending more than $1 million of their own on general election campaigns between 2002 and 2022, only forty-five won, all but four by taking open seats. Only twelve of the seventy-four similarly self-financed Senate candidates were successful over this period, and six were already incumbents. Nearly half of these candidates did not even get past the primary.[42] Steen found that, on average, candidates contributing substantial sums to their own campaigns did only slightly better than candidates financed by others, largely because they often lacked previous elective experience and the requisite ability to allocate the funds effectively.[43]

Despite this unimpressive record, BCRA's designers thought it necessary to accommodate the incumbent's nightmare of facing a multimillionaire opponent by including a provision that raised contribution and party spending limits for candidates facing self-financed opponents. The limits would be raised on a sliding scale depending on the level of self-financing; at maximum, the limits for individual contributions to Senate candidates could be increased sixfold, and the limits on party support would be entirely eliminated. In 2008, a 5–4 Supreme Court majority rejected this attempt at leveling, arguing, "It imposes an unprecedented penalty on any candidate who robustly exercises [his or her] First Amendment right, requiring him to choose between the right to engage in unfettered political speech and subjection to discriminatory fundraising limitations."[44] BCRA also tried to discourage high levels of self-financing by limiting the amount candidates may loan their campaigns to $250,000; anything more must be a personal donation to the campaign that cannot be recouped from contributors later (something winners would have been able to do before BCRA).

Obviously, great personal wealth is not a prerequisite for winning a seat in Congress. But candidates not enjoying the fund-raising advantages

[41]Jennifer A. Steen, *Self-Financed Candidates in Congressional Elections* (Ann Arbor: University of Michigan Press, 2006).

[42]Center for Responsive Politics, "Top Self-Funding Candidates," https://www.opensecrets.org/elections-overview/top-self-funders?cycle=2022, accessed February 10, 2023.

[43]Steen, *Self-Financed Candidates*, 2006.

[44]*Davis v. Federal Election Commission*, 554 U.S. 724 (2008).

that come with incumbency normally must be prepared to invest some of their own money—$50,000 or more—to pay startup costs and demonstrate commitment, with little hope of recouping any of it if they lose.

Fund-Raising Tactics and Donors

The most important aspect of fund-raising is convincing potential donors that their money will not be wasted. Donors must be persuaded that the candidate has a plausible chance of winning and would be more attentive than the opponent to their values and interests. Incumbents are, of course, in the best position to be persuasive. For nonincumbents, techniques of persuasion range from polls and old election returns to a smooth tongue backed by a lively imagination and from recitation of a political record to solemn promises. PACs and other contributors, wary of such salesmanship, often take cues from each other and, more importantly, from party campaign committees in deciding who is a worthy investment.

With or without party matchmaking, large contributions must usually be solicited face to face or in personal phone calls by the candidate or a prominent, high-status fund-raiser. Smaller contributions are sought at meetings, rallies, and dinners, through direct-mail appeals sent to individuals at home, and on campaign websites. Direct mail can be expensive; in 1992, Congressman Robert Dornan of California spent $1,151,338 to raise $1,407,922; $967,650 of the total went to direct-mail solicitation.[45] This form of fund-raising has raised some concern because direct-mail pleas are the most successful when they play on strong emotions, such as anger, fear, or frustration, to convince people to support the candidate. Extremist candidates—Dornan, a flamboyant conservative firebrand, again serves as an example—are thus best able to exploit this method.[46] Internet fund-raising, by comparison, is very cheap but typically requires even more intense commitment on the part of donors; as one veteran direct-mail fund-raiser put it: "You think of the mail as fundraisers as chasing donors. The Internet, when it works, is donors chasing fundraisers, which is a truly unnatural act."[47] Perhaps, but political passions in 2022 inspired millions of citizens to engage in it; online donations reached record levels, with more than $747 million raised from donors contributing $200 or less.[48] Most of this money went

---

[45]Dwight Morris and Mureille E. Gamache, *Handbook of Campaign Spending: Money in the 1992 Congressional Elections* (Washington, DC: Congressional Quarterly Press, 1994), 29.

[46]Xandra Kayden, "The Nationalizing of the Party System," in *Parties, Interest Groups, and Campaign Finance Laws*, ed. Michael J. Malbin (Washington, DC: American Enterprise Institute, 1980), 266.

[47]David B. Magleby and Kelly Patterson, eds., *War Games: Issues and Resources in the Battle for Control of Congress* (Provo, UT: Brigham Young University, Center for the Study of Elections and Democracy, 2007), 20.

to Democrats and a substantial amount was gathered using online fundraising tools provided by ActBlue, a nonprofit organization aiding Democrats and progressive causes by making it easier to connect with like-minded donors across the country. In 2022, approximately $2.24 billion was raised by this organization to assist Democratic candidates. Republicans, by contrast, were aided by a similar nonprofit organization known as WinRed that was formed in 2020. However, that entity only managed to raise about $1.18 billion on behalf of Republican candidates in 2022.[49]

No matter how candidates raise the money, timing is crucial. It is as important to have money available when it is needed as it is to have it in the first place. In general, money available early in the campaign is put to much better use than money received later. Early money is seed money for the entire campaign effort; it is needed to organize, plan, and raise more money. This circumstance adds to the advantage of personal wealth; it also enhances the importance of national party and other organizations willing to make contributions and provide help early in the campaign. EMILY's List, a PAC devoted to electing pro-choice women to Congress, takes its name from an acronym extolling this approach: "Early money is like yeast (it makes the dough rise)." EMILY's List is also the premiere proponent of bundling: Rather than contributing money directly to candidates, the PAC directs the individual contributions of its members to designated candidates. That way, it can provide help in excess of the $5,000 PAC contribution limit. The EMILY's List website boasts of having raised over $700 million for its candidates since 1985.[50]

Political elites, interest groups, and donors typically give money to candidates who share their values on important and salient issues. Recently, Adam Bonica developed a technique that enables researchers to place donors to local, state, and federal candidates in elections from 1979 through 2018 (the most up-to-date data available) on a common liberal–conservative scale. The donor data, in turn, serve to locate the candidates receiving the donations on the same scale. Prior to Bonica's measure, we could measure ideological leanings consistently only for candidates who won and thus subsequently compiled analyzable voting records.[51] Bonica's data include the losers as well as the winners.

---

[48]Ian Vandewalker and Mariana Paez, "4 Takeaways about Money in the Midterms," *Brennan Center,* November 16, 2022, https://www.brennancenter.org/our-work/analysis-opinion/4-takeaways-about-money-midterms.

[49]Open Secrets, "PAC Profile: ActBlue," https://www.opensecrets.org/political-action-committees-pacs/actblue/C00401224/summary/2022, "PAC Profile: WinRed," https://www.opensecrets.org/political-action-committees-pacs/winred/C00694323/summary/2022, accessed February 13, 2022.

[50]https://www.emilyslist.org, accessed February 13, 2022.

[51]See, for instance, Keith Poole and Howard Rosenthal, *Ideology and Congress* (New York: Transaction Publishers, 2007).

Figure 4.10 Ideology of Winning and Losing House Candidates, 1980-2018

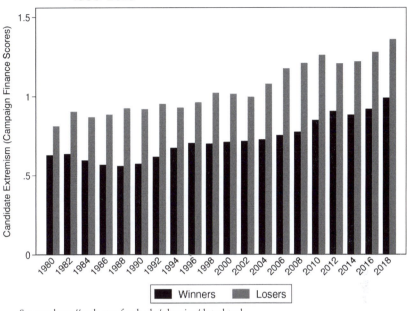

Source: http://web.stanford.edu/~bonica/data.html

Figure 4.10 displays the mean ideological location on Bonica's scale of all winning and losing House candidates in elections from 1980 to 2018. According to Bonica's measure, both winners and losers have become more extreme over time, and in every election year the losers have been, on average, more extreme than the winners. The same holds for winners and losers of Senate races (figure 4.11), although the difference between them is less pronounced in some election years (1994, 1996, 2006, 2008, and especially 2012). These figures document the increasing extremity of House and Senate winners over the past three decades—fueling the growing polarization of partisans in both chambers discussed in greater detail in chapter 7—but they also indicate that Congress might have polarized even more had a greater number of the losing candidates found a way to get elected.[52]

---

[52]On this point, see Jamie L. Carson and Ryan Williamson, "Candidate Ideology and Electoral Success in Congressional Elections," *Public Choice* 176 (2018): 175–92; Andrew B. Hall and Daniel M. Thompson, "Who Punishes Nominees? Candidates Ideology and Turning Out the Base in U.S. Elections," *American Political Science Review* 112 (2018): 509–24; Jordan Kujala, "Donors, Primary Elections, and Polarization in the United States," *American Journal of Political Science* 64 (2020): 587–602; Stephen M. Utych, "Man Bites Blue Dog: Are Moderates Really More Electable than Ideologues?" *The Journal of Politics* 82 (2020): 392–96.

Figure 4.11 Ideology of Winning and Losing Senate Candidates, 1980–2018

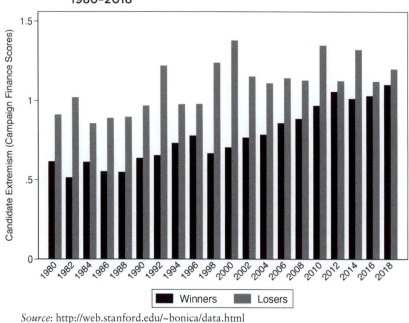

Source: http://web.stanford.edu/~bonica/data.html

INDEPENDENT, VOTER-EDUCATION, AND ISSUE-ADVOCACY CAMPAIGNS

Candidates and parties have never enjoyed exclusive control over congressional campaigns; independent campaigns conducted by PACs and other organizations have been part of the process since the adoption of the FECA in the early 1970s. But until the 1990s, their part was minor, with independent spending never accounting for more than 3 percent of total campaign spending; in most election years, it was closer to 1 percent. In the 1990s, however, interest groups developed a new avenue for large-scale involvement in electoral politics beyond the control of the candidates. The Court's *Buckley* decision construed the FECA "to apply only to expenditures for communications that in express terms advocate the election or defeat of a clearly identified candidate for federal office." Prior to the enactment of BCRA, the Court had ruled that the First Amendment protects the right to conduct unrestricted so-called voter-education or issue-advocacy campaigns, even if clearly intended to influence voters (for example, through tendentious comparisons of candidates' issue positions), as long as such words as "vote for," "elect," "vote against," "defeat," and "reject" are not used.[53] In 2007 the Court rejected BCRA's attempt to limit the effect of these campaigns via a ban on the mention of candidates' names in them during a fixed pre-election period (thirty days for primaries, sixty days for general elections),[54] then in 2010 decided, in *Citizens United*, that any limit at all on any independent campaigning violated the First Amendment.[55]

Independent campaigns are now conducted by so-called super PACs organized solely for this purpose, as well as by 527 and 501(c) organizations. The 527 groups may raise and spend unlimited sums for voter mobilization and issue advocacy. Although their campaign ads must still refrain from specifically advocating a vote for or against a candidate, forswearing the Court's forbidden "magic words" does not inhibit the production of ads that are indistinguishable from ordinary campaign ads.[56] The 501(c) organizations may engage in political activity, particularly internal communications with their members, but political activity is not supposed to be their primary purpose. Super PACs are under no fund-raising or spending restrictions, although they may not contribute directly to candidates. The Senate Leadership Fund, a super PAC organized to benefit Republican candidates, was the biggest outside spender in 2022, at $246 million, more than two and half times its spending in 2018.[57]

Spending by independent groups for and against congressional candidates grew slowly and was a relatively small part of the financial mix until 2006, when it increased more than fourfold, partly through a rechanneling of efforts in response to the ban on soft money contributions to parties.[58] That upward trajectory continued through 2022, with a particularly large jump for entities allied with the Republican Party and especially in Senate races. Table 4.2 lists the nonparty independent groups that spent at least $10 million in 2022. Coming second, after the

---

[53]Jonathan D. Salant, "GOP Bumps Up against Court Precedent in Trying to Block AFL-CIO," *Congressional Quarterly Weekly Report*, April 13, 1996, 996–97.

[54]*Federal Election Commission v. Wisconsin Right to Life, Inc.*, 551 U.S. 449 (2007).

[55]*Citizens United v. Federal Election Commission*, 130 S. Ct. 876 (2010).

[56]One study found that fewer than 10 percent of candidates' broadcast ads used any of the words deemed by the Court to be out of bounds for issue advocacy campaigns; see "Straight Talk on Campaign Finance: Separating Fact from Fiction," Paper No. 5, Brennen Center for Justice (undated), http://www.brennancenter.org/dynamic/subpages/paper5.pdf, accessed July 2, 2007.

[57]Center for Responsive Politics, "2022 Outside Spending, by Super PAC," https://www.opensecrets.org/outside-spending/super_pacs/2022?disp=O&type=S&chart=P, accessed February 13, 2023.

[58]Stephen R. Weissman and Ruth Hassan, "BCRA and the 527 Groups," in *The Election after Reform*, ed. Michael Malbin (Boulder, CO: Rowman & Littlefield, 2006), 79–111.

Table 4.2 Top Independent Spending Groups, 2022

Group	Total Spent ($)	Partisan Orientation
Senate Leadership Fund	246,008,258	Republican
Congressional Leadership Fund	227,141,883	Republican
Senate Majority PAC	162,490,161	Democrat
House Majority PAC	138,411,985	Democrat
Club for Growth Action	69,844,653	Republican
Americans for Prosperity Action	69,427,295	Republican
Georgia Honor	60,365,009	Democrat
LCV Victory Fund	33,299,173	Democrat
Women Vote!	29,851,924	Democrat
Wisconsin Truth PAC	28,874,330	Republican
United Democracy Project	25,957,513	Bipartisan
Saving Arizona PAC	25,405,565	Republican
Protect Our Future PAC	24,246,001	Democrat
VoteVets.org	22,829,825	Democrat
Future Forward USA	20,708,128	Democrat
American Leadership Action	19,569,461	Republican
Honor Pennsylvania	19,262,367	Republican
Protect Ohio Values PAC	15,985,849	Republican
Priorities USA Action	15,970,141	Democrat
Make America Great Again Inc.	15,030,834	Republican
Our American Century	13,615,265	Republican
American Dream Federal Action	12,649,179	Republican
Sentinel Action Fund	12,227,420	Republican
School Freedom Fund	10,465,158	Republican
Opportunity Matters Fund	10,009,606	Republican

Source: Center for Responsive Politics, "2022 Outside Spending, by Groups," Open Secrets .org, https://www.opensecrets.org/outside-spending/by_group/2022?chart=P&disp=O&type=I, accessed February 13, 2023.

Senate Leadership Fund, was the Congressional Leadership Fund (benefiting Republicans), and third was the Senate Majority PAC (benefiting Democrats). Most of the independent spending for Democrats came from a variety of issue-oriented groups. Only one of the twenty-five, the United Democracy Project, showed any bipartisan inclinations. Overall, independent groups favoring Republican candidates spent $797.9 million, and those favoring Democrats spent $633.9 million in 2022; groups not clearly allied with a party spent about $60 million.

Groups incorporated as 501(c) organizations are not required to disclose their donors. Thus, for example, the underlying sources of the $60 million spent by Georgia Honor in 2022 remain hidden. Democrats, fearing that *Citizens United* would allow corporations and wealthy donors to attack their candidates anonymously, proposed legislation in 2010 that would compel disclosure of most sources of funds spent on independent campaigns. Republicans successfully filibustered the bill in the Senate, arguing that disclosure would inhibit corporate free speech by exposing donors to retaliation (boycotts, protest demonstrations) by offended citizens—just the kind of accountability Democrats presumably wanted to impose.[59]

As the law now stands, it is possible for any individual or organization not only to spend without limit to influence congressional electorates but to do so anonymously. Some shadowy groups have exploited this opportunity by conducting stealth campaigns behind innocuous-sounding fronts. For example, three groups active in 2002 on the Republican side—the United Seniors Association, the Seniors Coalition, and the 60 Plus Association—were all creatures of the pharmaceutical industry, promoting candidates who supported the industry's prescription drug plan.[60] Stealth was carried to an extreme in some House races that year. Jill Long Thompson, Democratic candidate for Indiana's 2nd District, was hammered during the last three weeks of the campaign in a series of twelve automated phone calls, each of which reached at least forty thousand households. The calls, including one featuring the voice of Barbara Bush, the president's mother, reiterated Long Thompson's Republican opponent's campaign theme.[61] Chris Kouri, a Democrat competing for North Carolina's 8th District, faced a similar automated onslaught.[62] In neither case did anyone admit responsibility for the phone calls, and their origin remains a mystery. Both Long Thompson and Kouri lost. More systematic evidence that "voter-education" campaigns can be effective comes from a study of the AFL-CIO's $25 million to $35 million campaign against sixty-four Republican incumbents in 1996; the campaign deprived targeted freshmen of their sophomore surges and, arguably, cost seven of them their seats.[63]

Independent groups usually coordinate their campaigns with those of the parties and candidates, albeit tacitly in order to stay within the law. Indeed, most serve as reliable components of one or the other party's coalition.[64] Some, however, have their own agendas and are willing

---

[59]David M. Herszenhorn, "Campaign Finance Bill Is Set Aside," *New York Times*, July 27, 2010.

[60]"Pulling Strings from Afar," *AARP Bulletin Online*, February 3, 2003, http://www.aarp.org/bulletin/consumer/a2003-06-30-pullingstrings.html, accessed October 15, 2007.

[61]John Roos and Christopher Roderiguez, "Indiana Second District—Hoosier Values and Outside Money," in *The Last Hurrah?*, eds. David B. Magleby and J. Quin Monson (Brookings, 2004), 22.

[62]Eric S. Heberlig, "North Carolina's Eighth and Ninth Districts," in *The Last Hurrah?*, eds. David B. Magleby and J. Quin Monson (Brookings, 2004), 260.

[63]Gary C. Jacobson, "The Effect of the AFL-CIO's 'Voter Education' Campaigns on the 1996 House Elections," *Journal of Politics* 61 (1999): 185–94.

[64]Paul S. Herrnson, "The Role of Party Organizations, Party-Connected Committees, and Party Allies in Elections," *Journal of Politics* 71 (October 2009): 1207–24.

to sacrifice a party's interest to further their own. The Club for Growth, for example, a group dedicated to electing anti-tax purists, has mounted primary campaigns against Republican incumbents it considers insufficiently conservative. Contrary to the wishes of national Republican leaders, the group sponsored a primary challenge to moderate Republican senator Lincoln Chaffee of Rhode Island in 2006. The challenge fell short, 46–54, but it probably helped weaken the incumbent, who lost the general election to Democrat Sheldon Whitehouse by a similar margin. Had the conservative Republican backed by the Club for Growth won the nomination, he would certainly have done even worse than Chaffee. Thus the Club was willing to sacrifice Republican control of the Senate (which the Democrats won by a single seat in 2006) in order to move the Republican Party rightward.

CAMPAIGN ORGANIZATIONS

Campaigns require organization. Raising funds, handling the legal formalities, gathering intelligence, designing and executing advertising strategies, holding events, and identifying supporters and getting them to cast ballots are complex and demanding tasks that have to be carried out in a brief and inflexible time frame. It takes experience and savvy to do any one of them well. It is neither easy nor cheap to build a good campaign organization.

Many incumbents keep at least an embryonic campaign organization permanently in place, often as personal staff. Other candidates must normally build organizations from scratch—one reason seed money is so important. There was a time when, in many places, vigorous party organizations operated on a permanent basis and worked for entire party tickets. This is rarely the case now. Even when parties were more robust, congressional candidates were not centers of attention, since local parties were interested primarily in patronage, and members of Congress controlled little of that. Now that local party organizations have lost much of their value as campaign allies (at least until the national party decides to finance their federal campaign activities), party assistance comes primarily from the national party committees and can be abundant for candidates deemed competitive.

For candidates who can afford it, the easiest way of acquiring a campaign organization is to buy one. Professional campaign specialists have taken over many of the functions formerly performed by local parties and have pioneered a variety of new electoral techniques adapted to an age of television, computers, and the Internet. It is possible for a candidate to hire a single outfit that will handle the entire campaign. More commonly, candidates engage a team of specialists—campaign managers, accountants, media consultants, pollsters, fund-raisers, researchers, and the like. Professional services do not come cheap.[65] Incumbents can afford them; often challengers cannot and must soldier on without much professional assistance. A 2002 study, for example, found that about 90 percent of incumbents had a paid campaign manager, whereas a paid staffer or general consultant managed only 44 percent of challengers' House campaigns.[66] The rest relied almost entirely on volunteers to run their campaigns. No doubt most poorly financed challengers—120 reported spending less than $50,000 in 2022—continue to run campaigns without professional help. Senate challengers, with larger campaigns and bigger budgets, are considerably more likely to make use of professional campaign services. Hiring experienced professionals is now one way to signal a serious campaign, and candidates who cannot afford to do so are unlikely to attract much attention from PACs or party committees.[67]

Short of buying a complete team package, most nonincumbent congressional candidates can obtain an adequate campaign organization only by assembling one themselves (although the most promising candidates can expect extensive help from national party officials). Close political friends, the "personal constituency" that Richard F. Fenno Jr. noticed all of his congressmen had acquired, form the core. Other components get added as they become available. Some Democrats, for example, receive extensive organizational help from labor unions. Fragments of local parties can sometimes be used. Inner-city African American candidates may work through neighborhood churches. Christian fundamentalist congregations and other conservative organizations help Republican candidates espousing "family values." Local groups associated with the conservative Tea Party movement or Freedom Caucus have worked for like-minded Republican candidates in every election since 2010. Single-issue advocates, such as environmentalists, opponents of gun control, and those on opposite sides of the abortion issue, provide organizational help to supporters of their causes. A campaign organization can absorb almost any existing group with political interests. The kind of organization a candidate assembles depends on what kinds of groups are available, which ones he or she can appeal to, and the candidate's range of contacts, resources, and level of political skill.

The campaign organizations of poorly funded House challengers tend to be personal, ephemeral, and dependent on volunteers. Because they

---

[65]On this point, see Gregory J. Martin and Zachary Peskowitz, "Agency Problems in Political Campaigns: Media Buying and Consulting," *American Political Science Review* 112 (June 2018): 231–48.

[66]Computed from data in Herrnson, *Congressional Elections*, 6th ed., 78.

[67]Paul S. Herrnson, "Do Parties Make a Difference? The Role of Party Organizations in Congressional Elections," *Journal of Politics* 48 (1986): 612–13.

are ephemeral and rely on people giving their time and energy without pay, a great deal of effort goes into internal organizational maintenance. Xandra Kayden observed, "Most of the campaign staff devotes most of its time to creating and maintaining the campaign organization."[68] Such campaign organizations cannot be hierarchical because sanctions are so few. They cannot learn from their mistakes because they exist for such a short time and go out of business at the very time the real effectiveness of their work is measured—when the votes are counted. It is not surprising that so few are successful.

CAMPAIGN STRATEGIES

In a broad sense, everyone knows what campaigns are supposed to do: Find and expand the pool of eligible voters favoring the candidate and make sure that they vote. Figuring out just *how* to do this is another matter. As one political veteran told John Kingdon, "I don't know very much about elections. I've been in a lot of them."[69] In fact, the central motif of almost every discussion of campaign strategy is uncertainty.

What is the most efficient way to reach voters? No one knows for sure. The conventional view is that "half the money spent on campaigns is wasted. The trouble is, we don't know which half."[70] The effects of uncertainty about what does and does not work pervade campaign decision-making. Successful candidates are inclined to do what they did in the past—they must have done something right, even if they cannot be sure what; a degree of superstition is understandable. Other candidates follow tradition. Kayden concludes, "Basically, campaigns produce literature because campaigns have always produced literature."[71] The same may be said of yard signs, bumper stickers, and campaign buttons. They appear in every election year not so much because they have ever been shown to be effective but because everyone expects them and their absence would be noticed, if only by the campaign's activists.

On the other hand, uncertainty also invites innovation. Challengers, underdogs, and former losers have an incentive to try new tactics, if only to get desperately needed attention from the news media. For example, Lawton Chiles won a surprise victory in the 1970 Florida Senate election by walking the length of the state, talking and listening to people along the way. Other candidates quickly imitated him. While it was still

---

[68] Xandra Kayden, *Campaign Organization* (Lexington, MA: D. C. Heath, 1978), 61.
[69] John W. Kingdon, *Candidates for Office: Beliefs and Strategies* (New York: Random House, 1968), 87.
[70] One of Fenno's congressmen raised it to 75 percent; see Fenno, *Home Style*, 17.
[71] Kayden, *Campaign Organization*, 120.

fresh, the tactic generated abundant free publicity and far more attention than Chiles and the other candidates could afford to buy. Similarly, Tom Harkin, challenging the Republican incumbent for Iowa's 5th District in 1972, made news by working for one day at a time in a variety of blue-collar jobs, ostensibly to get close to the common experience. Others soon picked up the idea. Senator Bob Graham of Florida made such workdays his political trademark, logging more than 385 between his first successful campaign in 1978 (for governor) through the end of his third and final Senate term in 2004.[72]

Others imitate whatever seems to work,[73] so the novelty and therefore effectiveness of such tactics fade. But there is always something new. In 1980, Kenneth Snider, Democratic challenger in Indiana's 8th District, dropped in on voters with the helicopter he had purchased especially for the campaign; the news media loved it.[74] Snider lost the election but won a respectable 45 percent of the vote. Two years later, Republican Dan Burton, campaigning in his 1948 fire engine, was more successful and ended up representing Indiana's 5th District for the next thirty-three years.[75]

Other modes of transportation have not been overlooked. Challenger Gene Freund undertook what might be called the "Tour d'Iowa," pedaling his bicycle eight hundred miles through twenty-seven counties of Iowa's 5th District in 1988.[76] In 1986, another challenger had been desperate enough for publicity to bicycle 340 miles across the Nevada desert along the shoulder of Interstate 80 in August.[77] Neither of these cyclists crossed the finish line first, but David Minge's five-hundred-mile bike tour through forty-seven towns in nine days helped him win Minnesota's 2nd District in 1992. Minge repeated the tactic in 1994, narrowly holding off a challenger who, among other things, campaigned from a train.[78]

---

[72]Michael Barone and Richard Cohen with Charles E. Cook Jr., *The Almanac of American Politics 2004* (Washington, DC: National Journal, 2003), 384–85.

[73]Marjorie Randon Hershey, *Running for Office: The Political Education of Campaigners* (Chatham, NJ: Chatham House, 1984), 69–79.

[74]"The Outlook: Senate, House, and Governors," *Congressional Quarterly Weekly Report*, October 11, 1980, 3014, 3017.

[75]Alan Ehrenhalt, "House Freshmen: Campaign Traditionalists," *Congressional Quarterly Weekly Report*, January 8, 1983, 30.

[76]Jonathan Roos, "Freund Hopes to Grab Coattails," *Des Moines Register* (August 23, 1988), A2.

[77]"Outlook: Nevada," *Congressional Quarterly Weekly Report*, October 11, 1986, 2453.

[78]Michael Barone and Grant Ujifusa, *The Almanac of American Politics 1994* (Washington, DC: National Journal, 1993), 691; "Minnesota," *Congressional Quarterly Weekly Report*, October 22, 1994, 3032.

Sometimes a vehicle can even embody the campaign's central theme. In 1994, Greg Ganske campaigned for Iowa's 4th District in the Neal-mobile, a DeSoto manufactured in 1958, the year the incumbent, Neal Smith, was first elected to the House. A sign on the roof asked, "WHY is it still running?"[79] In a year when *career politician* was a nasty epithet, Ganske drove the Nealmobile right into the House. Candidates also travel in battered pickup trucks, old station wagons, and other humble vehicles to show that they are just plain folks, not out-of-touch Washington insiders. In 2006, as voters watched gas prices rise above $3.00 per gallon nationally, the fuel rather than the vehicle provided the gimmick. Mike Weaver, Democratic challenger to Ron Lewis in Kentucky's 2nd, "filled motorists' gas tanks for $1.20 per gallon, the price gasoline cost when Lewis was first elected to Congress in 1994," paying the difference out of pocket; Lewis thereupon accused Weaver of the federal crime of trying to buy votes.[80]

Occasionally, candidates will project unconventional images calculated to attract attention and votes. In 2008, two-term Illinois state representative Aaron Schock pursued an open House seat in Illinois's 18th District by featuring what might have been a liability: his age. Schock was only twenty-seven at the time. His winning campaign emphasized his youth and vigor, and he was by far the youngest member of the Congress inaugurated in 2009. Schock's age and physique attracted an inordinate amount of media attention for a freshman,[81] and he was later featured shirtless (with six-pack abs) on the cover of the June 2011 issue of *Men's Health* as "America's Fittest Congressman." Although Schock easily won reelection to a fourth term in 2014, he resigned from Congress a few months later while under investigation for improper use of federal funds, provoked in part by the expensive remodel of his Capitol Hill office in a style inspired by *Downton Abbey*.[82]

Youth was again a factor in 2018 when Alexandria Ocasio-Cortez (D-NY) and Abby Finkenaur (D-IA) were elected to the 116th Congress as the youngest and second youngest congresswomen, respectively, to ever take office. Both featured their youth as a campaign theme. In the

---

[79]"Challenger Hits Iowa's Smith with Incumbency, Earmarks," *Congressional Quarterly Weekly Report*, September 10, 1994, 2533.

[80]Nicole Duran, "GOP: Gas Gimmick Is Illegal," *Roll Call*, September 5, 2006.

[81]Caroline May, "Illinois Republican Rep. Aaron Schock's Path to Congress and His Hopes for the Country's Future," *Daily Caller*, July 31, 2010, http://dailycaller.com/2010/07/31/illinois-republican-rep-aaron-schocks-path-to-congress-and-his-hopes-for-the-country's-future.

[82]Ashley Parker, "Aaron Schock, Facing Questions on Spending, Is Resigning," *New York Times*, March 17, 2015, http://www.nytimes.com/politics/first-draft/2015/03/17/aaron-schock-facing-questions-on-spending-announces-resignation/?_r=0.

2018 Missouri Senate race, Republican Josh Hawley defeated incumbent Democrat Claire McCaskill, becoming, at age thirty-nine, the youngest senator in the 116th Congress. This distinction had previously belonged to Senator Tom Cotton (R-AR), who was forty-one when initially elected to the 115th Congress.[83] In 2022, Maxwell Frost (D-FL) became the first member of Gen Z to be elected to Congress at the age of 25.[84]

A clever ad can sometimes turn the tide. During the 2014 election cycle, Democrat Bruce Bailey was initially odds-on favorite to win Iowa's open Senate seat. His eventual opponent, a Republican state senator and former military commander, Joni Ernst, changed the dynamic with a now famous "squeal ad," introducing herself to voters with a simple message: "I'm Joni Ernst. I grew up castrating hogs on an Iowa farm, so when I get to Washington, I'll know how to cut pork. ... Because Washington is full of big spenders, let's make them squeal."[85] The ad resonated with Iowa voters, propelling her from near obscurity to a decisive victory over Bailey in the November election.

In 2022, candidates continued to broadcast ads designed to break through the clutter and grab the attention of voters. Author J. D. Vance (R), running for the Senate in Ohio, claimed in one ad that the media portrayed anyone who supported building Trump's wall along the Mexican border as a racist to stir up voter support. In Pennsylvania, losing Republican Senate candidate Mehmet (Dr.) Oz ran a TV ad showing him shooting both a handgun and a shotgun to dispel campaign rumors he maintained were "dead wrong" about him not supporting guns. Republican Senator Marco Rubio, running for reelection in Florida, denounced the radical left for trying to "destroy America." Perhaps the oddest TV ad featured Marjorie Taylor Green, a Republican House member from Georgia's 14th congressional district, flying over a field in a helicopter shooting at wild hogs with an AR-15.[86]

CAMPAIGN MEDIA

Two groups of activities are common to all full-scale campaigns. One is mass media advertising, which absorbs about 45 percent of a typical campaign budget.[87] The candidate's name and perhaps a short message are

[83]Beatrice Jin, "Congress's Incoming Class Is Younger, Bluer, and More Diverse Than Ever," *Politico*, January 7, 2019, https://www.politico.com/interactives/2018/interactive_116th-congress-freshman-younger-bluer-diverse/.

[84]Jennifer Liu, "25-Year-Old Maxwell Frost Will Be the First Gen Z Member of Congress," *CNBC*, November 9, 2022, https://www.cnbc.com/2022/11/09/maxwell-frost-will-be-the-first-gen-z-member-of-congress.html.

[85]Joni Ernst, "Squeal," YouTube, March 24, 2014, https://www.youtube.com/watch?v=zc8uLuHsNw0.

[86]Yahoo News, "2022 Midterm Political Ad Mashup," YouTube, October 14, 2022, https://www.youtube.com/watch?v=iRFm-9x-K2E.

[87]Morris and Gamache, *Handbook of Campaign Spending*, tables 1.5 and 1.6.

presented to voters via some combination of television, radio, and newspaper advertisements, billboards, mass mailings, automated telephone calls, e-mails, tweets, and instant messaging. The choice of media is partly strategic and partly dictated by cost and available resources. About one-third of House campaigns, for example, do not use paid television.[88] In large metropolitan areas, it is inefficient and too expensive for candidates without extraordinarily ample funds. Candidates must pay for the audience they reach; at the extreme (the greater New York City media market), constituents may comprise less than 5 percent of the audience. The more efficiently television markets fit a district, the more likely House candidates are to use television advertising.[89] The spread of cable television has made access to television less expensive, but the lower cost reflects the small size of the audiences reached through this much more fragmented medium.

Despite high costs, House candidates with enough money buy broadcast television time even if it is very inefficient, for it may be the only way to reach many potential voters. So do parties and organizations spending independently of candidates' campaigns. The notion that television advertising is essential regardless of price is perhaps the most important force driving up the cost of campaigning. In the hotly contested campaigns that attract the national parties' attention, multimillion-dollar broadcast campaigns that saturate the airwaves in the weeks leading up to the election are not uncommon. Radio advertising is also wasteful in large media markets, but the costs are much lower than those for television, and radio audiences tend to sort themselves out demographically for targeting, so campaigns often use radio ads where TV is beyond their means.

Senate campaigns are usually able to use television much more efficiently than House campaigns because constituencies are entire states, though cost and efficiency still vary considerably across states.[90] The use of television helps candidates who are not already well known (i.e., challengers) and can be added to the list of factors that make Senate campaigns so much more competitive, on average, than House campaigns.

With enough money on both sides, a television campaign can take on the character of an ongoing debate, where "one day's set of TV ads for one candidate [is] followed soon after by his [or her] opponent's set of counter

---

[88]Herrnson, *Congressional Elections*, 6th ed., 229.

[89]Edie N. Goldenberg and Michael W. Traugott, *Campaigning for Congress* (Washington, DC: Congressional Quarterly Press, 1984), 120; Stephen Ansolabehere, Alan Gerber, and James M. Snyder Jr., "Television Costs and Greater Congressional Campaign Spending: Cause and Effect or Coincidence?" (manuscript, August 1999).

[90]Charles Stewart III and Mark Reynolds, "Television Markets and U.S. Senate Elections," *Legislative Studies Quarterly* 15 (1990): 495–523.

ads, and the process [is] repeated several times in an intricate series of tactical moves."[91] There is no apparent limit to how much television advertising voters will tolerate. Back in 1984, Senator Jesse Helms's reelection campaign in North Carolina was on the air almost continuously for the eighteen months preceding the election; 150 different ads were produced for the campaign. His opponent, James Hunt, also saturated the airwaves, though for a shorter period.[92] Helms won, spending $16.5 million to Hunt's $9.5 million in what was up to then the most expensive Senate contest ever held. Twenty years later, John Thune won a narrow victory in South Dakota over Tom Daschle, then Democratic majority leader of the Senate, in a contest in which the candidates managed to spend more than $34 million between them in a state with fewer than 502,000 registered voters. The total amounted to a record $68 per voter. They spent more than $9 million on broadcast ads in a state where airtime is relatively cheap.[93] This record was later broken in the 2018 Senate contest in North Dakota in which Republican Kevin Cramer defeated Democratic incumbent Heidi Heitkamp, with the candidates and outside groups spending more than $49 million, or approximately $145 per voter.[94]

Well-funded House campaigns in districts with inefficient television coverage often rely heavily on direct mail, which can pinpoint the district's voters. House and Senate campaigns also use direct mail to send messages targeted to specific subgroups in the electorate. In a sample of hotly contested races in 2002, the candidates and parties combined to send an average of forty-four unique mail pieces during the campaign; voters reported receiving three or four pieces a day during the last week of the campaign. Some campaigns greatly exceeded these averages; in the contest for South Dakota's Senate seat, won by incumbent Democrat Tim Johnson by a margin of only 524 votes, some voters reported receiving as many as ten pieces of mail per day. A total of 174 unique direct-mail pieces were distributed during this race: "The blizzard of messages became intrusive and it was hard to break through the clutter and process all of the brief messages. The direct mail pieces were primarily visual, usually filled with distorted images of opponents, babies, or the

[91]Alan Ehrenhalt, "Technology, Strategy Bring New Campaign Era," *Congressional Quarterly Weekly Report*, December 7, 1985, 2559.

[92]Ehrenhalt, "New Campaign Era," 2563.

[93]Elizabeth Theiss Smith and Richard Braunstein, "The Nationalization of Local Politics in South Dakota," in *Dancing without Partners: How Candidates, Parties and Interest Groups Interact in the New Campaign Finance Environment*, eds. David B. Magleby, J. Quin Monson, and Kelly Patterson (Provo, UT: Brigham Young University, Center for the Study of Elections and Democracy, 2005), 246.

[94]See Center for Responsive Politics, "North Dakota 2018 Senate Race," https://www.opensecrets.org/races/summary?cycle=2018&id=NDS2, accessed July 10, 2019.

candidate and his family. The messages lacked substance and most were brief enough to be read on the way to the trash can."[95]

The growing sophistication of both data processing and lists segmenting the voting population into distinct subgroups has greatly increased the efficiency with which campaigns can target direct-mail appeals at specific audiences.[96] Improved databases and much cheaper technology have also led to increased use of the telephone to get out campaign messages and mobilize voters. "A telephone call, as unwelcome as it may be, cuts through … apathy and cynicism by forcing voters to listen to a political message," or so practitioners once claimed.[97] Robo call saturation has probably rendered this approach less effective, as people increasingly ignore calls from numbers they do not recognize.

Congressional candidates also regularly make use of the Internet and social media. A study of the 2002 campaigns found that 70 percent maintained websites, and 55 percent sought to raise funds online (via credit card transactions). Most sites featured newsletters and action alerts, as well as information about the candidates.[98] Since then, campaign websites and Internet fund-raising efforts have become virtually universal. They are a boon to researchers looking for a quick way to check out the candidates, but it is hard to gauge how effectively they serve the campaigns. Websites no doubt help to coordinate the candidate's active supporters, making it easy for them to keep in touch and send money, but the numbers involved are small. Candidates seeking to reach voters using newer technologies clearly recognize these trends, especially among younger citizens who are increasingly getting their news from sources such as social media even if they do not fully trust it.[99]

E-mail is also now part of the campaign arsenal, although some care must be taken to avoid irritating voters with unwanted spam. So is text messaging. For example, Rick Santorum, running (unsuccessfully) for reelection to his Pennsylvania Senate seat in 2006, encouraged attendees at a woman's outreach breakfast "to text 'LEADING' to a PA phone number to receive a return text message that read: 'From Keeping Women's Docs in PA to Allowing Parents the Freedom to Work from Home,

---

[95]James Meader and John Bart, "South Dakota: At-Large and Senate Race 2002," in *The Last Hurrah?*, eds. David B. Magleby and J. Quin Monson (Brookings, 2004), 164.

[96]"We've Got Mail," *Campaigns & Elections* (June 1999): 22.

[97]John Jameson, Chris Glaze, and Gary Teal, "Effective Phone Contact Programs and the Importance of Good Data," *Campaigns & Elections* (July 1999): 64–71.

[98]Phil Noble, "Internet and Campaign 2002 Analysis," Politics Online, July 15, 2005, http://www.politicsonline.com/pol2000/specialreports/campaign_analysis_2002, accessed May 15, 2003.

[99]Julie Ray, "Young People Rely on Social Media, but Don't Trust It," *Gallup,* November 18, 2021, https://news.gallup.com/opinion/gallup/357446/young-people-rely-social-media-dont-trust.aspx.

Rick Santorum is Leading 4 Women. Look 4 Msgs with More Information.'"[100] Because cell phone users have to sign up to receive the messages, the medium has traditionally been viewed as better suited to rallying the faithful than to attracting the undecided. The same was believed for Facebook and Twitter prior to the 2016 election. Now, candidates are increasingly using text messaging, Facebook, and social media platforms to raise money (via chat bots) and mobilize voters to go to the polls.[101]

During the past decade, candidates have also begun to rely on "micro-targeting" in their political campaigns. Micro-targeting allows candidates to tailor communications and messages to specific individuals in districts or states, much as Facebook targets advertisements at individual users based on the types of stories or posts they "like" in their newsfeeds. Micro-targeting has made political campaigns more customized and personal, but it may also have raised the stakes for candidates. Individuals may expect more from the winners because the appeals made during the campaign are so much more specific and personal than the older-style messages that targeted voters as members of large groups.[102] Micro-targeting on Facebook has also made it easier to manipulate the ads that users see during an election campaign, which has led Facebook to adopt procedures like the transparency initiative to help minimize this type of manipulation.[103] It has also lent itself to clandestine foreign interference in campaigns, as noted in recent election cycles.[104]

Regardless of the media combination chosen, a fundamental goal is to get the candidate's name before the public. Although little else is certain about the effects of mass communications, it is well established that mass media coverage is positively related to public awareness of people, products, messages, and events. As we shall see in chapter 5, the more nonincumbent candidates spend on a campaign, the more voters are likely to know who they are. Getting voters' attention is only one hurdle, of course, but clearing it is essential.

---

[100]"Consultants Corner: Sending Out an SMS," Hotline *on* Call, July 14, 2006, http://hotlineblog.nationaljournal.com/archives/2006/07/consultants_cor_2.html, accessed July 2, 2007.

[101]Elizabeth Germino, "How Social Media Has Changed the U.S. Congress," *CBS News*, November 6, 2022, https://www.cbsnews.com/news/social-media-u-s-congress-60-minutes-2022–11-06/

[102]Rick Ridder, "All Politics Is Customizable: The Pitfalls of Micro-targeting," Real Clear Politics, December 8, 2014, http://www.realclearpolitics.com/articles/2014/12/08/all_politics_is_customizable_the_pitfalls_of_micro-targeting_124856.html.

[103]See https://www.transparency-initiative.org.

[104]Kate Ackley, "Democrats Seek SEC Action on Foreign Influence in Elections," *Roll Call*, March 24, 2022, at https://rollcall.com/2022/03/24/democrats-seek-sec-action-on-foreign-influence-in-elections/

PERSONAL CAMPAIGNING

The second basic type of campaign activity centers on the candidate's personal contact with potential voters. Most politicians have faith in the personal touch; if they can just talk to people and get them to listen, they can win their support. There is some evidence backing this notion. Larry Pressler, who represented South Dakota in Congress from 1974 to 1996, won his first House election with a campaign that consisted largely of meeting people one on one. "I tried to shake five hundred hard hands a day," Pressler has said. "That is where you really take their hand and look at them and talk to them a bit. I succeeded in doing that seven days a week. I put in a lot of twelve-hour days, starting at a quarter to six in the morning at some plant in Sioux Falls or Madison."[105] Pressler estimates that he shook three to five hundred hands per day on about eighty days. "You would not believe the physical and mental effort this requires."[106] Shaking one hand per minute, a candidate would have to work for more than eight hours without stop to reach five hundred people.

The difficulty with this approach is that even the average House district now contains more than 761,000 people, and states can be much more populous than this. It is simply impossible to meet more than a small fraction of the electorate during a single campaign, which is part of the reason that candidates have begun to rely on impersonal contacts such as robo calls to introduce themselves to voters or encourage them to vote on election day.[107] But candidates often agree with Pressler that it is worth trying—especially for challengers whose only advantage may be the time they can devote to one-on-one campaigning. Some go door to door, "shoe-leathering" the neighborhoods. In his first House campaign in 1990, candidate Rick Santorum rang twenty-five thousand doorbells in his upset victory over the incumbent in Pennsylvania's 18th District;[108] four years later, he won election to the Senate.

Many candidates greet the early shift at the factory gate, shaking hands, passing out leaflets, and showing that they care enough to get up as early as the workers must. Most will accept any opportunity to speak

---

[105]Alan L. Clem, "The Case of the Upstart Republican," in *The Making of Congressmen: Seven Campaigns of 1974*, ed. Alan L. Clem (North Scituate, MA: Duxbury Press, 1976), 140.

[106]Clem, "The Case of the Upstart Republican."

[107]See Alan Gerber and Donald Green, "The Effects of Canvassing, Telephone Calls, and Direct Mail on Voter Turnout: A Field Experiment," *American Political Science Review* 94 (2000): 653–63, for evidence suggesting phone calls are much less effective at stimulating voter turnout. For an alternative perspective, see Kosuke Imai, "Do Get-Out-the-Vote Calls Reduce Turnout? The Importance of Statistical Methods of Field Experiments," *American Political Science Review* 99 (2005): 283–300.

[108]Barone and Ujifusa, *Almanac of American Politics 1994*, 1119.

to a group, and it is not uncommon for candidates to show up wherever people congregate in sufficient numbers: shopping malls, community picnics, parades, sporting events, religious services, and the like. As Santorum proved, energetic grassroots campaigns of this sort are occasionally successful even in this high-tech era,[109] and because they offer some hope to unknown candidates not blessed with great personal wealth, they remain common.

Even lavishly funded campaigns use the personal touch when feasible, and with adequate research resources, the touch can be personal indeed. Tim Johnson's successful campaign for reelection to the Senate in 2002 tried to personally visit as many households as possible. Either the candidate or a campaign worker went door to door carrying nine scripts that contained different issues. Before knocking, he or she already knew something about the occupant and selected the script developed for that demographic.[110]

Many of a candidate's activities are intended to reach voters beyond those in the immediate audience by attracting the attention of the news media. Indeed, campaigns work so hard to get free media exposure that campaign professionals commonly refer to it as "earned" media.[111] The main reason for walking the length of the state or pedaling across the district is that it makes news. Campaign events are designed not so much for the immediate audience as for the larger audience watching television, surfing the Internet, or reading the newspaper at home.

Campaigns do not always resist the temptation to resort to gimmickry. Ronald Machtley began his successful campaign to replace Fernand J. St Germain accompanied by a "250-pound hog named Lester H. Pork ('Les Pork') to symbolize his opposition to St Germain's big spending policies."[112] In 2010, a cash-short Republican challenger in Massachusetts reaped reams of publicity by distributing his campaign message on a barf bag (Sick of Congress? Then Vote Marty Lamb!). Ray Lutz, far behind in his challenge of Republican Duncan Hunter Jr., in California's 52nd District, went on an eleven-day hunger strike. Its stated purpose was to compel Hunter to debate him, but Lutz conceded that the tactic "got his name out there" and "from a publicity standpoint ... worked pretty well."[113] During the 2014 campaign, candidates sought to make their ads

---

[109]Ehrenhalt, "House Freshmen," 37, 41.

[110]Meader and Bart, "South Dakota," 165.

[111]Craig Varoga, "Lone Star Upset," *Campaigns & Elections* (March 1995): 35; Travis N. Ridout and Glen R. Smith, "Free Advertising: How the Media Amplify Campaign Messages," *Political Research Quarterly* 61 (2008): 598–608.

[112]Michael Barone and Grant Ujifusa, *The Almanac of American Politics 1990* (Washington, DC: National Journal, 1989), 1087.

[113]Michele Clock, "Hunger Strike Ends at Day 11 for Congressional Hopeful," *San Diego Union-Tribune*, August 24, 2010, B1.

memorable by featuring animals, including pigs, alligators, and monkeys. In 2022, more than a handful of Republican candidates appeared in ads brandishing either handguns or assault weapons to forcefully remind voters what they stood for.[114]

Paid campaign ads may also be used to gain media exposure; one consultant recommends using "shock mailers" to provoke opponents into outraged responses, which then give the charges much wider publicity when the news media report the squabble.[115] Russ Feingold used a gentler tactic in his successful challenge to Wisconsin senator Bob Kasten in 1992: humorous ads, including one featuring a mock personal endorsement by Elvis, that delighted the media. Kasten countered with his own Elvis spot attacking Feingold on the issues.[116] Sometimes the attention garnered by an ad backfires: Christine O'Donnell, Republican Senate nominee from Delaware in 2010, began her initial TV ad by gently informing voters, "I'm not a witch," inspiring parodies broadcast on Saturday Night Live and across the Internet on YouTube.[117]

A candidate's time is a scarce resource, so an important function of a campaign organization is to arrange for its effective use. An exhausting day of travel and meetings that results in few contacts with voters or little money raised is a campaign manager's nightmare. Time wasted cannot be retrieved. The reality of campaigns is that candidates and their aides cannot tailor the social and political world to suit their needs; they have to be ready to exploit opportunities to meet people and make news as they arise.

CAMPAIGN MESSAGES

Along with letting voters know who the candidate is, a campaign works to persuade them to vote for him or her. Uncertainty dominates here as well. There is no magic formula for appealing to voters; what works in one district or election year may not work in another. Nonetheless, according to campaign professionals, to be effective, every campaign needs to develop and project some consistent campaign theme. The theme explains why the candidate should be elected and why the opponent should not. It attempts to frame the choice—to establish what the election is about—in a way that underlines the candidate's strengths and plays down his or

---

[114]Yahoo News, "2022 Midterm Political Ad Mashup," YouTube, October 14, 2022, https://www.youtube.com/watch?v=iRFm-9x-K2E.

[115]Eva Pusateri, "Shock Mailers That Jolt Your Audience," *Campaigns & Elections* (May 1995): 41.

[116]Michael Barone and Grant Ujifusa, *The Almanac of American Politics 2000* (Washington, DC: National Journal, 1999), 1446.

[117]"Christine O'Donnell TV Ad: 'I'm Not a Witch,'" NPR, May 4, 2011, http://www.npr.org/blogs/itsallpolitics/2010/10/05/130346290/christine-o-donnell-tv-ad-i-m-not-a-witch.

her weaknesses. The goal is not to change people's political attitudes but rather to define the choice so that a vote for the candidate is consistent with existing attitudes.[118] The available themes and approaches are often rather different for incumbents, challengers, and candidates for open seats, so it is best to consider these categories separately.

Challengers' Campaigns

Challengers certainly hope to convince people of their own virtues—at minimum, that they are qualified for the office—but they are not likely to get far without directly undermining support for the incumbent. The trick is to find some vulnerable point to attack, and challengers are happy to exploit whatever is available. Inevitably, at least a few members are beset with scandal—moral or ethical lapses, felony convictions, signs of senility or alcoholism—and offer obvious targets, although a surprising number of incumbents with such liabilities manage to win reelection.[119] Democratic challengers to several Republicans defeated in 2006—including Richard Pombo (California's 11th), J. D. Hayworth (Arizona's 5th), and Senator Conrad Burns (Montana)—successfully exploited the incumbent's close association with convicted influence peddler Jack Abramoff. But William Jefferson, a Democrat representing Louisiana's 2nd District, won reelection that year, despite the discovery in his home freezer of $90,000 in marked bills from an FBI sting operation; Jefferson was indicted eight months after the election on multiple corruption charges and lost his bid for reelection in 2008.[120]

In 2022, numerous discrepancies came to light about Representative-elect George Santos's (R-NY) personal biography that featured a number of embellishments before he was eventually seated in Congress.[121] Four years earlier, two House Republicans—Duncan Hunter (California) and Chris Collins (New York)—were reelected to Congress despite being under federal indictments for, respectively, illegally using campaign funds for personal

---

[118]Joel Bradshaw, "Who Will Vote for You and Why: Designing Campaign Strategy and Theme," in *Campaigns and Elections American Style*, eds. James A. Thurber and Candice J. Nelson, 2nd ed. (Boulder, CO: Westview Press, 2004), 37–56.

[119]For example, Robert Leggett won reelection to California's 4th District in 1976, even after having been a principal subject of the "Koreagate" investigation and having it known publicly that he had fathered two children by an aide, had been supporting two households for years, and had even forged his wife's name to the deed for the second house. For a more general analysis of the electoral effects of corruption charges, see John G. Peters and Susan Welch, "The Effects of Charges of Corruption on Voting Behavior in Congressional Elections," *American Political Science Review* 74 (1980): 697–708; Susan Welch and John R. Hibbing, "The Effects of Charges of Corruption on Voting Behavior in Congressional Elections, 1982–1990," *Journal of Politics* 59 (1997): 26–39.

[120]"Louisiana Congressman Indicted in Bribery Probe," CNN, June 5, 2007, http://www.cnn.com/2007/POLITICS/06/04/jefferson.probe.ap/index.html.

[121]Jeremy Murn, "The Saga of Rep. George Santos: Inside His Many Fabrications, Exaggerations, and Embellishments," *ABC News*, January 23, 2023, https://abc7ny.com/george-santos-republican-congressman-anthony-devolder/12718559/

expenses and insider stock trading.[122] Back in 1992, the House Bank scandal had provided ammunition to challengers of the more than two hundred incumbents seeking reelection who had written unfunded checks on their House Bank accounts; most survived, but between retirements, defeats, and redistricting, only 60 percent returned to the next Congress, compared to 87 percent of those with clean banking records.[123]

Individual political failings—excessive junketing or lack of attention to the district or to legislative duties—also invite attack. Republican Mitch McConnell's defeat of incumbent Democrat Walter Huddleston in Kentucky's 1984 Senate race is widely attributed to a series of television ads that featured a pack of bloodhounds searching for him in places far from Washington, DC, and underlined the charge that Huddleston had neglected his duties.[124] Congressional travel became a common target in the 1990s, as challengers used it to symbolize insulation of "career politicians" from the lives of ordinary people. Any sign of neglecting the home folks also provides a ripe target. This was a winning theme in Kay Hagan's challenge to Republican senator Elizabeth Dole in North Carolina; one early mailing from the state's Democratic Party featured a "Where is Liddy Dole?" milk carton, reminding voters that she had spent only thirty-three days in the state during all of 2005 and 2006.[125]

Challengers also routinely try to show that incumbents are out of touch with district sentiments by attacking specific roll-call votes, the ideological or partisan pattern of votes, or a combination of the two. They also try to hang unpopular policies or politicians around their necks. Although cases exist in which a single "wrong" vote led to defeat, it is by no means easy to nail members with their voting records. Members are aware that they may be called to answer for any vote and on controversial issues take pains to cast an explainable one.[126] That is, a member will cast a vote likely to offend important groups in his or her electoral coalition or in the district at large only if it can be supported by

---

[122]"Indictment Caucus: Duncan Hunter and Chris Collins Win Reelection," *Roll Call*, November 7, 2018, https://www.rollcall.com/news/politics/indictment-caucus-duncan-hunter-chris-collins-win-reelection.

[123]Gary C. Jacobson and Michael Dimock, "Checking Out: The Effect of the House Bank Overdrafts on the 1992 House Elections," *American Journal of Political Science* 38 (August 1994): 601–24.

[124]The end of each ad criticizing Huddleston featured the pithy slogan "Switch to Mitch."

[125]Eric S. Heberlig, Peter L. Francia, and Steven H. Green, "The Conditional Party Teams of the 2008 North Carolina Federal Elections," in *The Change Election: Money, Mobilization, and Persuasion in the 2008 Federal Elections*, ed. David B. Magleby (Philadelphia: Temple University Press, 2011), 125.

[126]John Kingdon, *Congressmen's Voting Decisions* (New York: Harper & Row, 1973), 46–53.

a plausible explanation, one that does not make the member look bad if the vote is questioned.

Normally, a few wrong votes do not seriously weaken an incumbent, although a string of them lends plausibility to the charge that he or she is mismatched with the constituency and ought to be replaced. On occasion, challengers have been able to turn one or two key votes into potent symbols of the incumbent's divided loyalties. House Democrats running for reelection in 2010 did significantly worse if they had supported Barack Obama's health care reforms, economic stimulus package, clean energy bill, and financial reform legislation, particularly if they represented Republican-leaning districts.[127] The same was true for House Democrats in 1994: The more loyal they were to Bill Clinton and the party on key votes, the more electoral damage they suffered, and the more Republican the district's voting patterns in presidential elections, the more severe the damage.[128]

Democratic challengers in 2006 and 2018 and Republican challengers in 2010 and 2014 also effectively used the strategy of tying the incumbent to a locally unpopular president; a number of their campaigns featured ads depicting the president in close proximity to the incumbent, sometimes digitally morphing one into the other, suggesting the two were indistinguishable. This strategy probably contributed to the defeat in 2014 of Georgia congressman John Barrow, the last white, southern conservative Democrat in the House. With the increasing nationalization of politics, incumbents sharing the president's party affiliation now find it harder to separate their standing from his. They suffer more from his perceived shortcomings, as did Republicans in 2006 with Bush and 2018 with Trump, and Democrats with Obama in 2010 and 2014, but they also benefit more when he is popular, as did Democrats in 1998 and Republicans in 2002. Incumbents are also more vulnerable to attack for opposing locally popular presidents; several Republicans who voted to impeach Bill Clinton in 1998, despite representing districts he had won handily in 1996, paid the price in 2000.

General ideological or partisan attacks have been a mainstay of challengers' campaigns for decades. Incumbents are criticized for being too liberal or too conservative for the constituency or for their guilt by association with unpopular parties, causes, or leaders. This approach lost some of its punch in the 1960s and 1970s, as members strove to avoid

---

[127]Gary C. Jacobson, "The Republican Resurgence in 2010," *Political Science Quarterly* 126 (Spring 2011): 48–51; David W. Brady, Morris P. Fiorina, and Arjun S. Wilkins, "The 2010 Congressional Elections: Why Did Political Science Forecasts Go Awry?", *PS: Political Science & Politics* 44, no. 2 (2011): 247–50.

[128]Gary C. Jacobson, "The 1994 House Elections in Perspective," *Political Science Quarterly* 111, no. 2 (Summer 1996): 203–23.

ideological categorization or personal responsibility for party decisions when it would hurt them politically back home. By soliciting support as individuals rather than as representatives of a party or cause, they sought to undermine the force of such charges. As electoral politics took on a more ideological and partisan cast in the 1980s, incumbents—particularly Democrats—found it more difficult to sidestep attacks of this sort. Since then, the number of members representing districts where their party label suggests a poor ideological fit has dwindled (figure 2.2), but as the congressional parties have become increasingly polarized along ideological lines (see chapter 7), charges of extremism remain plausible (figures 4.10 and 4.11).

Going Negative

Until the 1980s, harsh personal attacks on an opponent were considered a sign of desperation, ineffective, and likely to backfire. Challengers on the ropes sometimes resorted to them; incumbents ignored the attacks on the theory that reacting would only bring them unwarranted attention. They were most common in campaigns of sure losers.[129] No longer. Campaign professionals have become convinced that negative advertising works, despite the general failure of academic studies to confirm this belief.[130] One Democratic consultant put it this way: "People say they hate negative campaigning. But it works. They hate it and remember it at the same time. The problem with positive is that you have to run it again and again to make it stick. With negative, the poll numbers will move in three or four days."[131] *Campaigns & Elections*, which bills itself as "the magazine for political professionals," devoted several articles in its July 1995 issue to helpful hints on "going negative" (e.g., "Attack Mail: The Silent Killer").[132] Campaign professionals distinguish between accurate *comparative* ads that highlight differences between the candidates (fair) and strictly personal attacks of questionable accuracy or relevance (unfair), although voters may not always appreciate the distinction.

In close races where party organizations are heavily involved, a division of labor usually emerges: the candidate's campaign takes the high

---

[129]Goldenberg and Traugott, *Campaigning for Congress*, 123.

[130]Richard R. Lau and Gerald M. Pomper, *Negative Campaigning: An Analysis of Senate Elections* (Lanham, MD: Rowman & Littlefield, 2004), 91; Richard R. Lau, Lee Sigelman, and Ivy Brown Rovner, "The Effects of Negative Political Campaigns: A Meta-analytic Reassessment," *Journal of Politics* 69, no. 4 (November 2007): 1176–209. Although they do not systematically swing elections, negative ads do have a downside, leaving voters with more negative impressions of the political process in general.

[131]Ehrenhalt, "New Campaign Era," 2561.

[132]Richard Schlackman and Jamie "Buster" Douglas, "Attack Mail: The Silent Killer," *Campaigns & Elections* (July 1995): 25.

road while the party does the dirty work. Commenting on the 2002 campaign in New Mexico's 2nd District, the Democrats' political director asserted that "the party's job was to act 'as the bad guy,' so Democratic candidates could focus on a more positive message." His Republican counterpart agreed: "Negative advertising is the job of the party, leaving candidates to stay above the fray longer."[133] Independent groups are even freer to sling mud; as the late Terry Dolan, whose National Conservative PAC pioneered independent campaigning in the early 1980s, observed in a moment of candor, "A group like ours could lie through its teeth and the candidate it helps stays clean."[134] BCRA has reinforced this division of labor by requiring candidates to say on camera, in every ad their campaigns broadcast, that they authorized and approved it. Still, candidates are not above going negative themselves; Republican Saxby Chambliss's successful 2002 Senate challenge of Georgia Democrat Max Cleland, who lost both legs and an arm in Vietnam, featured a television ad that followed footage of Osama bin Laden and Saddam Hussein with an unflattering shot of Cleland and a voiceover claiming that he had "voted against the president's vital homeland security efforts."[135]

The logic, if not the civility, of attacking opponents is compelling in a system of candidate-centered electoral campaigns. To the extent that members of Congress win and hold office by eliciting trust and regard as individuals, then the way to undermine their support is to destroy their constituents' trust and regard. Even national issues unfavorable to the incumbent's party—bad economic news, scandals, failed policies, an unpopular president—need to be personalized to serve effectively to weaken an incumbent. When national issues are scarce or favor the other party, character assaults are about the only tactic readily available.[136]

National issues helpful to challengers did become available in the early 1990s, and they were quick to exploit them. Intense public dissatisfaction with Congress's performance offered a potent theme to those challengers who could demonize the incumbent as a career politician guilty by association with the government's failings. Demonizing individual incumbents, as opposed to the class of officeholders, is not easy, however. For years, members of Congress managed to avoid the fallout from the public's routine dissatisfaction with Congress's institutional performance. Rather than defend the body, they would join

---

[133]Lonna Rae Atkeson, Nancy Carrillo, and Margaret C. Toulouse, "The 2002 New Mexico Federal Races," in *The Last Hurrah?*, eds. David B. Magleby and J. Quin Monson (Brookings, 2004), 276.

[134]Myra MacPherson, "The New Right Brigade," *Washington Post*, August 10, 1980, F1.

[135]Joel Roberts, "Big Brother Lends a Hand," CBS, October 28, 2002, http://www.cbsnews.com/stories/2002/10/28/politics/main527101.shtml, accessed May 15, 2003.

[136]Paul Taylor, "Accentuating the Negative," *Washington Post*, October 20, 1986, 6.

in the criticism: "Members of Congress run *for* Congress by running *against* Congress."[137] They defended their own personal performances vigorously but not at all the collective actions of Congress.

The effectiveness of this tactic began to break down in 1990, when voters reduced their support for incumbents of both parties in reaction to an unpopular October budget deal that cut programs and raised taxes.[138] The House Bank scandal undermined it further in 1992 by allowing challengers to connect members personally, through their record of bad checks, with congressional malfeasance.[139] The stratagem also failed conspicuously for Democrats in 1994, when Republicans succeeded in turning hostility to government into hostility to Democrats by depicting them as adherents of an intolerable status quo, exemplified by their unpopular president's "big government" solution to the health care system's shortcomings.[140] Nor did it work during four of the last five midterm elections, when the out party succeeded in framing the choice in national terms, as a referendum on the performance of the president, rendering the incumbents' emphasis on local service and political independence ineffective (see chapter 6).[141]

In the search for campaign issues, then, challengers are necessarily opportunists. It is a matter of finding and exploiting the incumbent's mistakes—neglect of the district, personal lapses, "bad" votes—or discovering a way to saddle him or her with personal responsibility for Congress's or the administration's shortcomings. A challenger cannot hope to win without reordering the campaign agenda. Incumbents thrive on campaigns that center on personal performance, experience, and services. Few members are vulnerable if they can persuade voters that this is what the contest is about; even losing incumbents usually get high marks on these dimensions. Challengers succeed only when they can frame issues in

---

[137]Fenno, *Home Style*, 168; emphasis is Fenno's.

[138]Gary C. Jacobson, "Deficit Cutting Politics and Congressional Elections," *Political Science Quarterly* 108 (1993): 390–96.

[139]Gary C. Jacobson and Michael A. Dimock, "Checking Out: The Effects of Bank Overdrafts on the 1992 House Elections," *American Journal of Political Science* 38 (1994): 601–24; see also chapter 6.

[140]Gary C. Jacobson, "The 1994 House Elections in Perspective," *Political Science Quarterly* 111, no. 2 (Summer 1996): 203–23.

[141]Gary C. Jacobson, "Referendum: The 2006 Midterm Congressional Elections," *Political Science Quarterly* 122 (2007): 1–24; Jacobson, "The Republican Resurgence in 2010," 27–52; Gary C. Jacobson, "Obama and Nationalized Electoral Politics in the 2014 Midterm," *Political Science Quarterly* 130 (Spring 2015): 1–26; Gary C. Jacobson, "Extreme Referendum: Donald Trump and the 2018 Midterm Elections," *Political Science Quarterly* 134 (Spring 2019): 1–30. Gary C. Jacobson, "The 2022 Elections: A Test of Democracy's Resilience and the Referendum Theory of Midterms." *Political Science Quarterly* 138 (Spring 2023): 1–22.

a way that makes these dimensions less relevant and other considerations more salient.

From this perspective, the burgeoning role of party committees and other institutional participants in congressional election politics takes on added importance. National campaign committees have helped their challengers by polling between elections to probe for soft spots in incumbents' support, tracking their votes to store up ammunition for the next election, attacking them between elections with negative advertising, and quickly spreading the word about successful innovations in strategy and tactics. Dozens of groups now rate roll-call votes, target incumbents opposing their views, advise favored challengers on tactics, and mobilize campaign volunteers—in addition, of course, to providing campaign money. All of these things add to incumbents' uncertainty and worry; aware of the resources available to be mobilized against them, most act as if they are anything but safe.

Incumbents' Campaigns

Incumbents pursue reelection throughout their terms in office, so their campaign strategies are visible in all their dealings with constituents. Naturally, they try to avoid mistakes that would give opponents campaign issues, but in an uncertain and complicated political world, in which the pressure for party loyalty is now higher than it has been in decades, that is not always possible. They therefore work to maintain the kind of relationship with constituents that will allow them to survive a damaging vote or contrary political tide. Fenno's insightful account of how House members do this, in fact, describes effective campaigning by any congressional candidate, incumbent or challenger.[142]

Fenno traveled extensively with eighteen House members as they made the rounds of their districts. He found that each projected a personal home style that defined his relationship with the groups he relied on for political support. Home styles varied according to the character of the district and the personality of the individual member, but in one way or another, all members basically sought to inspire trust among their constituents. They did this by emphasizing their personal qualifications, including moral character; by identifying with their constituents ("I am one of you," they implied, "so you can trust me to make the right decisions—those you would make under the same circumstances"); and by working to develop bonds of empathy with the groups and individuals they met.

Along with trust, members emphasized their accessibility. They reminded constituents continually that the lines of communication were

---

[142]Fenno, *Home Style*, 55.

open, that they had access to the member whenever they needed it. The payoffs are clear. Members who are trusted, accessible, and thought to be "one of us" will have much less trouble fending off personal attacks. Their explanations for controversial votes will get a more sympathetic hearing; institutional or partisan failures and even notorious ethical lapses may go unpunished.

This kind of relationship cannot be developed overnight; nor can it be maintained without continual reinforcement. Its importance is the reason that, as one congressman put it, "it's a personal franchise you hold, not a political franchise."[143] Nonincumbents may aspire to it, but they have little chance of achieving it in the brief period of a single election campaign. Those who have held other elective offices in the district or who are already familiar to district voters for other reasons—a previous campaign, a family name, or celebrity status as an athlete, entertainer, or newscaster—have a head start.[144]

The personal connection so important to Fenno's subjects is no doubt harder to cultivate now that districts contain a quarter million more constituents than when he initially did his research, but most members of Congress continue to try.[145] A polarized public has made the task harder; with many incumbents now avoiding open town hall meetings that would attract noisy, angry critics.[146] In addition to trying to keep district connections in good repair, incumbents have now begun to deal with the growing threat of harsh personal and political attacks and well-financed challenges by campaigning preemptively. Incumbents have always raised and spent money reactively, in proportion to what their challengers raise and spend against them. They now spend increasing amounts of money preemptively in order to inoculate voters against anticipated attacks.

Both patterns are evident when incumbents' expenditures are regressed on challengers' expenditures in House elections from 1972 through 2022; table 4.3 reports the results. For comparison, the dollar figures have been adjusted for inflation (2022 = 1.00). First, look at the intercept, which indicates how much, on average, an incumbent would spend if the challenger

---

[143]Fenno, *Home Style*, 114.

[144]Jamie L. Carson et al., "Constituency Congruency and Candidate Competition in U.S. House Elections," *Legislative Studies Quarterly* 36 (2011): 461–82.

[145]Richard F. Fenno Jr., *Congress at the Grassroots: Representational Change in the South, 1970–1998* (Chapel Hill: University of North Carolina Press, 2000), 129–40; Richard F. Fenno Jr., *The Challenge of Congressional Representation* (Cambridge, MA: Harvard University Press, 2013). For more recent evidence of this type of legislator–constituency connection, see Charles Hunt, *Home Field Advantage: Roots, Reelection, and Representation in the Modern Congress* (Ann Arbor: University of Michigan Press, 2022).

[146]Heather Caygle, "Lawmakers Ditch Town Halls: 'They Want to Avoid Those Gotcha Moments.'" *Politico*, August 21, 2018, https://www.politico.com/story/2018/08/21/congress-town-halls-gotcha-public-meetings-789430, accessed March 19, 2019.

Table 4.3 Incumbents' Expenditures as a Function of Challengers' Expenditures in House Elections, 1972–2022

Year	Number of Cases	Intercept		Regression Coefficient: Challenger's Expenditures		R²
1972	319	196.8	(13.3)	.56	(.04)	.34
1974	323	195.1	(12.9)	.63	(.04)	.42
1976	332	250.6	(14.4)	.55	(.04)	.36
1978	312	326.3	(18.0)	.50	(.04)	.38
1980	338	316.0	(25.7)	.74	(.05)	.41
1982	315	476.0	(24.6)	.58	(.05)	.34
1984	341	534.0	(24.1)	.63	(.04)	.39
1986	319	654.0	(36.5)	.73	(.07)	.27
1988	328	658.7	(31.1)	.79	(.06)	.32
1990	328	686.6	(27.9)	.70	(.07)	.24
1992	312	816.9	(39.6)	.82	(.08)	.23
1994	336	746.1	(37.4)	.64	(.06)	.24
1996	359	739.9	(40.2)	.87	(.05)	.42
1998	309	920.2	(54.1)	.44	(.06)	.13
2000	333	907.3	(43.6)	.89	(.05)	.54
2002	302	1,104.8	(42.4)	.44	(.04)	.27
2004	334	1,076.9	(45.9)	.91	(.06)	.40
2006	345	1,198.4	(49.8)	.91	(.04)	.55
2008	344	1,310.1	(51.3)	.61	(.04)	.38
2010	366	1,381.6	(69.4)	.69	(.05)	.32
2012	320	1,252.1	(118.3)	.98	(.10)	.22
2014	314	1,353.6	(85.7)	.64	(.08)	.17
2016	329	1,320.2	(71.6)	.94	(.09)	.26
2018	325	1,378.5	(76.7)	.46	(.03)	.40
2020	358	1,626.4	(170.4)	.85	(.08)	.25
2022	326	2,215.3	(195.9)	1.09	(.12)	.20

Note: Expenditures are in thousands of dollars, adjusted for inflation (2022 = 1.00); standard errors are in parentheses; all coefficient are significant beyond $p > .001$.
Source: Calculated by the authors.

spent nothing at all. It has increased dramatically, from $196,800 to $2,215,300 (in 2022 dollars), between 1972 and 2022; the average increase from one election to the next is about 10 percent. House incumbents have been raising and spending increasing sums of money, regardless of the kinds of challenges they face; the growing practice among safe incumbents of raising money to pass along to the party and other candidates explains only part of this growth. Second, the regression coefficients (slopes) vary but average around .72, indicating that, on top of their initial level of spending, an incumbent typically matches nearly three-fourths of the challenger's spending. The matching rate was notably higher in 2022 (1.09), reflecting incumbents' ability to significantly outspend challengers.

The same campaign professionals who promote negative campaigns recommend a preemptive strategy to cope with them. "Inoculation and preemption are what win campaigns," according to one Republican consultant. Said another, "If you know what your negatives are and you know where you are vulnerable, you can preempt it."[147] Hence, for example, Republican senator James Abdnor of South Dakota, expecting to be challenged by the state's governor for renomination on grounds of ineffectiveness, began broadcasting ads in November 1985 that had prominent Republican senators bearing witness to his effectiveness. Another Republican thought to be in trouble for the 1986 election, Senator Paula Hawkins of Florida, also began airing commercials in 1985. A year before the election she had already spent $750,000 on media advertising alone.[148] Both these attempts at preemption failed, however; evidently rhetoric could not mask the candidates' real weaknesses. More successful was Democratic senator Patrick Leahy, who ran an ad warning his Vermont constituents, "Oh boy, it's going to get knee-deep around here. Dick Snelling has hired some famous dirty tricksters to foul the airwaves with a big-bucks, political smear campaign. ... Do we really have to go through this in quiet, sensible, beautiful Vermont?"[149] Leahy did not seek reelection in 2022 after a 48-year career in the Senate.

Although incumbents, at least in the House, engage more or less continuously in activities aimed at ensuring reelection—including, now, preemptive campaigning—their real campaigns start when it becomes clear who the challenger will be in the primary or general election or both. Different challengers present different problems and inspire different campaign strategies. Routine maintenance of ties with groups in the electoral coalition can deal with inept, obscure, or underfinanced opponents, who can otherwise be ignored. Senator Daniel Inouye, for example, had little reason to mention his 1998 opponent, Crystal Young, who spent no money on the campaign but got some publicity when she "alleged that actress Shirley MacLaine implanted electromagnetic needles in her."[150] And Senator Jim De Mint could ignore his 2010 challenger, Alvin Greene, an unemployed veteran who raised no money and was under indictment on an obscenity charge.[151]

Ignoring the opposition is a standard tactic of incumbents who feel relatively secure: Why give an unknown opponent free publicity? More

---

[147]Ehrenhalt, "New Campaign Era," 2563.

[148]Ehrenhalt, "New Campaign Era," 2563–64.

[149]Taylor, "Accentuating the Negative," 6.

[150]Barone and Ujifusa, *Almanac of American Politics 2000*, 497.

[151]Katherine Q. Seelye, "Final Days of an Unlikely Run for Senate," *New York Times*, October 30, 2010.

serious opponents compel more vigorous campaigns, with the strategy adapted to the relative strengths and weaknesses of both candidates. Incumbents also adjust to opponents' campaign tactics once their effectiveness has been demonstrated. For example, counterattack or, better yet, preemptive assault on the challenger's character and credibility has replaced the older practice of ignoring personal attacks. Expecting to be on the defensive because of adverse national conditions in 2006, many Republican incumbents followed this strategy. Those who did so had plenty of help and encouragement from their party. As early as the summer of 2005, the NRCC began investigating prospective Democratic challengers, looking for anything it could use to discredit them: unpaid student loans, bankruptcies, op-ed pieces written in college advocating legalized pot, defense of criminals in court, tax delinquencies, and so on. It collected and catalogued anything from a challenger's past that it could portray as unsavory. Indeed, in an era of Google, Facebook, and YouTube, prospective candidates are on notice that no youthful indiscretion is safe from wide public exposure. Representative Thomas Reynolds from New York's 26th District, the NRCC's chair, boasted: "These candidates have been out there doing other things—they have never seen anything like this before. We haven't even begun to unload this freight train."[152] Consider the following example that went awry: In New York, the NRCC ran an ad accusing Democratic House candidate Michael A. Arcuri, a district attorney, of using taxpayer dollars for phone sex. "Hi, sexy," a dancing woman purrs. "You've reached the live, one-on-one fantasy line." It turns out that one of Arcuri's aides had tried to call the state's Division of Criminal Justice, which had a number almost identical to that of a porn line. The misdial cost taxpayers $1.25.[153]

Incumbents also adapt their strategies to the president's current standing with the public. Many Democrats who had been happy to link themselves with their party and Bill Clinton in 1992 sought to declare their independence in 1994. Similarly, many Republicans who had celebrated their connection with Donald Trump in 2016, when he was first elected, emphasized their differences with the president and avoided appearing with him at campaign events in 2018, when his approval ratings were down and his disapproval ratings up. With President Biden not actively campaigning in 2022, Democratic candidates were able to

[152]Adam Nagourney, "Theme of Campaign Ads: Don't Be Nice," *New York Times*, September 27, 2006, http://www.nytimes.com/2006/09/27/us/politics/27ads.html?ex=1317009600&en=5 b29b3a6fe35f5cc&ei=5088&partner=rssnyt&emc=rss, accessed July 3, 2007.

[153]Michael Grunwald, "The Year of Playing Dirtier: Negative Ads Get Positively Surreal," *Washington Post*, October 27, 2006, A1.

downplay their connections with the president in light of the high rates of inflation and his lower levels of approval.[154]

Common to most incumbents' campaigns are an emphasis on the value of experience and seniority (for the capacity it gives members to serve the district more effectively) and reminders of the things that the member has done over the years for constituents. When the insider image these accomplishments evoked became a potential liability in the early 1990s, some switched to emphasizing their status as outsiders opposed to the status quo by advocating term limits, balanced-budget amendments, and an end to congressional perks. This was a favorite (and uniformly successful) tack taken by Republican incumbents in 1994. In special circumstances, special ploys may be necessary. Milton Young, running for reelection to the Senate from North Dakota in 1974 at the age of seventy-six, countered suggestions that he was getting too old by running a TV spot showing him splitting a block of wood with a karate chop.[155]

Despite what members learn about their constituencies, uncertainty plagues incumbents as well as nonincumbents. Each election may present a new challenge and a new set of electoral variables. Because incumbents are not sure which of their actions got them elected previously, they cannot be sure what combination of activities will serve them in altered circumstances. Although in a normal election year most members are reelected easily (at least in the House), most have had close calls at one time or another, and all have vivid memories of seemingly entrenched colleagues who suffered sudden massive vote losses and unexpected defeats.

Because of uncertainty, members tend to exaggerate and overreact to electoral threats. They are inspired by worst-case scenarios—imagining what they would have to do to win if everything went wrong—rather than objective probabilities. Hence, some members conduct full-scale campaigns even though the opposition is nowhere to be seen. The desire to win decisively enough to discourage future opposition also leads many incumbents to campaign a good deal harder than would seem objectively necessary. The sense of uncertainty and risk felt by incumbents has grown in recent years, along with the money, professional talent, and technology potentially available to their opponents. The specter of fickle electorates, combined with active organizations ready to mobilize extensive campaign resources against them should they show signs of vulnerability, undermines whatever confidence comfortable reelection margins might otherwise inspire. The electoral shake-ups of the early 1990s and

---

[154]John Aldrich, Jamie Carson, Brad Gomez, and Jennifer Merolla, *Change and Continuity in the 2020 and 2022 Elections* (Lanham: Rowman & Littlefield, 2023), 302.

[155]Michael Barone, Grant Ujifusa, and Douglas Matthews, *The Almanac of American Politics 1980* (New York: E. P. Dutton, 1979), 669.

in midterms from 2006 through 2022 are a reminder that they are wise to take nothing for granted.

Candidates for Open Seats

Candidates for open seats face somewhat different electoral situations because none of the contestants is an incumbent or a challenger with the accompanying advantages or disadvantages. Contenders are much more likely to face difficult primary contests because the opportunity offered to ambitious politicians by an open seat attracts more and better-qualified candidates. As figure 4.12 shows, candidates with previous elective experience are much more likely to compete for nominations in primaries when seats are open than when incumbents are involved, with 1990 and 2008 attracting the highest proportion of experienced open-seat contestants during the 1980–2022 period. More generally, with so many congressional districts now lopsidedly partisan, the primary is often a more difficult hurdle than the general election.[156]

Both candidates in open-seat races are likely to have some experience in elective office and, therefore, some familiarity with at least part of the constituency and some useful relationships with electorally important segments of it (recall table 3.3). Both are more likely to have adequate campaign resources because contests for open seats are expected to be competitive; the best chance by far to take a seat from the opposing party occurs in the absence of an incumbent. As a consequence, candidates for open seats are typically better known and better liked than challengers—but not as well as incumbents.[157] No particular pattern of campaign strategy is typical of candidates for open seats other than a highly variable mixture of the approaches used by incumbents and challengers that coincides with the electoral position between the two.

Because candidates competing for open seats are normally much more closely balanced in skills and resources than are challengers and incumbents, partisan trends, both local and national, more strongly influence the outcomes. Without the pull of incumbency, votes get cast more consistently along party lines, so election results reflect state or district partisanship more consistently. Presidential coattails (discussed more

---

[156]Harvey L. Schantz, "Contested and Uncontested Primaries for the U.S. House," *Legislative Studies Quarterly* 5 (1980): 550; Jeffrey S. Banks and D. Roderick Kiewiet, "Explaining Patterns of Candidate Competition in Congressional Elections," *American Journal of Political Science* 33 (1989): 997–1015; Jason Byers, Jamie L. Carson, and Ryan D. Williamson, "Candidate Quality and Electoral Success in U.S. House Primary Elections" (paper presented at the 2018 Annual Meeting of the American Political Science Association); Rachel Porter and Tyler S. Steelman, "No Experience Required: Early Donations and Amateur Candidate Success in Primary Elections," *Legislative Studies Quarterly* 47(2022): https://doi.org/10.1111/lsq.12396

[157]The evidence is presented in chapter 5.

Figure 4.12 Candidate Emergence Patterns in US House Primary Races, 1980–2022

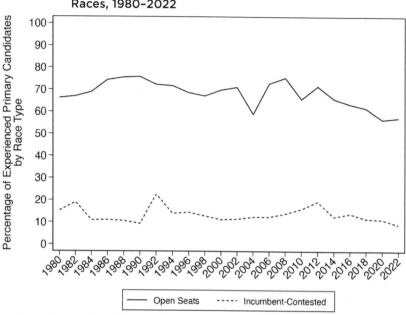

Source: Data collected by the authors.

fully in chapter 6) are stronger; that is, voters are more likely to cast congressional votes consistent with their presidential votes, so the fates of candidates for open seats are tied more closely to the top of the ticket in presidential election years.[158] Open seats also register partisan tides more strongly; in years with big swings, such as 1974, 2006, 2008, and 2018 (pro-Democratic), or 1980, 1994, 2010, and 2014 (pro-Republican), a disproportionate share of the winning party's gains come from open seats.[159]

SENATE CAMPAIGNS

As we observed in chapter 3, Senate elections are, on average, considerably more competitive than House elections. Senate incumbents win less consistently and by narrower margins than House incumbents. At least until recently, nearly every state was potentially winnable by either party;

---

[158]Jeffrey Mondak, "Presidential Coattails in Open Seats: The District-Level Impact of Heuristic Processing," *American Politics Quarterly* 21 (1993): 307–19; Gregory Flemming, "Presidential Coattails in Open-Seat Elections," *Legislative Studies Quarterly* 20 (1995): 197–211. The difference between open and incumbent-held seats has diminished in this century along with the decline in the incumbency advantage.

[159]See Ronald Keith Gaddie, "Congressional Seat Swings: Revisiting Exposure in House Elections," *Political Research Quarterly* 50 (1997): 699–710.

greater partisan sorting and party line voting has probably now taken more states out of play. Thirty-eight states have chosen senators from both parties in elections since 1996, and all but three of the remaining states have elected governors of the party opposite their senators' during this time. Greater partisan balance by itself makes Senate elections more competitive than House elections, but it also creates a strategic electoral environment that enhances competition in several ways.

First, Senate incumbents usually face formidable opponents.[160] About two-thirds of Senate challengers in recent elections had previously held elective office. Even the amateurs often have impressive résumés; among the successful first-time candidates have been two former astronauts (John Glenn and Harrison Schmitt), a former basketball star (Bill Bradley), a lawyer turned actor (Fred Thompson), a comedian (Al Franken), an author (J. D. Vance), and several prominent multimillionaire businessmen.

Formidable challengers attract campaign resources. Senate campaigns in general attract proportionately greater contributions because the donations are, in a sense, more cost-effective, especially in smaller states.[161] Senate contests are usually closer, so campaign resources are more likely to affect the outcome. Parties and groups with particular policy agendas are aware that, when it comes to passing legislation, one senator is worth 4.35 representatives. A party has to defeat far fewer incumbents to take over the Senate than the House. It makes strategic sense for donors to campaigns and the outside spending groups now investing huge sums in congressional races to focus on the Senate, and that is what they have done. Thus Senate challengers are much more likely than House challengers to enjoy adequate financial support for their causes.

Senate challengers can also use their campaign resources more effectively than House challengers. Most Senate constituencies have the size and structure to make television advertising cost-efficient. Resources are usually sufficient to justify using campaign professionals and the technical paraphernalia of modern campaigns: computers, micro-targeting data, polls, direct-mail advertising and solicitation, and so forth. The news media are much more interested in Senate campaigns, so they bestow much more free attention and publicity on Senate candidates than on their House counterparts.[162] It is little wonder that Senate challengers and

[160]Peverill Squire, "Challenger Quality and Voting Behavior in U.S. Senate Elections," *Legislative Studies Quarterly* 17 (1992): 247–64; David Lublin, "Quality, Not Quantity: Strategic Politicians in U.S. Senate Elections, 1952–1990," *Journal of Politics* 56 (1994): 228–41.

[161]David Magleby, "More Bang for the Buck: Campaign Spending in Small-State U.S. Senate Elections" (paper presented at the annual meeting of the Western Political Science Association, Salt Lake City, Utah, March 30–April 1, 1989).

[162]Kim Fridken Kahn, "Senate Elections and the News: Examining Campaign Coverage," *Legislative Studies Quarterly* 16 (1991): 349–74.

other nonincumbents are much better known by voters than are House challengers.

Furthermore, Senate incumbents find it more difficult to develop and maintain the kind of personal relationships with constituents that Fenno observed among House incumbents. The reason is obvious. Senate districts (states) are, with six exceptions for the states with a single representative, more populous than congressional districts—often very much so. The opportunities for personal contacts with constituents and attention to individual problems are proportionately fewer. It also follows that the larger the state, the more difficult it is for a senator to cultivate firm personal ties to constituents. The larger Senate staffs cannot make up the difference.[163]

Senators' activities in Washington are also more conspicuous than those of representatives. Action in the Senate is more visible than action in the House; the Senate has fewer members, and they receive more attention from the news media.[164] Senators are thus more likely than representatives to be associated with controversial and divisive issues.[165] As senators do not have the pressure of a two-year election cycle to keep them attuned to the folks back home, electoral coalitions may fall into disrepair, and a careless senator may discover that he or she must begin almost from scratch when reelection time rolls around.

Lavishly funded and professionally run Senate campaigns have been the proving ground for the latest innovations in campaign tactics and techniques. One development is interactive campaigning, in which the campaign themes and messages of each candidate are rapidly altered in response to what the opposition is saying and, more importantly, to what tracking polls say about the effectiveness of both campaigns. Polling technology is the key. In the words of a Democratic consultant: "It's relatively simple and not very expensive now to sample public opinion. In the last month of a campaign, both sides will poll nightly, test how that day's media and campaigning has played, and trace the results."[166] Instead of planning and executing

---

[163]Gary C. Jacobson and Raymond E. Wolfinger, "Information and Voting in California Senate Elections," *Legislative Studies Quarterly* 14 (1989): 518–19; John R. Hibbing and John R. Alford, "Constituency Population and Representation in the United States Senate," *Legislative Studies Quarterly* 15 (1990): 581–98. However, one careful study found little difference in the level of regard voters have for senators compared to representatives and little disadvantage for senators from large states compared to senators from small states. See Jonathan S. Krasno, *Challengers, Competition, and Reelection: Comparing Senate and House Elections* (New Haven, CT: Yale University Press, 1994), chapter 3.

[164]Timothy Cook, "House Members as Newsmakers: The Effects of Televising Congress," *Legislative Studies Quarterly* 9 (1986): 211.

[165]Barbara Sinclair, "Washington Behavior and Home-State Reputation: The Impact of National Prominence on Senators' Visibility and Likability," *Legislative Studies Quarterly* 15 (1990): 486–90.

[166]Ehrenhalt, "New Campaign Era," 2560.

a single strategy over the course of an entire campaign, campaign teams practice "strategic flexibility." Observed another consultant, "When candidates come in here now, their first questions to me are: Can you respond quickly? Can you attack quickly? Can you do a fast turnaround?"[167] With enough money, turnaround can be fast indeed. In California's 1994 Senate campaign, Dianne Feinstein saw her campaign ads answered within twenty-four hours by new commercials produced and distributed statewide by Michael Huffington's lavishly funded campaign team.[168]

MANIPULATING TURNOUT

The advent of multimillion-dollar media campaigns has not made organized, grassroots-level efforts to get out the vote any less crucial. In fact, campaigns that deluge voters with broadcast ads, mailings, and phone calls may just turn them off. Reviewing the 2002 South Dakota Senate campaign, in which candidates, parties, and interest groups spent some $24 million in a state with fewer than 476,000 registered voters, James Meader and John Bart concluded, "In the end, most voters probably tuned out the commercials, turned off the phone, and placed all the mail in the trash"; they cited as an example "one woman [who] wrote and explained that she started to watch public television and stopped answering the phone in the evening."[169] Thus the effort to mobilize potential supporters to vote either through absentee ballots (increasingly common) or at the polls on election day may be essential to offset voters' inclination to withdraw from the barrage of conflicting, often mean-spirited messages showered on them in competitive races.

For years, labor unions led the effort to get out the Democratic vote in many areas and were responsible for the Democrat's traditional superiority in this area. But Republicans have now caught up. In elections since 2002, the RNC has financed extensive pre-election drives to mobilize voters in key contests, using thousands of volunteers and paid workers. In 2006, it spent $30 million on the effort, which included, according to its organizer, "35 million live calls and door knocks with one-third of that (13 million) in the last 96 hours."[170] Such campaigns can be effective. A meta-analysis of 294 experimental field studies found that door-to-door canvassing increased turnout by an average of about 2.5 percentage points; volunteer phone calls raised it by about 1.9 points, compared to 1.0 points for calls from commercial phone banks; and automated phone

[167]Ehrenhalt, "New Campaign Era," 2560.

[168]David Lesher, "TV Blitz Fueled by a Fortune," *Los Angeles Times*, September 12, 1994, 1.

[169]Meader and Bart, "South Dakota," 170.

[170]Magleby and Patterson, *War Games*, 34.

messages were ineffective. Direct mail had a small (.16 percentage points on average) but nonetheless statistically significant effect.[171]

Both parties and their interest-group allies now mount extensive mobilization drives wherever tight competition makes them necessary. With the increase in early and absentee voting, these efforts now necessarily take place over weeks rather than days; in 2022, an estimated 37 percent of votes were cast prior to election day.[172] Voter mobilization efforts become more urgent because fewer voters seem willing to cross party lines and outcomes thus depend increasingly on turning out core party supporters. Both parties are fully aware of this and invest heavily in getting their people to the polls. The record turnout in the 2018 and 2022 midterms, especially among younger voters, demonstrates the efficacy of such efforts, although the continued and polarized sentiments provoked by Donald Trump were no doubt a large part of the explanation for the huge increase in participation.[173]

Not all efforts go into getting supporters to the polls. For purposes of winning an election, reducing the other side's vote by a given number is as valuable as raising one's own by the same number. Thus campaigns have an incentive to discourage the turnout of voters who would, if they participated, vote for the opposition. Because voting, as a duty and a right, is such a potent symbol of democracy, campaigns rarely admit openly to trying to keep people from the polls. Nonetheless, Republican activists are regularly accused of trying to dampen turnout in minority neighborhoods, which tend to be overwhelmingly Democratic. For example, an unsigned flyer appeared in minority neighborhoods in Baltimore in 2002 reading, "URGENT NOTICE. Come out to vote on November 6th. Before you come to vote make sure you pay your parking tickets, motor vehicle tickets, overdue rent and most important any warrants."[174] The election was actually on November 5. No one took credit, but it is not hard to guess which party's allies put out the flyer. More publicly, Republican donors financed a "Don't Vote" campaign in Nevada in 2010, urging Latinos to stay home to punish Democrats for failing to deliver on immigration reform.[175] In 2022, Republicans in

[171]Donald P. Green, Peter M. Aronow, and Mary C. McGrath, "Field Experiments and the Study of Voter Turnout," *Journal of Elections, Public Opinion, and Parties* 23 (2012): 27–48.

[172]Michael P. McDonald, United State Election Project, https://www.electproject.org, accessed February 15, 2023.

[173]Alana Wise, "Young Voters Helped Democrats Win the Senate and Other Midterm Elections," NPR, November 15, 2022, https://www.npr.org/2022/11/15/1136563709/young-voters-helped-democrats-win-the-senate-and-other-midterm-elections.

[174]Howard Tibit and Tim Craig, "Allegations Fly as Election Day Nears," *Baltimore Sun*, November 4, 2002, http://www.baltimoresun.com/news/elections/bal-te.md.turnout-04nov04,0,732693.story?coll=bal-election-governor, accessed May 16, 2003.

[175]The organization's statement may be found at http://www.latinosforreform.com.

battleground states, notably Georgia, were accused of passing stricter voting laws to dissuade African Americans from voting despite high levels of turnout.[176]

Negative ads are also used to depress opposition turnout; voters who could never be attracted to a candidate may nonetheless be induced to stay home if the alternative is discredited. Supposedly independent groups conducting "voter-education" campaigns and thus immune from FEC reporting requirements most often do the dirty work. In 2002, one such organization, calling itself the Council for Better Government, ran ads on urban radio stations accusing Democrats of taking African American voters for granted and making such statements as "Each year the abortion mills diminish the human capital of our community by another 400,000 souls. The Democratic Party supports these liberal abortion laws that are decimating our people."[177]

It is not clear, however, that negative campaigns actually depress turnout; they may even enhance it.[178] The intensely polarized and competitive electoral environments that encourage campaigns to go negative also excite voters and spur efforts to mobilize them. The 2006 campaigns, conducted in what was then characterized as "the most toxic midterm campaign environment in memory,"[179] featured an abundance of scurrilous and often dishonest attack ads from both sides. Yet turnout was the highest for any midterm since 1982 and the second highest since eighteen-year-olds got the vote. The 2010 campaigns were at least as nasty and turnout was, by a small margin, even higher (figure 5.1). The 2018 and 2022 campaigns featured their fair share of negative ads, but also had two of the highest midterm turnouts in over fifty years.

Another ploy to drain votes from the rival party is to run a spurious third-party campaign designed to attract some of its more gullible supporters. In 2002, the campaign manager for the incumbent Democrat running in Minnesota's 2nd District arranged for a liberal activist to run as the candidate of the previously nonexistent "No New Taxes" party, named for a favorite Republican campaign theme.[180] Similarly,

---

[176]Associated Press, "Effect of Georgia's Voting Law Unclear, Despite High Turnout," *Georgia Public Broadcasting*, December 12, 2022, https://www.gpb.org/news/2022/12/12/effect-of-georgias-voting-law-unclear-despite-high-turnout.

[177]Jay Barth and Janine Parry, "Provincialism, Populism, and Politics: Campaign Spending and the 2002 U.S. Senate Race in Arkansas," in *The Last Hurrah?*, eds. David B. Magleby and J. Quin Monson (Brookings, 2004), 61.

[178]Lau and Pomper, *Negative Campaigning*, 76–85; Ken Goldstein and Paul Freedman, "Campaign Advertising and Voter Turnout: New Evidence for the Stimulation Effect," *Journal of Politics* 64 (2002): 721–40.

[179]Nagourney, "Theme of Campaign Ads."

[180]John S. Schockley, "The Three-Peat in the 2nd Congressional District in Minnesota," in *Running on Empty? Political Discourse in Congressional Elections*, eds. L. Sandy Maisel and Darrell M. West (Lanham, MD: Rowman & Littlefield, 2004), 42–43.

Democratic incumbent John Adler's campaign in New Jersey's 3rd District sought to stem the Republican tide in 2010 by running an accomplice under the Tea Party label.[181] In both cases, the ploy was exposed and the perpetrator lost.

CONCLUSION

Congressional election practices have undergone a period of rapid development, as organizational, technical, and financial innovations have turned the closest contests into remarkably extravagant affairs. The emergence of evenly matched, strongly polarized national parties has put control of at least one house of Congress up for grabs in every election since 1994, raising the stakes in competitive races. The candidates and their organizations no longer control or even dominate the campaigns in such contests; the national parties and outside interest groups, with their own resources and agendas, strongly influence the tone and content of campaigns. From incumbents' perspective, the value—and difficulty—of scaring off serious opposition has never been greater, since abundant, centrally disposed resources are available to be mobilized against them quickly on any sign of vulnerability. New techniques and tactics may hold unpleasant surprises, and strategies for coping with them are still unsure. Sharpened sensitivity to the electoral implications of their activities in office is a natural result; so too is intensified partisan animosity on the Hill. Both of these developments have, as we shall see in chapter 7, important effects on how the House and Senate work as legislative institutions.

That said, it is also important to emphasize that a large majority of House incumbents and a smaller majority of Senate incumbents escape serious competition altogether and so win by quite comfortable margins. The impressive new technology for probing electorates, along with the growing cost of competitive campaigns and the growing number of seats securely in one party's hands, has led to a sharp bifurcation of effort. Under normal circumstances, electoral resources (including high-quality candidates) are now concentrated in a small subset of House districts and in selected Senate races, making life more difficult for those incumbents who appear sufficiently vulnerable to invite an all-out challenge. But those who avoid becoming targets face increasingly feeble opposition because promising challengers have little incentive to incur the growing cost in money, time, lost privacy, and diminished family life of conducting a serious challenge unless the prospects for victory are very good.

---

[181]Richard Perez-Pena, "Sham Candidacy Is Charged in House Race," *New York Times*, October 11, 2010, http://www.nytimes.com/2010/10/12/nyregion/12jersey.html.

5

Congressional Voters

★　★　★

WE EXAMINED VIRTUALLY EVERY ISSUE raised in the previous two chapters from the perspective of some implicit notions about how congressional voters operate. Discussions of the rise and decline of the incumbency advantage, the importance of campaign money, and House–Senate electoral differences, to mention a few examples, were grounded in particular assumptions about voting behavior in congressional elections. So, too, are the campaign and career strategies of congressional candidates. Their activities are guided by beliefs about what sways voters and, at the same time, help define what voters' decisions are supposed to be about. An adequate understanding of voting behavior in congressional elections is important to congressional scholars and politicians alike.

Neither political scientists nor candidates have reason to be fully satisfied; voters continue to surprise both. Studies over the past several decades have produced a great deal of fresh information about congressional voters, however, and we know much more about them than we once did. This chapter examines voting behavior in congressional elections and how it relates to the other phenomena of congressional election politics. We begin with a discussion of voter turnout and then turn to the fundamental question of how voters come to prefer one candidate over another. The answer to this question has evolved over the past several decades as part of the transition from the candidate-centered electoral politics of the 1970s and 1980s to the much more nationalized and party-centered electoral politics of today.

TURNOUT IN CONGRESSIONAL ELECTIONS

Voting requires not only a choice among candidates but also a decision to vote in the first place. With the exception of the highest midterm turnout in living memory in 2018, the 46.8 percent turnout in 2022 was the highest for a midterm since 1970 (figure 5.1).

Figure 5.1 Voter Turnout in Federal Elections, 1932–2022

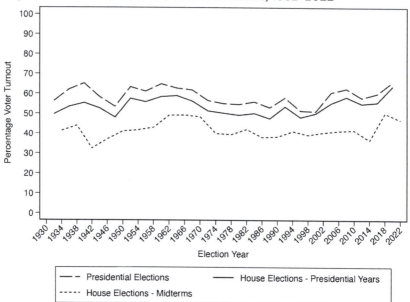

Sources: Norman J. Ornstein, Thomas E. Mann, and Michael J. Malbin, Vital Statistics on the American Congress, 2008 (Washington, DC: -Brookings Institutions Press, 2008), table 2-1. Data for 2008–2022 are from Michael P. McDonald, "Voter Turnout," at http://electionsproject.org/home/voter-turnout/voter-turnout-data (accessed March 2, 2023).

Obviously, participation in congressional elections is strongly influenced by whether there is a presidential contest to attract voters to the polls; turnout drops by an average of twelve percentage points when there is not. Even in presidential election years, House voting is about five percentage points lower than presidential voting. Turnout generally declined between 1960 and 2000. After that, it enjoyed a modest revival, although only in presidential election years, until 2018, when it jumped abruptly to the highest midterm rate since 1914, when people first voted directly for senators. This was unambiguously a Trump effect, with highly polarized reactions to his person and policies arousing the voting public directly as well as inspiring the huge influx of campaign money (discussed in previous chapters) that financed wide-ranging efforts to get out the vote. Turnout dipped slightly in 2022 but was still the highest for a midterm in over five decades.

The question of why turnout declined for several decades was the subject of intensive investigation, but political scientists never provided a definitive answer.[1] The mystery grows all the deeper because

[1]Michael P. McDonald and Samuel Popkin, "The Myth of the Vanishing Voter," *American Political Science Review* 95 (2001): 963–74; Eric R. A. N. Smith and Michael Dolny, "The Mystery of Declining Turnout in American National Elections" (paper presented at the annual meeting of the Western Political Science Association, Salt Lake City, Utah, March 30–April 1, 1989); Ruy Teixeira, *The Disappearing American Voter* (Washington, DC: Brookings Institution, 1992); Warren E. Miller and J. Merrill Shanks, *The New American Voter* (Cambridge, MA: Harvard University Press, 1996), 509–14.

the single demographic factor most strongly linked to participation—level of education—was increasing in the population at the same time that voting participation was dropping. A thorough examination of the question, undertaken by Steven Rosenstone and John Mark Hansen in the early 1990s, placed most of the blame on a decline in grassroots efforts by parties and other organizations (e.g., unions, social movements, and others) to get voters to the polls.[2] By implication, the extensive voter-mobilization work of parties and allied groups in recent presidential elections and especially in 2018 helps explain the uptick in participation. A full review of the question would take us too far afield; it is enough for our purposes to recognize that an unimpressive proportion of eligible voters elect members of Congress. Even with the increases in turnout for 2018 and 2022, on average in midterm elections since 1982, only about 42 percent of the eligible population has shown up at the polls.

WHO VOTES?

The low level of voting in congressional elections raises a second question: Who votes and who does not? This question is important because politicians wanting to get into or remain in Congress will be most responsive to the concerns of people they expect to vote.[3] If voters and nonvoters have noticeably different needs or preferences, the former are likely to be served and the latter slighted.

Jan Leighley and Jonathan Nagler have given Raymond Wolfinger and Steven Rosenstone's classic 1980 study of who votes and who does not a thorough updating.[4] Examining electorates from 1972 through 2008, Leighley and Nagler report that demographic differences in turnout have changed little since Wolfinger and Rosenstone's analysis. Voting rates continue to be substantially higher among people who are better educated, richer, older, and married; a new twist is that women are now about 5 percent more likely to vote than men. Voting rates remain significantly lower among Hispanics but not African Americans (once age and education are taken into account). Turnout is still significantly lower among people living in the South, a residue of the era when one-party

---

[2]Steven J. Rosenstone and John Mark Hansen, *Mobilization, Participation, and Democracy in America* (New York: Macmillan, 1993), 215.

[3]John D. Griffin and Brian Newman, "Are Voters Better Represented?" *Journal of Politics* 67 (November 2005): 1222–24.

[4]Raymond E. Wolfinger and Steven J. Rosenstone, *Who Votes?* (New Haven, CT: Yale University Press, 1980); Jan E. Leighley and Jonathan Nagler, *Who Votes Now? Demographics, Issues, Inequality, and Turnout in the United States* (Princeton, NJ: Princeton University Press, 2014), 24–26.

rule was fortified by formal and informal practices that kept African Americans and poor whites from the polls.[5]

The single most important factor in explaining turnout remains level of education, followed by income and age.[6] The finding that turnout varies most strongly with education comes as no surprise because every other study of American voting behavior has found this to be the case. Although some scholars have questioned the direct causal effects of education,[7] the common interpretation is that education imparts knowledge about politics and increases one's capacity to deal with complex and abstract matters such as those found in the political world.[8] People with the requisite cognitive skills and political knowledge find the cost of processing and acting on political information lower and the satisfaction greater. Politics is less threatening and more interesting. Similarly, learning outside formal education can facilitate participation. People whose occupations put them in close touch with politics or whose livelihoods depend on governmental policy—government workers and farmers, for example—vote more consistently, as do people who are older and simply have longer experience as adults.

Better-educated, wealthier, and older people are clearly overrepresented in the electorate. When their preferences and concerns substantially differ from those of nonvoters, governmental policy will be biased in their favor. Wolfinger and Rosenstone, citing survey data from the 1970s, argued that the views of voters did not differ much from those of the population as a whole, so differential participation did not impart any special bias.[9] In the 1980s and 1990s, policy issues that divided people according to economic status became more prominent, and the underrepresented groups suffered. Cuts in government spending to reduce federal budget deficits hit welfare recipients far harder than they hit senior citizens or business corporations. Yet, until recently, research suggested that the policy preferences of voters and nonvoters were not very different and that few, if any, election results would change

---

[5]Leighley and Nagler, *Who Votes Now?*, 84–87; Wolfinger and Rosenstone, *Who Votes?*, 94.

[6]Leighley and Nagler, *Who Votes Now?*, 80–81.

[7]One study found that people who shared the cognitive and personality characteristics typical of college attendees but for some reason did not attend college participated in politics at the same level as those who did; thus higher education is an indicator rather than a cause of a propensity to participate. See Cindy D. Kam and Carl L. Parker, "Reconsidering the Effects of Education on Political Participation," *Journal of Politics* 70 (July 2008): 621–31.

[8]Wolfinger and Rosenstone, *Who Votes?*, 18.

[9]Wolfinger and Rosenstone, *Who Votes?*, 104–14; see also Stephen D. Shaffer, "Policy Differences between Voters and Non-voters in American Elections," *Western Political Quarterly* 35 (1982): 496–510.

if every eligible person voted.[10] Leighley and Nagler, examining more recent evidence, found that, regarding redistributive policies (e.g., government guarantee of jobs and health insurance, preference for services over spending cuts), nonvoters are significantly more liberal (favoring redistribution) than voters, and the authors conclude that these preferences are thus likely to be underrepresented in Congress.[11]

Another question posed by the turnout data is whether congressional electorates differ between presidential and midterm election years. Do the millions of citizens who vote for congressional candidates only because they happen to be on the same ballot with presidential candidates change the electoral environment in politically consequential ways? One prominent study, based on surveys of voters taken in the 1950s, concluded that they did. It found the electorate in presidential election years to comprise a larger proportion of voters weakly attached to either political party and subject to greater influence by political phenomena peculiar to the specific election, notably their feelings about the presidential candidates. At the midterm, with such voters making up a much smaller proportion of the electorate, partisanship prevailed. This resulted in a pattern of "surge and decline," in which the winning presidential candidate's party picked up congressional seats (the surge), many of which it subsequently lost at the next midterm election when the pull of the presidential candidate was no longer operating (the decline). The theory of surge and decline explained why, in every midterm election between 1934 and 1998, the president's party lost seats in the House.[12]

We will examine aggregate shifts in congressional seats and votes from one election to the next at length in chapter 6. At this point, suffice it to say that later evidence has not supported the view of electorates underlying this theory. Subsequent research suggested that midterm voters were no more or less partisan than those voting in presidential election years and that the two electorates were demographically alike, except the midterm electorate tended to be older.[13] The addition or subtraction

---

[10]Teixeira, *The Disappearing American Voter*, 86–101; Benjamin Highton and Raymond E. Wolfinger, "The Political Implications of Higher Turnout," *British Journal of Political Science* 31 (2001): 179–223.

[11]Leighley and Nagler, *Who Votes Now?*, 158–77; the progressive agenda espoused by the House Democrats in 2019 suggests that higher turnout in 2018 served to reduce this bias.

[12]Angus Campbell, "Surge and Decline: A Study of Electoral Change," in *Elections and the Political Order*, eds. Angus Campbell et al. (New York: John Wiley, 1966), 40–62.

[13]See Raymond E. Wolfinger, Steven J. Rosenstone, and Richard A. McIntosh, "Presidential and Congressional Voters Compared," *American Politics Quarterly* 9 (1981): 245–55; see also Albert D. Cover, "Surge and Decline Revisited" (paper presented at the annual meeting of the American Political Science Association, Chicago, Illinois, September 1–4, 1983), 15–17; James E. Campbell, *The Presidential Pulse of Congressional Elections* (Lexington: University of Kentucky Press, 1993), 44–62.

of voters drawn out by a presidential contest did not routinely produce significantly different electorates. This does not appear to hold true for Barack Obama's presidency, however. Turnout among younger and minority voters was unusually high in 2008, followed by a more typical lower turnout among both groups in 2010, a pattern repeated in the 2012–14 election cycle, much to the benefit of Obama when he was on the ballot and of Republican candidates in the two midterm elections.[14] Turnout among younger and minority voters was lower in 2016 without Obama (or youth favorite Bernie Sanders) on the ballot. In 2018, turnout was as usual highest among older whites, but younger, minority, and better-educated voters made up a larger proportion of the electorate than in 2014 or 2016.[15] During the 2022 midterms, turnout among adults aged eighteen to twenty-nine was estimated at 27 percent, second only to the 2018 election four years earlier when turnout for the same age group was around 31 percent.[16]

These observations about turnout refer to the electorate as a whole, but congressional candidates are, of course, much more concerned about the particular electorates in their states and districts. As noted in chapter 2, turnout varies enormously across constituencies. One obvious source of variation is the demographic makeup of the district: average level of education, income, occupational status, age distribution, and so on. These factors are, at least in the short run, fairly constant in any individual state or district, but turnout also varies in the same constituency from election to election (quite apart from the difference between presidential and midterm elections), and these variations are, for our purposes, the most interesting.

The generally low level of voting in congressional elections means that a large measure of the fundamental electoral currency, votes, lies untapped. This affects campaign strategy in several ways. Even incumbents who have been winning by healthy margins recognize that many citizens did not vote for them (even if they did not vote against them) and that they could be in trouble if an opponent who can mobilize some of the abstainers comes along. This is not an idle worry. Generally, the higher the turnout, the closer the election; the lower the turnout, the more easily

---

[14]Gary C. Jacobson, "Obama and Nationalized Electoral Politics in the 2014 Midterm," *Political Science Quarterly* 130 (Spring 2015): 1–26.

[15]Matthew Yglesias, "The 2018 Electorate Was Older, White, and Better Educated than in 2016," *Vox*, November 12, 2018, https://www.vox.com/policy-and-politics/2018/11/12/18 083014/2018-election-results-turnout, accessed November 24, 2018.

[16]Gianna Melillo, "Researchers Say 2022 Election Had Second Highest Young Voter Turnout in Last 30 Years," *The Hill*, November 11, 2022, https://thehill.com/changing-america/respect/diversity-inclusion/3730922-researchers-say-2022-election-had-second-highest-young-voter-turnout-in-last-30-years/

the incumbent is reelected.[17] Despite the increased turnout rate in 2022 relative to many previous midterms, neither Democrats nor Republicans seemed to be significantly advantaged as was the case four years earlier when higher turnout was a key factor in flipping forty House seats to the Democrats. In that election, successful challengers evidently drew to the polls people who normally do not bother to vote.

Experienced campaigners know that getting one's supporters to the polls is as important as winning their support in the first place; as we saw in chapter 4, well-organized campaigns typically devote a major share of their work to getting out the vote. This effort presupposes that there is a vote to be gotten out and that people brought to the polls will indeed support the candidate. After all, what finally matters is what voters do in the voting booth. And this raises questions of fundamental interest to politicians and political scientists alike: What determines how people vote for congressional candidates? What moves voters to support one candidate rather than the other? The entire structure of congressional election politics hinges on the way voters reach this decision.

PARTISANSHIP IN CONGRESSIONAL ELECTIONS

The first modern survey studies of congressional elections conducted in the 1950s identified partisanship as the single most important influence on individuals' voting decisions, and it remained so even through the period of weakened party influence in the 1960s and 1970s. Since then, the impact of partisanship has returned to the point where it dominates congressional voting decisions at least as much as it did in the 1950s, with profound consequences for both electoral and congressional politics.

Alternative Interpretations of Party Identification

The pioneering survey studies of voting behavior in both presidential and congressional elections conducted in the 1950s found that a large majority of voters thought of themselves as Democrats or Republicans and voted accordingly. Particular candidates or issues might, on occasion, persuade a person to vote for someone of the other party, but the defection was likely to be temporary and did not

---

[17]Gregory A. Caldeira, Samuel C. Patterson, and Gregory A. Markko, "The Mobilization of Voters in Congressional Elections," *Journal of Politics* 47 (1985): 490–509; Franklin D. Gilliam Jr., "Influences on Voter Turnout for U.S. House Elections in Non-presidential Years," *Legislative Studies Quarterly* 10 (1985): 339–52; Robert A. Jackson, "A Reassessment of Voter Mobilization," *Political Research Quarterly* 49 (1996): 331–49. The anticipation of a close election itself increases turnout; see Stephen P. Nicholson and Ross A. Miller, "Prior Beliefs and Voter Turnout in the 1986 and 1988 Congressional Elections," *Political Research Quarterly* 50 (1997): 199–213.

dissolve the partisan attachment.[18] The leading interpretation of these findings was that voters who were willing to label themselves as Democrats or Republicans identified with the party in the same way they might identify with a region, ethnic or religious group, or sports team: "I'm a Bostonian, a Catholic, a Red Sox fan, and a Democrat." Partisanship was, in short, a component of a person's social identity. Identification with a party was rooted in powerful personal and collective experiences (best exemplified by the millions who became Democrats during the Great Depression) or was learned, along with similar attachments, from family, friends, and neighbors. In either case, identification with a party was thought to establish an enduring orientation toward the political world. The result, in aggregate, was a stable pattern of partisanship across the entire electorate—for people do not often revise their social identities.

This did not mean that the same party won every election, of course. Some voters did not think of themselves as belonging to a party, and even those who did would defect to the rival party if their reactions to particular candidates, issues, or recent events ran contrary to their party identification strongly enough. But once these short-term forces were no longer present, the long-term influence of party identification would reassert itself, and voters would return to their partisan moorings. For most citizens, only quite powerful and unusual experiences could inspire permanent shifts of party allegiance.

Challenges to this interpretation of party identification came from at least two directions during the 1960s and 1970s. First, the electoral influence of partisanship diminished. Fewer voters were willing to identify as partisans, and the party attachments of those who did were likely to be weaker. The proportion of people declaring themselves to be strong partisans fell from 37 percent in 1952 to 23 percent in 1978; the proportion declaring themselves either strong or not strong partisans fell from 77 to 60 percent over the same period.[19] Second, even those who still identified with a party were a good deal more likely to defect to candidates of the other party than they had been earlier.[20]

---

[18]See Angus Campbell et al., *The American Voter* (New York: John Wiley, 1960), chapter 6.

[19]Conventionally, party identification is measured by a series of questions: "Generally speaking, do you usually think of yourself as a Republican, a Democrat, an Independent, or what? [If Republican or Democrat] Would you call yourself a strong (Republican/Democrat) or a not very strong (Republican/Democrat)? [If Independent] Do you think of yourself as closer to the Republican or Democratic Party?" The responses locate the respondent on a seven-point scale: strong Democrat, not-strong Democrat, independent closer to Democrats, pure independent, independent closer to Republicans, not-strong Republican, strong Republican; the data are from the American National Election Studies Cumulative Data File.

[20]Warren E. Miller and Santa A. Traugott, *American National Election Studies Data Sourcebook, 1952–1986* (Cambridge, MA: Harvard University Press, 1989), 81; see also figure 5.2.

Although researchers have yet to agree on a definitive explanation for the period of decline in electoral partisanship, it no doubt relates to political events of the 1960s and 1970s. Each party brought disaster upon itself by nominating a presidential candidate preferred only by its more extreme ideologues—the Republicans with Barry Goldwater in 1964 and the Democrats with George McGovern in 1972. In 1968, the Vietnam War and the civil rights issue split the Democrats badly and fostered the strongest third-party showing since 1924. Republicans suffered in turn, as the Watergate revelations forced their disgraced president from office. Jimmy Carter's inept handling of the economy and troubles with Iran laid the Democrats low in 1980. More generally, the political alliances formed in the battle over the New Deal fractured along multiple lines as new problems and issues—most notably civil rights and social issues concerning abortion, crime, sexuality, and the environment—forced their way onto the political stage.

Voters responded to these political phenomena as they were expected to respond to short-term forces, defecting when their party preferences were contradicted strongly enough. As defections became more widespread and partisanship, in general, continued to decline, an interpretation of party identification that, among other things, more easily accommodated change gained plausibility. The alternative interpretation, presented most fully by Morris P. Fiorina, emphasized the practical rather than the psychological aspects of party identification. Fiorina argued that people attach themselves to a party because they have found through past experience that its candidates are more likely than those of the other party to produce the kinds of results they prefer.

Because it costs time and energy to determine the full range of information on all candidates who run for office, voters quite sensibly use the shorthand cue of party to simplify the voting decision. Past experience is a more useful criterion than future promises or expectations because it is more certain. Party cues are recognized as imperfect, to be sure, and people persuaded that a candidate of the other party will deal more effectively with their concerns vote for him or her. More importantly, if cumulative experience suggests that candidates of the preferred party are no longer predictably superior in this respect, the party preference naturally decays.[21] Party ties are subject to modification, depending on the answer to the proverbial voters' question, "What have you done for me lately?"[22]

---

[21]Morris P. Fiorina, *Retrospective Voting in American National Elections* (New Haven, CT: Yale University Press, 1981).

[22]Samuel L. Popkin et al., "Comment: What Have You Done for Me Lately? Toward an Investment Theory of Voting," *American Political Science Review* 70 (1976): 779–805.

Figure 5.2 Average Party Identification, All Respondents and Voters, by Decade

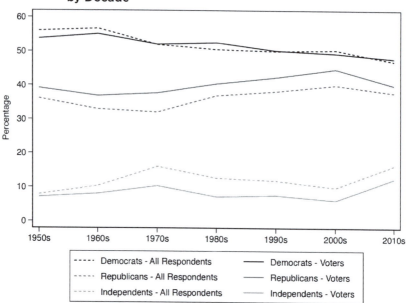

Source: American National Election Studies (ANES).

    The virtue of this alternative interpretation is that it can account for both the observed short-run stability and the long-run lability of party identification evident in individuals and the electorate. For example, it offers a plausible explanation for the evidence of a significant shift in party identification away from the Democrats and toward the Republicans after the 1970s evident in figure 5.2.[23] The Democrats' advantage in the population as a whole has diminished by more than half since the 1960s, but among voters it has narrowed even more, a clear consequence of higher Republican turnout rates. Republican identifiers also tend to vote more loyally for their party, so the national partisan division has been closely balanced in recent years.[24] (Notice also that pure independents, with much lower turnout rates than other citizens, comprised less than 10 percent of the electorate until very recently.)

    The greatest shift toward the Republican Party occurred in the South, largely in response to the civil rights movement (electing conservative Democrats was no longer an effective barrier to racial desegregation)

---

[23]Independents who consider themselves closer to a party are considered partisans because they are about as loyal to their party's candidates as are not-strong partisans; see figure 5.4.
[24]Alan I. Abramowitz, "The End of the Democratic Era? 1994 and the Future of Congressional Election Research," *Political Research Quarterly* 48 (1995): 873–89; Gary C. Jacobson, "Terror, Terrain, and Turnout: Explaining the 2002 Midterm Elections," *Political Science Quarterly* 118 (Spring 2003): 12–16.

and the Democratic Party's adoption of increasingly liberal positions on social issues. The proportion of white southern voters identifying as Republicans grew from an average of less than 20 percent in the 1950s to more than 67 percent in 2020, while the proportion identifying as Democrats dropped from 74 to 24 percent. About half of this realignment occurred through generational replacement (older Democrats dying off and younger whites entering the electorate as Republicans); the other half happened through people switching their party allegiances.[25] The southern realignment—and a small countermovement outside the South of socially moderate and liberal Republicans drifting toward the Democratic Party—showed that party identification, though resistant to change, is not immutable. Other evidence also suggested that partisanship is more sensitive to short-term influences than the social identification model would predict, but the durability of their effects remains in dispute.[26]

Partisanship and Voting

The issue of which interpretation of party identification makes more empirical sense (or which combination of the two views—they are by no means irreconcilable, and each may apply to a different subset of citizens) will not be settled here. What matters most for our purposes is that party identification, however understood, has always been the primary determinant of voting in postwar congressional elections. As the trends in party loyalty among House and Senate voters displayed in figure 5.3 demonstrate, however, that influence has varied widely over the postwar period. Back in the 1950s, the incidence of party-line voting averaged 88 and 86 percent in, respectively, House and Senate elections. Party loyalty among voters for both houses of Congress subsequently declined, dropping below 80 percent in most elections during the 1970s and 1980s. In the past two decades, however, it has returned to the levels of the 1950s and, in the three most recent elections, has reached some of the highest points ever in the full time series.[27] Readers should note that the data for

---

[25] Donald Green, Bradley Palmquist, and Eric Schickler, *Partisan Hearts and Minds: Political Parties and the Social Identities of Voters* (New Haven, CT: Yale University Press, 2002), 140–54.

[26] The sensitivity of aggregate distribution of party identification to political conditions is shown clearly in Michael B. MacKuen, Robert S. Erikson, and James A. Stimson, "Macropartisanship," *American Political Science Review* 83 (1989): 1125–42; see also Gary C. Jacobson, "The Effects of the George W. Bush Presidency on Partisan Attitudes," *Presidential Studies Quarterly* 39 (June 2009): 172–209. For a more skeptical view, see Green, Palmquist, and Schickler, *Partisan Hearts and Minds*, 87–103.

[27] Much of the data from 2020 used here and elsewhere in this book are from the 2020 CES in lieu of the 2020 ANES survey since the latter oversampled Biden supporters and undersampled Trump supporters. For more on this issue, see Gary C. Jacobson, "Explaining the Shortfall of Trump Voters in the 2020 Pre- and Post-Election Surveys," Paper presented at the 2022 Annual Meeting of the Midwest Political Science Association.

Figure 5.3 Party Loyalty in Contested House and Senate Elections, 1952–2022

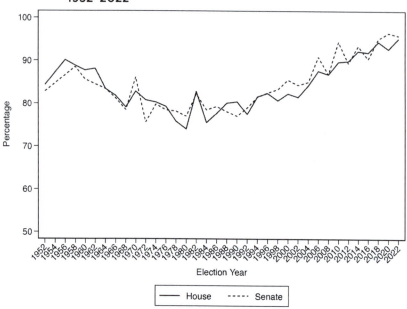

Source: American National Election Studies (ANES), 1952–2004, 2008, 2012, 2016; Cooperative Election Study (CES), 2006, 2010, 2014, 2018, 2020, 2022.

2006, 2010, 2014, 2018, 2020, and 2022 in figure 5.3 and several subsequent figures are from the Cooperative Election Study (CES) rather than the ANES, which no longer conducts midterm election studies; the CES data points are thus not strictly comparable to those from other years.[28] That said, the same upward trend is evident in the CCES series, with 2022 levels of party loyalty reaching 95.2 and 95.9 percent, respectively, in House and Senate elections.

The data in figures 5.2 and 5.3 include as partisans those voters who initially call themselves independents but then say they are closer to a party. The reason is that such voters behave like partisans, as figure 5.4 demonstrates. Voters who lean toward a party are nearly as loyal to that party's candidates in House elections as are weak party identifiers and are therefore appropriately treated as closet partisans; the same holds for

[28]Stephen Ansolabehere, "CCES Common Content, 2006," March 26, 2012, https://www.icpsr.umich.edu/icpsrweb/ICPSR/studies/30141; Stephen Ansolabehere, "CCES Common Content, 2010," 2010, http://hdl.handle.net/1902.1/17705; Stephen Ansolabehere, "CCES Common Content, 2012," Release 1: April 15, 2013; Stephen Ansolabehere, "CCES Common Content, 2014," Release 1: April 15, 2015. Data produced by Harvard University, Brian Schaffner, Stephen Ansolabehere, Sam Luks, 2019, "CCES Common Content, 2018," Brian Schaffner, Stephen Ansolabehere, Marissa Shih, 2023, "CES Common Content, 2022," March 20, 2023, https://dataverse.harvard.edu/dataset.xhtml?persistentId=doi%3A10.7910/DVN/PR4L8P

Figure 5.4 Partisanship and Voting in House Elections, 2004–2020

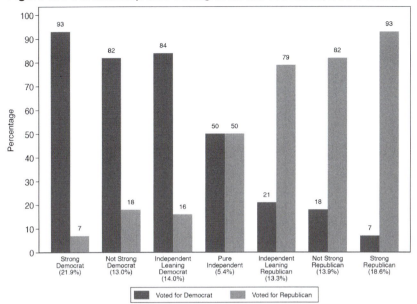

Source: ANES 2004, 2008, 2012, 2016, and 2020; the proportion of voters in each party category is in parentheses.

voters in Senate elections. This is important, because survey results that lump them with pure independents greatly exaggerate the share of the electorate potentially available to both parties. Although about a third of voters say they are independents, more than 80 percent of this group actually favors one of the parties, and the proportion of voters without any partisan inclination is very small.

The revival of party loyalty documented in figure 5.3 is a direct consequence of the gradual realignment of the mass parties into increasingly coherent and distinctive electoral coalitions since the 1970s.[29] The rise of the (white) Republican South is only one part, albeit an important one, of a long-term process in which voters have increasingly sorted themselves into the appropriate party, given their political opinions, values, and ideologies. Figure 5.5 illustrates the consequences. Since the 1970s, the ANES has asked respondents about where they would place themselves on seven-point scales regarding how far the government should go in guaranteeing people a good job and standard of living, in helping

---

[29]For fuller accounts of these trends, see Alan I. Abramowitz, *The Disappearing Center: Engaged Citizens, Polarization, and American Democracy* (New Haven, CT: Yale University Press, 2010); Matthew Levendusky, *The Partisan Sort: How Liberals Became Democrats and Conservatives Became Republicans* (Chicago: University of Chicago Press, 2010).

Figure 5.5 Correlations between Party Identification, Ideology, and Issue Positions for House Voters, 1972–2020

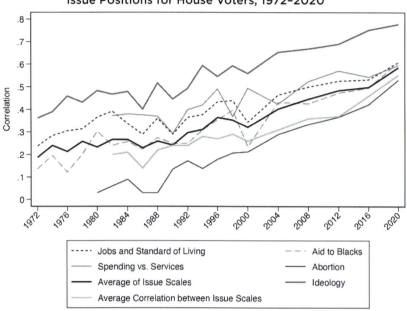

Source: ANES.

blacks and other minority groups, and in providing services that require government spending. Respondents have also been asked about their views on abortion in a format that generates a four-point scale measuring opinion on the issue and about where they would place themselves on a seven-point liberal–conservative scale.[30] As figure 5.5 shows, the relationships between voters' party identification, ideology, and position on these issues have grown steadily stronger. The correlation between partisanship and ideology has increased from .36 to .78, and the average correlation

---

[30] The end points of the first scale are "the government ... should see to it that every person has a job and a good standard of living" and "the government should just let each person get along on his own"; of the second, "the government should make every possible effort to improve the social and economic position of blacks" and "the government should not make any special effort to help blacks because they should help themselves"; of the third, "the government should provide fewer services, even in areas such as health and education, in order to reduce spending" and "it is important for the government to provide more services even if it means an increase in spending." The abortion measure offers four alternatives: never permitted, permitted only in case of rape or incest or danger to the woman's life, permitted for other reasons but only after the need has been clearly established, and always permitted as a matter of personal choice. Ideology is the respondents' self-location on a seven-point scale: extremely liberal, liberal, slightly liberal, moderate, slightly conservative, conservative, and extremely conservative. The proportion of voters calling themselves liberal or conservative has grown over time; typically, about 80 percent of voters can place themselves on the scale, and about 70 percent of those voters place themselves either to the left or right of center.

of partisanship with issue positions has risen from .15 to .59 over this period. Back in 1972, 61 percent of conservatives identified as Republicans and 31 percent as Democrats; in 2020, the comparable distribution was 82 and 7 percent. Similarly, in 1972, 71 percent of liberals identified as Democrats and 20 percent as Republicans; in 2020, the distribution was 91 and 5 percent. Fewer voters now face conflicts among their partisan identities, ideological leanings, and issue opinions, so fewer have a reason to defect to the other party's candidate.

PARTISANSHIP AND INCUMBENCY

Changes in the incidence of party-line voting contributed directly to the rise and subsequent decline in the congressional incumbency advantage discussed in chapter 3. Challengers' partisans have always been more inclined to defect to incumbents than have incumbents' partisans to challengers (or candidates for open seats), but the incidence of such defections rose in the 1960s and 1970s to remarkably high levels (figures 5.6 and 5.7). Changes in the wording of the vote choice question exaggerated these estimates beginning in 1978 (it was revised again to reduce the exaggeration after 1998),[31] but even with that caveat, it is obvious that the decline in party loyalty strongly favored incumbents, contributing to their growing electoral advantage. It is also evident that the revival of party loyalty in recent elections registers mainly as a decrease in partisan defections to incumbents, which in ANES data for 2008–16 and the CES data for 2020 have been lower than at any time since the 1950s. Data from Senate elections display the same trends, although Senate incumbents' advantage in defections is almost always smaller than that of House incumbents. Defections to challengers among voters sharing the incumbent's party affiliation have always been comparatively rare, but they, too, have declined significantly since the 1970s.

Figures 5.6 and 5.7 display, at the level of individual voters, the changes in the vote advantage of House and Senate incumbents found in the aggregate data examined in chapter 3 (figure 3.1) and confirm that

---

[31]Robert B. Eubank, "Incumbent Effects on Individual-Level Voting Behavior in Congressional Elections: A Decade of Exaggeration," *Journal of Politics* 47 (1985): 964–66; Gary C. Jacobson and Douglas Rivers, "Explaining the Overreport of Votes for Incumbents in National Election Studies" (paper presented at the annual meeting of the Western Political Science Association, Pasadena, California, March 18–20, 1993); Janet Box-Steffensmeier, Gary C. Jacobson, and J. Tobin Grant, "Question Wording and the House Vote Choice: Some Experimental Evidence," *Public Opinion Quarterly* 64 (Fall 2000): 257–70. Prior to 1978, support for the incumbent was overstated by about 1.5 percentage points; from 1978 through 1998, it was overstated by about 8.4 percentage points; from 2000 through 2012, the overestimate was about 3.5 percentage points in the ANES data. The CES is not afflicted by this problem.

Figure 5.6 Partisan Voters Defecting to Incumbents and Challengers in House Elections, 1956–2022

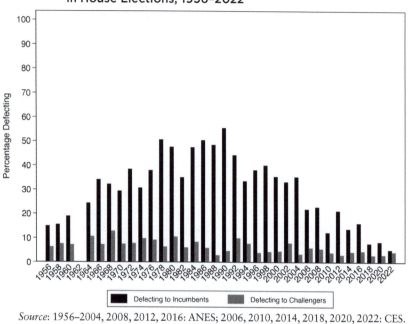

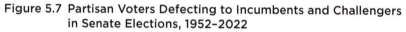

Source: 1956–2004, 2008, 2012, 2016: ANES; 2006, 2010, 2014, 2018, 2020, 2022: CES.

Figure 5.7 Partisan Voters Defecting to Incumbents and Challengers in Senate Elections, 1952–2022

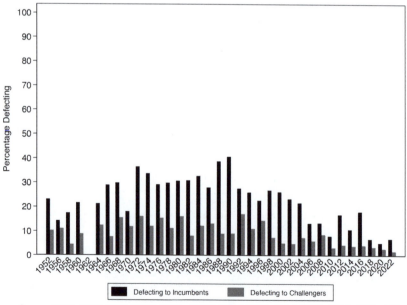

Source: 1952–2004, 2008, 2012, 2016: ANES; 2006, 2010, 2014, 2018, 2020, 2022: CES.

incumbency, though still a net asset in appealing to voters, is a considerably less valuable one now than it was in the 1970s and 1980s. The data also reveal enduring House–Senate differences in this regard: The balance of partisan defections is almost always more favorable to representatives (about 5:1) than to senators (about 2.5:1). Neither phenomenon is self-explanatory. As Albert Cover pointed out in his study of the initial rise in the incumbency advantage, there is no logical reason why weaker party loyalty could not produce defections balanced between incumbents and challengers or even favoring the latter.[32] Similarly, there is no logical reason why the incidence of defection should be less favorable to incumbent senators than to representatives. Other factors must be involved, and one such factor is unquestionably information.

INFORMATION AND VOTING

At the most basic level, people hesitate to vote for candidates they know nothing at all about. Among the most consistent findings produced by studies of congressional voters during the past generation is that simple knowledge of who the candidates are strongly influenced voting behavior. Prior to the 1978 ANES, knowledge of the candidates was measured by whether voters remembered candidates' names when asked by an interviewer. Very few partisans defected if they remembered the name of their own party's candidate but not that of the opponent; more than half typically defected if they remembered only the name of the other party's candidate; defection rates of voters who knew both names or neither fell in between. The pattern held for both Senate and House candidates.[33]

This suggested one important reason that incumbents were doing so well in congressional elections: Voters are much more likely to remember incumbents' names. In surveys taken during the 1980–2000 period, for example, 41 to 54 percent of voters (46 percent on average) could recall the House incumbent's name, but only 10 to 26 percent (16 percent on average) remembered that of the challenger. If voters could name only one of the two candidates, it was the incumbent 95 percent of the time. But understanding the effects of differential knowledge of the candidate's names does not clear up all the basic questions.

First, it does not explain the growth in partisan defections to incumbents through the 1980s. Beyond question, incumbents were comparatively much better known, through both past successful campaigns and

---

[32]Albert D. Cover, "One Good Term Deserves Another: The Advantage of Incumbency in Congressional Elections," *American Journal of Political Science* 21 (1977): 532.

[33]Gary C. Jacobson, *Money in Congressional Elections* (New Haven, CT: Yale University Press, 1980), 16.

vigorous exploitation of the abundant resources for advertising themselves that come with office. But as campaign spending and official resources grew, voter familiarity did not; indeed, it declined, with recall of their names dropping from an average of 61 percent in the 1960s to 45 percent in the 1990s.[34] Voters' familiarity with House challengers declined even more, from 39 to 17 percent over the same time span, but the difference was not enough to contribute much to the rising value of incumbency. Second, voters favored incumbents even when they could not recall either candidate's name, so there must be more to the choice than simple name recognition.[35] Voters are, in fact, often willing to offer opinions about candidates—incumbents and challengers alike—even without remembering their names.[36]

Recall and Recognition of Candidates

Such discoveries forced scholars to reconsider what "knowing" the candidates means. Thomas Mann was the first to show that many voters who could not recall a candidate's name could recognize it from a list—information always available on the ballot.[37] Beginning in 1978, the American National Election Studies thus included questions testing voters' ability both to recall (through the 2000 study) and to recognize each candidate's name. The studies also included a battery of questions designed to find out what else voters knew about the candidates, what sort of contact they had had with them, and what they thought of them on a variety of dimensions. The data collected between 1978 and 2000 allowed a much more thorough examination of voting behavior in congressional elections than was previously possible. Since 2000, unfortunately, ANES has sharply curtailed its coverage of congressional elections in presidential election year time-series studies and no longer covers midterm elections at all, so we can only speculate about how responses to many of these questions might have changed as the electorate has become more partisan and polarized.

---

[34]The reasons for this decline remain obscure; see Gary C. Jacobson, "The Declining Salience of U.S. House Candidates, 1958–1994" (paper presented at the annual meeting of the American Political Science Association, Boston, Massachusetts, September 3–6, 1998).

[35]John A. Ferejohn, "On the Decline of Competition in Congressional Elections," *American Political Science Review* 71 (1977): 171; Candice J. Nelson, "The Effects of Incumbency on Voting in Congressional Elections, 1964–1974," *Political Science Quarterly* 93 (1978/1979): 665–78.

[36]Jacobson, *Money*, 19–20; see also Alan I. Abramowitz, "Name Familiarity, Reputation, and the Incumbency Effect in a Congressional Election," *Western Political Quarterly* 28 (1975): 668–84.

[37]Thomas E. Mann, *Unsafe at Any Margin: Interpreting Congressional Elections* (Washington, DC: American Enterprise Institute, 1977), 30–34.

The available data leave no doubt that voters recognize candidates' names much more readily than they recall them. Table 5.1 shows that voters are twice as likely to recognize as to recall House candidates in any incumbency category. The same is true for Senate candidates, except in the case of incumbents and candidates for open seats, whose names more than half the voters already recall. These figures also leave no doubt that the House incumbents' advantage in recall is matched by an advantage in recognition. Typically, more than 90 percent of voters recognize the incumbent's name. The shift in focus from name recall to name recognition nicely resolves the apparent anomaly of voters favoring incumbents without even knowing who they are. Many more voters also recognize the challenger than recall his or her name, but these voters still amount to little more than half the electorate. (The apparent increase in recognition of challengers since 2000 is an artifact of a change in the order in which questions about House candidates were asked in the survey, not a sign of growing awareness of challengers.[38]) Candidates for open seats are better known than challengers but not so well known as incumbents; indeed, the data show that they fall between incumbents and challengers on almost every measure. This is exactly what we would expect, knowing the kinds of candidates and campaigns typical of open-seat contests.

Senate candidates are better known than their House counterparts in each category, and Senate incumbents are clearly better known than their challengers (though the more populous the state, the lower the proportion of voters who can recall the senator's name[39]). But the gap is smaller than it is for House candidates. Again, this is the kind of pattern we would anticipate, owing to the distinctive circumstances of Senate electoral politics outlined in chapter 4.

Familiarity is supposed to matter, of course, because of its connection to the vote; table 5.2 displays the connection for elections with the most recent available data on both recall and recognition of candidates.[40] In both House and Senate elections, the more familiar voters were with a candidate in these elections, the more likely they were to vote for him

---

[38]Prior to 2000, the survey asked a feeling thermometer question (used to test name recognition) before the vote question, in which respondents were shown a card listing the candidates' names; since 2000, the vote question has come first, so respondents have already been reminded of the candidates' names when they are asked to rate the (named) Democratic and Republican House candidates on the thermometer scale. This change raised the average recognition of challengers from 51.5 to 62.0 percent, of open-seat candidates from 79.6 to 84.4 percent, and of incumbents from 91.6 to 91.8 percent.

[39]John R. Alford and John R. Hibbing, "The Disparate Electoral Security of House and Senate Incumbents" (paper presented at the annual meeting of the American Political Science Association, Atlanta, Georgia, August 31–September 3, 1989), 14.

[40]The results are typical of every election for which we have data going back to 1980; see earlier editions of this book.

Table 5.1 Incumbency Status and Voters' Familiarity with Congressional Candidates, 1980–2020 (Percentages)

Year	INCUMBENTS		CHALLENGERS		OPEN SEATS	
	Recalled Name	Recognized Name[a]	Recalled Name	Recognized Name[a]	Recalled Name	Recognized Name[a]
House Elections						
1980	46	92	21	54	32	82
1982	54	94	26	62	29	77
1984	45	91	18	54	32	80
1986	42	91	13	46	43	84
1988	46	93	16	53	33	71
1990	45	93	10	37	26	78
1992	43	87	15	56	23	79
1994	51	93	22	57	36	82
1998	42	91	15	45	52	83
2000	42	91	13	57	29	80
2002	–	95	–	58	–	90
2004	–	92	–	64	–	84
2008	–	90	–	63	–	88
2012		93		64		84
2016		89		61		76
2020		92		67		83
Mean:	46	92	17	56	34	81
Senate Elections						
1980	61	99	40	81	47	89
1982	61	97	37	78	73	95
1986	61	97	41	77	61	94
1988	51	96	30	74	73	97
1990	57	98	31	69	31	86
1992	55	96	33	82	59	93
1994	–	98	–	84	–	92
1998	–	96	–	71	–	77
2000	–	93	–	73	–	90
2002	–	99	–	84	–	97
2004	–	92	–	69	–	92
2008	–	92	–	71	–	97
2012		97		81		90
2016		94		78		85
2020		96		71		87
Mean:	58	96	35	76	57	91

[a]Includes only respondents who reported voting and who could recognize and rate the candidates on the feeling thermometer or, if they could not rate the candidates, could recall the candidates' names.

Source: American National Election Studies and Cooperative Election Studies.

Table 5.2 Familiarity with Candidates and Voting Behavior in
Congressional Elections (Percentage of Voters Defecting)

	Familiarity with Own Party's Candidate		
	Recalled Name	Recognized Name[a]	Neither
House Elections (1994–2000) Familiarity with other party's candidate:			
Recalled name	15	39	74
Recognized name[a]	5	26	50
Neither	1	6	11
Senate Elections (1988–92) Familiarity with other party's candidate:			
Recalled name	20	49	75
Recognized name	9	30	63
Neither	8	7	25

Note: [a]Recognized name and could rate candidate on the thermometer scale but could not recall candidate's name.
Source: ANES, 1994–2000; Senate Election Studies, 1988–92.

or her, with the effect also depending, symmetrically, on the degree of familiarity with the other candidate. Partisan defections are concentrated in the upper-right corner of each table; party loyalty predominates in the lower-left corner. Only about 3 percent of House voters and 13 percent of Senate voters defected to candidates who were more familiar than their own. Independent voters, omitted from this table, voted for the better-known candidate 84 percent of the time in House races and 82 percent of the time in Senate contests.

More recent data show that familiarity with the candidates continues to have a notable influence on the vote, but its effects have diminished in parallel with the rise in party-line voting (figure 5.8). Back in 1978, voters who did not recognize their party's candidate's name remained loyal only 50 percent of the time; in 2020, that figure was up to 80 percent. Although the gap has clearly narrowed, voters unfamiliar with their party's candidate still defect at substantially higher rates than voters who recognize their party's candidate, who have been quite loyal all along. In contests involving incumbents, party loyalty has grown among challenger partisans to a similar degree regardless of whether they can recognize the challenger's name, although defections are still more common if they do not. In this more partisan era, voters have become more likely to vote for unfamiliar candidates—as long as they have the right party label.

Figure 5.8 Candidate Name Recognition and Party Loyalty in House Elections, 1978-2020

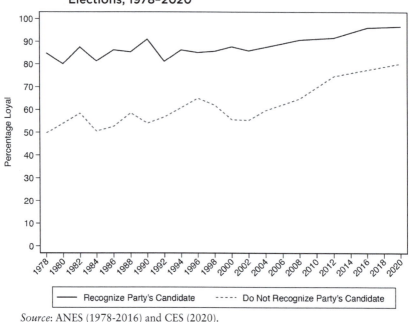

Source: ANES (1978-2016) and CES (2020).

Although somewhat diminished in electoral potency, name familiarity clearly remains an important influence on the congressional vote. Why? The answer proposed by Donald Stokes and Warren Miller in the 1960s, that "in the main, to be perceived at all is to be perceived favorably," has not found much support in later work.[41] From 1978 through 2000, the ANES surveys asked respondents what they liked and disliked about House candidates; the 1988–92 Senate Election Studies asked the same questions about Senate candidates. Responses showed that the more familiar voters are with candidates, the more likely they are to discover things they both like and dislike about them. Familiarity by no means breeds only favorable responses. Beyond that, however, the data showed that the benefits of incumbency extended well beyond greater familiarity. Incumbents were better liked—by a wide margin—as well as better known than challengers. At any level of familiarity, voters were more inclined to mention something they liked about the incumbent than about the challenger; negative responses were rather evenly divided, so

---

[41]Donald E. Stokes and Warren E. Miller, "Party Government and the Saliency of Congress," in *Elections and the Political Order*, eds. Angus Campbell et al. (New York: John Wiley, 1966), 205. Contrary findings are reported by Abramowitz, "Name Familiarity," 673–83, and Jacobson, *Money*, 16.

the net benefit was clearly to the incumbent. For example, the ratio of likes to dislikes among voters who knew the candidate's name averaged 71 to 32 percent for incumbents and 43 to 35 percent for their challengers. Voters tended to favor Senate as well as House incumbents on this dimension, though the difference was smaller; Senate candidates tended to attract a higher proportion of negative responses, reflecting the greater average intensity of these contests.[42]

No comparable data exist for more recent elections, but responses to another survey question document trends in voters' feelings about House and Senate candidates from 1978 through 2020. Respondents are asked to rate candidates on a thermometer scale of zero to one hundred degrees, with zero as the most unfavorable, one hundred as the most favorable, and fifty as neutral. Over the entire period, House incumbents have been rated more warmly than their opponents, averaging sixty-two degrees compared to fifty-two degrees for challengers. But that gap has declined over time, falling from twelve degrees between 1978 and 1992 (sixty-four to fifty-two) to eight degrees (sixty to fifty-two) thereafter. Senate incumbents have also been regarded more warmly than their challengers, but by a smaller margin (sixty degrees compared to fifty-three degrees) and with no trend over time. In both House and Senate contests, candidates for open seats are typically rated at temperatures somewhere between incumbents and challengers.[43]

CONTACTING VOTERS

Why are House incumbents typically better known and liked than their opponents? Why are Senate challengers more familiar to voters than House challengers? One obvious explanation is the extent to which voters come into contact with candidates in these various categories. The ANES studies undertaken from 1978 through 1994 asked a series of questions regarding ways in which voters might have interacted with House candidates; a separate survey posed the same questions for Senate candidates from 1988 through 1992. Table 5.3 summarizes responses to these questions. Voters were more than twice as likely to report contact of every kind with incumbents than with challengers in House races. The incumbent reached a large majority of voters in some way, while less than half of respondents reported contact of any kind with the challenger. The incumbents' advantage was greatest in forms of contact facilitated by official resources—staff and mail (a benefit of the congressional frank).

---

[42]For details on the data, see Gary C. Jacobson, *The Politics of Congressional Elections*, 8th ed. (Boston: Pearson, 2013), 135.

[43]For details on the data, see Jacobson, *The Politics of Congressional Elections*, 8th ed., 136.

Table 5.3 Voters' Contacts with House and Senate Candidates (Percentages)

Type of Contact	House Candidates (1978–1994)			Senate Candidates (1988–1992)		
	Incumbents	Challengers	Open Seats	Incumbents	Challengers	Open Seats
Any	87	42	72	99	85	96
Met Personally	18	4	10	25	9	10
Saw at Meeting	16	3	8	26	9	11
Talked to Staff	12	2	7	21	7	12
Received Mail	66	17	49	83	51	66
Read about in Newspaper	62	28	55	93	75	85
Heard on Radio	31	13	27	60	45	55
Saw on TV	53	24	57	94	75	85
Family or Friend HAD Contact	34	10	16			

Source: American National Election Studies, 1978–94; Senate Election Studies, 1988–92.

Senate incumbents had a substantially smaller advantage over their challengers in frequency of reported contacts, and voters reported higher rates for every type of contact for Senate challengers than even for well-financed House challengers. The differences between House and Senate challengers were widest in mass media contacts. Notice especially the difference in the proportion of voters reached through television. Richard F. Fenno Jr.'s observations of senators and Senate candidates led him to conclude that a major difference between House and Senate elections is the much greater importance of the mass media in the latter. The news media are much more interested in Senate candidates than in House candidates because they are much more interested in senators.[44] As noted in chapter 4, Senate campaigns are also usually better financed and can use paid television more extensively and more efficiently than can most House campaigns. The consequences are evident in the survey data; both factors enhanced the Senate challenger's ability to catch the attention of voters, an essential ingredient of electoral success.

Although it is no surprise that senators and Senate candidates reached a larger proportion of voters through the mass media, it is certainly a surprise that more voters reported meeting them personally and talking to their staffs than reported equivalent contacts with their counterparts in the House. We would expect that the much larger constituencies represented by senators would make personal contacts less common. Part of the reason these data show the opposite pattern is that the Senate Election Studies have equal-sized samples from every state, so voters from smaller states are overrepresented. Even adjusting for state size, however, House members and candidates evidently have no advantage in personal contacts. Only in the very largest states—those with voting-age populations in excess of five million—did voters report significantly fewer personal contacts with Senate candidates than with House candidates.[45] The main House–Senate difference, then, is in mass media contacts.

For Senate incumbents, the news media's greater interest is a mixed blessing. Senators are accorded more attention but are also subject to higher expectations. A House member running for the Senate explained it to Fenno this way: "People don't treat me differently. They don't see any difference between the two jobs. Maybe they think it's a higher office, but that doesn't make any difference. But the media hold me to a much higher standard than they did as a House member. They expect me to

[44]Richard F. Fenno Jr., *The United States Senate: A Bicameral Perspective* (Washington, DC: American Enterprise Institute, 1983), 11.

[45]Jonathan S. Krasno, *Challengers, Competition, and Reelection: Comparing Senate and House Elections* (New Haven, CT: Yale University Press, 1994), 47.

know more details. Am I treated differently running for the Senate? By the people, no; by the media, yes."[46]

During the 1978–94 period, House incumbents who avoided scandal normally did not attract much attention from the news media. This meant that, except during campaigns, they usually produced and disseminated much of the information about themselves that reached the public. To the extent they controlled their own press, it was a good press, and voters thus tended to think highly of them.[47] In recent elections, however, incumbents showing any sign of vulnerability have almost without exception attracted well-funded challengers, often assisted by lavish independent campaigns financed by party and ideological organizations, saturating the electorate with information critical of the incumbent's character and performance. The media environment has also expanded to include a diverse ecology of bloggers eager to dig up and disseminate stories about the supposed failings and peccadilloes of politicians. Consequently, individual representatives now have much less control than they once did over the information conveyed to constituents about them.

Table 5.3 illustrates another important point: Not all nonincumbent candidates are alike. Voters reported more contact of all sorts with candidates for open seats than with challengers, with figures often closer to those for incumbents than to those for the average challenger. House incumbents held a wide advantage over challengers in these categories, but not simply because they were incumbents and their opponents were not. Their opponents were, rather, much weaker candidates than they might be—or than appear when no incumbent is running. This is a natural consequence of the strategies followed by potential House candidates and their potential supporters, as discussed in chapter 3.

When stronger challengers did appear, the incumbents' advantage in contacting voters shrank. The more challengers spent, the more likely voters were to have heard them on the radio or seen them on television, to have received mail from them, and to recognize their names. For incumbents, in contrast, levels of campaign spending were unrelated to the extent of recognition or contacts. A large majority of challengers (68 percent) were in the lowest spending category during this period. Those who spent more were able to diminish the incumbent's advantage on these measures, but even the highest spenders could not close it completely.[48] As noted in chapter 3, the returns on campaign spending are

---

[46]Fenno, *Senate*, 18–19; the Senate Election Study confirms this candidate's view that voters have very similar expectations of senators and representatives; see Krasno, *Challengers, Competition, and Reelection*, 17–35.

[47]Alan I. Abramowitz, "A Comparison of Voting for U.S. Senator and Representative in 1978," *American Political Science Review* 74 (1980): 639.

[48]See Jacobson and Carson, *The Politics of Congressional Elections*, 9th ed., 167.

Figure 5.9 Campaign Spending and Familiarity with House Candidates, 2022

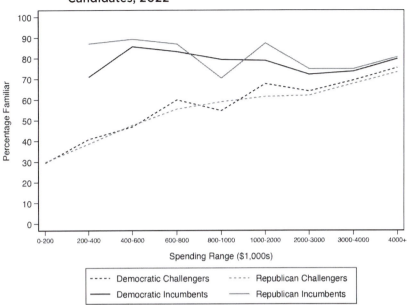

Source: Federal Election Commission and 2022 Cooperative Election Study data.

considerably greater for challengers than for incumbents, and these data on name recognition and contacts helps to explain why this is the case.

The contact questions have not been asked since 1994, but every election produces additional evidence that challengers can close the gap in candidate awareness by spending large sums on their campaigns. Figure 5.9 shows, for example, that familiarity with challengers (measured here by the ability of voters to place the candidate on the seven-point liberal–conservative scale) increases with increasing levels of spending, growing from 46 percent for challengers spending less than $1 million to 75 percent for those spending more than $4 million. Familiarity with incumbents also grows modestly with their levels of spending, but their advantage in familiarity narrows as spending on both sides increases.

CHANGING EVALUATIONS OF INCUMBENTS

The period during which the ANES fully covered congressional elections was also the era in which these elections were in their most candidate-centered and incumbent-friendly phase. In keeping with aggregate and survey data on the advantages of incumbency (figures 3.3 and 5.6), surveys taken during the 1980s found that incumbents not only won high approval ratings but also were widely regarded as in touch, responsive

Figure 5.10 House Incumbents' Performance on Keeping in Touch, 1986–2020

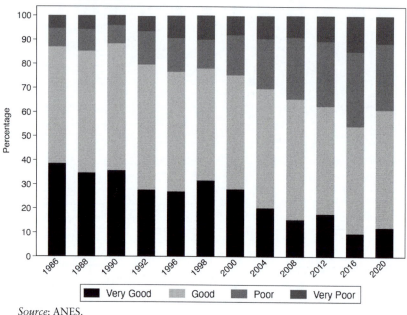

Source: ANES.

to constituents' requests, in agreement with constituents' policy views, and better able to solve national problems than their opponents.[49] Most of the relevant questions have not been asked for the past two decades, but the question about how good a job the incumbent is doing at keeping in touch with the district has been asked fairly regularly since 1986. The distribution of responses, displayed in figure 5.10, documents the very high scores incumbents enjoyed on this question in the 1980s and their subsequent decline through 2020. Over the past three decades, the proportion of voters rating their representative's performance on keeping in touch as very good has dropped by more than half, from 39 to 12 percent, while the proportion who rated it as somewhat or very poor has tripled, from 13 to 39 percent; among partisans of the rival party, the increase in poor or very poor ratings was even greater, from 18 to 76 percent. (Among incumbent partisans, it grew only a modest amount, from 16 to 20 percent.)

Why this decline? There is no evidence that members of Congress have become any less diligent in sending out newsletters, spending time in the district, pursuing media attention, or performing casework than

---

[49]See chapter 5 in any of the earlier editions of this book.

they have been in the past. And most of them now have websites and use social media extensively to reach out to constituents.[50] Part of the reason for the decline may be the greater difficulty of reaching an ever-growing citizenry amid increasing competition for its limited attention. But the main reason is probably the more negative opinions people, especially those identifying with the rival party, have developed about their representatives (and of Congress as an institution), which find expression whenever questions about their performance are posed.

Shifts in the criteria voters use to evaluate congressional candidates have accompanied these more negative performance ratings. Between 1978 and 2000, the ANES regularly asked respondents what they liked and disliked about the House candidates, recording multiple answers. The content of responses to these open-ended questions changed across these years for both incumbent and nonincumbent candidates. The proportion of candidate-related comments (about personal character, service to the public, experience, and individual performance in office) declined, from 80 percent in 1978 to 53 percent in 1996, while the proportion of comments relating to party, ideology, and policy grew from 15 to 42 percent.[51] These questions have not been repeated since 2000, but other evidence of the continuing emergence of a more party- and issue-centered electoral process suggests that if they were, the balance would have shifted even more away from the personal and toward the political.

Whether voters' responses to these questions reveal the actual criteria they use to evaluate candidates remains uncertain, however. Experimental research has shown that voters often form affective responses to candidates based on information that they then forget, remembering only the affective sentiment. When later asked why they like or dislike a candidate, they give some reasons that rationalize their feelings, but they are not necessarily the reasons that led to the feelings in the first place.[52] The reasons voters give for liking or disliking candidates depend on what is on their minds at the time they are asked, and that, in turn, is determined by whatever political events or campaign messages have caught their recent attention.[53] Despite this caveat, there is little doubt that the content of electoral politics—at least as refracted through the

---

[50]Dennis Johnson, *Congress Online: Bridging the Gap between Citizens and Their Representatives* (New York: Routledge, 2004), chapters 4–6.

[51]The most recent figures, from 2000, are 59 and 35 percent, respectively; for more details, see Jacobson, *The Politics of Congressional Elections*, 8th ed., 150–51.

[52]Milton Lodge and Marco R. Steenbergen with Shawn Brau, "The Responsive Voter: Campaign Information and the Dynamics of Candidate Evaluation," *American Political Science Review* 89 (1995): 309–26.

[53]John Zaller and Stanley Feldman, "A Theory of Survey Response," *American Journal of Political Science* 36 (1992): 586–89.

minds of voters—became considerably less personal and more explicitly political in the 1990s. Such changes in the terms by which voters evaluated candidates worked to the detriment of incumbents. Members thrive when voters focus on their personal virtues and services to the district and its inhabitants. They become more vulnerable when the focus is on their party, ideology, or policy stances, for these repel as well as attract voters. Thus negative comments about House incumbents were twice as common in the 1990s as in the 1980s, and the ratio of positive to negative comments was also much smaller in the 1990s (an average of 2.6:1, compared with more than 4.5:1 for the earlier election years). Although comparable data are lacking, it is almost certain that incumbents have become even worse off in this respect since the 1990s.[54]

The distribution of evaluative comments about Senate candidates (recorded during the 1988–92 election cycle) was not very different from the distribution of comments about House candidates during the same period. The incidence of personal comments was about the same; references to party, ideology, and policy were also distributed similarly. Once again, voters did not think much differently about House and Senate candidates. They did, however, have more thoughts about Senate candidates; the number of comments per respondent was generally larger for Senate candidates, particularly nonincumbents.

Although these data point to a measurable decline from the remarkably high levels of regard for incumbents found in the late 1970s, they still suggest that all of the actions members of Congress undertake in pursuit of reelection continue to pay off in some way. Individual voters respond, for example, to the advertising (familiarity, contacts), credit claiming (mention of personal and district services), and position taking (expressing general and specific agreement with members' votes and issue stances) that David Mayhew identified as the characteristic means by which incumbents pursue reelection.[55] On the other hand, the home styles developed by the House members whom Fenno observed no longer seem quite so effective as they once did. Fenno found that, in the 1970s, members typically worked to project images devoid of partisan or even programmatic content, presenting themselves instead as trustworthy, hardworking people who deserved support for their experience, services, and personal qualities more than for their political beliefs or goals.[56] Partisan, policy, and ideological considerations have become much more

---

[54]For details, see Jacobson, *The Politics of Congressional Elections*, 8th ed., 150–52.

[55]David R. Mayhew, *Congress: The Electoral Connection* (New Haven, CT: Yale University Press, 1974), 49–68.

[56]Richard F. Fenno Jr., *Home Style: House Members in Their Districts* (Boston: Little, Brown, 1978), chapters 3 and 4.

prominent since Fenno did his research, and the strategy he described conspicuously failed a substantial number of Democrats in 1994 and 2010 and Republicans in 2006 and 2018; it no longer appears to be viable in the face of adverse partisan conditions.[57]

Finally, it is also apparent that the electoral strategy of discouraging the opposition before the campaign begins is very effective—if it can be accomplished. Even in recent elections, most incumbent House members have continued to face obscure, politically inexperienced opponents whose resources fall far short of what it takes to mount a serious campaign. It is obvious from the survey data how this would ease incumbents' task of retaining voters' support. Typically, House incumbents are doubly advantaged compared with their Senate counterparts in this regard: They are more highly regarded and more likely to face obscure opponents. These are not separate phenomena. Not only do popular incumbents discourage serious opposition, but in the absence of vigorous opposition, information that might erode incumbents' popularity seldom reaches voters. Nonetheless, with national party and ideological groups now so deeply involved in recruiting and financing challengers to incumbents who show any signs of vulnerability, only members representing districts solidly in their own partisan camp can expect to enjoy the benefits of feeble general election opposition—and even they have to watch out for serious primary challenges if they displease their party's more fervent ideologues.[58]

---

[57]Gary C. Jacobson, "It's Nothing Personal: The Decline in the Incumbency Advantage in U.S. House Elections," *Journal of Politics* 77, no. 3 (July 2015): 861–73.

[58]Robert G. Boatright, *Getting Primaried: The Changing Politics of Congressional Primary Challengers* (Ann Arbor: University of Michigan Press, 2014); Shigeo Hirano and James M. Snyder, Jr., *Primary Elections in the United States* (New York: Cambridge University Press, 2019).

6

National Politics and Congressional Elections

★ ★ ★

WHEN THE 118TH CONGRESS CONVENED in early 2023, things started off a bit rocky for the House Republicans when it took four days, and a total of fifteen ballots, to select a new speaker. Many in the party initially believed that Kevin McCarthy was the natural choice for the position, given his previous role as the minority leader and his proven track record in raising money for Republican candidates over previous election cycles. However, McCarthy faced a rather tenuous situation, given the narrow majority of House seats controlled by the Republicans following the election. On top of that, at least five members of the Freedom Caucus, including Andy Biggs (R-AZ), Matt Gaetz (R-FL), Ralph Norman (R-SC), Matt Rosendale (R-MT), and Bob Good (R-VA), announced shortly after the midterms that they intended to oppose McCarthy's selection as the new speaker, which would make it extremely difficult for him to be selected.[1]

Prior to the start of the 118th Congress, McCarthy and other key members of the Republican conference met with the potential holdouts to determine what it would take for them to support McCarthy for speaker and to start advancing their conservative agenda. Although some members, like Representative Gaetz, initially indicated they would never back down from their opposition to a McCarthy speakership, several others simply wanted a variety of concessions to be made before they would support McCarthy. After several very tense days in the House with little accomplished despite rumors of various backroom agreements being

---

[1]Emily Brooks, "Frustration Swirls in House GOP over McCarthy Speakership Opposition," *The Hill*, December 8, 2022, https://thehill.com/homenews/house/3766102-frustration -swirls-in-house-gop-over-mccarthy-speakership-opposition/

made, a sufficient number of the holdouts opted either to vote for McCarthy or switch their vote to present (thus reducing the total number of yea votes needed), finally allowing McCarthy to be sworn in as the new speaker after failing on the first fourteen ballots.[2] Meanwhile, the Democrats increased their narrow majority in the Senate as a result of their win in Pennsylvania, giving them some wiggle room as they contended with divided government and legislative gridlock for the next two years.

Four years earlier, Democrats assumed control of the House of Representatives for the first time in eight years. Although the Republicans managed to shore up their Senate majority by exploiting the highly favorable distribution of seats up for reelection in 2018, the Democrats' House takeover guaranteed divided government for at least the next two years. President Donald Trump got his first taste of what this meant when, after a five-week shutdown of parts of the federal government in a dispute over funds to build his promised wall on the Mexican border, he capitulated to Speaker Nancy Pelosi's Democrats and signed a spending bill without the funds.

In 2014, Republicans enjoyed majorities in both chambers for the first time since 2006 and were in their strongest position on Capitol Hill since the onset of the Great Depression in the late 1920s. Flush with victory, the Republican House and Senate majorities adopted a budget resolution that envisioned reducing government spending by $5.3 trillion over the next decade by repealing the Patient Protection and Affordable Care Act (ACA), restructuring and cutting funding for the Medicare and Medicaid programs, and imposing drastic reductions in spending on other domestic programs. Only national defense was spared. The budget resolution was more aspirational than practical, however, because even most Republicans were not ready to take the political heat that would come with, for example, depriving as many as 27,000,000 Americans of health insurance and slashing spending on school lunches, food stamps, tax credits for low-income workers, and nutritional programs for poor mothers.[3] And, of course, Barack Obama stood ready to veto appropriations legislation intended to carry out the resolution. But it did reaffirm the Republican's dream of dramatically contracting the American welfare state and set the stage for the real budget battles to come with the administration.

This was not the first time in recent history that congressional Republicans had sought to conduct major surgery on the welfare state. In 1995, the first Republican-controlled Congress in more than forty years had also sought to dismantle programs and overturn policies that had accumulated under decades of Democratic rule. Their targets were similar, including

---

[2]John Aldrich, Jamie Carson, Brad Gomez, and Jennifer Merolla, *Change and Continuity in the 2020 and 2022 Elections* (Lanham: Rowman & Littlefield, 2023), 318–20.

[3]Jonathan Weisman, "Senate Passes Cost-Cutting Budget Plan," *New York Times*, May 5, 2015.

welfare programs for poor families, regulations protecting the environment and consumers, and Medicare spending. In both instances, the goal of balancing a federal budget that had been running large deficits justified the spending cuts. Republican leaders in 1995 had also pushed for large tax cuts skewed toward upper-income families. This combination of policies would redistribute income from poorer to wealthier citizens, extending a trend initiated in 1981 under the Ronald Reagan administration. Many of the programs scheduled for elimination had first seen the light of day in the explosion of social welfare legislation that followed the 1964 elections. Others had been enacted in the 1930s as part of the New Deal, the last time such a radical shift in national policy had been attempted.

Each of these moves to force changes in the direction of national policy was the product of the preceding congressional election. A major shift of seats from one party to the other made possible the New Deal, the Great Society, Barack Obama's health care reforms of 2009, and the Republicans' conservative counterattacks on the welfare state in 1981, 1995, and 2015. The New Deal happened because the 1932 election gave Franklin D. Roosevelt large and cooperative majorities in Congress, with reinforcements in 1934 and 1936. Lyndon B. Johnson's War on Poverty went into high gear when Democrats increased their share of House seats from 59 to 68 percent in 1964; it was stopped cold when Democratic representation dropped back to 57 percent following the 1966 elections. The Reagan administration's early victories on tax and welfare spending reduction were possible because the 1980 election had given Republicans control of the Senate for the first time since 1952 and thirty-three additional House seats, raising their share in that body from 36 to 44 percent; their much broader assault on welfare and regulatory programs had to wait, however, until 1994, when they won majorities in both chambers. The Democrats' dream of extending the welfare state to include guaranteed health insurance for everyone, dashed by the failure of Bill Clinton's proposal and the 1994 election, was revived in 2008 when Democrats added to the congressional majorities they had won in 2006 and put Obama in the White House. The Supreme Court finally determined the fate of the resulting ACA, which became an ongoing target of the resurgent Republicans after their victories in the 2010 election, when in 2015 it upheld insurance subsidies as legal in a 6–3 ruling in *King v. Burwell*.[4] The unified Republican government following Trump's election in

---

[4] Abby Goodnough, "Before Justices Rule, Floridians Consider Life without Health Subsidies," *New York Times*, February 27, 2015, http://www.nytimes.com/2015/03/01/us/florida-health-care-supreme-court.html. On June 28, 2012, the Supreme Court upheld the legality of the Affordable Care Act in a 5–4 ruling (*National Federation of Independent Business v. Sebelius*, 132 S. Ct. 1133 [2012]). For more details on *King v. Burwell*, 135 S. Ct. 475 (2014), see Sarah Kliff, "Supreme Court Rules in Favor of Obamacare in King v. Burwell," *Vox*, June 25, 2015, http://www.vox.com/2015/6/25/8804053/king-v-burwell-obamacare-scotus-in-favor.

Figure 6.1 House Margins, 1866–2022

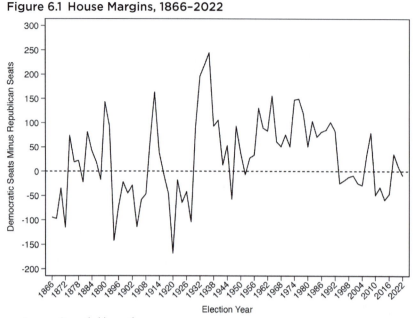

Source: Compiled by authors.

2016 failed, barely, to repeal the ACA but succeeded in enacting the major tax cuts for wealthy individuals and corporations that the party had been pursuing for years. Under President Biden's leadership following the 2020 elections, Democrats in control of both chambers successfully enacted several major legislative initiatives prior to the Republicans narrowly regaining a majority in the House during the 2022 midterms.

These pivotal election years stand out in figures 6.1 and 6.2, which display the net Republican or Democratic seat advantage in the House and Senate beginning in 1866. The charts underline the crucial importance of congressional elections as collective as well as individual events. When the wins and losses in all the separate contests are added up, the sums determine which party controls the House and Senate and with what size majority. The aggregate outcome also gives everyone in national politics at least a speculative sense of what is on the public's mind. The raw numbers and their interpretation establish the opportunities and constraints that guide the direction of national policy for at least the next two years and often a good deal longer.[5] The electoral politics of Congress may center largely on individual candidates and campaigns, but it is the collective results of congressional elections that shape the course of national politics.

---

[5]Midterms can be as important as presidential election years in this regard; see Andrew E. Bush, *Horses in Midstream: U.S. Midterm Elections and Their Consequences, 1894–1998* (Pittsburgh, PA: University of Pittsburgh Press, 1999).

Figure 6.2 Senate Margins, 1866–2022

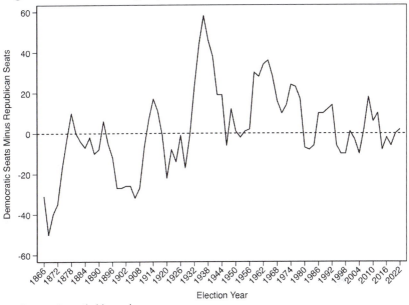

Source: Compiled by authors.

This is true not only in a specific and practical sense—take, for example, the Republican gains in 2010 leading directly to a focus on reducing the deficit instead of stimulating the economy—but also more fundamentally. The possibility of responsible representative government in the United States depends on the capacity of congressional elections to influence the course of public policy. This, in turn, is contingent on aggregate election results reflecting, in a meaningful way, the basic concerns of the public. This chapter discusses how the millions of individual voting decisions in hundreds of distinctly individual contests combine to produce intelligible election results.

POLITICAL INTERPRETATIONS
OF CONGRESSIONAL ELECTIONS

Before the tools of survey research came into common use, politicians and political analysts had little problem interpreting aggregate congressional election results. It was widely believed that economic conditions (prosperity or recession, unemployment, or price levels) and presidential politics (the popular standing of presidents or presidential candidates, influenced by economic conditions and policy triumphs or blunders) shaped the electoral prospects of congressional candidates. Thus it was possible to make sense of sets of data such as those in figures 6.1 and 6.2 and table 6.1 with a little knowledge of contemporary events.

Table 6.1 Net Party Shift in House and Senate Seats, 1946-2022

Year	House[a]	Senate[a]	President's Party[b]
1946	56 R	13 R	D
1948	75 D	9 D	D
1950	28 R	5 R	D
1952	22 R	1 R	R
1954	19 D	2 D	R
1956	2 D	1 D	R
1958	49 D	15 D	R
1960	22 R	2 R	D
1962	1 R	3 D	D
1964	37 D	1 D	D
1966	47 R	4 R	D
1968	5 R	6 R	R
1970	12 D	2 R	R
1972	12 R	2 D	R
1974	49 D	4 D	R
1976	1 D	0	D
1978	15 R	3 R	D
1980	33 R	12 R	R
1982	26 D	1 R	R
1984	14 R	2 D	R
1986	5 D	8 D	R
1988	2 D	0	R
1990	8 D	1 D	R
1992	10 R	0	D
1994	54 R	8 R	D
1996	3 D	2 R	D
1998	4 D	0	D
2000	1 D	5 D	R
2002	8 R	1 R	R
2004	3 R	4 R	R
2006	31 D	6 D	R
2008	24 D	8 D	D
2010	63 R	6 R	D
2012	9 D	2 D	D
2014	13 R	9 R	D
2016	6 D	2 D	R
2018	41 D	1 R	R
2020	14 R	3 D	D
2022	9 R	1 D	D

Note: Listed is the change in the number of seats won compared to the previous general election, not the number gained on election day; the two numbers sometimes differ because of changes created by special elections and party switches between elections.

[a]D indicates Democrats; R indicates Republicans.

[b]Denotes party of winning candidate in presidential election years.

Source: Norman J. Ornstein, Thomas E. Mann, and Michael J. Malbin, *Vital Statistics on Congress, 1997–1998* (Washington, DC: Congressional Quarterly Press, 1998), table 2.2; data for 1998 to 2022 compiled by the authors.

The Republicans were the "natural" majority in Congress prior to the 1930s but lost this status with the onset of the Great Depression and the subsequent popularity of Franklin D. Roosevelt's New Deal. Republicans managed to win majorities in 1946 because of economic dislocation and inflation brought on by postwar demobilization; Democrats made a comeback in 1948 behind Harry S. Truman's spirited campaign in defense of the New Deal and because of economic problems—strikes and rising prices—that could be blamed on the Republican Congress. The 1950 and 1952 elections clearly expressed public dissatisfaction with the second Truman administration. A major recession took its toll on Republicans in 1958. The Barry Goldwater debacle lengthened Johnson's coattails in 1964, but the Republicans came back strong in 1966 as discontent with Johnson's policies spread.

The electorate punished Republican congressional candidates in 1974 for Richard Nixon's Watergate sins and a recessionary economy. Inflation, Iran, and incompetence at the top of the ticket spelled disaster for Democrats in 1980, but they rebounded in 1982 on the strength of a recession that produced the highest unemployment levels since the Great Depression. In elections from 1984 through 1988, voters registered relative satisfaction with the status quo in both congressional and presidential elections; when they became disgusted with both parties in 1990, the administration's party naturally suffered more. With the end of divided government in 1992, popular discontent focused fully on the Democrats as the party in power, so the Republicans swept to a historic victory in 1994. Republican overreaching on the budget and on Bill Clinton's impeachment reduced their House majorities in 1996 and 1998.

In 2002, George W. Bush's popularity as national leader in the war on terrorism helped Republicans pick up House seats and take control of the Senate—but in 2006, his low approval ratings, largely generated by the increasingly unpopular Iraq War, cost Republicans their majorities in both chambers. Bush's even greater unpopularity, augmented by the onset of the deepest recession since World War II, fueled further Democratic gains in 2008, but the Republicans roared back in 2010 as unemployment remained stubbornly high and Obama's domestic initiatives proved unpopular. With Obama's popularity at the low point of his presidency in the fall of 2014, the Republicans gained a net thirteen seats in the House and nine in the Senate, leaving them with their largest seat margins in both chambers since the 71st Congress (1929–30). After his surprising win in the 2016 presidential election, Trump's highly polarizing rhetoric and policies over the next two years provoked strong Democratic opposition and unusually low approval ratings, turning the 2018 election into a consummate referendum on his performance. Democrats picked up a net forty seats in the House even as the Republicans shored up majority control in the Senate. Despite Biden winning the presidency in 2020, Republicans managed to win back fourteen seats in the House while the Democrats won a 50–50 majority in the Senate (with Vice President Kamala Harris serving as the tie-breaking vote). Two years later, Republicans only gained a narrow majority in the House despite unfavorable national conditions while the Democrats managed to pick up one seat in the Senate. Plainly, it is no great challenge to interpret congressional elections as national events controlled by national political conditions. Most political professionals do so routinely.

MODELS OF AGGREGATE CONGRESSIONAL ELECTION RESULTS

Social scientists have examined the impact of national forces on congressional elections rather more systematically without upsetting the conventional wisdom. Numerous studies have investigated the effects of national economic conditions, variously measured, on the national division of the two-party vote for representative.[6] Although the variety of approaches taken to the question (different economic indices, time periods, and control variables) has engendered important disagreements, most specifications produce the expected systematic relationship between the state of the economy and aggregate congressional election outcomes: The better the economy is performing, the better the congressional candidates of the president's party do in an election.

---

[6]Gerald H. Kramer, "Short-Term Fluctuations in U.S. Voting Behavior, 1896–1964," *American Political Science Review* 65 (1971): 131–43; Francisco Arcelus and Allan H. Meltzer, "The Effects of Aggregate Economic Variables on Congressional Elections," *American Political Science Review* 69 (1975): 1232–39; Howard S. Bloom and H. Douglas Price, "Voter Response to Short-Run Economic Conditions: The Asymmetric Effect of Prosperity and Recession," *American Political Science Review* 69 (1975): 1240–54; Brian Newman and Charles Ostrom Jr., "Explaining Seat Changes in the U.S. House of Representatives, 1950–98," *Legislative Studies Quarterly* 27 (August 2002): 383–405.

For arguments that the economy makes no difference in midterm elections, see Alberto Alesina and Howard Rosenthal, "Partisan Cycles in Congressional Elections and the Macroeconomy," *American Political Science Review* 83 (1989): 373–98; Robert S. Erikson, "Economic Conditions and the Congressional Vote: A Review of the Macrolevel Evidence," *American Journal of Political Science* 34 (1990): 373–99; G. Patrick Lynch, "Midterm Elections and Economic Fluctuations: The Response of Voters over Time," *Legislative Studies Quarterly* 27 (May 2002): 265–94.

For critiques of these arguments, see Gary C. Jacobson, "Does the Economy Matter in Midterm Elections?" *American Journal of Political Science* 34 (1990): 400–407; Gary C. Jacobson, *The Electoral Origins of Divided Government: Competition in U.S. House Elections, 1946–1988* (Boulder, CO: Westview Press, 1990), 77–80. For a study examining state-level data, see Andrew Rudalevige, "Revisiting Midterm Loss: Referendum Theory and State Data," *American Political Research* 29 (January 2001): 25–46.

Edward Tufte took this work a step further by adding a measure of the popular standing of the president to the analysis. Tufte began with the familiar fact of political life that the president's party nearly always loses seats in midterm elections; the figures in table 6.1 attest to it. The president's party lost House seats in every postwar midterm election until 1998 and 2002, dropping an average of twenty-four. And in twelve out of nineteen postwar presidential election years, the party of the winning presidential candidate picked up House seats. (The postwar average is twenty.) The surge-and-decline theory, outlined in chapter 5, attempted to explain these phenomena as part of a single system. Investigations of individual voting behavior produced little support for the theory. The theory also failed to explain the size of the midterm swing affecting the president's party, which has varied from a gain of eight to a loss of sixty-three House seats in postwar elections.

Tufte showed that the division of the congressional vote in midterm elections was strongly and systematically related to simple measures of the economy (change in real income per capita over the election year) and presidential approval (percentage approving of the president's performance in office in the Gallup poll closest to election day). He also applied his model to presidential election years, using relative candidate evaluations in place of presidential approval ratings.[7]

The regression equation reported in table 6.2 is an updated variant of Tufte's model. The dependent variable is the change in the percentage of House seats held by the president's party before and after the election. We include a control for the party's exposure—the share of seats it holds above or below its average over the previous eight elections—because the more seats a party holds, the more of its seats are vulnerable to the opposition.[8] We adjust the exposure figure to incorporate the sharp and sustained swing favoring the Republicans that followed the redistricting for the 1990s.[9] National conditions are

---

[7]Edward R. Tufte, *Political Control of the Economy* (Princeton, NJ: Princeton University Press, 1978), tables 5.2 and 5.4; see also Edward R. Tufte, "Determinants of the Outcomes of Midterm Congressional Elections," *American Political Science Review* 69 (1975): 812–26.

[8]Bruce I. Oppenheimer, James A. Stimson, and Richard W. Waterman, "Interpreting U.S. Congressional Elections: The Exposure Thesis," *Legislative Studies Quarterly* 11 (1986): 227–47.

[9]Gary C. Jacobson, "Reversal of Fortune: The Transformation of U.S. House Elections in the 1990s," in *Continuity and Change in Congressional Elections*, eds. David W. Brady, John Cogan, and Morris P. Fiorina (Stanford, CA: Stanford University Press, 2000), table 1. Based on this analysis and updating it through 1998, we estimate that the "expected" number of seats held by House Democrats fell by forty-two after 1990. All the coefficients in the equation remain statistically significant without this adjustment, but with it, the adjusted R^2 rises from .50 to .72.

Table 6.2 Effects of National Conditions on US House Elections, 1946–2022

Variable	Coefficient	Standard Error
Intercept	−16.0	2.80
Exposure	−.76	.09
Change in real income per capita (%)	1.04	.38
Presidential approval (%)	.23	.06
Adjusted R^2	.72	
Durbin-Watson statistic	2.21	
Number of cases	39	

Note: The dependent variable is the percentage of seats gained or lost by the president's party; see the text for a description of the independent variables; standard errors are in parentheses; all coefficients are statistically significant at $p < .01$.

Source: Calculated by the authors.

represented by the change in real income per capita in the year preceding the election and the president's level of popular approval in the Gallup poll taken closest to the election.

The equation explains 72 percent of the variance in the share of House seats a party wins or loses, and all of the other variables work as expected. According to the coefficients, the difference between the highest and lowest values of presidential approval (74 and 25 percent) translates into a difference of fifty-one House seats, and the difference between the highest and lowest values of income change (6.0 and −2.6 percent) translates into a difference of forty-eight House seats. Of course, the equation also leaves 28 percent of the variance unexplained, a fact of considerable importance when we consider differences in results across individual election years.

The results of this and other analyses leave little doubt that economic conditions and presidential performance ratings affect aggregate House election results. Both also have a significant impact on aggregate Senate election results, although there is, not surprisingly, more unexplained variance on the Senate side.[10] Furthermore, congressional electorates behave rationally, holding the party of the administration responsible for the performance of both the president and the economy. Tufte recognized that "many different models of the underlying electorate are consistent with electoral outcomes that are collectively

---

[10]Alan I. Abramowitz and Jeffrey A. Segal, "Determinants of the Outcomes of U.S. Senate Elections," *Journal of Politics* 48 (1986): 433–39.

rational,"[11] but less cautious scholars have interpreted collective rationality as a demonstration of equivalent individual rationality. The problem with this interpretation is that it finds only modest support in survey studies of individual voters.

The strong connection between aggregate economic variables and aggregate election results naturally inspired scholars to investigate the effects of economic conditions on individual voting behavior. At least four kinds of economic variables might influence the vote choice: personal financial experiences and expectations, perceptions of general economic conditions, evaluations of the government's economic performance, and party images on economic policies.[12]

Most aggregate-level studies are based on the assumption that personal financial well-being is voters' primary criterion: "Rational voters are concerned with their real income and wealth."[13] The aggregate economic variables (change in real per capita income, percentage unemployed) were chosen because they represent direct economic effects on individual citizens. Survey studies have turned up very little evidence that personal finances directly influence individual congressional voters, however. The occasional effects that do appear in some election years are generally indirect and much too weak to account for the robust relationships that Tufte and others have found between national measures of economic conditions and election outcomes.

Survey research does produce some evidence suggesting that economic conditions may influence the vote in one or more of the other ways. But the reported effects are almost always modest and explain little additional variance in the vote once other variables (of the kind examined in chapter 5) are taken into account. Part of the reason is that partisanship shapes views of the economy: Voters identifying with the president's party tend to be more positive about it than those of the opposing party.[14] But whatever the reason, the behavior of individual

---

[11]Tufte, "Midterm Congressional Elections," 826.

[12]M. Stephen Weatherford, "Social Class, Economic Conditions, and Political Translation: The 1974 Recession and the Vote for Congress" (paper presented at the annual meeting of the Western Political Science Association, Portland, Oregon, March 22–24, 1979), 3–7.

[13]Arcelus and Meltzer, "Congressional Elections," 1234.

[14]Partisan differences on the economy were especially large during the administrations of George W. Bush, Barack Obama, and Donald Trump; see Gary C. Jacobson, *A Divider Not a Uniter: George W. Bush and the American People* (New York: Pearson, 2007), 249; John Sides, Michael Tesler, and Lynn Vavreck, *Identity Crisis: The 2016 Campaign and the Battle for the Meaning of America* (Princeton: Princeton University Press, 2018), 208; and Gary C. Jacobson, *Presidents and Parties in the Public Mind* (Chicago, University of Chicago Press, 2019), 80.

voters does not consistently conform to any straightforward model of economic rationality.[15]

Survey findings about the electoral effects of voter evaluations of presidents are somewhat more consistent with the aggregate evidence. Samuel Kernell found that in midterm elections from 1946 through 1966, approval or disapproval of the president's performance correlated with congressional preferences (with party identification controlled) and that disapproval had a greater effect than approval.[16] Other evidence from elections in the 1960s also showed voter evaluation of presidents to influence congressional voting.[17] Studies from the 1970s reported contrary findings; evaluations of Gerald Ford (in 1974) and Jimmy Carter (in 1978) made little difference. Since then, however, midterm assessments of presidents from Reagan to Biden have had a substantial influence on the individual House vote, an effect that has become especially pronounced in a more nationalized political context.[18]

Various attempts have been made to account for the occasionally feeble connection between the economic variables and individual congressional voting without abandoning the original premise of individual

---

[15]See Morris P. Fiorina, "Economic Retrospective Voting in American National Elections: A Micro Analysis," *American Journal of Political Science* 22 (1978): 426–43; Donald R. Kinder and D. Roderick Kiewiet, "Economic Discontent and Political Behavior: The Role of Personal Grievances and Collective Economic Judgments in Congressional Voting," *American Journal of Political Science* 23 (1979): 495–527; M. Stephen Weatherford, "Economic Conditions and Electoral Outcomes: Class Differences in the Political Response to Recession," *American Journal of Political Science* 22 (1978): 917–38; Weatherford, "The 1974 Recession and the Vote for Congress"; Alan I. Abramowitz, "Economic Conditions, Presidential Popularity, and Voting Behavior in Midterm Congressional Elections," *Journal of Politics* 47 (1985): 31–43; D. Roderick Kiewiet, *Macroeconomics and Micropolitics* (Chicago: University of Chicago Press, 1983), chapter 6; David W. Romero and Stephen J. Stambaugh, "Personal Economic Well-Being and the Individual Vote for Congress: A Pooled Analysis, 1980–1990," *Political Research Quarterly* 49 (1996): 607–16.

[16]Samuel Kernell, "Presidential Popularity and Negative Voting: An Alternative Explanation of the Midterm Congressional Decline of the President's Party," *American Political Science Review* 71 (1977): 44–66.

[17]Candice J. Nelson, "The Effects of Incumbency on Voting in Congressional Elections, 1964–1974," *Political Science Quarterly* 93 (1978/1979): 665–78.

[18]Morris P. Fiorina, *Retrospective Voting in American National Elections* (New Haven, CT: Yale University Press, 1981), 165; Gary C. Jacobson, "Congressional Elections 1978: The Case of the Vanishing Challengers," in *Congressional Elections*, eds. Louis Sandy Maisel and Joseph Cooper (Beverly Hills, CA: Sage Publications, 1981), 238; Jacobson, "Reagan, Reaganomics, and Strategic Politics in 1982," 16; Abramowitz, "Voting Behavior in Midterm Congressional Elections," 36; Gary C. Jacobson and Samuel Kernell, "National Forces in the 1986 U.S. House Elections," *Legislative Studies Quarterly* 15 (1990): 74–82; Alan I. Abramowitz, "It's Monica, Stupid: The Impeachment Controversy and the 1998 Midterm Election," *Legislative Studies Quarterly* 26 (May 2001): 211–26; Gary C. Jacobson, "Referendum: The 2006 Midterm Congressional Elections," *Political Science Quarterly* 122 (2007): 1–24; Gary C. Jacobson, "Extreme Referendum: Donald Trump and the 2018 Midterm Elections," *Political Science Quarterly* 134 (2019): 9–38.

economic rationality; none has been fully convincing.[19] Morris P. Fiorina has made the strongest empirical case, arguing that personal economic experiences "affect more general economic performance judgments, both types of judgments feed into evaluations of presidential performance, and more general judgments, at least, contribute to modifications of party identification,"[20] which is known to be strongly related to the vote. Even granting this complex process, the effects are a good deal weaker than the strong aggregate relationships would predict.

PRESIDENTIAL COATTAILS

The impact of voters' feelings about presidential candidates is puzzling in a different way. Customarily, this has been discussed in terms of *coattail effects*. The term reflects the notion that successful candidates at the top of the ticket—in national elections, the winning presidential candidate—pull some of their party's candidates into office along with them, riding on their coattails, as it were. Just how this works is a matter of considerable debate. Perhaps the presidential choice has a direct influence on the congressional choice; people prefer to vote for candidates sharing their presidential favorite's party affiliation. Or perhaps the same considerations—for example, disgust with the failures of the current administration or delight with a party platform to which both candidates are committed—influence both choices, which thus move in the same direction. It is even conceivable that, on occasion, support for popular candidates for lower offices spills over into support for the head of the ticket.[21]

Regardless of the mechanisms in operation, if a large number of fellow partisans are swept into office along with the president, political interpretation usually favors the traditional view embodied in the term itself. A presidential winner whose success is not shared by other candidates of his party is presumed to have no coattails.

The question of whether the president has strong coattails is of more than academic interest. Sheer numbers matter; administrations get more of what they want from Congress the more seats their party holds in the House and Senate. Roosevelt's New Deal, Johnson's Great Society,

---

[19]See Gary C. Jacobson and Samuel Kernell, *Strategy and Choice in Congressional Elections*, 2nd ed. (New Haven, CT: Yale University Press, 1983), 12–13.

[20]Morris P. Fiorina, "Short- and Long-Term Effects of Economic Conditions on Individual Voting Decisions," in *Contemporary Political Economy*, eds. D. A. Hibbs and H. Fassbender (Amsterdam: North Holland, 1981), 73–100.

[21]On this point, see Jamie L. Carson and Joel Sievert, *Electoral Incentives in Congress* (Ann Arbor: University of Michigan Press, 2018). For a discussion linking presidential coattail effects to ballot structure across time, see Erik J. Engstrom and Samuel Kernell, *Party Ballots, Reform, and the Transformation of America's Electoral System* (New York: Cambridge University Press, 2014).

and Reagan's budget victories all depended on large shifts in party seats. George H. W. Bush, in contrast, had no choice but to compromise with a strongly Democratic Congress from the beginning of his presidency, and Bill Clinton found himself in a similar position when his party failed to regain its congressional majorities in 1996. Aside from sheer numbers, members of Congress who believe they were elected with the help of the president are more likely to cooperate with him, if not from simple gratitude then from a sense of shared fate: They will prosper politically as the administration prospers. Those convinced that they were elected on their own or despite the top of the ticket have less reason to cooperate.

Finally, a partisan sweep that extends to Congress also sends a potent message to the incumbents who have survived (and to other Washington politicians). If the electorate seems to have spoken clearly and decisively, political wisdom dictates that its message be heeded, at least for a while.[22] The resistance of recalcitrant senior Democrats to the John F. Kennedy–Lyndon Johnson programs collapsed for a time after the 1964 election. Republican gains in 1980 transformed more than a few congressional Democrats into born-again tax and budget cutters. The 1988 congressional election returns, in contrast, left Democrats under little pressure to follow George H. W. Bush's lead, and the 1992 elections, in which the Democrats lost a net ten House seats, were scarcely a ringing endorsement of Bill Clinton's plans. Similarly, George W. Bush's narrow victories in 2000 and 2004 brought little change to the House (and were accompanied by inconsistent results in the Senate—a five-seat Democratic gain in 2000 and a four-seat Republican gain in 2004) and left congressional Democrats with little reason to worry about opposing the president's policies.

Obama's election in 2008 brought reinforcements to the Democratic House and Senate majorities elected in 2006 that were crucial to his signature legislative achievements on health care (the ACA), financial regulation (Dodd-Frank Wall Street Reform and Consumer Protection Act), and economic stimulus (Reinvestment Act of 2009). The huge Democratic losses in the House two years later left him on the defensive for the remainder of his presidency, as the 2010 election left the House in Republican hands and the 2014 election gave Republicans the Senate as well. In 2016, Donald Trump lost the popular vote and Republicans lost seats in the House (six) and Senate (two), so the election did not signal an upsurge in support for Republican policies. Despite the luxury of unified partisan control of Congress during his first two years in office, Trump's main accomplishments were limited to placing two conservative justices

---

[22]James A. Stimson, Michael B. MacKuen, and Robert S. Erikson, "Dynamic Representation," *American Political Science Review* 89 (1995): 543–65; Lawrence J. Grossback, David M. Peterson, and James A. Stimson, *Mandate Politics* (New York: Cambridge University Press, 2006).

on the US Supreme Court and a tax reform bill; the Democrats' take-over of the House after the 2018 midterms severely limited what he could accomplish legislatively during the next two years. Notwithstanding the loss of fourteen seats in the House during the 2020 elections, President Biden was able to accomplish several of his signature policy objectives as a result of unified control of the House and Senate; that ended abruptly when the Republicans picked up nine seats in the House during the 2022 midterms and regained a narrow majority.

We discuss how election results and their interpretation affect congressional politics more thoroughly in chapter 7. We mention the political significance of coattail effects (or, more precisely, the perception of them) here because most of the aggregate evidence available indicates that coattails became increasingly attenuated between the 1950s and the 1980s. Both *cross-sectional* (relating the presidential and congressional vote at the district level) and *time-series* (relating the national presidential and congressional vote over a series of election years) studies show a diminishing connection between presidential and congressional voting over that period.[23] Evidence from elections since 1992, however, indicates that the linkage has tightened up once again.

One perspective on the link between presidential and congressional elections is provided by the data in figure 6.3, which displays the percentage of House districts that delivered split verdicts—majorities for the presidential candidate of one party and for the House candidate of the other party—in presidential election years from 1920 through 2020. The increase between 1952 and 1972 is striking. The proportion of split results is naturally larger in years with presidential landslides—it reached peaks of 44 and 45 percent, respectively, in 1972 and 1984—but from 1964 through the 1980s, it exceeded 29 percent even in years with comparatively close presidential contests. In the 1990s, however, the proportion of split districts fell off, and the figure for 2020 (4 percent) was the lowest in one hundred years. Bill Clinton, George W. Bush, Barack Obama, Donald Trump, and Joseph Biden may not have had lengthier coattails than their recent predecessors (table 6.1), but partisan consistency at the House district level has risen sharply over the past two decades.

---

[23]Walter Dean Burnham, "Insulation and Responsiveness in Congressional Elections," *Political Science Quarterly* 90 (1975): 411–35; Randall L. Calvert and John A. Ferejohn, "Coattail Voting in Recent Presidential Elections," *American Political Science Review* 77 (1983): 407–19; John A. Ferejohn and Randall L. Calvert, "Presidential Coattails in Historical Perspective," *American Journal of Political Science* 28 (1984): 127–46; George C. Edwards III, *Presidential Influence in Congress* (San Francisco: W. H. Freeman, 1980), 74–75; Richard Born, "Reassessing the Decline of Presidential Coattails: U.S. House Elections, 1952–1980," *Journal of Politics* 46 (1984): 60–79; James E. Campbell, "Predicting Seat Gains from Presidential Coattails," *American Journal of Political Science* 30 (1986): 397–418; Jacobson, *The Electoral Origins of Divided Government*, 80–81; Gregory N. Flemming, "Presidential Coattails in Open-Seat Elections," *Legislative Studies Quarterly* 20 (1995): 197–212.

Figure 6.3 Proportion of Districts with Split Results in Presidential and House Elections, 1920–2020

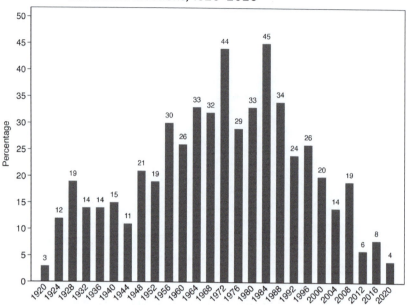

Note: Prior to 1952, percentages are based on from 344 to 364 districts rather than the full 435 because of missing data.

Source: Norman J. Ornstein, Thomas E. Mann, and Michael J. Malbin, "Vital Statistics on Congress, 1997–1998" (Washington, DC: Congressional Quarterly Press, 1997), table 2-16; data for 2000 to 2020 compiled by authors.

Figures 6.4 and 6.5 offer further evidence of the growing influence of presidents on congressional voting in recent elections. Figure 6.4 displays trends in the simple correlation between the district-level House and state-level Senate and presidential votes, and figure 6.5 shows the incidence of ticket splitting reported in the American National Election Studies (ANES) and Cooperative Election Study (CES) surveys from 1952 through 2020. The correlation between the House and presidential vote, which stood at .86 in 1952, declined to as low as .54 in 1972 and then rose again, reaching .95 in 2012 and 2016 before setting a record of .99 in 2020. The trend for the Senate is similar, although the correlation remains noticeably smaller than that for the House for each election year since 1956 with the exception of 2016 when the Senate correlation was .94. This is not merely a consequence of realignment in the South—where conservative voters now vote Republican at the congressional level, as they have at the presidential level since Barry Goldwater's candidacy in 1964—for the same trends appear if we confine the analysis to nonsouthern districts.[24] The incidence of major-party ticket splitting—voting for

[24]Gary C. Jacobson, "Party Polarization in National Politics: The Electoral Connection," in *Congress and the President in a Partisan Era*, eds. Jon R. Bond and Richard Fleisher (Washington, DC: Congressional Quarterly Press, 2000), 21.

Figure 6.4 Correlations between District-Level House and Senate and Presidential Voting, 1952–2020

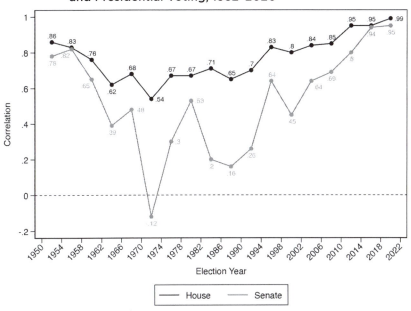

Source: Compiled by authors.

Figure 6.5 Ticket Splitting in National Elections, 1952–2020

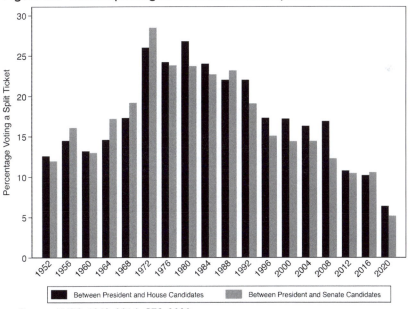

Source: ANES, 1952–2016; CES, 2020.

a Democrat for one office and a Republican for the other—depicted in figure 6.5 shows the same pattern inverted, with a sharp rise in ticket splitting from the 1950s to the 1970s, followed by a nearly steady decline that culminated in 2020 with the lowest ticket-splitting levels for both the House and Senate in six decades.[25]

Because the extent to which presidential and congressional election results coincide has such profound implications for national politics, it is worth considering some of the individual-level evidence in more detail. The evidence suggests that even in elections with a high incidence of split results and split-ticket voting, such as in 1980 and 1984, presidential coattails continue to exert a pull. We can make a simple test for the presence of individual-level coattail effects of some kind by adding a variable representing the presidential vote to variants of the logit models of the individual House vote examined in chapter 5. The results shown in table 6.3 derive from equations for each election year estimating the effects of an individual's presidential vote on the House vote, controlling for party identification, incumbency, and the thermometer ratings of the two House candidates. The entries indicate the difference in the probability of

Table 6.3 Effect of Presidential Coattails and Party Identification on the House Vote, 1980–2020

Estimated Effect	Election Year										
	1980	1984	1988	1992	1996	2000	2004	2008	2012	2016	2020
Presidential vote	.28	.42	.38	.33	.54	.48	.50	.36	.59	.68	.79
Party identification	.55	.37	.50	.39	.56	.53	.54	.52	.68	.89	.64

Note: Entries are based on logit equations for each election that estimate the effects of the presidential vote on the House vote, controlling for party identification, incumbency, and the thermometer ratings of the two House candidates (missing thermometer ratings are set at 50 degrees to avoid losing cases). The entries indicate the difference in the probability of voting for the Democratic House candidate between voters for the Democratic presidential candidate and voters for the Republican presidential candidate (first line) and between strong Democrats and strong Republicans (second line), with the other variables set at their mean values.

Source: American National Election Studies; data for 2012 and 2016 are from the face-to-face component of the survey; Cooperative Election Study, 2020.

---

[25]Ticket-splitting rates are of course higher in years with substantial independent or third-party presidential candidacies (1968, 1980, 1992, and 1996) if we include these candidates' supporters in the analysis. Such voters are forced to split their tickets if they vote in the House election because there is no House candidate of their presidential favorite's party to vote for.

voting for the Democratic House candidate between voters for the Democratic presidential candidate and voters for the Republican presidential candidate (first line) and, for comparison, between strong Democrats and strong Republicans (second line). Coattail effects, so measured, tend to be larger after 1996, although 2008 is an exception. In 2016, the estimated effect of both presidential coattails and party identification were the largest for the entire series to date, reflecting that election's status as the most partisan, nationalized, and president-centered in at least six decades. Four years later, the effect of presidential coattails increases even further, but we also observe a decline in the effect of party identification on vote choice.

Yet another way to check for coattail effects is to observe the consequences of partisan defection in the presidential campaign on the congressional vote. Figures 6.6 and 6.7 show the pattern for the 1952 through 2020 elections. Clearly, party identifiers who voted for the other party's presidential candidate were a good deal more likely also to vote for the other party's House or Senate candidate as well in every election year. On average, about 50 percent of the presidential defectors also defected in both House and Senate elections, compared with only about 12 percent of presidential loyalists. Also notice the rise and then decline of defections among presidential loyalists over this period. In the 1980s,

Figure 6.6 Partisan Defections to House Candidates, by Presidential Loyalty, 1952–2020

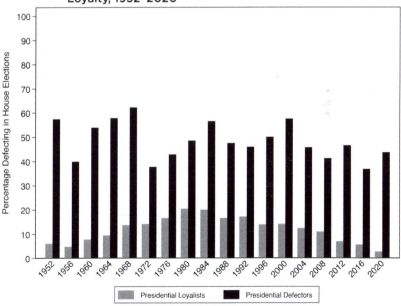

Source: ANES, 1952–2016; CES, 2020.

Figure 6.7 Partisan Defections to Senate Candidates, by Presidential Loyalty, 1952–2020

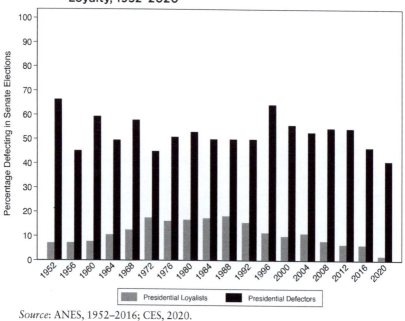

Source: ANES, 1952–2016; CES, 2020.

as many as 20 percent of presidential loyalists defected in House elections and 18 percent in Senate elections; in 2020, defection rates were below 3 percent in both.

The aggregate effects of presidential coattails depend on how defection rates differ between the two parties' identifiers. For example, about 80 percent of the defectors in 1980 and 85 percent in 1984 were Democrats voting for Reagan, so this pattern must have helped Republican congressional candidates. A simple calculation shows that, had presidential defections been divided equally while other things remained the same, the reported vote for House Republicans would have been three percentage points lower in 1980 and five percentage points lower in 1984; the Republican vote for senator would have been two points lower in 1980 and four points lower in 1984. Presidential defections were more evenly balanced in 1988—about 60 percent entailed Democrats voting for George H. W. Bush—so the net effect is smaller, adding about one percentage point to the Republican vote in both House and Senate contests. Defections in every presidential election since 1992 (except 1996) were so evenly balanced that neither party enjoyed any net benefit; in 1996, the balance, for once, favored Democrats, adding about 2.6 percentage points to their overall House and Senate totals.

Plainly, nontrivial coattail effects have been discernible in recent elections. The effects were evidently stronger in 1996, 2004, 2012, and especially 2016 than in the other years under examination. This is a curious result because the aggregate results imply that in none of these years were the winner's coattails substantial; Democrats gained only three House seats in 1996, Republicans only three in 2004, and Democrats only nine in 2012 (table 6.1). In 2016, the Republicans actually lost seats in the House despite Trump winning the presidency. A similar outcome occurred in 2020 when Biden won the presidency and Democrats lost 14 seats in the House.

These are not the only elections for which aggregate and survey evidence of coattail effects conflict. In 1972, Richard Nixon won more than 60 percent of the vote; yet Republicans gained only twelve House seats and lost two Senate seats. Nonetheless, coattail effects were detectable at the level of individual voters. Just as in more recent elections, voters in 1972 who defected to the other party's presidential candidate were significantly more likely to defect to the other party's House candidates as well.[26] Almost 90 percent of the defectors were Democrats voting for Nixon; again, it is possible to calculate that, had defections been divided evenly and the other patterns remained stable, the Republican House vote would have been five percentage points lower.

Here, then, is evidence of a connection at the level of individual voters that is not apparent at the aggregate level, whereas for national economic conditions and midterm presidential popularity, strong aggregate relationships tend to atrophy at the individual level. The solution to both puzzles lies in understanding the interactions between national conditions and the career and campaign strategies of individual congressional candidates.

NATIONAL CONDITIONS AND STRATEGIC POLITICS

It is entirely possible for national conditions, personalities, and issues to affect congressional election results without directly impinging on individual voters at all. Gary C. Jacobson and Samuel Kernell have presented the full explanation of how this can be so in *Strategy and Choice in Congressional Elections*,[27] so we will merely summarize it here.

A great deal of evidence, some of which we presented in chapter 5, indicates that, in present-day congressional elections, voters' knowledge and evaluations of the particular set of candidates running in the district or state strongly influence the vote decision. National issues such as the state of the economy or the performance of the president may influence

---

[26]Gary C. Jacobson, "Presidential Coattails in 1972," *Public Opinion Quarterly* 40 (1976): 194–200; Calvert and Ferejohn, "Coattail Voting," 415.

[27]Jacobson and Kernell, *Strategy and Choice*, 33.

some voters some of the time—for example, those who think that one candidate will do a better job dealing with the most important national problem almost invariably vote for that candidate—but for many voters, evaluations of candidates as individuals, often with little conscious reference to national policies or personalities, determine the congressional choice. Even in the past nine elections (2006–22), when national issues have had a major impact on voters' decisions, the choice offered locally among a set of candidates has remained crucial, and the relative political talents and campaign resources of congressional challengers have helped frame that choice.

Variations in the attractiveness of challengers and the vigor of their campaigns are by no means random. The decisions to run for Congress and to contribute to campaigns are subject to strategic calculation. As we pointed out in chapter 3, the strongest potential candidates—those already holding a place on the political-career ladder—also have the greatest incentive to engage in careful strategic behavior, for they have the most to lose if a bid for a higher office fails. A reading of the odds of winning invariably condition their plans. People who contribute to campaigns also take full account of the candidate's electoral chances. Table 3.3 and figure 3.7 present some clear evidence of strategic behavior on the part of candidates and contributors. More experienced nonincumbent candidates run more lavishly financed campaigns when the incumbent seems vulnerable or when no incumbent is running.

Another important consideration is whether it promises to be a good or bad year for the party—and that, it is widely believed, depends on national economic and political conditions. A booming economy and a popular president (or presidential candidate) are assumed to favor the party in power; economic problems and other national failings blamed on the administration are costly to its congressional candidates. Exactly those forces that politicians and political scientists who look at aggregate data believe influence congressional voters also guide the strategic decisions of potential candidates and contributors.

This means that when the partisan outlook is gloomy, shrewd and ambitious politicians figure that the normally long odds against defeating an incumbent are even worse than usual, and they wait for a better day. People who supply campaign resources to the party's candidates also decline to waste resources on trying to defeat incumbents they dislike and, instead, deploy them to defend their own favorite incumbents, who may be in more trouble than usual.

Politicians of the other party, sensing that electoral tides are moving in their direction, view the chances of winning as better than usual, so more and better candidates compete for the nomination to challenge incumbents.[28] One thing encouraging them to run is easier access to campaign funds; contributors are also more willing to invest in challenges because political conditions seem favorable. Because the marginal effects of campaign spending are greater for challengers than for incumbents, the contrasting offensive and defensive contribution strategies do not simply cancel one another out; rather, they add to the vote totals of the party favored by national political conditions.

Thus, when conditions appear to favor one party over the other, the favored party fields an unusually large proportion of formidable challengers with well-funded campaigns, while the other party fields underfinanced amateurs willing to run without serious hope of winning. In addition, incumbents of the disadvantaged party are marginally more likely to retire when facing the prospect of a tougher-than-usual campaign; the struggle for one more term may not be worth the effort.[29] This, too, means that the disadvantaged party will have relatively fewer strong candidates.

The choice between pairs of candidates across states and districts in an election year thus varies systematically with the strategic decisions of potential candidates and associated activists. Perceptions of national political and economic conditions systematically inform these decisions. Voters need only respond to the choice between candidates and campaigns at the local level to reflect, in their aggregate behavior, national political forces. It is not necessary for individual-level analogs of national forces—the voter's personal economic experiences and feelings about the president or presidential candidates—to influence the vote directly in order to affect the aggregate results. Some voters are no doubt moved by such considerations—the favored party's candidates certainly strive to show how national conditions affect voters' lives—but pervasive individual rationality of this sort is not essential for the process to work. The intervening strategic decisions of congressional elites provide a mechanism sufficient to explain how congressional election outcomes can come to express national forces.

---

[28]Jacobson and Kernell, *Strategy and Choice*, 33; Cherie D. Maestas and Cynthia R. Rugeley, "Assessing the 'Experience Bonus' through Examining Strategic Entry, Candidate Quality, and Campaign Receipts in U.S. House Elections," *American Journal of Political Science* 53 (July 2008): 530–35; Kevin Arceneaux, Johanna Dunaway, Martin Johnson, and Ryan Vander Wielen, "Strategic Candidate Entry and Congressional Elections in the Era of Fox News," *American Journal of Political Science*, 64 (July 2019): 398–415; Costas Panagopoulos, *Congressional Challengers: Candidate Quality in U.S. Elections to Congress* (Philadelphia: Routledge, 2021).

[29]Jacobson and Kernell, *Strategy and Choice*, 49–59; Walter J. Stone et al., "Incumbency Reconsidered: Prospects, Strategic Retirement, and Incumbent Quality in U.S. House Elections," *Journal of Politics* 72 (January 2010): 178–90.

The logic of this explanation is straightforward enough; there is also considerable evidence for it. Politicians routinely sniff the political winds early in the election year; speculation about what will happen in the fall is a common feature of political news in January and February—and even earlier in some election years, notably 2008, 2010, 2014, 2018, and 2022. Predictions rest explicitly on economic conditions and the public standing of the administration. Other information, from polls and special elections, for example, is also sifted for clues. Signs and portents are readily available, widely discussed, and taken seriously.[30]

They are also usually heeded. In 1974, for example, Watergate, the recession, and Nixon's low standing in the polls made it very difficult for Republicans to recruit good candidates at all levels. Republicans expected it to be a bad year, and candidates and activists refused to extend themselves in a losing cause.[31] Democrats saw it as a golden opportunity, and an unusually large proportion of experienced candidates challenged Republican incumbents.[32] Their strategic decisions contributed to one of the Democrats' best years since the 1930s.

Campaign contributors also respond to election year expectations. In 1974, for example, Democratic challengers typically spent more than 2.8 times as much as Republican challengers; they even outspent Democratic incumbents. Republican incumbents, on the defensive, spent 74 percent more than Democratic incumbents. In 1994, it was the Republicans' turn to go on the offensive and the Democrats' turn to try to save endangered incumbents. Republican challengers outspent Democratic challengers by 60 percent that year; Democratic incumbents spent 32 percent more than Republican incumbents. Conditions strongly favored Democrats in 2006, and their challengers raised and spent, on average, 2.3 times as much as Republican challengers, while Republican incumbents felt compelled to spend 47 percent more than their Democratic counterparts. With the national tide running the opposite way in 2010, Republican challengers outspent Democratic challengers 2.5 to 1, and Democratic incumbents spent 32 percent more than Republican incumbents. During the 2014 midterm elections, Republican challengers spent, on average, 40 percent more than Democratic challengers. In 2018, the pattern was reversed dramatically as Democratic challengers spent on average more than ten times as much as Republican challengers. Four years later, Republican

---

[30] Jacobson and Kernell, *Strategy and Choice*, 27–29.

[31] "Running Hard in Watergate's Shadow," *Congressional Quarterly Weekly Report*, February 16, 1974, 353; "Southern Republicans: Little Hope This Year," *Congressional Quarterly Weekly Report*, October 26, 1974, 2959–61.

[32] Linda L. Fowler, "Candidate Perceptions of Electoral Coalitions: Limits and Possibilities," *American Politics Quarterly* 8 (1980): 483–94; Jacobson and Kernell, *Strategy and Choice*, 32.

challengers spent 27 percent more on average than Democratic challengers in the 2022 midterms.[33] Clearly, campaign contributions—and hence expenditures—responded sharply to perceived political trends in these election years.

Not all election years follow this pattern so decisively. For example, all the signs for 1982 pointed to a very good year for Democrats; yet Democratic challengers were not especially well funded and were actually outspent by Republican challengers. The pattern of expenditures for 1984 seemed to reflect a good Republican year, and so it was; yet Republican House gains were rather limited, especially compared with 1980 (table 6.1). Overall, though, the relationship between the relative levels of spending by the two parties' challengers (measured by log of the ratio of Republican to Democratic challenger spending) and the size of the partisan seat swing across these elections remains quite strong ($r = .76$).

Campaign finance data do not exist for elections prior to 1972, so there is no way to know whether campaign contributions reflected strategic advantages and disadvantages in earlier election years. It is possible, however, to show that variations in the relative quality of each party's candidates are strongly related to national conditions and aggregate election results in the way necessary for the explanation to be valid. The regression equations in table 6.4 demonstrate that the relative aggregate quality of each party's challengers reflects, among other things, national conditions.

For this analysis, the quality of a party's challengers is measured as the percentage of those who have held elective office. The independent variables are presidential approval and real-income change, plus the current partisan division of House seats (to consider the opportunities created by exposure). Because the administration's party (not just the Democratic Party) is supposed to be rewarded or punished for the administration's performance, presidential approval and income change are multiplied by –1 when a Republican is in the White House, and a fourth variable, the party of the administration, is included as a control. National conditions are measured in the second quarter (April–June) of the election year because most final decisions about candidacy must be made during that period.[34] We have also included a variable that controls for the effects of the sustained shift in favor of Republicans in the 1990s, which has reduced the proportion of strong Democratic challengers.[35]

---

[33] According to Federal Election Commission data, the average Republican challenger spent $787,000, the average Democratic challenger, $617,000, on their campaigns. Democratic incumbents, on the defensive, spent nearly 28 percent more than Republican incumbents in 2022.

[34] Jacobson, *The Electoral Origins of Divided Government*, 73.

[35] Jacobson, "Reversal of Fortune," 12.

Table 6.4 Determinants of the Percentage of Experienced House Challengers, 1946–2022

Variable	Democrats (Equation 1)		Republicans (Equation 2)		Democrats–Republicans (Equation 3)	
Intercept	52.72[a]	(10.02)	−11.12	(8.65)	61.72[a]	(12.26)
Party of administration	−24.78[a]	(8.51)	7.59	(4.21)	−30.72[a]	(8.47)
Seats won by Democrats last election (%)	−.24	(.14)	.40[a]	(.13)	−.61[a]	(.17)
Change in real income per capita (2nd quarter)	.80[a]	(.28)	.08	(.25)	.66[a]	(.34)
Presidential approval (2nd quarter)	.24[a]	(.08)	−.05	(.04)	.28[a]	(.08)
1992 or later	−13.09[a]	(2.11)	2.15	(1.50)	−15.53[a]	(2.11)
Adjusted R^2	.59		.32		.63	
Number of cases	39		39		39	

Note: The dependent variable in Equations 1 and 2 is the percentage of challengers of the designated party who have held elective office; for Equation 3, it is the difference between the two; the independent variables are described in the text; standard errors are in parentheses.

[a]Statistically significant at $p < .05$

Source: Calculated by the authors.

The coefficients from equation 1 indicate that both economic conditions and the level of public approval of the president have a large and significant impact on the quality of Democratic challengers. Neither factor matters to Republicans, who are sensitive only to the opportunities offered by the current level of Democratic strength in the House (equation 2). However, all these variables significantly affect a composite variable measuring the relative quality of challengers. This is the key variable because relative quality matters for aggregate election results. Table 6.5 presents the evidence. The dependent variable here is the change in the percentage of House seats won by the Democrats from the prior to the current election. As before, we control for the Democrats' exposure and for the party of the administration. The other variables are measured as in table 6.4, except that real-income change is the average for the election year and presidential approval is taken from the last Gallup poll before the election.

The first equation in table 6.5 presents another variant of the standard referendum model discussed earlier. In this model, both presidential

Table 6.5 National Forces, Strategic Politicians, and Inter-election Seat Swings in House Elections, 1946–2022

Variable	(Equation 1)		(Equation 2)		(Equation 3)	
Intercept	65.51[a]	(8.16)	49.14[a]	(7.63)	20.14[a]	(4.52)
Party of administration	−33.73[a]	(4.41)	−25.63[a]	(4.88)		
Seats won by Democrats last election (%)	−.81[a]	(.13)	−.61[a]	(.11)	−.36[a]	(.09)
Change in real income per capita	.69[a]	(.36)	.39	(.32)		
Presidential approval	.27[a]	(.05)	.21[a]	(.05)		
Quality of Democratic challengers			.25[a]	(.08)	.50[a]	(.08)
Quality of Republican challengers			−.39[a]	(.10)	−.74[a]	(.13)
1992 or later	−9.33[a]	(1.80)	−5.47[a]	(1.90)		
Adjusted R^2	.80		.86		.71	
Number of cases	39		39		39	

Note: The dependent variable is the change in the percentage of seats won by the Democrats from the previous election; standard errors are in parentheses.

[a]Statistically significant at $p < .05$

Source: Calculated by the authors.

approval and the economic variables have a significant impact on party fortunes. The second equation adds the aggregate quality variable for each party's challenger; each of these variables has a strong, statistically significant impact on the House seat swing; Democrats gain more seats the more experienced their challengers are, and lose more seats the more experienced the Republican challengers are. Note that the quality of Republican challengers is, if anything, more strongly related to election results than is the quality of Democratic challengers, even though high-quality Republican challengers appear to be less strategic in their behavior than high-quality Democratic challengers. Note also in the second equation that the effect of real-income change is reduced substantially (compared to equation 1) and becomes statistically insignificant; presidential approval continues to have a significant influence, although its estimated impact is reduced somewhat. This is evidence that the effects of the economy and presidential approval derive, in part, from their effects on the relative quality of challengers.

A model that includes the quality variables but not income change or presidential approval (equation 3) is less accurate in predicting seat swings than the model that does the opposite (equation 1). Still, just three variables can explain more than two-thirds of the variance in postwar House seat shifts: the quality of Republican challengers, the quality of Democratic challengers, and exposure. The coefficients from equation 2

Figure 6.8 The Quality of Challengers and Party Fortunes in House Elections, 1946–2022

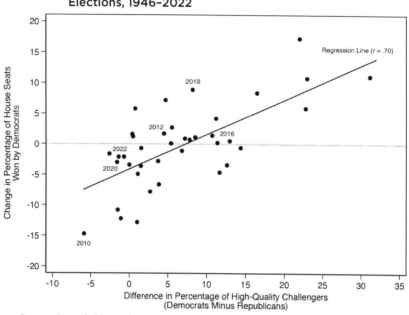

Source: Compiled by authors.

indicate that, controlling for other factors, a difference of one percentage point in quality of Democratic candidates is worth about one House seat; the range between the coefficient's highest and lowest values (thirty-two) covers thirty-one seats. A difference of one percentage point in the quality of Republican challengers is worth about 1.6 House seats; the range between the coefficient's highest and lowest values (twenty-one) covers thirty-four seats. Figure 6.8 displays the simple relationship between relative candidate quality and party fortunes in postwar House elections. Note that 2010 featured the largest Republican advantage in quality and the largest swing in House seats to the Republican side during the entire period covered. By contrast, Democrats did slightly worse in 2022 than their advantage in experienced challengers would predict.

In general, then, the political strategies of congressional elites respond to and help translate national forces into aggregate election results.[36] Complete evidence—on candidates, campaign finances, and

---

[36]For further evidence on these points, see Gary C. Jacobson, "Strategic Politicians and the Dynamics of U.S. House Elections, 1946–1986," *American Political Science Review* 83 (1989): 775–93; Michael Berkman and James Eisenstein, "State Legislators as Congressional Candidates: The Effects of Prior Experience on Legislative Recruitment and Fundraising," *Political Research Quarterly* 52 (1999): 481–98.

voting behavior—is available only as far back as the early 1970s, and until recently, data on experienced challengers extended back only to 1946. Additional research has found evidence of consequential strategic entry by high quality challengers in the late-nineteenth and early-twentieth centuries as well, so the pattern is not unique to the post–World War II era.[37] Still, it is very likely that in some earlier electoral periods, national forces influenced voters much more directly. It would be difficult to argue, for instance, that many congressional voters in 1932, 1934, and 1936 were not responding directly to their economic experiences during the Great Depression or to their feelings about Franklin D. Roosevelt. Individual congressional candidates were important only insofar as they were committed to a position for or against the New Deal. Elections such as these were, of course, the source of the conventional wisdom about the effects of national forces on the fates of congressional candidates. Observing them, shrewd politicians would be well advised to adjust their career strategies to take advantage of favorable national tides and avoid contrary currents.

The strong postwar trend toward a more candidate-centered style of electoral politics would reduce the electoral importance of national forces while enhancing that of individual candidates and campaigns. In more candidate-centered electoral politics, the resources and talents of challengers would have a larger impact on district-level results. Elite strategies would thus make a greater independent contribution to a party's electoral performance. As elections have become more party-centered in recent years, the quality of individual candidates should matter less and national conditions more in shaping district-level election results (see chapter 3). Quality challengers may now be, to a greater extent, riders on than creators of national tides, but they still contribute importantly to electoral turnover.

CAMPAIGN THEMES

At the district level, in addition to shaping alternatives by influencing strategic decisions to run or contribute money, national conditions affect the success or failure of candidacies by defining the campaign themes available to candidates in different situations. They shape the substantive content of campaigns and thus determine the form in which national

[37]Jamie L. Carson and Jason M. Roberts, "Strategic Politicians and U.S. House Elections, 1874–1914," *Journal of Politics* 67 (2005): 474–96; Jamie L. Carson, Erik J. Engstrom, and Jason M. Roberts, "Redistricting, Candidate Entry, and the Politics of Nineteenth-Century U.S. House Elections," *American Journal of Political Science* 50 (2006): 283–93; Jamie L. Carson and Jason M. Roberts, *Ambition, Competition, and Electoral Reform: The Politics of Congressional Elections across Time* (Ann Arbor: University of Michigan Press, 2013).

issues are presented to, and therefore influence, individual voters. The connections between national issues and individual voting decisions are forged by the rhetoric of campaigns and so vary, as do the campaigns. Variation occurs both across districts in a single election year and across election years. The latter helps to explain why survey findings about the determinants of the vote are so often inconsistent from one election to the next.[38] Variation across districts helps explain why there can be so much diversity among district-level vote swings between elections (recall table 3.2).

To succeed, challengers must accomplish two basic tasks: build support for themselves and undermine that of their incumbent opponents. The first task is insufficient without the second. Adverse conditions for the incumbent contribute to the first task by encouraging better-qualified challengers to run and by increasing the campaign resources available to them when they do. They contribute to the second task by giving challengers a campaign theme that has some prospect of undermining the incumbent's support.

Incumbents are, as a class, remarkably adept at taking credit for the good things that government does while avoiding responsibility for its failures. Under neutral or favorable conditions, a member of Congress who cultivates his or her district diligently and avoids personal scandal makes an extremely difficult target. But if people are sufficiently unhappy with the administration or the Congress, if the economic situation is sufficiently dire, or if a war is sufficiently unpopular, it may become a good deal more difficult to avoid guilt by association if an energetic challenger is continually reminding voters of the connection. This is crucial. A vigorous campaign is still essential to defeat incumbents, no matter how bad the political conditions become for them personally or for their party.

Thus national conditions continue to create problems or opportunities for congressional candidates; but how they are handled or exploited makes a difference, and this varies among candidates, between parties, and across election years. When a party does not field enough challengers with sufficient resources and skills to take full advantage of the opportunities created by national conditions, partisan swings are dampened; when it does, partisan swings are enhanced. Similarly, incumbents often survive individual political or personal shortcomings if they avoid challengers capable of exploiting them. These are among the clearest lessons of recent electoral history, to which we now turn.

---

[38]Morris P. Fiorina, "Who Is Held Responsible? Further Evidence on the Hibbing-Alford Thesis," *American Journal of Political Science* 27 (1983): 158–64; Kiewiet, *Macroeconomics and Micropolitics*, 102–08.

HOUSE ELECTIONS, 1992-2022

1992-2000

This section briefly recounts some of the more dramatic electoral changes in the House that have occurred since the early 1990s. After substantial upheavals in 1980 and 1982, House elections for the rest of the decade were uneventful, with weak challengers, low turnover, and small partisan swings (figure 6.1 and table 6.1). The static results reflected national conditions that, for different reasons in different years, were not conducive to changes.[39] The cycle of uneventful House elections ended with a bang in 1992 and foreshadowed the dramatic reversal of partisan fortunes to come two years later, in 1994. The 1992 elections yielded the largest crop of new representatives in more than forty years, with 110 newcomers joining the House in January 1993. The influx of new members sharply altered the House's demographic makeup. The number of women representatives rose from twenty-eight to forty-seven; of African Americans, from twenty-five to thirty-eight; and of Hispanics, from eleven to seventeen.

Although the 1992 elections brought high turnover and sharp changes in the House's demography, they registered little partisan change. Republicans, though losing the presidency, picked up ten seats in the House, leaving the Democrats with a reduced but still comfortable 258–176 majority. The forces that generated turnover did not have a consistent partisan thrust. Conditions that favored Democrats (the stagnant economy, George H. W. Bush's unpopularity, and Bill Clinton's vigorous and successful presidential campaign) offset conditions that favored Republicans (reapportionment, the House Bank scandal [more Democrats than Republicans had written overdrafts on their bank accounts], the low repute of a Congress run by Democrats, and perhaps the Gulf War).[40]

The 1992 elections, extraordinary as they were, turned out to be only a prelude to an even greater upheaval in 1994. For the first time in forty years, Republicans captured the House of Representatives. The fifty-two-seat gain that gave them a 230–204 majority was the largest net partisan swing since 1948. Why did Republicans, after four decades of futility, suddenly win a clear majority of House seats? The short answer is that they won by inverting political patterns that had given Democrats comfortable House majorities despite a generation of Republican superiority in presidential elections. In 1994, the Republicans won the House by fielding (modestly) superior candidates who were on the right side of the issues that were important to

---

[39]For a more detailed discussion of these elections, see Gary C. Jacobson, *The Politics of Congressional Elections*, 5th ed. (New York: Longman, 2000).

[40]Gary C. Jacobson, "Congress: Unusual Year, Unusual Election," in *The Elections of 1992*, ed. Michael Nelson (Washington, DC: Congressional Quarterly Press, 1983), 153–82.

voters in House elections and by persuading voters to blame a unified Democratic regime for government's failures. They exploited favorable national issues more successfully than any party in decades. But marketable national campaign themes did not by themselves give the Republicans their House majority. To win House seats, Republicans still needed plausible candidates with enough money to get their messages out to district voters. Even in 1994, the effects of national issues, important as they were, depended on how they were injected into local campaigns.

House Democrats had long thrived by adhering to former House Speaker Tip O'Neill's dictum that "all politics are local." All politics were *not* local in 1994. Republicans succeeded in framing the local choice in national terms, making taxes, social discipline, big government, and the Clinton presidency the dominant issues. They did so by exploiting three related waves of public sentiment that crested simultaneously in 1994. The first was public disgust with the politics, politicians, and government in Washington. The second was the widespread feeling that American economic and social life was out of control and heading in the wrong direction. The third was the visceral rejection of Bill Clinton by a crucial set of swing voters, the "Reagan Democrats," and supporters of Ross Perot, who as an independent candidate for president had won 19 percent of the vote in 1992.

The electoral effect of national issues in 1994 varied across districts and regions, depending on incumbency, candidate quality, the level of campaign spending, the partisan makeup of the district, and the behavior of the incumbent. Wielding potent campaign themes drawn from national issues, Republicans needed only reasonably attractive and well-financed candidates to take seats from Democrats in districts that leaned Republican in presidential elections. Democratic retirements from such districts created a host of open-seat opportunities that well-funded Republican candidates exploited to the hilt. Against incumbent Democrats, Republicans did best where they fielded experienced, well-financed challengers against Democrats whose votes tied them to the Clinton administration in districts where the president (and his party more generally) was relatively unpopular—in other words, where the local campaign could give their national themes the most extensive publicity and the local context gave these themes their greatest resonance. Poorly funded Republican challengers were largely unsuccessful even in districts where the Democrat should have been vulnerable.[41] The central issues in the 1994 House elections may have been national, but how they played out depended strongly on local circumstances.

---

[41]Against incumbent Democrats in Republican-leaning districts, 49 percent (nineteen of thirty-nine) of Republican challengers who spent in excess of $300,000 won, whereas only 6 percent (two of thirty-two) of the challengers who spent less than this sum managed to defeat the incumbent. If analysis is further confined to Democratic incumbents who supported the Clinton administration on at least two of three key votes, the respective percentages are 52 percent (fourteen of twenty-seven) and 13 percent (two of fifteen).

After the upheavals of 1992 and 1994, the next two congressional elections appear positively mundane. Despite Bill Clinton's easy reelection, Republican candidates did remarkably well in the 1996 House races. They lost only eight House seats on election day; moreover, because five opportunist Democrats had switched to the Republican side of the aisle after the 1994 election and Republicans enjoyed a net gain in special elections held during the 104th Congress, the party ended up with only three fewer House seats in 1996 than it had won in 1994. That a Democrat could win the White House by eight million votes without winning control of Congress would have been unthinkable only a few years earlier; every one of the twenty-six successful Democratic presidential candidates from Thomas Jefferson in 1800 through Bill Clinton in 1992 had brought Democratic majorities into the House with them. Yet by the time it happened, few informed political observers were surprised, a sign of how profoundly the balance of partisan competition had shifted in the 1990s.

From one perspective, the results of the 1998 House elections were stunning. For only the second time since the Civil War, the president's party increased its strength in the House at midterm.[42] Democrats gained five seats, leaving the Republicans with a narrow 223–211 majority.[43] Shocked and angered by their losses, House Republicans drove Speaker Newt Gingrich, architect of their historic 1994 victory, to resign. From another perspective, however, there is little remarkable about what happened in 1998. The national conditions that normally shape midterm elections had their usual effects: the voters, for good and familiar reasons, delivered a ringing endorsement of the political status quo. What makes the election nonetheless remarkable is, of course, that despite the president's involvement in a scandal that transfixed Washington throughout 1998 and led to his impeachment in the House and trial and acquittal in the Senate, the status quo that voters endorsed clearly included keeping Bill Clinton in the White House.

That voters did opt for the status quo in 1998 is beyond question. Only six House incumbents met defeat, and only seventeen House seats switched party control; the former ties and the latter sets the record for the least change in any midterm election. Both Democratic and Republican incumbents enjoyed an average vote gain of 2.8 percentage points over 1996. The 395 members returned to office in 1998 are the most for any midterm House election ever. The contrast between the first and second midterm elections of the Clinton presidency could scarcely be starker.

[42]The Democrats picked up seats in 1934 during the New Deal realignment; both parties had added seats in 1902 when the House grew by twenty-nine seats, but the president's Republicans had picked up fewer than the opposition Democrats and so were relatively weaker after the election.

[43]Bernard Sanders, the lone independent who normally votes with the Democrats, was also reelected.

The triumph of the status quo in 1998 was fully consistent with national conditions. House Democrats went into the 1998 elections with only two more seats than they had held after their 1994 disaster, so their exposure was minimal. The economy was booming, with both inflation and unemployment at thirty-year lows. Moreover, the federal budget was in surplus for the first time in nearly thirty years, and violent crime and welfare dependency were dramatically lower than they had been just a few years earlier. In keeping with these highly favorable trends, Bill Clinton's job approval rating stood at 66 percent in the final Gallup poll taken before the election, the highest for any president in any midterm preelection poll since Gallup had begun asking the question more than fifty years before.[44]

The 2000 elections, by contrast, were as close to a dead heat across the board as we are ever likely to see. As such, they accurately represented the close partisan balance now prevailing in the United States. As we saw in chapter 5, the substantial popular majority among party identifiers that Democrats had enjoyed since the New Deal was largely gone by the mid-1980s, a change traceable largely to realignment of southerners and social conservatives into the Republican camp.[45] Democrats have since retained a small advantage among party identifiers in most polls,[46] but because self-identified Republicans are more likely to vote than Democrats and are slightly more loyal to their party when they do, the normal electoral balance is now nearly even.

The congressional election results in 2000 mirrored this close partisan balance because national forces were essentially neutral. The narrow margin separating George W. Bush and Al Gore (Bush won 49.7 percent of the major-party popular votes and 50.4 percent of the electoral votes) meant that neither party benefited nationally from presidential coattails. Nor did any other national conditions clearly favor one party over the other. Unlike in 1994, but as in 1996 and 1998, the electoral environment in 2000 broadly favored the congressional status quo. The economy continued to look strong through election day. Modest inflation, low unemployment, rising family incomes, a

---

[44]Gary C. Jacobson, "Impeachment Politics in the 1998 Congressional Elections," *Political Science Quarterly* 114 (1999): 33–40.

[45]Alan I. Abramowitz, "The End of the Democratic Era? 1994 and the Future of Congressional Election Research," *Political Research Quarterly* 48 (1995): 873–89; Warren E. Miller and J. Merrill Shanks, *The New American Voter* (Cambridge, MA: Harvard University Press, 1996), chapter 7.

[46]In twenty Gallup polls taken between January and September 2000, the Democrats averaged 51.5 percent of the major-party identifiers (with leaners included among the partisans); the two-party split among voters in the 2000 National Election Study sample was 53 to 47 percent, but the survey probably overstates Democratic strength, as the presidential vote was reported as 50.6 percent for Gore and 45.5 percent for Bush.

growing federal budget surplus, and declining rates of crime and welfare dependency had left the public largely content with the direction of the country and approving of its elected leaders. In the end, relatively few seats changed party control (seventeen, tied for third lowest among the twenty-seven post–World War II congressional elections), but on balance the changes that occurred increased the partisan match between districts and members, extending one of the most important developments of the Clinton era.

2002-2010

In 2002, for the second midterm election in a row, the president's party gained seats in the House. Prior to 1998, this had happened only once since the Civil War, and some postelection analysts read the Republicans' upset of naïve expectations based on the historical pattern as both surprising and indicative of a pro-Republican national tide.[47] But just as in 1998, nothing in the 2002 results challenged our current understanding of the processes that shape midterm congressional elections. Rather, the Republican gain of six House seats (seven more than its 2000 total) was entirely consistent with models treating midterm elections as a referendum on the administration and economy.[48] It was also a consequence more of redistricting than of any national shift in public sentiment toward the Republican Party. And it was the undeniable if unintended gift of Osama bin Laden, for the attacks of September 11, 2001, and Bush's responses to them, generated a huge spike in presidential approval that was still above 60 percent a year later.

In the end, 2002 produced the smallest number of successful House challenges (four) of any general election in US history. To be sure, incumbents did not survive redistricting entirely unscathed; four also lost general elections to other incumbents, four were defeated in primaries by other incumbents, and four were defeated in primaries by challengers. But the total number of defeated incumbents, sixteen, was less than half the average (thirty-five) for postwar election years ending in 2. The number of voluntary retirements was also lower than normal for a reapportionment year. As a consequence, only 54 new members entered the House when the 108th Congress met in 2003, fewer than half of the 110 newcomers seated in 1992 and well below the average for other postwar reapportionment years (eighty-two).

---

[47]See, for example, James Carney and John Dickerson, "W. and the 'Boy Genius,'" *Time*, November 11, 2002, 41–45; Howard Fineman, "How Bush Did It," *Newsweek*, November 11, 2002, 29–31.

[48]The equation in table 6.2 predicted a three-seat Republican House gain in 2002.

The 2004 elections left the Republican Party in its strongest position since Herbert Hoover was elected president back in 1928. George W. Bush won reelection by a modest but unambiguous margin (50.7 percent to John Kerry's 48.3 percent of the popular vote), while the Republicans solidified their congressional majorities by adding three House seats and four Senate seats. The election was not, however, a ringing electoral endorsement of the administration's or the Republican Congress's performance; nor did it represent any global shift in public sentiment to the Republican side. Rather, it was the product of two salient features of American politics during the first decade of the twenty-first century: the substantial structural advantage Republicans enjoyed in the struggle for control of Congress (see chapter 2) and the extraordinarily polarized public reactions to the Bush administration, sentiments that found their fullest expression in the presidential contest but also spilled over into congressional races.

The election brought little change to the House of Representatives. Only seven of the 402 incumbents who sought reelection were defeated, and four of the seven were casualties of a Republican gerrymander in Texas (see chapter 2), not swings in voter sentiment. The party already in control held onto twenty-seven of the thirty-four open seats, and two of the three lost by Democrats were also a result of the Texas redistricting, as was the Republican pickup of the state's new open seat. Without the Texas remap, only eight House seats would have changed party hands, an all-time low.

Few districts were in play in 2004 because the ingredients of a competitive race were missing in so many places; not only was no partisan tide running, but there were few seats where local partisanship or missteps by the incumbent gave the out-party hope. In the end, five of the seven open seats that switched party control in 2004 went to the party with the 2000 presidential majority, as did the new open seat in Texas, the two Texas seats where incumbents faced off, and four of the five other seats where challengers were successful. Thus, although the House elections produced very little change, they extended the long-term trend toward increasing district-level consistency in House and presidential voting (figure 6.3) and in partisan loyalty among voters (figure 5.1).

The decade of low turnover and partisan stasis ended abruptly in 2006. Democrats picked up thirty House seats to win a 233–202 majority, one seat larger than held by the Republicans in the previous Congress. They also gained six Senate seats to win a one-seat majority in the upper house. Remarkably, Democrats lost not a single seat in either chamber, making this the first election in US history in which a party retained all of its congressional seats. Although a number of factors contributed to the pro-Democratic national tide—notably, scandals that weakened some Republican members and sullied the congressional party's brand name—its primary source was the electorate's unhappiness with the Iraq

War and the president responsible for it. Midterm elections are usually at least to some extent popular referendums on the current administration, although, as noted earlier in this chapter, the electoral effects of attitudes toward the president vary from year to year. But by any measure, opinions on George W. Bush's job performance shaped individual voting in 2006 to an extraordinarily large degree.

Well before the election, surveys provided ample reason for believing that opinions of Bush would have an unusually large effect on voters in 2006, especially among those holding negative views of his performance. Compared to electorates in previous midterms going back to 1978, voters in 2006 were more likely to say that their congressional vote would be about the president (54 percent, compared to between 34 and 46 percent in the earlier midterms); more important, more than one-third of voters said that their vote for Congress would be a vote against Bush, a noticeably larger proportion than for any of his three predecessors at midterm, including Bill Clinton in 1994. The reversal from 2002, when 31 percent of voters said their vote would be an expression of support for President Bush, is especially notable, as is the increase of 13 percent of voters who said they would be casting a vote to affect which party controlled Congress.[49]

Postelection surveys found that voters did what they said they would do. The proportion of the electorate whose prospective vote for US representative in preelection polls and reported vote after the election was consistent with their evaluations of President Bush—voting Republican if they approved of his performance and Democratic if they disapproved— exceeded 85 percent, more than ten percentage points higher than in any of the previous eight midterm elections (figure 6.9). The problem for Republican candidates was that Bush was also considerably less popular than any of his midterm predecessors in this set; Bush's 38 percent approval rating in the Gallup poll taken just before the election was in fact the lowest for any president at midterm since Harry Truman in 1950.

The strong pro-Democratic national tide running in 2006 was not by itself sufficient to deliver control of Congress to the Democrats. The Democrats' share of the total House vote nationally increased by nearly five percentage points over 2004, and the vote swing to Democrats in districts contested in both 2004 and 2006 averaged a little less than five points. But only five of the thirty Democratic pickups would have been achieved with a five-point increase in the Democratic vote over 2004; nineteen required swings of ten or more points to put the Democrats above 50 percent. The actual swing in the districts Democrats took from Republicans averaged fourteen points, exceeding ten points in twenty-four of them. These results underline the crucial contribution of

---

[49]See previous editions for visual representations of these data.

Figure 6.9 Congruence between Presidential Approval and the House Vote in Midterm Election Polls, 1946–2022

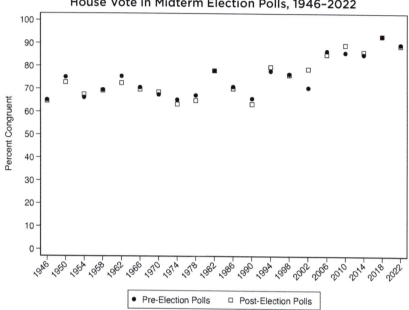

Source: Gallup, ABC News/Washington Post, CBS News/New York Times, CCES, ANES, NBC News/Wall Street Journal, Pew, Quinnipiac, Time, USC Dornsife, Suffolk, Roper, Newsweek, Marist, CNN, and Economist/YouGov polls.

the Democrats' strategic deployment of campaign resources—candidates, money, personnel—to their success in turning a favorable partisan tide into the victories that produced their House majority.

The congressional elections of 2008 extended the national trend that had given control of Congress to the Democrats two years earlier. Democrats picked up twenty-one seats in the House of Representatives and seven in the Senate. The House victories, added to the thirty-one seats they gained in 2006 and some pickups in subsequent special elections, left them holding 257 seats to the Republicans' 178, a gain of fifty-five seats over the two elections. The cumulative results of the two elections overturned the verdict of 1994—temporarily, as it turned out—reducing Republican representation to its level before the party's historic rise to majority status fourteen years earlier.

The 2008 elections shared a number of notable similarities with the 2006 elections, although important differences were also evident. Like 2006, 2008 was largely a referendum on George W. Bush's administration and, by extension, his Republican Party. Independents favored Democratic House candidates by a solid margin for the second time running. Finally, just as in 2006, most of the new Democratic House gains occurred in Republican-leaning districts, with the effect of moderating the party's caucus for the ensuing Congress.

Not all parallels held. Although voters took an even more unfavorable view of Bush and the Republican Party in 2008 than they had in 2006, the leading source of disaffection had shifted from the Iraq War to the recessionary economy. Unlike the Iraq War, the economic crisis soured many Republicans as well as Democrats and independents on the administration. As always, voters held even dimmer views of Congress than of the president, but unlike in 2006, the majority party in Congress did not suffer at the polls. And, of course, 2008 featured Barack Obama's remarkable victory in the presidential election, the product of an unusually well-financed and organized campaign that produced palpable spillover benefits for Democratic House and Senate candidates—benefits that turned out to be very short-lived.

The 2010 midterm elections erased all of the Democrats' House gains from 2006 and 2008 and more. The Republicans gained a net sixty-three seats to win a 242–193 majority, their best showing since 1946. The huge electoral swing to the Republicans reflected the usual fundamentals: the president's party's exposure (the surplus of House seats it holds above its "normal" level), the state of the economy, and the public's assessment of the president's job performance. The presidential component was extraordinarily strong in 2010, even stronger than in 2006 (figure 6.9), as Republicans succeeded in framing the election as an explicit referendum on Obama and his policies. The high level of animosity and anger among the president's opponents also augmented the Republican tide and, combined with tepid support among his supporters, left Republicans with the lion's share of highly motivated voters. It also reflected Obama's and his party's failure to persuade most Americans—most importantly, political independents—that the president's policies, including his landmark legislative victories, were to their or the nation's benefit. That is, Obama's legislative successes were, overall, political failures, and his party's congressional candidates paid the price.

Although President Obama's approval ratings were mediocre rather than dismal, his detractors tended to be considerably more adamant in their opinions than his supporters.[50] Members of the Tea Party movement, an assortment of populist conservatives and libertarians whose anger and energy made them a major force in the 2010 elections, expressed the most intense hostility toward Obama. Adopting the view of Obama promoted by the John McCain–Sarah Palin campaign in 2008, Tea Party sympathizers were nearly unanimous in their rejection of Obama's policy agenda

---

[50]For example, in the nine ABC News/*Washington Post* polls taken in the first ten months of 2010, 80 percent of the disapprovers disapproved of Obama's performance strongly, compared with 56 percent of the approvers who approved strongly; see "Washington Post Poll," *Washington Post*, July 2010, http://www.washingtonpost.com/wp-srv/politics/polls/postpoll_10302010.html?sid=ST2010103100110, accessed November 15, 2010.

and belief that it was moving the country toward socialism.[51] Their antipathy toward Obama was manifest in the refusal of so many of them to acknowledge Obama as an American-born Christian; for example, only 46 percent of voters expressing a favorable view of the Tea Party movement in the 2010 Cooperative Congressional Election Study (CCES) said he was a Christian and born in the United States; 21 percent said he was a foreign-born Muslim. Among respondents in the CCES who expressed a strongly favorable opinion of the Tea Party (29 percent in the sample), 96 percent voted for the Republican House candidate.

With the fundamentals on their side and buoyed by the anger and enthusiasm of their Tea Party faction, Republicans sought to nationalize the election, urging voters to treat it as a referendum on Obama and the unified Democratic government. They largely succeeded. An average of 56 percent of respondents said their vote for Congress would be a vote either for or against the president, the highest average to that point for any of the midterms for which data are available.[52] In contrast to the two midterms during the George W. Bush administration, the balance of support and opposition was quite even in 2010. The Republican's advantage lay in the greater enthusiasm of their voters, where they enjoyed a notably wider lead than had Democrats in 2006 or Republicans in 1994.[53]

Aggregate election results also suggest that the 2010 midterm was nationalized to an unusual degree and that the president was the primary focus. House (and Senate) election results bore an uncommonly strong relationship to district and state-level presidential voting two years earlier. Figure 6.10 displays correlations between the Democratic presidential candidate's share of the prior presidential vote in the district or state and the Democratic candidate's vote share in midterm elections since 1954.[54] How well Obama had run in 2008 in the district (or state) strongly conditioned how well the Democrats ran in 2010.[55] The correlations for 2010 House (.92) and Senate (.84) races extended the long-term

---

[51]Only 7 percent of Tea Party supporters in the April 5–12 CBS News/*New York Times* poll approved of Obama's performance; 88 percent disapproved, and 92 percent said his policies were leading the country toward socialism; see "Tea Party Movement: What They Think," CBS News, April 14, 2010, http://www.cbsnews.com/htdocs/pdf/poll_tea_party_041410 .pdf, accessed April 15, 2010.

[52]The data for 2010 are from ABC News/*Washington Post*, NBC News/*Wall Street Journal*, CBS News/*New York Times*, Pew, Gallup, and Associated Press–GfK surveys; for the sources of earlier data, see Jacobson, "Referendum," 18.

[53]Gary C. Jacobson, "The Republican Resurgence in 2010," *Political Science Quarterly* 126 (Spring 2011): 27–52.

[54]Both are measured as the percentage of the major-party vote, excluding third-party and independent candidates.

[55]Regression of the Democrats' vote share on Obama's 2008 votes share produces nearly identical results for the House and Senate. Democratic House candidates are estimated to get 109 percent of Obama's vote, minus 10.7 percentage points; Democratic Senate candidates are estimated to win 110 percent of Obama's vote, minus 11.3 percentage points.

Figure 6.10 Correlation between Prior Presidential Vote and the Midterm Vote across House Districts and States, 1954-2022

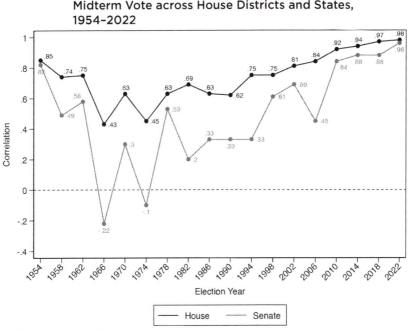

Source: Compiled by authors.

trend toward greater electoral coherence across federal offices. Survey data reiterate this point; as the data in figure 6.9 indicate, the consistency between voters' evaluations of the president and the reported House vote was a remarkable 89 percent, again the highest recorded to that date.

2012-2020

The 2012 elections reiterated the political status quo, with President Obama winning reelection to a second term with 51.0 percent of the vote (compared with 47.3 percent for Mitt Romney) and the Democrats making modest gains in Congress by adding eight House and two Senate seats. The Republicans retained a 234–201 House majority and thus a base from which to challenge the president's agenda in the 113th Congress. With the Senate still in Democratic hands, now with a 55–45 margin, the president had to contend with a divided Congress for the next two years. House incumbents who pursued reelection were only slightly less successful than average; aside from the thirteen defeated in primary (eight) or general (five) elections by other incumbents they faced after redistricting, about 90 percent who sought reelection were successful.[56]

---

[56]Gary C. Jacobson, "How the Economy and Partisanship Shaped the 2012 Presidential and Congressional Elections," *Political Science Quarterly* 128 (Spring 2013): 1–38.

Despite considerable unhappiness about the slow recovery from the Great Recession and the lowest congressional approval ratings on record (see chapter 7), voters ended up electing a new Congress only marginally different from the one that they fundamentally disdained. No strong national tide was present in 2012 (compared with the three previous elections), but the election extended the trend toward nationalized electoral politics that has been the hallmark of the twenty-first century. The linkages between electoral behavior and outcomes across national races were the strongest in at least sixty years, with individual ticket splitting and split-district outcomes hitting postwar lows (figures 6.3 and 6.5). Like Obama, congressional Democrats enjoyed a modest victory despite the burden of lingering high unemployment and weak economic growth, aided on the Senate side by the Obama campaign's mobilization efforts in some battleground states. Despite Obama's five-million-vote margin over Romney, the Republican House majority, protected by the formidable Republican structural advantage discussed in chapter 2, was never at risk. Democrats won a majority of the major-party national vote cast for House candidates, their share rising from 46.6 percent in 2010 to 50.7 percent in 2012; but with party loyalty so high and split outcomes so rare, their seat share only grew from 44.4 to 46.2 percent.

Republicans sought to make the 2014 election a referendum on Obama's performance as they had in 2010, and again they succeeded, although the outcome was not as dramatic as it had been four years earlier. The results left the Republican Party in its strongest position on Capitol Hill in over eight decades. A net gain of thirteen seats gave Republicans a 247–188 House majority, their largest since 1928, but the more dramatic victory occurred in the Senate contests, where the Republicans picked up nine Democratic seats while losing none of their own to take a 54–46 majority. Obama's standing with the public in the fall of 2014 was near the lowest point of his presidency (with about 42 percent approving), and Democrats could not escape his shadow. With that shadow so dominant, the fact that both congressional parties and Congress itself were held in even lower regard than the president—suffering their lowest popular ratings in any election season on record—turned out to be inconsequential.

The decline in Obama's job approval reflected administrative problems (e.g., with the Affordable Care Act rollout and problems in the Veterans Health Administration's medical services) and dissatisfaction with his responses to overseas challenges posed by the Syrian civil war, the rise of the Islamic State, and Russia's aggression in Ukraine. Improvements in the economy, which grew an average of 2.9 percent per quarter following Obama's reelection, with unemployment falling from 7.9 to 5.8 percent, did not help, as most Americans, experiencing stagnant wages and family incomes, did not think the economy was improving. The standard referendum model in table 6.2 predicted Democrats would lose about eleven seats, very close to the thirteen they actually lost.

The public was even less happy with Congress than with the president in 2014, expressing overwhelming dissatisfaction with the institution, its leaders, and its members; disapproval of Congress averaged a record 80 percent in polls taken in the three months leading up to the election. Yet, despite these sentiments, 96 percent of the House incumbents (98 percent of Republicans and 93 percent of Democrats) who sought reelection won, with only four losing primaries and only thirteen losing in the general election. The stunning upset of Republican House majority leader Eric Cantor by a Tea Party insurgent in his June 2014 primary in Virginia turned out to be an anomaly rather than a harbinger.

In the end, then, the electorate's nearly universal disdain for Congress in 2014 was inconsequential. With control of the Congress divided between the parties, each side could, and did, blame the other for its dysfunction. Voters were not particularly happy with their own congressional parties and perhaps even their local candidates, but their opinions of the other party and its leaders were much lower, so they had no reason to defect to the other side.[57] As a result, House incumbents won reelection at a rate higher than the 94 percent average of the past three decades. Incumbents were as successful in winning reelection in 2014 as they had been in the 1970s and 1980s, when the incumbency advantage was at its peak, not because they were incumbents but because a very large majority of them represented districts where their party was locally dominant, and they were protected by the high levels of party-line voting that have become the norm.

The 2016 presidential election produced two historic firsts: the Republican Party nominated Donald J. Trump, a candidate without any previous political or military experience (he had, however, been in the public eye since the 1980s as the billionaire host of a popular reality TV show on NBC, *The Apprentice*, for fourteen seasons). The Democrats nominated former first lady and New York senator Hillary Clinton, the first woman to head the ticket for either political party. Both candidates were unusually unpopular, Trump more so than Clinton, yet on election night, Trump shocked the nation, winning a 304–227 majority in the Electoral College, despite losing the popular vote to Clinton by 2.86 million votes and 2.1 percentage points.

---

[57]On average in six surveys taken in the fall of 2014, only 40 percent of Republicans approved of their party or party leaders in Congress, but only 7 percent approved of the congressional Democrats; the respective figures for Democratic voters were 61 and 10 percent; from CBS News/*New York Times*, Quinnipiac, Marist-McClatchy, and Gallup surveys.

Trump's peculiar candidacy and path to the presidency, as well as the unpopularity of both candidates within their own parties, raised the possibility that the high levels of party-line voting and low levels of ticket-splitting that had emerged in this century might fall off. They did not, and the congressional elections were as cohesively partisan as they were in 2008 and 2012. Despite the election of an antiestablishment outsider promising to "drain the swamp" in Washington, the congressional elections produced little change. Trump's victory yielded unified control of the federal government for the first time in eight years, although the Republicans lost a net six House seats. On average, 78 percent of Americans disapproved of Congress's performance in 2016, but more than 96 percent of House incumbents pursuing reelection were returned to office.

Even with unified government, the Republican majorities in the 115th Congress struggled to pass legislation fulfilling their and Trump's campaign pledges. First and foremost was repeal and replacement of the Affordable Care Act, which Republicans had been promising to do since its enactment in 2010. The House managed to pass legislation repealing "Obamacare" (as it was popularly known) by a narrow margin but the effort died in the Senate. Congress did eventually pass a sweeping tax bill cutting rates on corporations and the wealthy, but overall the 115th Congress served as a reminder that unified party control is not by itself sufficient for legislative success. Trump and the Republican Senate succeeded, however, in stacking the courts and administrative agencies with staunch conservatives.

Sharply polarized opinions of the first two years of the Trump presidency ensured that the 2018 midterm would be a referendum on his performance, a framing Trump encouraged while campaigning for Republican candidates: "pretend I'm on the ballot."[58] This turned out to be a good strategy in the Senate elections but not in the House elections. Despite a growing economy, with very low unemployment and inflation, and few Americans soldiers dying in overseas conflicts, Trump's overall approval remained anomalously low, averaging around 41 percent in the months leading up to the election. His approval ratings on the economy were about ten points higher but still much lower than would be expected given the economy's robust performance. Trump's low approval probably cost Republicans control of the House. A model akin to that in table 6.2, focusing on midterm elections, predicted the actual Republican losses on the nose: forty seats, giving Democrats their 235–200 majority for the 116th

Congress. The same model estimates that—had Trump's overall level of approval been at least 52 percent—the Republicans would have retained control of the House.[59] The president's popular standing was especially important in 2018 because vote intentions before the election and reported votes after the election were so strongly related to opinions of Trump: 93 percent of intended and reported votes matched opinions of Trump, for the Republican House candidate if approving, for the Democrat if disapproving, a level of congruence unmatched in any previous election (figure 6.9).

Presidents usually shape the political environment that guides the strategic decisions of candidates and campaign contributors, and 2018 was no exception. Observing the administration's general unpopularity, forty Republican representatives declined to run for reelection, the highest number and percentage of Republican departures in the postwar period. Only twelve sought higher office. Seven of the retirees represented districts won by Hillary Clinton in 2016, and several more were from districts Trump won only narrowly. Only twenty Democrats retired, nine of them to pursue higher office. Democrats also held a clear lead in the proportion of challengers with previous experience in elective office, but as noted in chapter 3, that proportion was comparatively low for a party favored by national conditions.[60] Their advantage stemmed, rather, from an exceptional crop of first-time candidates, half of them women, and the extensive grassroots activism and astonishing sums of money that supported their candidacies.

As documented in chapter 4, Democratic candidates pursuing Republican House seats in potentially winnable districts raised and spent record sums and then saw that total increased by an average of more than 80 percent by outside spending on their behalf by party and independent groups. Competitive Democratic challengers were backed by 31 percent more campaign money than their opponents, although endangered Republican incumbents were also generously supported, by an average of $8.5 million. It is unusual for incumbents to be outspent in competitive races; in elections since 2002, even successful challengers have been outspent by the losing incumbent 79 percent of the time. In 2018, Democrats enjoyed a financial advantage in twenty-one of the twenty-four races against incumbents in winnable districts and in all twelve competitive open seats.[61] The Democrats' ample finances were strongly associated

[59]Gary C. Jacobson, "Extreme Referendum: Donald Trump and the 2018 Midterm Elections," *Political Science Quarterly* 134 (Spring 2019): 1–30.

[60]Thirteen percent of Republican incumbents faced experienced challengers, compared to 5 percent of incumbent Democrats.

[61]The financial data are from the FEC, accessed at https://www.fec.gov/data/advanced/?tab=candidates, and the Center for Responsive Politics, accessed at https://www.opensecrets.org/outsidespending/summ.php?cycle=2018&disp=C&type=G.

with success in these districts; they defeated twenty of the twenty-four incumbents and won all twelve open seats. Twenty of these lavishly financed victors were women.

Midterm referenda depend in part on systematic shifts in voting behavior between elections, but with so few voters now willing to contemplate crossing party lines and the proportion of swing voters declining,[62] the outcome depends increasingly on the capacity of each side to motivate and mobilize its core supporters. Both sides recognized this reality in 2018 and made extraordinary efforts to get their supporters to the polls. Both succeeded, but Democrats did so to a much greater extent than Republicans. These efforts produced the highest midterm voting participation in a century, with an estimated 50.3 percent of eligible citizens casting ballots, turnout more than 13 percentage points higher than in 2014 and 11 points higher than the average for the past four decades.[63] In House elections, the total for Republican candidates nationally was about 10.9 million votes higher than in 2014, but the total for Democratic candidates was 25.1 million votes higher. In the thirty-two districts Democrats took from Republicans where comparisons with 2014 are possible,[64] the average Republican vote was up 21 percent over 2014, but the average Democratic vote was up more than 100 percent.

The 2018 House elections were, in sum, off the charts on a variety of dimensions. Spending by candidates and outside groups was by a wide margin the highest ever for a midterm. Grassroots activism surged. Turnout was higher than in any midterm in the past hundred years. Party-line voting reached a postwar high; Democrats took the House not by attracting Republican voters but because there were more Democrats in the electorate and, according to exit poll data, independents preferred Democrats, 54–42. All of these extremes reflected the public's highly polarized responses to Donald Trump's presidency and the influence assessments of Trump had on voting in the 2018 election, which was also off the charts.

After a divisive four years in the White House, the 2020 elections represented a referendum on Donald Trump and his policies as president. Former Vice President Joseph Biden defeated the sitting president with 51.3 percent of the vote compared to 46.9 percent for Trump. Turnout in the election was incredibly high despite the ongoing COVID-19 pandemic, with approximately 100 million people voting early via absentee

---

[62]Corwin Schmidt, "Polarization and the Decline of the American Floating Voter," *American Journal of Political Science* 61 (October 2017): 365–81.

[63]Michael P. McDonald, "2018 November General Election Turnout Rates," United States Election Project, December 18, 2018, http://www.electproject.org/2018g, accessed January 2, 2019.

[64]That is, excluding redrawn districts in Pennsylvania and those won by the Republican unopposed in 2014.

or mail-in ballots, setting a record in the process. President Trump decried the results for weeks following the election in light of the record use of mail-in voting necessitated by the pandemic, suggesting that Biden's victory was fraudulent and called on various state courts and legislatures to overturn the results, thus awarding him another four years in the White House. When he did not get the outcome he desired (all of his appeals were either dismissed or ignored), Trump spoke for over an hour at a rally held on January 6, 2021, headlined as the "Save America March." Immediately following Trump's remarks, a mob marched down Pennsylvania Avenue and invaded the Capitol while both chambers were seeking to ratify Biden's electoral victory, shutting down the ratification for several hours as a result.[65] Even with the delay, Biden was declared the winner early the following morning. Less than a week later, Trump was impeached for the second time during his first term as president but was ultimately acquitted in mid-February for his role in inciting the Capitol insurrection.[66]

Despite the highly nationalized election and low levels of approval for the president leading up to the election, Trump's electoral defeat did not translate into more widespread losses for Republicans in the House as many pundits initially predicted. In total, 23 Republican incumbents retired rather than run for reelection, and five sought higher office. (By contrast, only five Democrats retired and four pursued higher office.) Only eight incumbents were defeated in their primaries, and twelve were defeated in the general election, resulting in an incumbency reelection rate of about 95 percent. In total, not a single Republican incumbent was defeated in the general election and the Republicans managed to pick up 14 seats in the House, five votes shy of controlling a majority of the chamber. With the Republicans losing three seats in the Senate, resulting in a 50/50 split (thus requiring Vice President Kamala Harris' tie-breaking vote on occasion), Biden had unified control of Congress, but with very little margin of error when it came to passing legislation.[67]

The 2022 Midterm Election
Leading up to the 2022 elections, Republicans were initially optimistic that they would make notable gains in the US House. As discussed

---

[65]Gary C. Jacobson, "The President and Congressional Elections of 2020: A National Referendum on the Trump Presidency," *Political Science Quarterly* 136 (2021): 11–45.

[66]Domenico Montanaro, "Senate Acquits Trump in Impeachment Trial—Again." *NPR*, February 13, 2021, https://www.npr.org/sections/trump-impeachment-trial-live-updates/2021/02/13/967098840/senate-acquits-trump-in-impeachment-trial-again

[67]Jamie L. Carson, Spencer Hardin, and Aaron A. Hitefield, "You're Fired! Donald Trump and the 2020 Congressional Elections," *The Forum* 18 (2021): 627–50; John H. Aldrich, Jamie L. Carson, Brad T. Gomez, and Jennifer L. Merolla, *Change and Continuity in the 2020 Elections* (Lanham: Rowman & Littlefield, 2022).

throughout this book, midterm elections are often viewed as referenda on sitting presidents, and President Biden's relatively low levels of approval, along with the high rates of inflation throughout most of 2022, were not viewed as favorable conditions for the Democrats in the months preceding the election. However, two independent factors likely worked to the advantage of Democratic candidates in the midterm: Republican candidates' embrace of Donald Trump's Big Lie about the previous election being stolen and the Supreme Court's decision in the *Dobbs* case to end nearly fifty years of abortion rights at the federal level.[68] Republicans managed to win control of the House, but by a much narrower majority than expected, as they ended up with 222 seats to the Democrats' 213. Based upon initial assessments of the midterm, Trump's involvement in the election and the Court's decision to put abortion on the agenda served to mobilize Democrats and redefined the stakes of the 2022 midterms.[69]

In light of President Biden's declining levels of popularity and the growing levels of inflation leading up to the election, twenty-two Democrats elected not to seek reelection in the House, compared to ten Republicans. Likewise, nine Democrats decided to pursue higher office as did eight Republicans. Of the fifteen incumbents defeated in their primaries, six were Democrats and nine were Republicans. Six of these fifteen lost to other incumbents as a result of the redistricting that occurred following the decennial census. Only nine incumbents lost in the general election, two of whom were defeated by fellow incumbents against whom they were forced to run in the same congressional district. The 118th Congress elected 79 new members, which was slightly lower than the average number for a reapportionment year. Republicans had a greater number of experienced candidates run in both the primaries and the general election, but they were not able to convert that advantage into significant electoral gains in the midterms.[70]

For the second midterm election in a row, voter turnout was much higher than average, with an estimated 112.2 million people voting in the election—about 46.8 percent of the eligible voting age population—reflecting the increased stakes felt by partisans.[71] Republicans who turned out to vote were more likely to attribute their decision to issues such as inflation, crime, or the economy whereas Democrats indicated that abortion, protecting democracy, or keeping election deniers out of

---

[68]Dobbs v. Jackson Women's Health Organization, 597 U.S. __ (2022).

[69]Gary C. Jacobson, "The 2022 Elections: A Test of Democracy's Resilience and the Referendum Theory of Midterms," *Political Science Quarterly* 138 (Spring 2023): 1–22.

[70]Jamie L. Carson and Aaron A. Hitefield, "A Red Wave or a Ripple? Nationalized Politics and the 2022 Midterm Elections," *The Forum*: https://doi.org/10.1515/for-2023-2002.

[71]Data compiled by the United States Elections Project (http://www.electproject.org), accessed March 1, 2023.

office were their principal motivating factors.[72] Moreover, the overall consistency between perceptions of President Biden's performance and vote preferences in the 2022 midterms approached 90 percent, as shown in figure 6.9. Although this declined slightly from a record high of 93 percent set under Trump, it was still quite high by historical standards and likely reflected a modest but significant share of voters who chose to support the Democrats despite disapproving of Biden.

As was the case in prior years, money was an important factor in electoral success, and candidates set new records in spending during the 2022 midterms. According to the Center for Responsive Politics, Democrats spent on average $2.1 million in the election compared to $1.8 million for Republicans. When factoring in incumbency, Democrats spent nearly $3.3 million on average, whereas Republicans spent over $2.5 million in 2022. Additionally, outside spending eclipsed records set in previous elections by hundreds of millions of dollars even when factoring in inflation. Most notably, outside groups spent more than all the candidates combined in 49 House races in the 2022 midterms, reflecting the intensely partisan and fierce level of competition for control of the House.[73] Despite these record spending amounts, relatively few House seats changed hands in the election, and the value of incumbency fell to its lowest level in over 60 years, as noted in chapter 3 (figure 3.3).[74]

SENATE ELECTIONS, 1992–2022

1992–2000

The 1992 Senate elections, like the House elections, brought striking demographic changes without altering the partisan balance. Of the twelve newly elected senators, four were women, one of them (Carol Moseley Braun of Illinois) an African American; the election tripled the number of women senators from two to six. Another of the entering senators, Ben Nighthorse Campbell of Colorado, was the first Native American ever elected to the Senate. Yet the elections again produced no net partisan change at all, leaving the Democrats with the same 57–43 majority they had enjoyed before election day.

---

[72]Paul Blumenthal, "New Polling Shows Democracy Mattered in the 2022 Midterm Elections," *Huffington Post*, December 1, 2022, https://www.huffpost.com/entry/democracy-2022-election- poll_n_6388ce76e4b0151bdb1efbb2.

[73]https://www.opensecrets.org/elections-overview?cycle=2022&display=A&type=R, data accessed on March 29, 2023; https://www.opensecrets.org/outside-spending/outvscand, accessed on April 18, 2023.

[74]Gary C. Jacobson, "The 2022 Elections: A Test of Democracy's Resilience and the Referendum Theory of Midterms," *Political Science Quarterly* 138 (Spring 2023): 1–22.

As in the House, the advances made by women in the Senate were rooted in the primaries. Three of the four newly elected women—all Democrats—won open Senate seats; the fourth, Dianne Feinstein of California, defeated an appointed senator, John Seymour, who was an incumbent in name only. In contrast, the six women (five Democrats, one Republican) who faced elected incumbent senators in the general election lost. (The lone incumbent woman, Barbara Mikulski of Maryland, won reelection.) All the victors had previously held elective office, whereas four of the six losers were pursuing their first.[75]

Only one of the new women senators—Feinstein, who had narrowly lost a race to be California's governor in 1990—would have been a sure bet to win nomination without the special stimulus of the Anita Hill–Clarence Thomas confrontation. Carol Moseley Braun defeated incumbent Democrat Alan Dixon, who had voted to confirm Thomas, in the Illinois primary and then held on to win the general election against a relatively obscure first-time candidate. Patty Murray's self-described status as "a mom in tennis shoes" helped her emerge on top in Washington's jungle primary (in which candidates from all parties run on a single ballot, with the top Democratic and Republican vote-getters winning each party's nomination). Barbara Boxer took the California nomination despite having 143 overdrafts at the House Bank, in large part because of the attention and support her gender attracted in the primary.

The 1994 Republican tide flowed just as strongly in Senate as in House elections. Republicans took control of the Senate by taking eight seats from the Democrats, immediately adding a party-switching opportunist (Richard Shelby of Alabama) to end up with a 53–47 majority, which grew to 54–46 a few months later, when Democrat Ben Nighthorse Campbell of Colorado also switched sides. The Republican Senate victory was less surprising than the House victory, to be sure, because the party had controlled the Senate from 1981 to 1987 and because most Senate seats can be won by either party under the right conditions. But it was just as decisive.

As in the House elections, open seats made the difference. Republicans won all six open seats vacated by Democrats, defeated two of sixteen Democratic incumbents, and kept all the seats they already held (ten incumbents, three open seats). Also as in the House, Senate Democrats tended to retire where constituency voting patterns promised to make life difficult. Democrats vacated six of twelve seats in states where, on average, the two-party vote for Democratic presidential candidates fell below 50.5 percent; they vacated none of the ten seats where the presidential vote exceeded this amount. Strategic retirements thus hurt Democrats in Senate as well as House elections.

---

[75]Jacobson, "Congress," 173.

It could have been even worse for the Democrats. Three of their winners received less than 52 percent of the vote; only one winning Republican cut it that close. Still, it would not have taken a very large vote shift to alter the results. A careful redistribution of about 174,000 votes (.3 percent of the votes cast) would have let the Democrats retain four seats and thus their majority; but then a shift of only 112,000 votes (.2 percent of those cast) could have given the Republicans three additional seats.

As usual, experienced candidates both reflected and enhanced the competitiveness of these elections. Although much was made of the victories of two political novices in Tennessee (Fred Thompson, a lawyer and actor, and Bill Frist, a surgeon), seven of the eleven new Republican senators had served in the House, and another had been his state's governor.

In 1996, despite Clinton's victory, the Republicans added two new seats to the majority they had won in 1994, increasing their margin to 55–45. Both the luck of the draw and retirements hurt Democrats. Thirteen senators retired in 1996, the largest number of voluntary departures since 1914, when senators were first directly elected by voters. Eight of the thirteen were Democrats, four of them from the South. The timing of their retirement announcements again suggests strategic withdrawal; all eight of the Democrats but only one of the Republicans announced their retirement before Clinton's successful showdown with the Republican Congress in late 1995. Republicans won three of the seats vacated by Democrats, two in the South (Alabama and Arkansas) and one in Nebraska, a state won handily by Bob Dole. Republican senator Larry Pressler of South Dakota was the only incumbent defeated in the general election, and his was the only Republican Senate seat lost in 1996.

In 1998, the parties broke even in the Senate, preserving the status quo and the Republicans' 55–45 majority. Democrats defeated two Republican incumbents but lost two open seats. Republicans defeated one Democratic incumbent while losing one open seat. Although six Senate seats thus changed hands, the switches were much more a consequence of local issues and personalities than of any general thirst for change. Still, the outcome was disappointing to Republicans—for Democrats were defending most of the vulnerable seats, and Republicans had entertained dreams of winning a filibuster-proof sixty-seat majority.[76] There is some evidence that popular opposition to Clinton's impeachment hurt Republican Senate candidates even more than it did Republican House candidates, even though the Senate had not yet addressed the issue.[77] The potential effect of the issue was limited, however, because the number of

---

[76]Karen Foerstel, "Senate: GOP on the March," *Congressional Quarterly Weekly Report*, October 24, 1998, 2868–72.
[77]Abramowitz, "It's Monica," 8.

close elections was comparatively small—only nine were won with less than 55 percent of the two-party vote, compared to fifteen in 1996—and only two contests were won by margins of less than thirty-eight thousand votes. In contrast to the 1994 and 1996 elections, the 1998 elections disturbed neither the partisan nor the ideological balance in the Senate.

Unlike the uneventful House elections, the Senate elections shook up the status quo in 2000. Republicans lost five seats, leaving the Senate evenly divided between the parties for only the second time in US history. Democrats had picked up one seat in July, when Republican Paul Coverdell of Georgia died and Georgia's Democratic governor appointed Democrat Zell Miller to take his place; Miller easily won a special election on November 7 to fill out the remaining four years of Coverdell's term. The Democrats gained four additional seats on election day, defeating five incumbent senators to the Republicans' one, with each party losing a single open seat.

The 2000 Senate elections were the first test for several of the staunchly conservative Republicans who were first elected on the strong Republican tide in 1994. Three of the five Republican losers in 2000—John Ashcroft of Missouri, Rod Grams of Minnesota, and Spencer Abraham of Michigan—were members of this class. All three were burdened with images that put them well to the right of their constituents. Part of the reason Democrats pulled even in the Senate is that the strong Republican tide that had prevailed in 1994 was no longer present.

The 2000 Senate elections produced several historic firsts: Hillary Clinton, by winning the New York Senate seat left open by the retirement of Democrat Daniel Patrick Moynihan, became the first First Lady to be elected to any public office, let alone the Senate. In Missouri, John Ashcroft lost to a dead man. Ashcroft's opponent, Democratic governor Mel Carnahan, had been killed in a plane crash on October 16. The Democratic lieutenant governor thereby became governor and quickly promised voters that he would appoint Carnahan's widow, Jean Carnahan, to the seat if the late governor, whose name remained on the ballot, were to win—which he did. Finally, victories by Clinton, Carnahan, Maria Cantwell (Washington), and Debbie Stabenow (Michigan) raised the number of women senators from nine to thirteen, then an all-time high. Considering that until 1993 no more than two women had ever sat in the Senate at the same time, these gains extended a notable trend.

There was a modest but observable relationship between statewide presidential and Senate election results. The incumbent party lost six of fourteen Senate seats in states won by the other party's presidential candidate but only two of nineteen seats in states won by its own party's presidential candidate. One of the two was Florida, where Al Gore may actually have been voters' first choice (we'll never know). The other was Missouri, which George W. Bush won by a narrow margin. With the exception of Missouri's Ashcroft, every losing incumbent was from a state won by the other party's presidential candidate. Overall, twenty-four of thirty-four states cast a plurality of their votes for Senate and presidential candidates of the same party, precisely the same as in 1992 and 1996 (figure 6.12).

It is also possible to detect traces of the impeachment struggle in the Senate results. Twelve Republican incumbents represented states won by Clinton in 1996. The two who voted against conviction were reelected easily. Five of the ten voting for conviction lost, as did Bill McCollum, the House impeachment manager who tried to move up to the Senate in Florida. Five Republican incumbents represented states that Dole had won in 1996; all of them voted for conviction, and all were reelected. This is not to say that impeachment was a decisive issue in any of these races, but votes for conviction may have contributed to the impression that Republican conservatives such as Rod Grams (Minnesota), Spencer Abraham (Michigan), Ashcroft, and McCollum were ideologically out of step with their pro-Clinton constituencies.

Democrats won the close elections in 2000, taking five of six seats won with less than 52 percent of the major-party vote. With the exceptions of Clinton, Carnahan, and Jon Corzine, who spent more than $60 million on his election, both parties' newcomers were experienced politicians; three were former governors, and five were former US representatives.

2002–2010

The Senate tie was broken in May 2001 when James Jeffords of Vermont abandoned the Republican Party to become an independent who would vote with the Democrats on organizational matters. Jeffords's defection set the stage for a titanic battle for control of the Senate, provoking the huge investment of campaign resources by candidates, parties, and outside groups that was examined in chapter 4 (see figure 4.4). The Republicans came out on top in 2002, adding a net two seats by defeating two incumbent Democrats (Jean Carnahan of Missouri, running for the remainder of the term to which she had been appointed in 2000, and Max Cleland of Georgia) and adding an open seat while losing one incumbent of their own. Their open-seat pickup was in Minnesota, where Democratic incumbent Paul Wellstone, ahead in most polls, had died in a plane crash eleven days before the election; Republican Norm Coleman defeated former senator and vice president Walter Mondale, hastily chosen to replace Wellstone. The results left the Republicans with fifty-one seats and thus control of the Senate.

The key to Republican victories in Minnesota, Missouri, and Georgia, as well as in several states where Republican Senate seats had been at risk, was superior mobilization of Republican voters. Bush's near-universal approval among Republicans in 2002, energetic fund-raising, and frenzied last-minute campaigning in competitive states, combined with effective Republican grassroots drives to get out the vote, put Republicans over the top.[78] The Republicans also made effective use of the homeland security issue in races against Cleland and Carnahan; as in the House elections, the legacy of September 11 clearly worked to the Republicans' benefit.

It was a narrow victory. Republicans took a larger share of the close contests, winning four of the six won by less than 53 percent of the vote. Redistribution of about forty thousand votes (less than .1 percent of the total votes cast), properly allocated, could have given Democrats control of the Senate or Republicans two additional seats. Still, Senate outcomes, like those of House contests in 2002, usually reflected the constituency's underlying partisan balance; of the thirteen Senate races considered to be in doubt in October, ten went to the party that had won the state's presidential vote in 2000.[79] Minnesota was the only state won by Gore (barely, with 51 percent of the vote) where Republicans took a Senate seat from the Democrats.

The same trend toward greater consistency in voting for president and US representative in 2004 (figure 6.3) appeared in Senate elections as well, resulting in a four-seat addition to the Republicans' Senate majority. Although Democrats had entertained some hope of adding the two seats they needed to become the majority party, they would have had to win all of the close ones. Instead, Republicans won six of the seven tightest races. The Democrats' main problem was structural: They had to compete with the more efficient distribution of Republican voters. Although Gore had won the national vote in 2000, Bush carried thirty of the fifty states, including twenty-two of the thirty-four states with Senate contests in 2004. Democrats had to defend ten seats in states Bush had won, including five left open by retirements, all in the South, where support for Democrats has been eroding for several decades. Meanwhile, Republicans were defending only three seats in states won by Gore. In the end, Republicans won all five of the open southern Democratic seats, plus majority leader Tom Daschle's seat in South Dakota. Democrats picked up two open Republican seats with Barack Obama's victory over Alan Keyes in Illinois and Ken Salazar's over Peter Coors in Colorado. Seven of

---

[78]Mary Clare Jalonick, "Senate Changes Hands Again," *Congressional Quarterly Weekly Report*, November 9, 2002, 2907–09; Rebecca Adams, "Georgia Republicans Energized by 'Friend to Friend' Campaign," *Congressional Quarterly Weekly Report*, November 9, 2002, 2892–93.

[79]"Six Tossups Muddy Forecast for the Senate," *Congressional Quarterly Weekly Report*, October 26, 2002, 2792–93; the exceptions were Minnesota, Arkansas, and South Dakota (lost by Republican challenger John Thune by 534 votes).

Figure 6.11 Ticket Splitting by Republican Presidential Voters in the Southern Senate Elections, 1952–2020

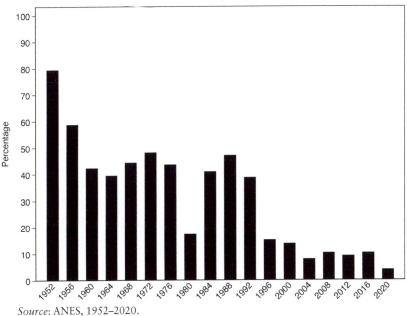

Source: ANES, 1952–2020.

the eight Senate seats that changed party hands in 2004 went to the party that won the state in the 2000 and 2004 presidential elections; Salazar's victory was the lone exception.

Most devastating to Democrats' hopes was the loss of the open seats they were defending in the South. Figure 6.11 shows why they were shut out. For many years, a substantial proportion of southerners who preferred Republican presidential candidates had nonetheless been willing to vote for Democrats for Senate; between 1960 and 1992, an average of 40 percent did so. After the Republican takeover of the Senate in 1994, that average fell to 15 percent; in 2004, it was down to 8 percent, and if we confine the analysis to open seats, it becomes a mere 4 percent.[80] Consequently, the five Democrats defending open Senate seats in the South ran only slightly ahead of Kerry (three percentage points on average), dooming their candidacies in states where Bush was very popular and won handily.[81] Tom Daschle's narrow defeat by John Thune in South

---

[80]The percentages were slightly higher in 2008 and 2012 but remain far below the levels recorded prior to 1992, suggesting a permanent shift in the voting behavior of southerners. The same trend shown in figure 6.11 is evident in southern voting for US representatives, although it is not so pronounced and was lowest in 2012, not 2004.

[81]According to the 2004 ANES survey, Bush's approval rating was 63.9 percent in these five states, compared to 49.4 percent elsewhere.

Figure 6.12 States Won by Same Party in Senate and Presidential Elections, 1952–2020

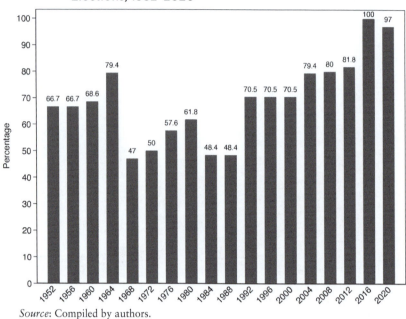

Source: Compiled by authors.

Dakota (49.4 to 50.6 percent) was also probably a consequence of tightening party lines. Daschle had run ninety-two thousand votes ahead of Bill Clinton in 1992 but outpolled Kerry by only forty-four thousand votes in 2004, not enough in a state that Bush won with 61 percent of the major-party vote.

More generally, twenty-seven of the thirty-four Senate contests were won by the party whose presidential candidate won the state's electoral votes, tying 1964 for the highest level of congruence in president-Senate election results in the past half century (figure 6.12). When the 2004 winners were added to the continuing Senate membership, fully 75 percent of senators represented states where their party's candidate won the most recent presidential election, the highest proportion in at least fifty years (figure 6.13).

In 2006, it was the Democrats' turn to sweep the competitive races. They took six seats from Republicans (all from incumbents) and lost only one of the hotly contested races. As in the 2006 House races, national conditions—the Iraq War, Bush's unpopularity, and congressional scandals—gave Democrats a strong edge. And as in House races, Democrats fielded formidable challengers to Republican senators wherever prospects

Figure 6.13 Senate Seats Held by Party Winning the State in the Most Recent Presidential Election

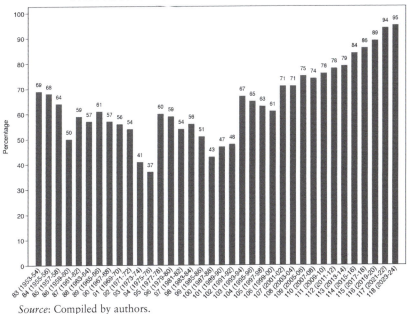

Source: Compiled by authors.

looked at all promising,[82] and the campaign of every Democrat (and Republican) in any of the Senate races where the outcome was at all in doubt was lavishly funded through a combination of contributions, party spending, and independent spending campaigns. The amounts put into the campaigns of competitive Democrats ranged from more than $9 million in the low-population states of Montana and Rhode Island to more than $23 million (Missouri); their Republican opponents were at least as well funded. Four of the defeated Republicans had themselves entered the Senate by defeating Democratic incumbents, underlining the basic competitiveness of these states. The Senate results repeated the pattern evident in several other elections (notably 1980, 1982, 1986, 1994, and 2004) in which one party won a large majority of the hotly contested races.

In 2008, the pro-Democratic tide fueled by disaffection with the Bush administration registered even more strongly in Senate than in House elections. The Democrats picked up eight seats, defeating five incumbents and taking three open seats to raise their total to fifty-nine (including the

---

[82]The list of Democratic challengers in the seven tightest races includes three candidates who had held statewide offices (governor, attorney general, auditor), two U.S. representatives, a president of the state senate, and a former secretary of the navy. The Democrats who retained open seats for the party were also experienced candidates: the attorney general for Minnesota's largest county and two US representatives (counting Bernie Sanders, an independent who caucuses with the Democrats).

two independents who voted to organize with the Democrats). For the second consecutive election, the Democrats held every Senate seat they were defending. Most of their victories were not even close.[83] The conspicuous exception was comedian Al Franken's win in Minnesota; after a lengthy recount (and litigation—he was not sworn in until July 2009), Franken was elected with 50.006 percent of the major-party vote.

Responding to favorable national conditions, experienced Democratic candidates flocked to contest every potentially winnable Republican Senate seat. The roster of Democratic contenders for the twelve Republican seats listed at any time during the election year as being in play by the authoritative *Cook Political Report* included two governors, a former governor, two US representatives, three state legislators, and the mayor of a state's largest city. Only two of the twelve were novices, one of whom was Franken. In contrast, nine of the twelve Senate Democrats seeking reelection faced Republicans who were political novices, as did five of the eleven Republicans whose states were never listed as in play.

The competitive Senate candidates of both parties were amply funded, but Democrats enjoyed a modest advantage because the Democratic Senatorial Campaign Committee raised so much more money than the National Republican Senatorial Committee. Republicans held a small edge in spending by the candidates' campaigns in the ten tightest races (nine held by Republicans, the tenth by Mary Landrieu of Louisiana), but once independent party spending is added to the totals, the advantage belonged to the Democrats; 43 percent of the money spent for Democrats in these races came from the party.

As in the House contests, the electoral fates of Senate candidates were clearly linked to the performance of their party's presidential candidate. Obama won the White House by carrying all of the states that had voted for John Kerry in 2004 plus nine that had voted for Bush. To a remarkable degree, Democratic Senate gains coincided with Obama's victories. The Democrats took all four Republican Senate seats in states that switched from Bush to Obama and three of the four seats in states that voted for both Kerry and Obama. Their only victory in a consistently red state came in Alaska, where Senator Ted Stevens's felony conviction for corrupt behavior (later overturned) shortly before the election no doubt made the difference. Overall, the share of states in which the same party came out ahead in the Senate and presidential races reached a then postwar high of 80 percent in 2008 (figure 6.12).

Democrats were fortunate to have had such a good year in 2008, for it saved their Senate majority when the tide turned back to the Republicans

---

[83]Only three Democratic victors—Mike Begich in Alaska, Jeff Merkley in Oregon, and Franken—won with less than 53 percent of the vote.

in 2010. Exploiting the same sentiments that produced their party's House victories, Republican Senate candidates defeated two incumbents and won four open seats that had been occupied by Democrats, while holding on to all seventeen of the seats they defended. Their six-seat gain left them with forty-seven and within striking distance of a majority in 2012, when Democrats would be defending twenty-three of the thirty-three seats at stake.

Tea Party candidates were especially prominent in the Senate campaigns, with mixed consequences for the Republican cause. Two Tea Party favorites denied Republican incumbents renomination: Mike Lee defeated Robert F. Bennett in Utah, and Joe Miller defeated Lisa Murkowski in Alaska, although Murkowski managed to win the general election as a write-in candidate. Four others—Rand Paul (Kentucky), Marco Rubio (Florida), Sharron Angle (Nevada), and Christine O'Donnell (Delaware)—won nominations over more conventional Republicans.[84] Lee, Paul, and Rubio won open Republican seats in the general election, and two of the five Tea Party candidates running for seats held by Democrats also won (Pat Toomey in Pennsylvania and Ron Johnson in Wisconsin). The other three, however, cost their party winnable seats. This is certainly true of Angle and O'Donnell and probably true of Ken Buck in Colorado. Angle lost to majority leader Harry Reid, whose unpopularity in Nevada would have doomed him against a challenger with less extreme views. O'Donnell, an eccentric repeat candidate who, as noted in chapter 4, introduced herself to voters by announcing "I am not a witch," took the nomination from Mike Castle, a moderate who had won Delaware's at-large House seat with 62 percent of the vote in 2008. Buck was not quite as extreme (although he did, for example, propose to privatize the Veterans Administration) and came much closer to victory. Of the thirteen newly elected Republican senators, then, five had strong Tea Party ties but were outnumbered by more conventional Republican freshmen, including six who had served in the House, a former governor, and a former state attorney general.[85]

Potentially competitive Senate races were generously funded on both sides, and therefore relative spending was not decisive. Independent campaign spending played a conspicuous role in a number of high-profile races. A remarkable 64 percent of campaign money spent in the Colorado race was not legally under the candidates' control; in six other Senate contests, outside spending accounted for between 35 and 55 percent of the total. Typically, Democratic candidates got more party assistance,

---

[84]Rubio's strength forced moderate Republican Charlie Crist out of the party and into an independent campaign.

[85]Toomey also once served in the House, and Rubio was majority leader of the Florida House; the other three Tea Party winners were political newcomers.

but Republican candidates enjoyed a greater share of nonparty spending. Not surprisingly, Tea Party favorites (Buck, Toomey, Angle, Paul, and Rubio) tended to receive extensive outside help, but so did several more mainstream Republicans.

As in the 2010 House elections, Barack Obama and his policies were central issues in the Senate elections. According to the CCES data, the consistency between voters' opinions on Obama's performance and their vote choice was even higher in Senate races (91 percent) than in House races (89 percent). The correlation between Obama's vote in 2008 and the Democratic Senate candidate's vote in 2010 was the highest for any such matching in nearly sixty years (figure 6.10), again indicating a highly nationalized election. The better Obama had run in 2008, the better the Democrats did in 2010—but with about a six-percentage point penalty (difference between Obama's vote and the Democratic Senate candidate's vote), reflecting public unhappiness with the weak economy and administration policies. Democrats won Senate elections in eleven of the thirteen states where Obama had won at least 56 percent of the vote in 2008; Republicans won twenty-two of the twenty-four states where Obama's vote had been below 56 percent. The 2010 elections maintained the high level of consistency between presidential results and party representation in the Senate that had been the norm for the past decade (figure 6.13).

2012-2020

At the beginning of 2012, Democrats had reason to be nervous about their chances in the upcoming fall elections—as noted earlier, twenty-three of the seats that comprised their 53–47 Senate majority were on the ballot in 2012, whereas Republicans held the remaining ten seats. Nevertheless, Obama had in 2008 carried eighteen of the contested Democratic seats as well as four of the Republican seats. By the time the election was over, Democrats ended up holding onto twenty of the twenty-one seats previously won by the president, losing only Nevada. They also managed to win five of the twelve states holding Senate elections in 2012 whose electoral votes ultimately went to Mitt Romney. At the beginning of the 113th Congress, Democrats had a 55–45 advantage over the Republicans, guaranteeing another two years of divided partisan control in Congress.

As was the case in 2010, the nomination of two extreme Tea Party favorites in the party primaries hurt the Republicans' chances of picking up additional Senate seats in 2012. In Indiana, Richard Mourdock defeated six-term Republican incumbent Richard Lugar by running to his right and claiming Lugar was out of touch with the conservative voters in the state. In Missouri, Tea Party favorite Todd Akin narrowly defeated two other Republican candidates in the primary in his bid to challenge

Democrat Claire McCaskill in the general election. Both of these candidates expressed rather extreme views in the fall campaign—especially on abortion and rape—which helped Democrats to win two Senate seats that the Republicans would otherwise have won.[86]

In line with the new normal, outside groups poured millions of dollars into the most competitive Senate races in 2012. Democratic candidates had a significant advantage in party spending, with $50 million to the Republicans' $32 million. Following the Court's decision in *Citizens United v. Federal Election Commission*,[87] spending by nonparty outside groups in the Senate races far eclipsed the totals observed two years earlier; Republican candidates had a sizable advantage in such support, with $137 million compared to the Democrats' $88 million. These extreme levels of spending appear to have had little effect on the overall election results, however; the saturation spending on both sides in competitive contests appears to have been a wash, with the outcomes determined by a variety of other factors.[88]

The 2014 Senate elections represented another low point for the Obama administration, with the Republicans gaining control of the chamber for the first time since 2006. When the election results were finally settled following the Louisiana runoff in early December, Republicans had picked up nine additional seats in the Senate, defeating five incumbent Democrats—Kay Hagan (North Carolina), Mark Udall (Colorado), Mark Pryor (Arizona), Mark Begich (Arkansas), and Mary Landrieu (Louisiana)—and picking up four open seats. The Republicans managed to hold onto every seat they were defending, including open seats in Georgia, Kansas, and Oklahoma, leaving them with a 54–44 advantage going into the 114th Congress. With both chambers firmly in their control, Republicans could turn their energies to trying to roll back policies advanced by the Democrats during the Obama administration.

As in 2012, enormous sums of money poured into the 2014 Senate elections to sway the outcome of individual races. According to data from the Center for Responsive Politics, outside groups spent over $565 million in 2014, nearly twice as much as in 2010. The largest chunk of this outside money ($440 million of the total) was invested in the competitive Senate races in Alaska, Arkansas, Colorado, Georgia, Iowa, Kentucky, Louisiana, Michigan, New Hampshire, and North Carolina.[89] The North Carolina race between incumbent Kay Hagan and Republican challenger Thom

---

[86]Jacobson, "The 2012 Presidential and Congressional Elections."

[87]S. Ct. 876 (2010).

[88]Jacobson, "The 2012 Presidential and Congressional Elections."

[89]"2014 Outside Spending, by Race," OpenSecrets.org, http://www.opensecrets.org/outside-spending/summ.php?disp=R.

Tillis set a new total-spending record of well over $100 million, of which nearly $78 million was spent by outside entities.

Although sums of outside money pouring into the 2014 election were vast and largely unprecedented, there is little evidence that they determined the outcomes of the targeted Senate races.[90] The Democrats' real problem was the sheer number and location of Senate seats they were defending.[91] With the exception of Maine's Republican senator Susan Collins, the 2014 results align tightly with Obama's 2012 vote; indeed, without Collins, the correlation between the two is .95 rather than the .88 displayed in figure 6.10. The election results also underline the Republican advantage in the set of states contested in 2014; seven states defended by Democrats had gone to Romney in 2012, and they lost all of them in 2014. They also lost two states—Colorado and Iowa—that Obama had won by a narrow margin. The Democratic candidates in these states ran significantly behind what would be predicted from Obama's 2012 vote, confirming observers' accounts of major flaws in their campaigns.[92] In contrast to 2010 and 2012,[93] Republican operatives and donors made a concerted and successful effort to prevent the nomination of extreme ideologues or otherwise weird Senate candidates in winnable states in 2014 and so were able to take full advantage of the favorable partisan landscape.[94]

Leading up to the 2016 elections, Democratic leaders hoped that Donald Trump's negatives would allow them to regain control of the Senate. One reason for optimism was that Republicans were defending twenty-four seats and the Democrats were defending ten. Seven of the Republican seats were in states that Obama had won in 2012, and six of them were listed as being at risk according to the *Cook Political Report*.[95] Believing that Clinton would easily defeat Trump, Democrats hoped to

---

[90]Alan I. Abramowitz, "Why Outside Spending Is Overrated: Lessons from the 2014 Senate Elections," Sabato's Crystal Ball, February 19, 2015, http://www.centerforpolitics.org/crystalball/articles/why-outside-spending-is overrated-lessons-from-the-2014-senate-elections.

[91]Benjamin Highton, Eric McGhee, and John Sides, "Constitutional Design and 2014 Senate Election Outcomes," *Forum* 12 (2014): 653–61.

[92]Jennifer Jacobs, "Iowa's Braley Named 'Worst Candidate of 2014,'" *Des Moines Register*, November 11, 2014, http://www.desmoinesregister.com/story/news/elections/2014/11/11/iowas-bruce-braley-named-worst-candidate-of-2014/18875387, accessed November 14, 2014; Nia-Malika Henderson, "How 'Mark Uterus' Lost in Colorado," *Washington Post*, November 5, 2014, http://www.washingtonpost.com/blogs/the-fix/wp/2014/11/05/how-mark-uterus-lost-in-colorado, accessed November 14, 2014.

[93]Jacobson, "The 2012 Presidential and Congressional Elections," 32–37.

[94]Elaine Kamarck, "The Primaries Project: Where's the Money Coming From," Brookings Institution, October 1, 2014, http://www.brookings.edu/blogs/fixgov/posts/2014/10/01-primaries-project-where-is-the-money-coming-from-kamarck.

[95]"2016 Senate Race Ratings for March 25, 2016," *Cook Political Report*, March 25, 2016, http://cookpolitical.com/senate/charts/race-ratings/9421.

pick up at least the four additional seats they needed to win back the Senate. Despite Trump's Electoral College victory, Democrats did manage to pick up two additional Senate seats, but that still left the Republicans with a 52–48 majority.[96]

The two Republican senators defeated by Democrats in 2016, Mark Kirk (Illinois) and Kelly Ayotte (New Hampshire), defended the only seats that changed party hands in 2016. Kirk had been in electoral trouble from the outset and had carefully distanced himself from Trump but to no avail. Ayotte had initially embraced Trump as the Republican nominee but abandoned him following the release of the videotape of him bragging about sexual assaults on women. That didn't help her, either. What mattered in 2016 was the top of the ticket. For the first time in history, every Senate contest in 2016 was won by the party that won the state's electoral votes (figure 6.12), further evidence that Senate elections, like their House counterparts, have become highly nationalized, party- and president-centered affairs.[97]

As was the case in other recent Senate elections, candidates, parties, and independent groups spent enormous sums of money in 2016. Senate candidates spent nearly $675 million on their campaigns,[98] and independent spending by parties and non-party groups continued its upward trend, rising 25 percent above the 2014 totals.[99] A remarkable $116 million was spent independently to influence the race between Pat Toomey and Kathleen McGinty in Pennsylvania, won narrowly by Toomey. In lightly populated New Hampshire, the total exceeded $68 million, and between them, the candidates and outside groups spent a whopping $95 per eligible voter. In six other contests, total outside spending exceeded $40 million. More than 70 percent of the money spent in the nine most competitive states was deployed by outsiders rather than the candidates' campaigns.[100]

The set of states up for election in 2018 gave Republicans a solid advantage in retaining control of the Senate because Democrats were defending nearly three times as many seats as Republicans. Ten of the Democratic incumbents seeking reelection were running in states that Trump had carried in 2016, five with more than 59 percent of the major party vote. In the end, Republicans were able to shore up their narrow

[96]Gary C. Jacobson, "The Triumph of Polarized Partisanship in 2016: Donald Trump's Improbable Victory," *Political Science Quarterly* 132 (2017): 9–41.

[97]Jacobson, "The Triumph of Polarized Politics in 2016," 31–33.

[98]Center for Responsive Politics, "Election Overview," https://www.opensecrets.org/overview/index.php?cycle=2016, accessed July 10, 2019.

[99]Campaign Finance Institute, "Independent Spending in Senate Races over $500 Million," news release, November 4, 2016.

[100]Jacobson, "Congress: Nationalized, Polarized, and Partisan."

majority with a net gain of two seats, defeating four incumbent Democrats in the process: Bill Nelson (Florida), Joe Donnelly (Indiana), Claire McCaskill (Missouri), and Heidi Heitkamp (North Dakota). Democrats defeated Dean Heller (Nevada) and won the Arizona seat vacated by Jeff Flake's retirement.[101] Although Republican Martha McSally narrowly lost to Kyrsten Sinema in a contest between two of Arizona's US Representatives, she was later appointed to fill the vacancy opened by the retirement of Senator Jon Kyl, who had been appointed to fill John McCain's seat after his death in August 2018.[102]

Spending by and for Senate candidates set a new record of more than $1.4 billion in 2018, 21 percent higher than in any previous election. The two most expensive Senate races in 2018 took place in Florida and Texas. In the former, incumbent Democrat Bill Nelson sought reelection to a fourth Senate term but was defeated by Republican Governor Rick Scott. Based on campaign estimates from the Center for Responsive Politics, the candidates spent a combined $116.5 million with Rick Scott spending over $63 million of his own money.[103] Adding outside spending (estimated at nearly $76 million), the total spent in Florida reached a record $192 million. The combined candidate spending in the Texas Senate race between incumbent Republican Ted Cruz and US Representative Beto O'Rourke amounted to about $125 million, of which O'Rourke raised approximately $79 million.[104] Including the $14 million in outside spending, the total was $138 million. But taking state population into account, the most extravagant campaign was in North Dakota, where the $46 million spent by and for the candidates amounted to $146 per vote cast.

The record sums spent on Senate races in 2018 both reflected and contributed to the extreme nationalization of these elections. Five of the six Senate seats that switched parties in 2018 went to the party that had won the state's electoral votes in the 2016 election, and the number of senators in the 116th Congress representing states won by their party in the most recent presidential election reached a then all-time high of 89 (figure 6.13). Two Senate Democrats managed to win states where Trump had won handily in 2016 and majorities continued to approve of his

---

[101] Jamie L. Carson and Aaron A. Hitefield, "Donald Trump, Nationalization, and the 2018 Midterm Elections," *The Forum* 16 (2018): 508.

[102] See Nicholas Riccardi and Terry Tang, "McSally Lost Senate Race but Will Fill McCain's Arizona Seat," *Associated Press*, December 18, 2018, https://www.apnews.com/cb8eee21e5484e31a5e042dcbadc6e52.

[103] Campaign spending estimates were collected by the Center for Responsive Politics (OpenSecrets.org) and include figures for money spent by each of the candidates. The figures we cite were downloaded on February 7, 2019.

[104] Karl Evers-Hillstrom, "Cruz, O'Rourke Break Spending Record," Center for Responsive Politics, October 29, 2018, https://www.opensecrets.org/news/2018/10/cruz-orourke-break-spending-record-texas-senate/.

performance in 2018: Joe Manchin of West Virginia, who won 52 percent of the vote in a state where Trump won 64 percent in 2016 and averaged 61 percent approving in 2018, his best for any state; and Jon Tester of Montana, where Trump had taken 61 percent in 2016 and was approved by 52 percent in 2018. The other results fall close to the diagonal produced by plotting the 2018 Senate results on the 2016 presidential results.[105] With record levels of party loyalty in these contests and the enormous sums of money available to challengers, there was no detectible advantage for incumbents in the 2018 Senate elections.[106]

As in the House elections, voter participation was up sharply in the Senate elections, generally to the benefit of the locally dominant party. Turnout was up by an average of 48 percent compared with 2014 in the ten most competitive states (rated tossup or leaning by the *Cook Political Report*); in the remaining states, it was up an average of 36 percent. Turnout increases of 64 percent in Indiana, 66 percent in Missouri, and 62 percent in Nevada helped turn these states over, and the increase of 64 percent in Texas put that once reliably red state in play.

Prior to the 2020 Senate elections, the *Cook Political Report* indicated that 14 of the 35 Senate seats up for election that fall were vulnerable, two controlled by the Democrats and 12 held by the Republicans. Additionally, three Republicans—Lamar Alexander (TN), Mike Enzi (WY), and Pat Roberts (KS)—did not seek reelection in 2020, nor did Democrat Tom Udall from New Mexico. Georgia had two Senate seats on the ballot that fall—one held by incumbent Republican David Perdue, who had first been elected in 2014. The other was held by incumbent Republican Kelly Loeffler, a financial services executive who had been appointed by Governor Kemp shortly after Senator Johnny Isakson left office at the end of 2019, and before the end of his term, due to health reasons. When Isakson announced his retirement earlier that fall, President Trump had lobbied Kemp to replace Isakson with Representative Doug Collins, a staunch ally of the president, but Kemp chose to defy him by appointing Loeffler instead.[107]

Despite the large number of competitive seats in the election, 85 percent of those senators up for reelection managed to win. Only one Democrat—Doug Jones from Alabama—lost in 2020, but this was not especially surprising since he had been elected in a 2017 special election to replace Republican incumbent Jeff Sessions, who had been appointed US

---

[105]See figure 6.15 in the tenth edition of this book.

[106]Jacobson, "Extreme Referendum: Donald Trump and the 2018 Midterm Elections," 2019.

[107]Yelena Dzhanova, "Georgia Gov. Brian Kemp Defies Trump in Appointing Kelly Loeffler to Senate Seat," *CNBC*, December 4, 2019, https://www.cnbc.com/2019/12/04/georgia-gov-brian-kemp-defies-trump-with-loeffler-senate-appointment.html

Attorney General by President Trump. Jones ended up narrowly defeating Alabama Supreme Court Justice Roy Moore in the general election, after widespread allegations of sexual assault by Moore surfaced about a month before the election. He was running for a full term in 2020.[108] The other four senators defeated were all Republicans, including Martha McSally (AZ), Cory Gardner (CO), David Perdue (GA), and Kelly Loeffler (GA). The latter two races went to a runoff held on January 5, 2021 (since no candidate in either race received more than 50 percent of the vote), with the two Democratic candidates—Jon Ossoff and Raphael Warnock—prevailing in both contests. Since the winners of these Senate races would eventually determine control of the chamber, both elections witnessed record levels of spending with over $500 million spent in these two runoff elections alone—the equivalent of approximately $50 spent per person living in the state.[109]

Senate elections held in 2020, like those occurring in the House, were primarily influenced by voter reactions to the candidates at the top of the ticket rather than the large sums of money that were spent—although there was plenty of that as well when you factor in the total spending in Senate races (besides the ones in Georgia) in states that initially looked competitive, such as Maine and South Carolina. As noted in figure 6.12, all but one Senate seat in 2020 went to the same party that won the state's electoral vote for president; the lone exception was Republican Susan Collins from Maine, who was easily reelected despite Biden carrying the state by more than 7 points. The proportion of split outcomes in 2020 is the second lowest to date, exceeded only by the record set in 2016. Additionally, the number of senators who represented states where their party won a greater number of votes in the most recent presidential election set a new record at 94 (figure 6.13) and the number of states with split Senate delegations (one from each party), dropped to an unprecedented low of six.[110]

The 2022 Senate Elections
The US Senate was evenly divided at 50–50 heading into the 2022 midterm elections, and Republicans needed a net pickup of at least one seat

---

[108]Kim Chandler and Steve Peoples, "Democrat Jones Wins Stunning Red-State Alabama Senate Upset," *AP News*, December 13, 2017, https://apnews.com/article/donald-trump-us-news-ap-top-news-elections-north-america-e2f3c87b2f6b4c05b5e8f8cab38dd48c

[109]Emma Green, "Georgia's Billion-Dollar Bonfire," *The Atlantic*, January 5, 2021, https://www.theatlantic.com/politics/archive/2021/01/money-spent-georgia-senate-runoffs/617545/

[110]Gary C. Jacobson, "The Presidential and Congressional Elections of 2020: A National Referendum on the Trump Presidency," *Political Science Quarterly* 136 (Spring 2021): 36–38.

to win control of the chamber. This was no easy task, however, since thirty-five seats were up for reelection in 2022—fourteen that were held by the Democrats and 21 held by Republicans. This total included two special elections, one held in California and the other in Oklahoma, that would be taking place along with the thirty-three regular Senate contests. Compared to two years earlier, the *Cook Political Report* included only four toss-up races just prior to the election (Arizona, Georgia, Nevada, and Pennsylvania), with five more leaning toward either the Democratic or Republican candidate. Only one Democratic incumbent—Patrick Leahy (VT)—and five Republicans—Richard Shelby (AL), Roy Blunt (MO), Richard Burr (NC), Pat Toomey (PA), and Rob Portman (OH)—announced prior to the election that they did not intend to seek reelection in 2022.[111]

After the electoral results were tallied, and following yet another runoff in Georgia between incumbent Democrat Raphael Warnock and former football player Herschel Walker held in early December, every incumbent senator who sought reelection was successful for the first time in the Senate's history. Democrats managed to pick up the open Senate seat in Pennsylvania that Pat Toomey previously held, where Lieutenant Governor John Fetterman defeated Mehmet Oz, giving them a one-seat majority in the chamber and reducing the need to rely on Vice President Harris to cast a tie-breaking vote. In addition to large sums of money spent by individual candidates in nearly all Senate races, nearly $2 billion was spent by outside groups in 2022, far eclipsing the $1.1 billion that had been spent by similar groups in the 2018 midterms. In the Georgia Senate race, for instance, about $225 million of outside money was spent in this close race in addition to the nearly $249 million spent by the individual candidates where Warnock prevailed by less than 100,000 votes in the runoff. The open seat contest in Pennsylvania also generated enormous sums of outside spending with more than $223 million flowing into the state beyond the nearly $124 million spent by the individual candidates.[112]

As we have seen in recent election cycles, the record sums of candidate and outside money spent in the 2022 Senate races continued to reflect and contribute to the extreme nationalization of these elections. The significant investments in many of these closely fought Senate contests reflected both the intense levels of competition for control of the Senate and the political passions invoked by both former President

---

[111] Jamie L. Carson and Aaron A. Hitefield, "A Red Wave or a Ripple? Nationalized Politics and the 2022 Midterm Elections," *The Forum* (2023): https://doi.org/10.1515/for-2023-2002

[112] *Ibid.*

Figure 6.14 The 2020 Presidential Vote and 2022 Senate Vote

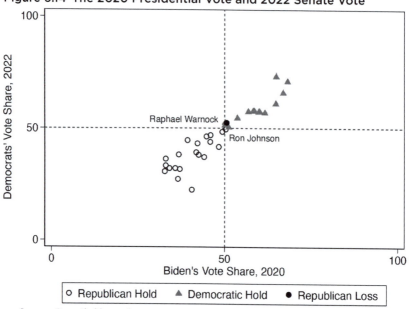

Source: Compiled by authors.

Trump's involvement in the election and the *Dobbs* decision handed down by the Court in late June.[113] Democrats appear to have done a somewhat better job getting their voters to the polls, and their success in making the election as much about Trump, abortion rights, and election denial likely offset many of the negatives associated with Biden's lagging approval numbers and the economy. Additionally, figure 6.13 illustrates that the total number of Senate seats held by the party of the winner of the most recent presidential election now stands at a record 95, indicating that only five states have split delegations in the 118th Congress.[114] Finally, we see that the Senate outcomes line up fairly well to the diagonal produced by plotting the 2022 Senate results on the 2020 presidential results (figure 6.14) with Raphael Warnock's and Ron Johnson's extremely close wins highlighted.

[113]Savannah Kuchar, "Democrats Spent Millions Boosting Ultra Right Candidates in Midterms. The Strategy Worked," *USA Today*, November 15, 2022, https://www.usatoday.com/story/news/politics/2022/11/15/democrats-boosted-trump-gop-primaries-helping-midterms/10670042002/; Jared Gans, "ActBlue Says It Processed $89 Million in Roughly a Week Following *Roe v. Wade* Reversal," *The Hill*, July 20, 2022, https://thehill.com/homenews/campaign/3567445-actblue-says-it-processed-89-million-in-roughly-a-week-following-roe-v-wade-reversal/

[114]Gary C. Jacobson, "The 2022 Elections: A Test of Democracy's Resilience and the Referendum Theory of Midterms," *Political Science Quarterly* 138 (Spring 2023): 1–22.

CONCLUSION

The Senate has changed party hands eight times since 1980. In four instances—1980, 1994, 2006, and 2014—the switch was part of a broader partisan tide that was visible in other elections as well. In contrast, when the Democrats won control in 1986, the shift was entirely idiosyncratic to the Senate elections. The switch in 2001 was set up (though not accomplished until Jeffords's defection) by Democratic gains in 2000, an election with no perceptible partisan tide at all. Republicans benefited from a modest national swing in 2002, a consequence of differential turnout and issues put on the agenda by the attacks of September 11, but they probably would have controlled the Senate only by the grace of Vice President Dick Cheney had Paul Wellstone not died in a plane crash. There have also been several elections since 1980—namely, 1982, 1984, 1996, 2018, and now 2022—when the Senate swings, though small, actually went against the national partisan trend. Clearly, the close competitive balance in so many states creates a potential for dramatic swings in party fortunes. Yet, at the same time, along with the idiosyncratic variety offered by local candidates, campaigns, and issues, it can also allow large swings to occur without strong partisan tides and partisan tides to surge without producing large partisan swings. The six-year Senate cycle, which alternates presidential and midterm years for each class of senators, also contributes to varied shifts in partisan fortunes.

Despite considerable idiosyncratic volatility in competition for control of the Senate, the trend toward greater partisan stability and consistency in Senate election voting patterns and outcomes is unmistakable (figures 6.5 and 6.10 to 6.14), with the four most recent elections displaying the highest partisan coherence yet observed. Both Senate and House election patterns confirm that the United States has entered an era of nationalized, polarized, party-centered electoral politics that is very different from the candidate-centered world of the 1970s and 1980s.[115] The campaign activities of outside groups—the national parties and independent campaign organizations—that now invest heavily in virtually all of the competitive races have strengthened the national component of congressional elections. With control of the House and Senate now at stake in an era of relatively even partisan balance and highly polarized national politics, these investments will only grow. The kind of congressional politics these trends have encouraged is the subject of the next, and final, chapter.

---

[115]Jacobson, "Extreme Referendum," 2019.

7

Elections, Representation, and the Politics of Congress

★ ★ ★

CONGRESSIONAL ELECTIONS MATTER because the US Congress matters. Though often overshadowed in the popular imagination by forceful presidents, Congress retains so much of its institutional autonomy that it remains, in Morris P. Fiorina's apt phrase, the "keystone of the Washington establishment." Experience with divided government in recent decades suggests that parties can advance their agendas far more effectively by controlling Congress but not the White House than by controlling the White House but not Congress. Even during the George W. Bush administration, when defense against terrorism and the prosecution of wars in Afghanistan and Iraq vastly increased the power and status of the executive branch, Congress's influence over domestic policy remained decisive; the president was by no means uniformly successful in achieving his legislative goals even with both houses in Republican hands. Barack Obama's legislative victories in the 111th Congress (2009–10) required not only Democratic majorities in Congress but the astute leadership of Nancy Pelosi and Harry Reid. And the Republican takeover of the House after 2010 and, even more so of the Senate after 2014, put Obama on the defensive for the remainder of his presidency, forcing him to rely on veto threats and executive orders to try to shape the direction of national policy. His successor Donald Trump's chief legislative proposals won (tax cuts) or lost (repealing and replacing the Affordable Care Act) depending on the actions of a Republican-controlled Congress, and the 2018 election put Trump in Obama's position, immediately signaled by his capitulation to Nancy Pelosi's House Democrats after a partial five-week government shutdown provoked by their refusal to fund his promised wall on the Mexican border. President Biden accomplished several of his key policy objectives during the 117th Congress despite narrow Democratic control of the House and Senate, but Republican control of the House after the 2022 midterms made that task eminently more challenging.

Because Congress plays such a pivotal role in American politics, its performance as an institution inevitably has a profound effect on how—and how well—the United States is governed. The workings of Congress and its strengths and weaknesses as a governing institution are in turn intimately connected to how its members win and hold office. This chapter examines how the electoral politics depicted in the first six chapters affect the workings of the House and Senate as institutions and the policy choices they make. Its central point is simple: how members win and hold office powerfully affects the internal organization of the houses of Congress, the kind of legislation they produce, and the kind of representation Americans therefore receive. The trend toward increasingly partisan and nationalized electoral politics over the past three decades documented in this edition has thus deeply affected all aspects of congressional life.

REPRESENTATION

Congress is a representative assembly. Put most simply,[1] it is a representative assembly because its members are chosen in competitive popular elections, and if voters do not like what the members are doing, they can vote them out of office. Voters can hold representatives accountable for their actions as long as members care about their own reelection or their party's future, and nearly every member does. Representation is an effect of electoral politics; the electoral process determines the kind of representation Congress provides.

Reflecting the multidimensional electoral process described in earlier chapters, representation in Congress is also multidimensional, and its main elements, while always present, have varied in salience over time. The electoral politics of the late 1960s and 1970s invited a focus on representation of the interests, values, and needs of local constituencies. Since that time, the growing electoral involvement of organized interest groups has increasingly directed members' attention to issues and concerns extending beyond the boundaries of their districts and states. Even more importantly, the expanding electoral role of national parties—organizationally, financially (aided by allied outside groups), and as the locus of intensified ideological conflict—has made the partisan

---

[1] It is a complicated concept; see Hanna Pitkin, *The Concept of Representation* (Berkeley: University of California Press, 1967). For a more recent discussion, see Charles Hunt, *Home Field Advantage: Roots, Reelection, and Representation in the Modern Congress* (Ann Arbor: University of Michigan Press, 2022).

component of representation much more salient than it was a generation ago. As electoral politics have changed, so too has the nature of representation and, consequently, the particular advantages and pathologies associated with its alternative forms.

POLICY CONGRUENCE

The foremost question regarding representation, at least as judged by research effort, is the extent to which the policy views of people in a state or district are reflected in the policy stances (usually measured by roll-call votes) of the people they elect to Congress. This has not been an easy question to answer. Information on constituency opinion has until very recently been scarce and often unreliable, and it is doubtful that there is any "constituency opinion" on many of the issues Congress faces. Measuring constituents' attitudes challenged the ingenuity of generations of scholars because the one obvious solution—regular, adequately sized sample surveys of a large number of states and districts—has only in the past two decades become feasible.

Earlier studies used demographic indicators, simulations, referendum voting, aggregated national surveys, and small-sample district- and state-level surveys to estimate district and state attitudes. Each of these approaches had drawbacks, and there was the additional problem of establishing some kind of comparability between any of these measures and measures of congressional behavior.[2] Still, researchers could draw a number of general conclusions from this work. Most research suggested that congressional roll-call votes were indeed related to district opinion, however estimated, although the strength of the connection varied across issue dimensions and was never overwhelmingly large. The relationships were strongest when votes and attitudes were combined and reduced to a few general dimensions—for example, domestic welfare policy or civil rights for minorities—and weaker for specific votes on single pieces of legislation.[3] The connection was also stronger if the constituency was defined as the member's supporters

---

[2]Walter J. Stone, "Measuring Constituency-Representative Linkages: Problems and Prospects," *Legislative Studies Quarterly* 4 (1979): 624–26; Catherine Shapiro et al., "Linking Constituency Opinion and Senate Voting Scores: A Hybrid Explanation," *Legislative Studies Quarterly* 15 (1990): 599–622; Larry M. Bartels, "Constituency Opinion and Congressional Policy Making: The Reagan Defense Buildup," *American Political Science Review* 84 (1991): 457–74.

[3]Compare Stone, "Linkages," with Gillian Dean, John Siegfried, and Leslie Ward, "Constituency Preference and Potential Economic Gain: Cues for Senate Voting on the Family Assistance Plan," *American Politics Quarterly* 9 (1981): 341–56.

(defined by voting or partisanship).[4] In the past two decades, survey samples large enough for estimating district-level preferences have allowed for more precise estimation of district-level ideological preferences, and analyses of these data have found the roll-call voting patterns of Democrats to be related strongly to their district's ideological median, the more so as it becomes increasingly conservative, whereas Republicans are responsive primarily to their own district partisans' ideological median and to the proportion of extreme conservatives they represent.[5] A direct comparison of the influence of the median constituent and the median primary voter in the member's party on twenty specific roll-call votes taken in the 111th to 113th Congresses produced a similar result. Members' votes on the bills reflected the preferences of both district and party medians, but the party median dominated, especially among Republicans, who were estimated to be about five times as responsive to the primary as to the general electorate, with Democrats by comparison only about twice as responsive to their core supporters.[6]

Broad ideological responsiveness is accompanied (and sometimes subverted) by narrower responsiveness to politically important constituency subgroups. Members form differentiated images of their constituencies and have a good idea of whose votes keep them in office. It is thus no surprise that they are attuned to the demands of some groups more than others—particularly those who express intense preferences and form part of a member's electoral coalition.[7] Members are under no great pressure to vote with the median district or party voter on the many specific votes about which most constituents are uninformed and comparatively indifferent. Members need only take care to cast "explainable" votes, freeing them to vote with party leaders or to please influential subgroups. On the other hand, anyone who consistently or conspicuously votes contrary to the wishes of his or her constituents is likely to run into trouble. Voters, in aggregate, do form passably accurate notions of their

---

[4]Stone, "Linkages," 632–34.

[5]Chris Tausanovitch and Christopher Warshaw, "Representation in the U.S. House: The Link between Constituents and Roll Calls in the 108th–111th Congresses" (manuscript, Department of Political Science Stanford University, April 2011); Joshua D. Clinton, "Representation in Congress: Constituents and Roll Calls in the 106th House," *Journal of Politics* 68 (2006): 397–409.

[6]Seth Hill, "Two Steps to Win: Balancing Representation of Primary and General Electorates in Congress" (paper presented at the annual meeting of the Midwest Political Science Association, Chicago, Illinois, April 16–18, 2015).

[7]For a set of careful case studies demonstrating this reality, see Benjamin G. Bishin, *Tyranny of the Minority: The Subconstituency Politics Theory of Representation* (Philadelphia: Temple University Press, 2009).

representatives' voting patterns, and members who stray too far from home suffer at the polls.[8]

Most members become adept at anticipating how their voters will respond to their actions. As Richard F. Fenno Jr. pointed out, the pursuit of reelection is what makes representation of this sort possible:

> There is no way that the act of representing can be separated from the act of getting elected. If the congressman cannot win and hold the votes of some people, he cannot represent any people. Further, he cannot represent any people unless he knows, or makes an effort to know, who they are, what they think, and what they want; and it is by campaigning for electoral support among them that he finds out such things. During the expansionist stage of his constituency career, particularly, he probably knows his various constituencies as well as it is possible to know them. It is, indeed, by such campaigning, by going home a great deal, that a congressman develops a complex and discriminating set of perceptions about his constituents.[9]

This knowledge is the basis for making judgments about what constituents want or need from politics. Two-way communication is essential to representation. The stress that members of Congress put on their accessibility invites communication from constituents at the same time that it attracts their support. The knowledge and work it takes to win and hold a district not only establish the basis for policy congruence but also let the member know when it is irrelevant or unnecessary.

CONSTITUENTS, INTERESTS, AND CAUSES

Research by Fenno and other scholars makes it clear that there is much more to representation than policy congruence. Members certainly "represent" their constituents in important ways by helping them cope with the federal

---

[8]Robert S. Erikson, "Roll Calls, Reputations, and Representation in the U.S. Senate," *Legislative Studies Quarterly* 15 (1990): 623–42; Patricia A. Hurley, "Partisan Representation, Realignment, and the Senate in the 1980s," *Journal of Politics* 53 (February 1991): 3–33; Amy B. Schmidt, Lawrence W. Kenny, and Rebecca B. Morton, "Evidence on Electoral Accountability in the U.S. Senate: Are Unfaithful Agents Really Punished?," *Economic Inquiry* 34 (July 1996): 545–67; Brandice Canes-Wrone, David Brady, and John F. Cogan, "Out of Step, Out of Office: Electoral Accountability and House Members' Voting," *American Political Science Review* 96 (March 2002): 127–40; Stephen Ansolabehere and Philip Edward Jones, "Constituents' Responses to Congressional Roll Call Voting, "*American Journal of Political Science* 54 (July 2010): 583–97; Jamie L. Carson et al., "The Electoral Costs of Party Loyalty in Congress," *American Journal of Political Science* 54 (July 2010): 598–616; Brandice Canes-Wrone and Michael R. Kistner "Out of Step and Still in Congress? Electoral Consequences of Incumbent and Challenger Positioning across Time," *Quarterly Journal of Political Science*: 17 (July 2022): 389–420.

[9]Richard F. Fenno Jr., *Home Style: House Members in Their Districts* (Boston: Little, Brown, 1978), 233.

bureaucracy, bringing in public works projects, helping local governments and other groups take advantage of federal programs, or helping an overseas relative get permanent resident status. Particularized benefits, as these are called, are still benefits, and an important part of representation is making sure one's constituents get their share.

Members who become spokespeople for interests and causes not confined to their constituencies provide representation of yet another kind. Some African American members of Congress, notably former representative John Lewis of Georgia for example, tried to speak for all African Americans. Representative Henry Hyde spent much of his lengthy career leading the legislative fight against abortion for the right-to-life movement. Carole Maloney of New York persistently advocated feminist positions on women's issues. Senator Marco Rubio champions global climate change denial. Senator Elizabeth Warren battles for consumers. Most members are not so careless that their commitment to a group or cause upsets their supporting constituency; more often it becomes a way of pleasing constituents (especially core supporters and donors) and so coincides nicely with electoral necessities. But not always. A few members invite consistently strong opposition and regularly court defeat in representing their vision of the national interest. The electoral process, however, tends to weed them out.

On a somewhat more mundane level, the current electoral structure gives representation of a sort to any group that can mobilize people or money to help in campaigns. The views of conservative Christian leaders enjoyed much more respectful attention once they demonstrated their ability to deliver millions of votes. The Tea Party movement pulled congressional Republicans sharply to the right after showing their clout in the 2010 elections. Many of the Democratic women elected in 2018, 2020, and 2022 owe a debt of gratitude to progressive women's organization. Various groups—corporate political action committees (PACs), trade associations, labor unions, and ideological groups that supply campaign resources—help elect congenial candidates and acquire access to them, ensuring that these groups' interests are represented in Congress. Whether this is a manifestation or subversion of democratic representation is the subject of endless debate, but it would be hard to argue that some mechanism is not essential for representing the enormous variety of economic and social interests that the framework of single-member districts cannot encompass.

REPRESENTATION BY REFERENDUM

Congress is broadly representative on another dimension. As we saw in chapter 6, aggregate election results are responsive to national economic and political conditions. When citizens are unhappy with the government's performance—including that of the Congress—the administration's party suffers the consequences. The opposing party picks up more seats, and even those who remain in Congress get the message that they had better recognize new realities. Ronald Reagan was able to win budget victories not only because more Republicans sat in the 97th Congress but also because the remaining Democrats read the election results as a demand that something drastic be done about taxes and inflation. The issue in 1981 was not whether the budget and taxes would be cut but which package of cuts—those of the administration or those of the House Democrats—would be adopted.[10] Similarly, the influx of new House Republicans in 1994 made cuts in domestic spending and action on other items in the Contract with America the top priorities for many of the holdovers as well. After 2006, some congressional Republicans began to go their own way on the Iraq War, abandoning the unwavering support for the Bush administration's policies that had been common only a couple of years earlier. After 2010, the Republican victory compelled both parties to focus for a time on deficit reduction. And after 2018 and especially 2022, some Republicans' fealty to Donald Trump began to wane and they began to take more interest in issues such as global warming.

Aggregate representation of this kind is necessarily crude, and it can operate only when there is some detectable public consensus on the general direction of policy, which is by no means always the case. The energy crisis, designated by Jimmy Carter as the "moral equivalent of war," was certainly the dominant national issue when gas lines developed and energy prices skyrocketed in the late 1970s. But Congress could not produce any systematic plan to cope with it because all of the proposed solutions would impose major costs on politically powerful groups. Budget politics during the Ronald Reagan–George H. W. Bush years assumed a similar character, with the public fed up with the problem—continuing deficits—but badly divided on the solution. Moreover, aggregate shifts are subject to misinterpretation; Clinton's victory in 1992 and Obama's in 2008 were, it turned out, no mandate for liberal domestic policies; nor were the Republican victories in 1994, 2010, 2014, and 2016 mandates for dismantling the welfare state.

DESCRIPTIVE REPRESENTATION

In one particular way, Congress does not represent the American public well at all: demographically. Congress contains a much greater proportion of white, male, college-educated, professional, higher-income people than the population as a whole; the Senate is especially unrepresentative

---

[10]Barbara Sinclair, "Agenda Control and Policy Success: Ronald Reagan and the 97th House," *Legislative Studies Quarterly* 10 (August 1985): 291–314.

by these criteria. Even the creation of minority-majority districts after 1990 did not eliminate racial underrepresentation in the House, although the gap did narrow. African Americans now comprise 12 percent of voting-age citizens and made up 13 percent of the House and 3 percent of the Senate in the 118th Congress (2023–24); Latinos make up 13 percent of eligible voters but comprised 12 percent of the House and 6 percent of the Senate. And despite the striking success of women candidates in the past three elections (2018–2022), women, who make up a majority of the voting-age population (51 percent), held only 29 percent of House seats and 25 percent of Senate seats in the 118th Congress.[11]

These numbers mask a stark demographic difference between the congressional parties. After the 2022 election, the Democrats, already comparatively diverse, became more so; 43 percent of House Democrats in the 118th Congress are women, 47 percent are ethnic or racial minorities, and only 35 percent are white men. In contrast, nearly 80 percent of House Republicans are white men; only 16 percent are women, and only 11 percent are nonwhite. Of the record twenty-five women senators, sixteen are Democrats. Ten House and two Senate Democrats are from the lesbian, gay, bisexual, transgender, and queer (LGBTQ) community; only one congressional Republican identifies as other than straight. Every Republican senator and all but two Republican representatives are Christians; about 13 percent of House Democrats and 15 percent of Senate Democrats are not. Descriptively, the congressional parties represent starkly different Americas in the 118th Congress.[12]

Occupationally, 30 percent of House members and 51 percent of senators are lawyers; a blue-collar background or an advanced science degree is rare.[13] Congress also boasts a much higher proportion of millionaires—about half of its current membership—than the population at large.

Yet Congress is probably quite representative of the kinds of people who achieve positions of leadership in the great majority of American institutions. It would be unlikely in the extreme for an electoral system such as the one described in this book to produce a Congress that looks

---

[11]Katherine Schaeffer, "U.S. Congress Continues to Grow in Racial, Ethnic Diversity," *Pew Research Center*, January 9, 2023, https://www.pewresearch.org/fact-tank/2023/01/09/u-s-congress-continues-to-grow-in-racial-ethnic-diversity/; Rebecca Leppert and Drew Desilver, "118th Congress Has a Record Number of Women," *Pew Research Center*, January 3, 2023, https://www.pewresearch.org/fact-tank/2023/01/03/118th-congress-has-a-record-number-of-women/.

[12]Katherine Schaeffer, "The Changing Face of Congress in 8 Charts," *Pew Research Center*, February 7, 2023, https://www.pewresearch.org/fact-tank/2023/02/07/the-changing-face-of-congress/.

[13]Jennifer Manning, "Membership of the 118th Congress: A Profile," *Congressional Research Service*, March 13, 2023, https://crsreports.congress.gov/product/pdf/R/R47470.

anything like a random sample of the voting-age population. What it does produce is a sample of local elites from a remarkably diverse nation. And from this perspective, at times the electoral politics of Congress generates legislative bodies that are too representative of the myriad divisions in American society.

Like the members of Congress whom we elect, we Americans want to have it both ways. We enjoy the programs and benefits that the federal government provides, but we dislike paying the price in the form of increased taxes, higher inflation, and greater government regulation. Public opinion surveys routinely find solid majorities in favor of government guarantees of jobs and current or greater levels of spending on the environment, education, the homeless, Social Security, and health care. The same polls find equally solid majorities believing that the federal government is too large, spends too much money, and is too intrusive in people's lives. We want Congress to balance the budget, but we want it to do so without raising taxes or reducing benefits and services.[14] When Congress is stalemated, enacts self-contradictory policies, or produces large budget deficits, it accurately reflects our own disagreement, confusion, and self-contradictory preferences. As David Mayhew pointed out, "Half the adverse criticism of Congress … is an indirect criticism of the public itself."[15]

POLICY CONSEQUENCES

Electoral incentives and processes have characteristic policy consequences—and pathologies. The electoral individualism characteristic of the 1970s and 1980s, and the much more party-centered electoral politics of recent years, have thus shaped congressional policy making in distinct ways that have posed a distinct set of problems for the institution.

Particularism

During the heyday of candidate-centered, incumbent-dominated electoral politics, a familiar target for congressional critics' scorn was members' notorious affection for policies that produce particularized benefits.[16] Electoral logic inspired members to promote narrowly targeted programs, projects, and tax breaks for constituents and supporting groups without worrying about their impact on spending or revenues. Recipients notice and appreciate such specific and identifiable benefits and show

---

[14]Gary C. Jacobson, *The Electoral Origins of Divided Government: Competition in U.S. House Elections, 1946–1988* (Boulder, CO: Westview Press, 1990), 106–12.

[15]David R. Mayhew, *Congress: The Electoral Connection* (New Haven, CT: Yale University Press, 1974), 140.

[16]Mayhew, *Congress*, 53–54.

their gratitude to the legislator responsible at election time. Because the benefits come at the expense of general revenues, no one's share of the cost of any specific project or tax break is large enough to notice. It thus made political sense for members to pursue local or group benefits that were paid for nationally even if the costs clearly outweighed the benefits.[17] Conversely, there is no obvious payoff for opposing any particular local or group benefit because the savings are spread so thinly among taxpayers that no one notices.

The influence of Congress's fondness for particularized benefits went beyond public works and tax breaks. Virtually any proposal would attract more support if the benefits it conferred could be sliced up and allocated in identifiable packages to individual states and districts. Because everyone in Washington knew this, policies were deliberately designed to distribute particularized benefits broadly, even when that made no objective sense. As a consequence, resources were not concentrated where they were needed most (or where they could be used most efficiently by any objective criterion). They were wasted, and their impact was diluted. Grandly conceived programs emerged in a form that often ensured that they would fail to achieve their objectives, feeding doubts that the federal government could do anything well.[18]

A more fundamental problem with particularized benefits was that Congress was always tempted to overproduce them. Individual members gained politically by *logrolling*, supporting each other's projects or tax breaks in return for support for their own. But when everyone followed such an individually productive strategy, all could end up in worse shape politically when shackled with collective blame for the aggregate consequences. When spending rises, revenues fall, the deficit grows, inefficient government programs proliferate, and the logrolling coalition—the majority party—becomes vulnerable to attack for wastefulness and incompetence.

Indictments of Congress have always included attacks on the traffic in particularized benefits, under the more familiar pejorative label, "pork." In reality, spending for traditional pork-barrel projects has been a small part of the federal budget for years, and such projects have contributed relatively little to budget deficits. The $29 billion spent on 9,963 earmarked projects in the 2006 budget set a new record but still

---

[17]Jeffrey Lazarus, "Giving People What They Want: The Distribution of Earmarks in the U.S. House of Representatives," *American Journal of Political Science* 54 (April 2010): 351–52.

[18]See, for example, R. Douglas Arnold, "The Local Roots of Domestic Policy," in *The New Congress*, eds. Thomas E. Mann and Norman J. Ornstein (Washington, DC: American Enterprise Institute, 1981), 272.

amounted to only about 1 percent of federal outlays; by 2010, the total was down to $16.5 billion, just .4 percent of federal spending.[19] As symbols of waste, however, earmarked pork-barrel projects are irresistible; for example, the $223 million earmarked in an appropriations bill for a "bridge to nowhere" in Alaska became the target of universal ridicule that contributed to the congressional Republicans' woes in 2006.[20]

Many of the Republicans first elected in the 1990s portrayed themselves as scourges of pork, but few of them declined to support local projects that would benefit their constituents. For example, Enid Green Waldholtz of Utah, while celebrating her part in a vote to balance the budget, circumvented a Transportation Appropriations Subcommittee rule against earmarked highway projects to secure a $5 million grant for work on Interstate 15 in Salt Lake City. Greg Ganske of Iowa fought to continue funding for local mass-transit and recreational projects initiated by an incumbent he had tagged as a wasteful spender and defeated in 1994. As Ganske put it, "I see my primary role as trying to [help] government be more fiscally responsible than it has been in the past," but "it's also part of a congressman's job to represent his district."[21] Exactly. Pork drew the special scorn of the Republican's Tea Party conservatives in the 2010 campaigns, and after the election the new Republican House majority formally swore off earmarks. A true end to earmarking would be a remarkable transformation, however, because most members have long been convinced that delivering such local benefits pays important electoral dividends. A comment by Minnesota Republican Michele Bachman, then a leading voice of the Tea Party faction, suggests that idealism would not trump more practical considerations: "Advocating for transportation projects for one's district does not in my mind equate to an earmark."[22]

The earmark moratorium was readopted for the 114th and 115th Congresses, but members have discovered alternative ways to channel federal resources to their districts, for the incentives to deliver particularized benefits to constituents remain powerful. Walter Oleszek catalogued "earmarks by another name. The techniques employed included 'lettermarks,' members writing to administrators to urge that home-related

[19]Robert Longley, "The Decade in Pork: Ten Years of Ear Mark Spending," *About US Government*, http://usgovinfo.about.com/od/federalbudgetprocess/a/porkdecade.htm, accessed April 1, 2010.

[20]The bridge would connect the small Alaskan city of Ketchikan (population 14,770) to an island with about fifty residents, which also has the city's airport, replacing a seven-minute ferry ride.

[21]Juliana Gruenwald, "Freshmen Walk Tightrope to Satisfy Voters," *Congressional Quarterly Weekly Report*, May 27, 1995, 1524–26.

[22]Kerry Young, "An Earmark by Any Other Name," *CQ Weekly*, November 22, 2010, 2700.

projects be funded; 'phonemarks,' calling executive officials to request money for projects in their states or districts; and 'soft marks,' simply 'suggesting' to agency officials that money should be spent on the lawmaker's project."[23] Still, the formal ban on earmarks has made trafficking in particularized benefits more difficult, denying House Speakers John Boehner and Paul Ryan as well as Senate Majority Leader Mitch McConnell an important bargaining chip that earlier party leaders had routinely traded for support as they sought to build legislative coalitions. House Republicans considered lifting the ban during the 115th Congress but did not act. Rules adopted by the new Democratic majority in the 116th Congress allowed earmarks, subject to transparency requirements and other safeguards against corruption they had adopted in 2007. In a conference rules meeting held in November 2022, Republicans voted against a proposed earmark ban, allowing earmarks to continue to be utilized in the 118th Congress.[24]

Serving the Organized

Another important consequence of electoral politics—in any era or form—is that Congress serves the vocal, organized, and active.[25] The system naturally favors any politically attentive group that is present in significant numbers in a large number of states or districts. The best examples are veterans (widely distributed, well organized) and Social Security and Medicare recipients (widely distributed, large in numbers, consistent as voters). Large numbers are not, however, essential for groups to be influential. Organization and money also matter. It is easy to exaggerate the threat that PACs and independent campaign organizations pose to democracy,[26] but their electoral importance is undeniable, and it would be surprising if their political clout were not proportionate. They need not "buy" members with their contributions to be effective. Some of the most successful groups—the National Rifle Association (zealous opponents of gun-control legislation) is perhaps the best example—win by the implicit threat to finance and work for the opponents of members who

---

[23]Walter J. Oleszek, *Congressional Procedures and the Policy Process*, 9th ed. (Washington, DC: Congressional Quarterly Press, 2014), 61; see also Ron Nixon, "Congress Appears to Be Trying to Get around Earmark Ban," *New York Times*, February 5, 2012.

[24]Aidan Quigley and Lindsey McPherson, "House GOP Votes Down Earmark Ban Proposal," *Roll Call*, November 30, 2022, https://rollcall.com/2022/11/30/pressure-builds-on-mccarthy-as-house-gop-earmarks-vote-nears/

[25]Mayhew, *Congress*, 130–31.

[26]Michael J. Malbin, "Of Mountains and Molehills: PACs, Campaigns, and Public Policy," in *Parties, Interest Groups, and Campaign Finance Laws*, ed. Michael J. Malbin (Washington, DC: American Enterprise Institute, 1980), 152–210; Frank J. Sorauf, *Money in American Elections* (Glenview, IL: Scott, Foresman, 1988), 307–17.

do not support their positions. A few instances where such groups have helped to defeat seemingly entrenched incumbents are sufficient to keep most members representing districts where such groups are a force from taking them on.

The prospect of being targeted by any group with formidable campaign resources is unsettling; most members prefer to keep a low profile, avoiding votes that consistently offend active, well-organized interests. During the 1970s, for example, Environmental Action, a conservation lobbying group, compiled and publicized a list of the "Dirty Dozen," twelve congressmen who had (by Environmental Action's standards) bad records on environmental issues and seemed vulnerable. Over the course of five elections, twenty-four of the fifty-two who made the "Dirty Dozen" list were defeated. A consultant who worked on the campaigns claimed that the tactic "was very effective at making congressmen think twice about certain votes. There were numerous examples of members or their staff calling and saying 'Is the congressman close to being on the list?' or 'Is this vote going to be used to determine the list?'"[27] The League of Conservation Voters (LCV) revived the tactic in 1996, again with considerable success. In elections from 1996 through 2012, more than half of the 118 candidates targeted were eventually defeated, including more than forty incumbents and nine House members trying to move up to the Senate. The tactic's potential was underlined by the reaction of Bob Dornan, a flamboyant conservative with a career LCV score of about ten on a hundred-point scale, to being put on the list in 1998. "In my heart," he said, "I'm a Greenpeace kind of guy."[28]

Keeping a low profile to avoid becoming a target became more difficult after the congressional reforms of the 1970s. Rule changes intended to open congressional activities to greater public scrutiny worked; the action became more visible, with more public meetings and more recorded votes. Members were thereby exposed to more pressure from interest and constituency groups. Lobbyists were quick to take advantage, with increasing sophistication and effectiveness. Shrewd interest groups learned to combine their work in Washington with work at the grassroots level, organizing a stream of messages from the district that, at the very least, encouraged members to listen attentively to the pitch made by the group's Washington agents. Conducting such campaigns has

---

[27]Bill Keller, "The Trail of the 'Dirty Dozen,'" *Congressional Quarterly Weekly Report*, March 21, 1981, 510.

[28]League of Conservation Voters, http://www.lcv.org/dirtydozen/callahan_postmt.htm, accessed June 3, 1999; more recent data are at League of Conservation Voters, "Elections: 2013–2014 Endorsements," http://www.lcv.org/campaigns/endorsements, accessed March 12, 2015.

become easier with the spread of modern communications technology and the emergence of professionals who organize grassroots campaigns for a living—if a group has the money to pay for them.

The growth of interest-group activity, combined with the expanding financial role of PACs, transformed congressional lobbying. Raymond Bauer, Ithiel de Sola Pool, and Lewis A. Dexter's classic study of lobbying in the 1950s described a process dominated by insiders. It was mainly a matter of friends talking to friends. Lobbyists worked through allies in Congress, encouraging them to pursue legislative projects that they were already inclined to favor by helping them do the necessary work. Opponents were ignored; pressure tactics in the insular social world of Congress were felt to be counterproductive. Not surprisingly, members regarded lobbying as basically benign and lobbyists as a resource to exploit.[29]

Few members would take such a sanguine view today. Insiders still lobby in the old way, although most of them now supplement their work with outside activities. Some PACs have been created at the behest of Washington lobbyists, who view them as a means of making inside work more effective.[30] But a host of activists and organizations working to influence Congress from the outside have joined them. An effective outside strategy does not rely on maintaining friendly relations with members, so outsiders are free to use pressure tactics, including explicit threats of electoral revenge, against members who oppose their views. The threats may come from factions within the party; for example, Republican incumbents deemed insufficiently conservative by right-wing advocacy groups risk being targeted in primary elections.

All of these developments reduce members' political maneuverability. The visibility of action and the growing capacity of organized groups to raise electoral trouble make it harder to engage in a politics of accommodation and compromise. It is not surprising that congressional enthusiasm for sunshine waned in the 1980s and that much of the important legislative action moved back behind closed doors or that House leaders of both parties became increasingly inclined to adopt more restrictive rules on bills sent to the floor, seeking to exercise tight control over the entire legislative process in order, among other goals, to minimize opportunities for interest groups to persuade backbenchers to bolt the party on bills important to the leadership.[31]

---

[29]Raymond A. Bauer, Ithiel de Sola Pool, and Lewis Anthony Dexter, *American Business and Public Policy* (New York: Atherton, 1968).

[30]Theodore J. Eismeier and Philip H. Pollock III, "Political Action Committees: Varieties of Organization and Strategy," in *Money and Politics in the United States*, ed. Michael J. Malbin (Washington, DC: American Enterprise Institute, 1984), 124–26.

[31]Barbara Sinclair, *Unorthodox Lawmaking: New Legislative Processes in the U.S. Congress*, 4th ed. (Washington, DC: Congressional Quarterly Press, 2012).

Responsiveness without Responsibility

The scramble for local benefits, the sensitivity to organized interests, and the dilemmas created by a public demanding mutually contradictory policies point to the fundamental danger in the kind of representation encouraged by candidate-centered electoral politics: individual responsiveness without collective responsibility. The safest way to cope with contradictory policy demands is to be acutely sensitive to what constituents and other politically important groups want in taking positions or providing benefits but to avoid responsibility for the costs they would impose. It does not help matters when members are rewarded individually for taking pleasing positions but are not punished for failing to turn them into national policy or, when they do become policy, seeing that they work.[32] Nor does it help when members thrive by delivering concentrated benefits to localities or special interests without being held accountable for the diffuse costs they impose on everyone else. As long as members are not held individually responsible for their collective performance in governing, a crucial form of representation is missing. Responsiveness is insufficient without responsibility.

The only known instrument for imposing collective responsibility on legislators is the political party.[33] Fiorina put the classic argument cogently:

> A strong political party can generate collective responsibility by creating incentives for leaders, followers, and popular supporters to think and act in collective terms. First, by providing party leaders with the capability (e.g., control of institutional patronage, nominations, etc.) to discipline party members, genuine leadership becomes possible. Legislative output is less likely to be a least common denominator—a residue of myriad conflicting proposals—and more likely to consist of a program actually intended to solve a problem or move the nation in a particular direction. Second, the subordination of individual office holders to the party lessens their ability to separate themselves from party actions. Like it or not their performance becomes identified with the performance of the collectivity to which they belong. Third, with individual candidate variation greatly reduced, voters have less incentive to support individuals and more to support or oppose the party as a whole. And fourth, the circle closes as party-line voting in the electorate provides party leaders with the incentive to propose policies which will earn the support of a national majority, and party backbenchers with the personal incentive to cooperate with leaders in the attempt to compile a good record for the party as a whole.[34]

---

[32]Mayhew, *Congress*, 115.

[33]Mayhew, *Congress*, 174–77; Morris P. Fiorina, "The Decline of Collective Responsibility in American Politics," *Daedalus* 109 (Summer 1980): 25–45.

[34]Fiorina, "Decline of Collective Responsibility," 26–27.

Pristine party government has never been characteristic of American politics, to be sure, but all of its necessary elements eroded with the electoral changes of the 1960s and 1970s. The emerging issues raised by the civil rights movement, the Vietnam War, the energy crisis, the environmental movement, *Roe v. Wade*, and the women's movement initially split both parties, but they cut across people, states, districts, and thus members of Congress in different ways. Coherent and consistent battle lines were absent, so policy coalitions tended to be ad hoc and fluid.[35] Conditions encouraged members to operate as individual political entrepreneurs and rewarded them when they did.

These developments exacerbated the unresolved tension between individual and collective goals inherent in congressional life. Although members won and held seats in good part through their own personal efforts, their collective rather than individual achievements shaped their parties' reputations and determined Congress's institutional significance. The problem is that party reputations and Congress's institutional strength are, for members, collective goods. Everyone in the majority benefits if their party builds a reputation for governing well, and all members benefit from belonging to a powerful and respected legislative body. Members enjoy these benefits, however, regardless of whether they contribute to achieving them.

The electoral needs of individual members and the practices required to make the House and Senate effective governing institutions often generate conflicting demands. The potential cost of ignoring the former is specific and personal: loss of office. The potential cost of ignoring the latter is diffuse and collective: an imperceptible marginal weakening of authority or decline in party stature. It is obvious where the balance of incentives lies. David Mayhew spelled out the danger nearly fifty years ago in his classic *Congress: The Electoral Connection*: "Efficient pursuit of electoral goals by members gives no guarantee of institutional survival. Quite the contrary. It is not too much to say that if all members did nothing but pursue their electoral goals, Congress would decay or collapse."[36] The same holds true for the congressional parties.

THE CONGRESSIONAL PARTIES: DECLINE AND REVIVAL

Congress has not collapsed. Because its members do care about more than reelection, they adopt institutional structures and processes designed to harness individual energies to collectively important ends.

---

[35]Barbara Sinclair, "Coping with Uncertainty: Building Coalitions in the House and Senate," in *The New Congress*, eds. Thomas E. Mann and Norman J. Ornstein (Washington, DC: American Enterprise Institute, 1981), 215.

[36]Mayhew, *Congress*, 141.

The most important of these institutional structures by far are the congressional parties. Even in periods when party government as outlined by Fiorina has not been remotely descriptive of American realities, the congressional parties have been at the center of collective action. Party leaders have always been responsible for producing results that bolster the party's collective reputation in the face of persistent incentives for individual members to ride free on the efforts of others.[37] Moreover, Congress's decentralized, specialized legislative committee systems—another set of institutions offering incentives for individual members to provide collectively beneficial goods[38]—could not work effectively without some means of coordinating the activities of its diverse parts.

Members of Congress recognize that the parties make a vital contribution to partisan and institutional achievement, and not a little of the deference accorded to party leaders derives from that knowledge.[39] Still, party leaders face the basic reality that members keep their jobs by pleasing voters, not the congressional party. Leaders can count on loyalty only to the degree that members believe that the ultimate career payoff is higher for loyalty than for defection.

To be effective, party leaders need the authority to reward cooperation with, or punish defection from, the party's collective enterprise. Just how much authority members are willing to delegate to leaders depends on how worried they are that leaders might use it in ways harmful to their careers or commitments. In general, the more unified that party members are in terms of ideology and policy preferences, the more authority they are willing to delegate to leaders. The more internally divided a party, the more reluctant its members are to give leaders the resources necessary to enforce party discipline, for who knows what a leader representing the wrong faction might do with them?[40]

During the 1950s and 1960s, Democratic leaders had to contend with a fractious membership whose differences were rooted in the diverse constituencies they were elected to represent. Hence, they considered it their job not so much to compel members to toe a party line

---

[37]Gary W. Cox and Mathew D. McCubbins, *Legislative Leviathan: Party Government in the House* (Berkeley: University of California Press, 1993).

[38]Mayhew, *Congress*, 85–96.

[39]Mayhew, *Congress*, 145–49.

[40]See John Aldrich and David Rohde, "The Logic of Conditional Party Government: Revisiting the Electoral Connection," in *Congress Reconsidered*, eds. Lawrence C. Dodd and Bruce I. Oppenheimer, 269–92 (Washington, DC: CQ Press, 2001).

as to discover it, to find and promote policies that party members could willingly support because doing so enhanced their own local reputations as well as their party's image. They were quick to recognize electoral necessity; members were expected to "vote the district first" when conflicts with the party's position arose, and they were encouraged to serve their constituents diligently in order to keep the seat for the party. There was nothing odd about this, for Democratic leaders were chosen to serve their party's members as they wish to be served. Such permissiveness simply reflected a widely acknowledged necessity arising from the diversity of the party's national coalition and its members' notions about how to win reelection.

The Democrats were well aware of the costs as well as the benefits of tolerant party leadership and in the 1970s introduced changes designed to strengthen the party's hand. The Speaker, who leads the majority party in the House, was given effective control of the Rules Committee, which directs the flow of legislation coming to the floor of the House, and dominant influence on the caucus's Steering and Policy Committee, which, among other things, makes committee assignments. The party's whip organization was enlarged substantially. These and other changes gave the party leaders more tools to coordinate the work of a fragmented legislative body and to exercise party control over lawmaking.

Democrats were willing to strengthen their party's capacity to act collectively because the division that had threatened to split the New Deal Coalition from the beginning—between northern liberals and southern conservatives—had begun to fade. The influx of northerners, industrial development, the movement of conservative southern white voters from the Democratic into the Republican camp, and the Voting Rights Act, which brought African American voters into southern Democratic electorates, gradually undermined the southern Democrats' ideological distinctiveness. As the electoral constituencies of Democrats became more similar across regions, their electoral interests became more consonant. The result was greater party cohesion, permitting stronger leadership.[41] House Democrats also accepted stronger leadership in the 1980s because they recognized the need to act collectively to make a public record as they contended with hostile Republican presidents and, from 1981 to 1987, a Republican Senate. Still, Democratic leaders rarely found it easy to assemble legislative coalitions on major issues, for the party was and remains an ideologically diverse coalition of groups and interests.[42]

---

[41]Cox and McCubbins, *Legislative Leviathan*, 153–57.

[42]David W. Rohde, *Parties and Leaders in the Postreform House* (Chicago: University of Chicago Press, 1991), 162–77.

Republicans delegated much more authority to their leaders when they took over the House in 1995. Unified by the party's Contract with America, as well as by their shared conservative ideology, House Republicans made Newt Gingrich the most powerful Speaker since the revolt against Joseph Cannon in 1910. Meeting in caucus, the Republicans ignored seniority in appointing committee chairs, ratifying without dissent the slate proposed by Gingrich. They also gave Gingrich a strong say in committee assignments, which he used to stack committees with junior allies firmly committed to the Contract with America.

House Republicans gave their leader an unusually strong hand because they believed that his strategy—embodied not only in the Contract with America but also in the guidance he had given so many of them through GOPAC—had given them their majority; they also believed that their performance on the promises in the contract would determine whether they would keep it. Although the contract's influence on voters was small, its impact on the Republican House was enormous, for its promise of quick, focused action made strong leadership indispensable. It did not, however, guarantee that the Speaker would always get his way; for the most zealous of the new Republican representatives, commitment to the spirit of the contract was even more powerful than commitment to Gingrich, and they resisted every compromise on the grounds that voters would punish them for selling out if they did not. Gingrich had to squash a backbench coup in 1997 and eventually resigned from the speakership and Congress after the Republicans' loss of House seats in 1998 was blamed on his mishandling of Clinton's impeachment.

Gingrich's successor, Dennis Hastert, relying on the political skills and strong-arm tactics of Tom DeLay (chief whip in the 104th to 107th Congresses, majority leader in the 108th and part of the 109th), maintained high levels of party discipline through the last Congress of the Clinton administration and the first three congresses of George W. Bush's administration. Democratic Speaker Nancy Pelosi (110th and 111th Congresses) continued the pattern of strong party leadership established by her Republican predecessors. Subsequent Republican Speakers John Boehner (2011–15) and Paul Ryan (2015–19) had rocky tenures, struggling, not always successfully, to prevent splits between the extremely conservative Tea Party faction, later organized as the Freedom Caucus, and the party's more orthodox conservatives. Both retired rather than continue the struggle. Pelosi resumed the speakership in 2019, but not without accepting a three-term limit for her and other senior leaders under pressure from newly elected Democrats who had promised to shake up the Washington establishment.

After a shaky start requiring fifteen ballots to be elected as the new Republican speaker at the beginning of the 118th Congress, Kevin

McCarthy spent the next few months trying to advance the party's agenda without upsetting members of the Freedom Caucus who had initially opposed his selection as speaker. Very little legislation was passed during that time since the Senate was narrowly controlled by Democrats, who had little interest in advancing what many perceived to be the extreme Republican agenda in the House. Meanwhile, former Speaker Nancy Pelosi and her top deputies kept their promise to step aside in favor of a much younger leadership team moving forward. Without any opposition from the rank-and-file membership, Democrats elected Rep. Hakeem Jeffries (NY) as the new minority leader of the party, making him the first Black legislator to lead either party in Congress.

The winds of change flowing from 1994 disturbed even the Senate's tradition of unbridled individualism. In July 1995, the Republican majority imposed six-year term limits on committee chairs and voted to adopt a formal legislative agenda at the start of each Congress. Committee chairs would also henceforth be subject to ratification by a secret vote of the Republican Conference (all Republican members meeting in caucus). These changes (and several more rejected and unsuccessful proposals) were intended to make senior members more responsive to party majorities, making it easier for the party to act collectively. In the 104th Congress, even Senate Republicans were acting as if they had an expanded personal stake in their party's collective performance.[43] Since then, under both Republican and Democratic regimes, individual senators, while remaining a good deal more autonomous than their counterparts in the House, have found themselves under increasing pressure to stick with their parties.

THE REVIVAL OF PARTY COHESION, 1980–2022

The organizational basis for much stronger party government, particularly in the House, developed during the last quarter of the twentieth century. The strengthening of congressional party organizations coincided with and contributed to the clarification of partisan divisions and the increase in party conflict that followed the election of Ronald Reagan in 1980. The budget crunch brought on by the energy crisis of the 1970s deserves a good deal of the credit for the initial change. Congress's electoral and institutional needs mesh most harmoniously when politics can

---

[43]David S. Cloud, "GOP Senators Limit Chairmen to Six Years Heading Panel," *Congressional Quarterly Weekly Report*, July 22, 1995, 2147. There is some evidence that majority party supporters, at least, do have an electoral stake in the Senate's collective reputation; see Monika L. McDermott and David R. Jones, "Congressional Performance, Incumbent Behavior, and Voting in Senate Elections," *Legislative Studies Quarterly* 30 (2005): 235–57.

focus on distributing benefits. In periods of prosperity and growth, public and private resources expand together, and members can busy themselves with the happy chore of figuring out how to divide up a growing pie. Universalistic distributive criteria—something for everyone, regardless of party—are applicable, and logrolling coalitions are relatively easy to assemble. The 1960s were just such a period. The 1970s, however, brought slower growth, higher inflation, and the need for higher taxes to pay for the benefits so generously provided when the economy was booming. Instead of the pleasant prospect of distributing benefits, Congress increasingly faced the bleak task of distributing costs.

Constraints on distributive politics drew even tighter in the 1980s, and although many sources of political cleavage remained, party coherence made a notable comeback. It did so in part because of a development that erected yet another barrier to responsible party government in the full sense, however: the division of government between a Republican White House and a Democratic Congress. After the brief period in 1981 when the Reagan administration won its major budget initiatives by splitting the House Democrats, divided government helped to unify both parties in both houses. On roll-call votes, Republicans continued to line up loyally behind their president. Democrats became increasingly loyal to their party throughout the 1980s and 1990s, and by the George W. Bush administration, both parties in both chambers were achieving the highest party unity scores since *Congressional Quarterly* began keeping track in 1954.

As figures 7.1 and 7.2 indicate, the upward trend in party unity continued through the Obama administration and into the first year of the Biden administration. The figures display the percentage of party unity votes (votes in which majorities of Democrats and Republicans took opposite sides) and the percentage of votes in which party members voted with their party's majority on these votes in the House and Senate since 1954. After falling to a low point during the Richard Nixon and Gerald Ford administrations, party unity in both parties and houses has grown steadily, rising by sixteen to twenty percentage points in both chambers. The proportion of party unity votes also grew irregularly over this period, reaching a high point during Biden's first year before declining somewhat during his second year. Rising party unity reflects both increasing partisan polarization in Congress and majority party leaders' efforts to prevent floor votes on issues that divide their caucuses.

In addition to incentives for the parties to resist administrations controlled by their rivals and to project an image of party competence, members may have also found it more expedient to remain loyal to their parties in recent congresses because of the expanded role of national party committees, leadership PACs, and other allied PACs in recruiting, training, and financing congressional candidates. Members elected as part of

Figure 7.1 House Party Unity, Eisenhower through Biden Administrations

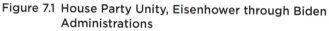

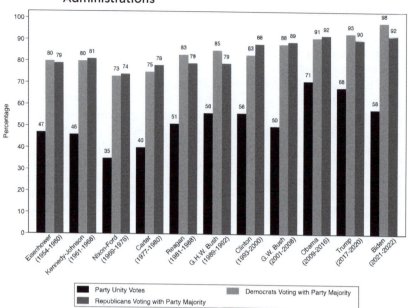

Source: Congressional Quarterly Weekly, online edition.

Figure 7.2 Senate Party Unity, Eisenhower through Biden Administrations

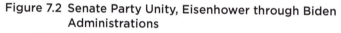

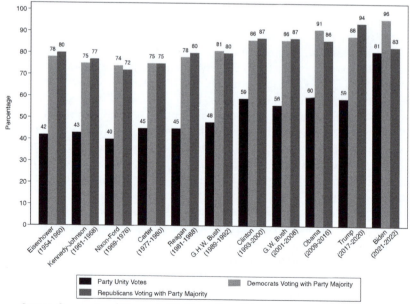

Source: Congressional Quarterly Weekly, online edition.

a team, using common campaign themes and issues and with considerable help from party committees, should be more disposed to cooperate on legislative matters. Members hoping for generous party assistance in future campaigns should be more susceptible to persuasion by leaders who influence the distribution of the party's funds.[44] That said, however, the most crucial contribution to party unity has been the growing ideological distance between the congressional parties.

Ideological Polarization in Congress and the Electorate

The congressional parties have grown more unified internally as they have separated ideologically. Ideological differences between the party coalitions in both houses have widened appreciably since the 1970s, as figures 7.3 and 7.4 demonstrate. The figures display party averages on Poole and Rosenthal's first-dimension NOMINATE score in the House and Senate, respectively, in the 80th to 117th Congresses.

Congressional Republicans have been growing steadily more conservative for more than four decades, and their rightward drift accounts for most of the increase in the ideological gap between the parties over this period. Democrats moved in the opposite direction as Republicans gradually replaced their party's conservative southern members in Congress. Southern Democrats are now ideologically indistinguishable from other Democrats in the House; the few remaining Southern Democrats in the Senate (five in the 117th Congress) continue to vote more moderately than other Democrats. Figure 7.5 shows how the ideological distance between the two parties widened in both chambers; in depicting the longer post-Reconstruction time span, it also shows that these differences were at a historical low during the middle years of the twentieth century but have since grown to their widest extent ever.

Polarization in Presidential Support

A parallel and related trend has been the growing partisan disparity in congressional support for presidential initiatives and preferences, as displayed in figures 7.6 through 7.8. For this analysis, presidential support is measured as the percentage of votes for the president's position on divisive roll calls, defined as those on which fewer than 80 percent of

---

[44]Paul S. Herrnson, *Party Campaigning in the 1980s* (Cambridge, MA: Harvard University Press, 1988); Kevin Leyden and Stephen A. Borelli, "An Investment in Good Will: Party Contributions and Party Unity among U.S. House Members in the 1980s," *American Politics Quarterly* 22 (1994): 421–52; Paul S. Herrnson, "The Impact of Reform on National Party Financing and Campaigning," in *Guide to U.S. Political Parties*, ed. Marjorie R. Hershey (Washington, DC: CQ Press, 2014), 196–208.

Figure 7.3 Ideological Positions of House Party Coalitions, 80th through 117th Congresses

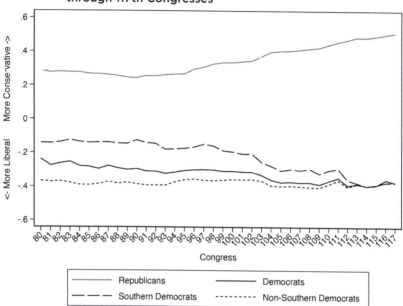

Congress

Republicans   Democrats

Southern Democrats   Non-Southern Democrats

Source: Jeffrey B. Lewis, Keith Poole, Howard Rosenthal, Adam Boche, Aaron Rudkin, and Luke Sonnet, Voteview: http://voteview.com/, accessed March 1, 2023.

Figure 7.4 Ideological Positions of Senate Party Coalitions, 80th through 117th Congresses

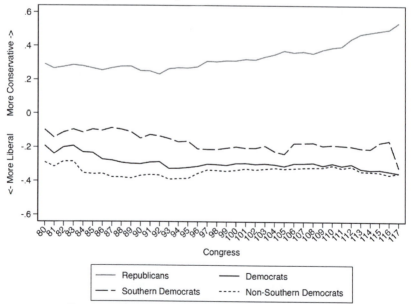

Congress

Republicans   Democrats

Southern Democrats   Non-Southern Democrats

Source: Jeffrey B. Lewis, Keith Poole, Howard Rosenthal, Adam Boche, Aaron Rudkin, and Luke Sonnet, Voteview: http://voteview.com/, accessed March 1, 2023.

Figure 7.5 Ideological Differences between the Congressional Parties, 46th through 117th Congresses

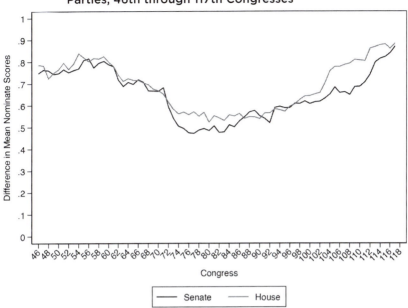

Source: Jeffrey B. Lewis, Keith Poole, Howard Rosenthal, Adam Boche, Aaron Rudkin, and Luke Sonnet, Voteview: http://voteview.com/, accessed March 1, 2023.

Figure 7.6 Presidential Support in the House of Representatives, 83rd through 117th Congresses

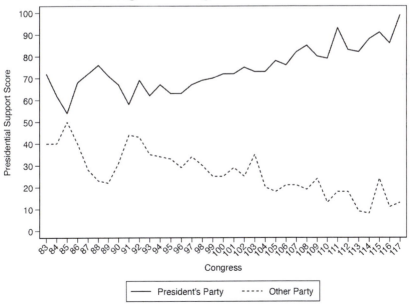

Source: Compiled by George C. Edwards III and posted at Presidency Research (http://presdata.tamu.edu) and Congressional Quarterly Weekly, online edition; annual scores are averaged for each Congress.

Figure 7.7 Presidential Support in the Senate, 83rd through 117th Congresses

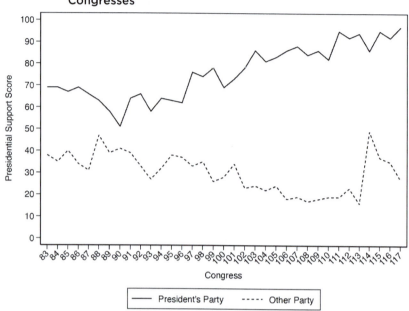

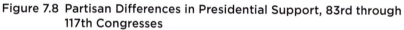

Source: Compiled by George C. Edwards III and posted at Presidency Research (http:// presdata.tamu.edu) and Congressional Quarterly Weekly, online edition; annual scores are averaged for each Congress.

Figure 7.8 Partisan Differences in Presidential Support, 83rd through 117th Congresses

Source: Computed from data in figures 7.6 and 7.7.

members in a chamber voted with the president.[45] Despite some noticeable differences, the figures reveal the same pattern of increasing partisan polarization in presidential support scores that we observe in NOMINATE scores. The trends are clearest in figure 7.8, which traces the partisan gap in average presidential support scores from the Dwight D. Eisenhower administration through the 117th Congress during the Biden administration. The House parties were somewhat more polarized on presidential initiatives than on ideology during the John F. Kennedy and Lyndon B. Johnson administrations, and the Senate parties were somewhat less polarized on presidential initiatives than on ideology during Bill Clinton's first Congress. Still, the widening partisan disparity in presidential support from the Nixon administration onward is unmistakable, and party differences increased during the early years of the Obama administration, although they shrank in the Senate during the final two years of Obama's presidency. The first two years of the Trump administration produced an uptick in the Senate and a modest decline in the House, with an increase in the final two years of the Trump presidency that continued into the first two years of the Biden administration. Both the president's partisans and opposition partisans contributed equally to the trends.

Party Polarization: The Electoral Connection

Plainly, policy representation in Congress has taken on an increasingly partisan cast over the past several decades. If elections shape congressional behavior as strongly as we have argued in this book, then growing party divisions in Congress must reflect concurrent changes in electoral politics, as indeed they do. But the sharpening of partisan conflict in Congress also affects electoral politics by shaping and clarifying the choices faced by voters.

The standard explanation for the rise in party cohesion in Congress since the 1970s is party realignment in the South, which left both congressional parties with more politically homogeneous electoral coalitions, reducing internal disagreements and making stronger party leadership tolerable. This explanation is certainly correct as far as it goes. The realignment of southern political loyalties and electoral habits has been

---

[45]Data on presidential support in Congress were previously compiled by George C. Edward III. More recent data were collected from various issues of *CQ Weekly*. For these figures, the annual scores are averaged for each Congress.

thoroughly documented.[46] As noted in chapter 5, starting from almost nothing in the 1950s, Republicans now enjoy solid majorities of southern partisans, as well as of House and Senate seats.[47] Realignment in the South certainly contributed to the increasing ideological homogeneity of the parties, but it is by no means the whole story. Other forces have also necessarily been at work, for the parties have become more divided ideologically and homogeneous internally outside the South as well.

Both aggregate and survey data reveal a clear constituency basis for the widening of party and ideological divisions in the House and Senate. For example, the district-level presidential vote, taken as a proxy for district partisanship, shows a growing partisan disparity in the electoral constituencies of House Republicans and Democrats (figure 7.9).[48] In 1972, for instance, the vote for Richard Nixon was only 7.6 percentage points higher in districts won by Republicans than in districts won by Democrats. Increasing steeply since then, the difference reached twenty-nine percentage points in 2016 before declining to nearly twenty-seven in 2020. Similarly measured, the electoral bases of the Senate parties have also become more polarized, although in absolute terms the differences are considerably smaller than those in the House (figure 7.10).[49] The gaps between the winners' electoral constituencies have been particularly

---

[46]Earle Black and Merle Black, *Politics and Society in the South* (Cambridge, MA: Harvard University Press, 1987); Paul Frymer, "The 1994 Aftershock: Dealignment or Realignment in the South," in *Midterm: The Elections of 1994 in Context*, ed. Philip A. Klinkner (Boulder, CO: Westview Press, 1995); Richard Nadeau and Harold W. Stanley, "Class Polarization among Native Southern Whites, 1952–1990," *American Journal of Political Science* 37 (August 1993): 900–19; Harold W. Stanley, "Southern Partisan Changes: Dealignment, Realignment, or Both?," *Journal of Politics* 50 (February 1988): 64–88; Martin P. Wattenberg, "The Building of a Republican Regional Base in the South: The Elephant Crosses the Mason-Dixon Line," *Public Opinion Quarterly* 55 (1991): 424–31; M. V. Hood III, Quentin Kidd, and Irwin L. Morris, "Of Byrd[s] and Bumpers: Using Democratic Senators to Analyze Political Change in the South, 1960–1995," *American Journal of Political Science* 43 (1999): 456–87.

[47]Gary C. Jacobson, "Party Polarization in National Politics: The Electoral Connection," in *Congress and the President in a Partisan Era*, eds. Jon R. Bond and Richard Fleisher (Washington, DC: Congressional Quarterly Press, 2000).

[48]Entries for midterm elections are calculated from the presidential vote in the previous election, adjusted for changes in district boundaries, if any; the statistic could not be calculated for 1962 and 1966 because information for reconfigured districts is not available.

[49]The presidential vote gap between the parties' Senate constituencies is smaller than for House districts in part because, with two senators each, some states have split delegations, netting out to zero. But the growth in electoral consistency has also produced a decrease in the proportion of split Senate delegations; at the high point in the 96th Congress (1979–80), 54 percent of the states' Senate delegations were split between the parties; the proportion of split delegations declined to a low of 24 percent in the 108th Congress (2003–04) before rising again modestly to 28 percent in the 114th Congress (2015–16). Since then, the proportion of split delegations has fallen irregularly, reaching a low of 10 percent in the 118th Congress (2023–24).

Figure 7.9 The Polarization of US House Districts, 1952–2022

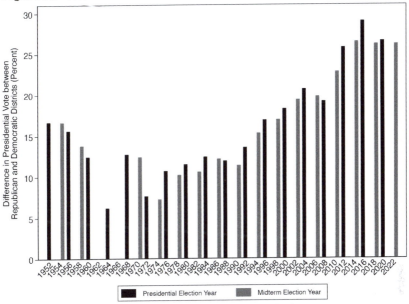

Note: Data for 1962 and 1966 are unavailable because of redistricting.
Source: Compiled by authors.

Figure 7.10 The Polarization of State Constituencies, 1952–2022

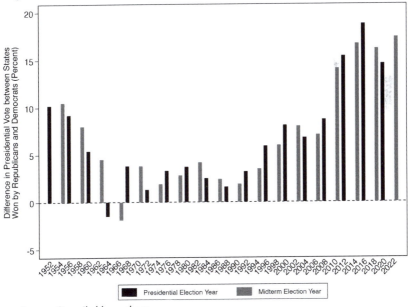

Source: Compiled by authors.

striking during the current decade. Such differences in the respective congressional parties' electoral bases are strongly related to party differences in presidential support as well as in roll-call ideology (as measured by NOMINATE scores), so these trends have clearly contributed to widening the partisan divisions in Congress.[50]

Survey data also provide evidence that the congressional parties represent increasingly distinctive electoral constituencies. Since 1972, the American National Election Studies (ANES) surveys have asked respondents to place themselves on a seven-point ideological scale ranging from extremely liberal to extremely conservative.[51] On average, nearly 80 percent of respondents who say they voted in the House elections are able to locate their position on the scale (and the proportion of voters able to place themselves on the scale has grown over time). As noted in chapter 5 (figure 5.5), the relationships among voters' ideological self-placement, party identification, views on political issues, and voting decisions have all become stronger over the past thirty years, and citizens sort themselves into the appropriate party (given their ideological leanings and positions on issues) a good deal more consistently now than they did in the 1970s, with the largest increases in consistency occurring in the 1990s.[52] In particular, voters locating themselves to the right on the liberal–conservative scale have become much more Republican in their voting habits, as figure 7.11 demonstrates. Comparable data from the exit polls conducted between 1980 and 2022 and the CES surveys conducted since 2006 show the same pattern of change.

Diverging Electoral Constituencies

The growth in partisan coherence, consistency, and loyalty among voters (see chapters 5 and 6) has made the two parties' respective electoral constituencies—that is, the voters who supported the party's winning candidates—politically more homogeneous and more dissimilar. We can measure differences in the ideological makeup of electoral constituencies by subtracting the mean ideological self-placement of ANES and CES respondents who voted for one set of winning candidates from the mean for respondents who voted for another set of winning candidates. Figure 7.12 displays the changes in the ideological distinctiveness of the electoral constituencies of House and Senate Republicans and Democrats

---

[50]Gary C. Jacobson, "Partisan Polarization in Presidential Support: The Electoral Connection," *Congress and the Presidency* 30 (Spring 2003): 8–11.

[51]The categories are extremely liberal, liberal, slightly liberal, moderate or middle-of-the-road, slightly conservative, conservative, and extremely conservative.

[52]Jacobson, "Party Polarization"; Matthew Levendusky, *The Partisan Sort: How Liberals Became Democrats and Conservatives Became Republicans* (Chicago: University of Chicago Press, 2009).

Figure 7.11 Ideology and the House Vote, 1972–2022

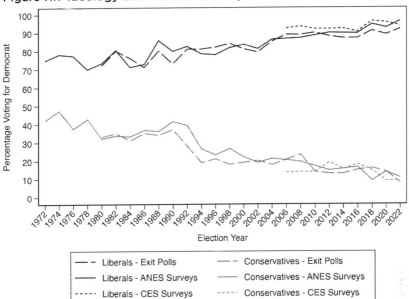

Figure 7.12 Ideological Divergence of Electoral Constituencies of House and Senate Parties, 1972–2022

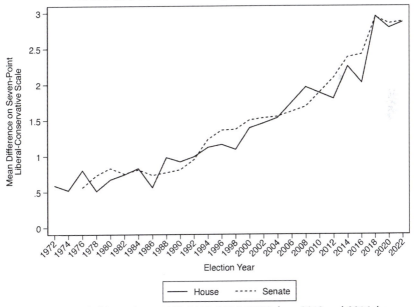

Source: Compiled by authors; 1972–2012, 2016 ANES data; 2012 and 2016 data are from the face-to-face component of the survey; 2014, 2018, 2020, 2022: CES.

Figure 7.13 Shared Electoral Constituencies, US Representative and President, 1956–2020

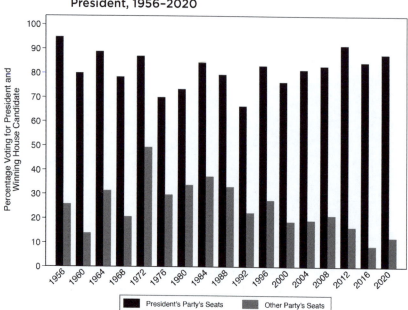

Source: Compiled by authors from ANES data; 2012 and 2016, face-to-face component of the survey; 2020: CES.

since 1972. In the 1970s, the ideological differences between the two parties' electoral constituencies were modest, in the neighborhood of .5 points on this seven-point scale. By 2020, the gaps had more than tripled for both chambers. Realignment in the South explains only part of this change, since the gap between Republican and Democratic constituencies outside the South also grew (from .7 to 2.0 points in the House and from .6 to 2.3 points in the Senate).[53]

Greater partisan consistency in voting has also reduced the proportion of electoral constituents shared by the president and members of Congress representing the opposition party. Figures 7.13 and 7.14 display this trend. For example, when Ronald Reagan took office in 1981, he faced a Congress in which 34 percent of House Democrats' voters and 37 percent of Senate Democrats' voters had also voted for him. When Joseph Biden took office in 2021, he shared only 12 percent of the House Democrats' voters and only 8 percent of the Senate Democrats' voters. The decline in presidential support among opposition-party senators and representatives displayed in figures 7.6 and 7.7 thus accurately reflects

---

[53]Entries for Senate electoral constituencies are calculated from the three biennial surveys up to and including the year indicated on the chart, so that data from voters electing the entire Senate membership are used to calculate each observation.

Figure 7.14 Shared Electoral Constituencies, US Senator and President, 1952–2020

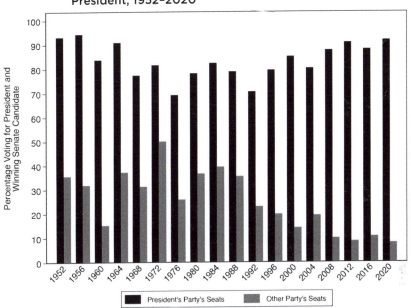

Source: Compiled by authors from ANES data; 2012 and 2016, face-to-face component of the survey; 2020: CES.

changes in their electoral constituencies; with fewer of their own voters favoring the president, they have less reason to support his initiatives.

Chicken or Egg?

The survey evidence, then, is consistent with the idea that partisan polarization in Congress reflects electoral changes that have left the parties with more homogeneous and more dissimilar electoral coalitions. When the focus of analysis is Congress, electoral change seems to be the independent variable: Changes in roll-call voting reflect changes in electoral coalitions. When the focus is on elections, however, it becomes apparent that causality works at least as strongly in the opposite direction: Voters sort themselves out politically by responding to the alternatives represented by the two parties.

Realignment in the South followed the national Democratic Party's decision to champion civil rights for African Americans and the Republican Party's choice of Senator Barry Goldwater, who voted against the Civil Rights Act of 1964, as its standard-bearer that year. Partisan divisions on the abortion issue emerged first in Congress and then in the electorate.[54] Electorates diverged ideologically after the parties had diverged ideologically; the divisions in Congress during and after the Reagan years

---

[54]Greg D. Adams, "Abortion: Evidence of an Issue Evolution," *American Journal of Political Science* 41 (1997): 718–73.

left the two parties with more distinctive images, making it easier for voters to recognize their appropriate ideological homes. Conservatives moved into the Republican ranks, while liberals remained Democrats.[55]

This is not to say, however, that members of Congress simply followed their own ideological fancies, leaving voters no choice but to line up accordingly. As vote-seeking politicians, they naturally anticipated voters' potential responses and so were constrained by them. The Republican "southern strategy" emerged because Republican candidates sensed an opportunity to win converts among socially conservative white southerners. Ambitious Republicans adopted conservative positions on social issues to attract voters alienated by the Democrats' tolerance of nontraditional lifestyles but indifferent at best to Republican economic policies. Democrats emphasized choice on abortion because they recognized its appeal to well-educated, affluent voters who might otherwise think of themselves as Republicans. In the budgetary wars of the past few decades, Democrats have vigorously defended middle-class entitlements such as Social Security and Medicare, while Republicans have championed tax cuts because each position has a large popular constituency. In adopting positions, then, politicians are guided by the opportunities and constraints presented by configurations of voter opinion on political issues. The growth of party polarization in Congress has depended on members' expectations that voters would reward, or at least not punish, their voting with their party's majority.[56]

The relationship between partisan consistency within Congress and within the electorate is thus inherently interactive. Between the 1970s and the 1990s, changes in electoral and congressional politics reinforced one another, encouraging greater partisan consistency and cohesion in both. An important consequence of the increased party loyalty among members of Congress and the ideological polarization of the congressional parties is that the linkage between citizens' voting decisions and the actions of the

---

[55]Alan I. Abramowitz and Kyle L. Saunders, "Ideological Realignment in the U.S. Electorate," *Journal of Politics* 60 (1998): 634–52; Edward G. Carmines and Geoffrey C. Layman, "Issue Evolution in Postwar American Politics: Old Certainties and Fresh Tensions," in *Present Discontents: American Politics in the Very Late Twentieth Century*, ed. Byron E. Shafer (Chatham, NJ: Chatham House, 1997); Alan I. Abramowitz, *The Disappearing Center: Engaged Citizens, Polarization, and American Democracy* (New Haven, CT: Yale University Press, 2010). Geoffrey C. Layman and Thomas M. Carsey, in "Party Polarization and 'Conflict Extension' in the American Electorate," *American Journal of Political Science* 46 (October 2002): 786–802, argue that the ideological realignment among voters is confined mainly to strong partisans.

[56]For an interesting discussion of the interplay between party loyalty and district preferences over time, see Stephen Ansolabehere, James M. Snyder Jr., and Charles Stewart III, "Candidate Positioning in U.S. House Elections," *American Journal of Political Science* 45 (January 2001): 136–59.

Figure 7.15 Variance in Roll-Call Ideology Explained by District Presidential Vote and Party, 83rd through 117th Congresses

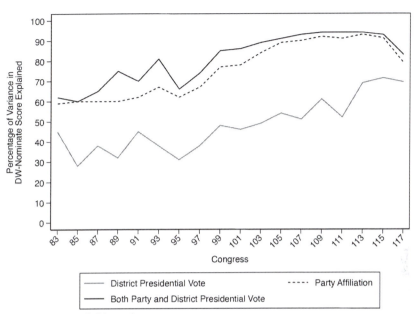

Source: Compiled by authors.

winners once they assume office has become much tighter. Indeed, election results predict congressional roll-call voting on issues that fall along the primary liberal–conservative dimension accurately enough to meet one of the fundamental conditions for responsible party government. This is evident when we regress NOMINATE scores on two variables, party and the district-level presidential vote, and observe how much of the variance they explain. Summarizing the results, figure 7.15 tracks the proportion of variance in first-dimension NOMINATE scores explained by party and presidential vote, individually and in combination, in the congresses immediately following each presidential election since 1952. Since 1976, both variables have become increasingly accurate predictors of congressional voting, to the point where, in the congresses elected in this century, party and district presidential vote together account for about 92 percent of the variance in representatives' positions on the scale.

The voting patterns of House members, then, are increasingly predictable from elementary electoral variables—the party of the winner and the district's ideology as reflected in its presidential leanings (with these two variables themselves correlated in 2020 at the highest level in the entire series at .82). With this development, voters have a much clearer idea of how their choices in national elections will translate into members' actions on national issues. Because party labels are so much more predictive of congressional behavior than they were in the 1970s, voters have good reason to use them more consistently to guide voting decisions. The consequences, however, are not those envisioned by advocates of strong party government. The electoral conditions for strong party government have been realized, but the results have been stalemate and inaction rather than responsible governance.

THE DOWNSIDE OF STRONG PARTY GOVERNMENT

The fundamental problem with candidate-centered electoral politics and consequent legislative individualism is, as we have argued, responsiveness without responsibility. The conventional solution, strong parties, turns out to have its own pathologies, at least in the particular context of present-day American politics. The problem is captured in a simple equation: Partisan polarization + divided government = gridlock. In the model of responsible party government outlined by Fiorina, parties compete for support by proposing alternative sets of policies; the winning party then enacts a program on which voters can pass judgment in the next election. But this presupposes a single winning party (or coalition) that actually controls the levers of government and can thus act. This is true of parliamentary systems, where a legislative majority chooses the executive and has full authority to make laws. But the system of checks and balances embodied in the US Constitution—two equally powerful legislative chambers, a separately elected president wielding a veto over legislation, and distinct electoral bases and calendars for representatives, senators, and presidents—was deliberately designed to thwart simple majority rule, and it nearly always has.

The electoral process has delivered a unified national government—a single party in control of the House, Senate, and White House—for only fifteen of thirty-nine congresses of the postwar era. Unified government has been even rarer in the latter part of this period, prevailing in only six of the twenty-two congresses elected since 1980. Historical experience shows that divided government need not always produce stalemate, gridlock, and intense partisan conflict in Washington.[57] But when, as now, the president and one or both houses of Congress owe their election to starkly divergent and barely overlapping electoral coalitions, the range of mutually agreeable policy options is severely limited. Insofar as each side loyally represents the voters who elected them, they find little common ground, and thwarting the other party becomes the highest priority.

---

[57]David R. Mayhew, *Divided We Govern: Party Control, Lawmaking, and Investigations, 1946–1990* (New Haven, CT: Yale University Press, 1991).

Ironically, then, the extraordinary electoral coherence characteristic of elections during the past decade documented in earlier chapters—high levels of party-line voting, low levels of ticket splitting, very few split verdicts, and so forth—has most often delivered incoherent divided government. Divided government persists for two reasons. First, it emerges from the confluence of the Constitution's Madisonian architecture and the current distribution of partisans across electoral units. In the presidential election, high rates of party-line voting tend to favor Democratic candidates because Democrats outnumber Republicans in the electorate, although as 2000 and 2016 showed, Democratic majorities can be thwarted by the electoral college; the Democrat has outpolled the Republican in seven of the last eight presidential elections. In House and Senate elections, however, party-line and straight-ticket voting favor Republicans because of their structural advantage in the distribution of partisans across states and congressional districts documented in chapter 2.

Second, divided government emerges from midterm referendums on unpopular presidents, which currently derive less from ruptured party loyalty than from differential turnout. All five unified governments elected in presidential years since 1992 (1992, 2004, 2008, 2016, and 2020) have been undone by out-party victories in the following midterm; in every case, the president's approval rating was 46 percent or lower, and opposition party's turnout surged while the president's party's sagged. The modest national tide that carried the House for the Republicans in 2022 was almost offset by high Democratic turnout across many congressional districts, while Democrat loyalty in blue states kept the Senate in Democratic hands (see chapter 6).

With both voters and politicians so sharply divided along partisan and ideological lines, divided government has produced acrimonious conflict, repeated games of chicken between the president and a Congress controlled by the opposition, multiple threatened and actual government shutdowns, and frequent legislative impasses. Instead of (however grudgingly) accepting the compromises necessary to reach durable agreements, each side puts its energy into posturing and position taking aimed at breaking the deadlock by winning full control in the next election, postponing crucial choices through short-term stopgap measures.[58] The partisan struggle has also encouraged unrestrained use of the procedural devices available to House and Senate leaders to obstruct or to circumvent obstruction that make legislative politics so frustrating to participants and so ugly to the public.[59]

---

[58]Sarah Binder, "The Dysfunctional Congress," *Annual Review of Political Science* 18 (May 2015): 85–101; Francis Lee, "How Party Polarization Affects Governance," *Annual Review of Political Science* 18 (May 2015): 261–82.

[59]Sinclair, *Unorthodox Lawmaking*, 141–65.

Figure 7.16 Approval of Congress, 1989–2023 (Quarterly Averages)

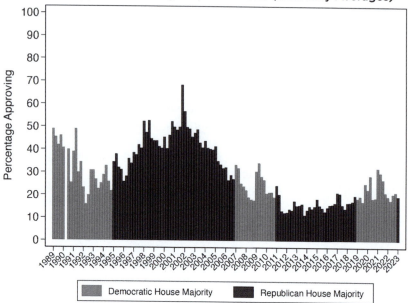

Source: Compiled by authors from surveys taken by 21 national polling firms over this period.

THE PUBLIC'S EVALUATIONS OF CONGRESS

Gridlock and stalemate during the Obama administration brought public approval of Congress to the lowest levels ever recorded and it has only recently begun to recover. Figure 7.16 displays the quarterly averages for congressional approval from polls taken from 1989 through early 2023. Congress is rarely very popular—average approval exceeds 50 percent in only 5 of the 137 quarters during this period—but the consistently terrible reviews earned by Congress since the middle of 2011 are unusual. The average approval rating in polls taken since July of that year through early 2023 is an abysmal 19 percent, with disapproval averaging 76 percent. Moreover, unlike in almost every other political evaluation, partisans differ little in their (thoroughly negative) assessments.

Congress has always been far less popular than its individual members. Even when the incumbency advantage was at its peak and members were typically very well regarded by their constituents, negative views of Congress consistently outnumbered positive views. In the most thorough study of congressional unpopularity to date, John Hibbing and Elizabeth Theiss-Morse argue that congressional unpopularity is almost inevitable because the public objects to the way Congress does its normal business. Hibbing and Theiss-Morse found that people want legislators to be fair and efficient. Fairness means looking out for the interests of "the people," not "special interests." Efficiency means making policy without the posturing, haggling, threatening, and compromise it normally entails—that is, without the politics.[60] But if Hibbing and Theiss-Morse are right, as long as Congress remains the venue in which intense political disagreements among competing, often narrow interests, as well as incompatible visions of the public good, are thrashed out in public view, Congress will always be unpopular. "Just as people want governmental services without the pain of taxes, they also want democratic procedures without the pain of witnessing what comes along with those procedures."[61] Thus,

> a major part of [the public's] distaste for Congress is endemic to an open legislative body in a large and complicated modern democratic polity. When the issues are complex and far-reaching, and when interests are diverse and specialized, the democratic process will be characterized by disagreements and a pace that can be charitably described as deliberate. And these disagreements will likely be played out by surrogates rather than by ordinary people.
>
> The public performs no useful purpose by adopting the attitude that these surrogates, whether they be members of Congress, leaders of the parties, or officials of interest groups, have messed everything up and all would be right if they would only listen to ordinary people again. The truth is that ordinary people disagree fundamentally on vital issues. The noise and acrimony we despise so much in politics is a reflection of our own diversity and occasional convictions.[62]

From this perspective, Congress's standing is bound to suffer from the inevitable conflicts that arise when it tries to make national policy.[63] Moreover, divided government, which popular majorities consistently say they do like, exacerbates the very things people don't like about Congress. The Democratic takeover of Congress in 2006 from an unpopular Republican majority boosted the institution's job-approval ratings modestly for a couple of months (figure 7.16), but they soon fell back under 30 percent as the Democratic majorities battled the Republican president and his allies in the House and Senate over the direction of the Iraq War and issues of governance and domestic policy. Ordinary Republicans disdained the Democratic Congress for what it was trying to do, ordinary Democrats soured on it for not succeeding in its efforts, and nearly

---

[60]John R. Hibbing and Elizabeth Theiss-Morse, *Congress as Public Enemy: Public Attitudes toward American Political Institutions* (Cambridge: Cambridge University Press, 1995), 14–20.

[61]Hibbing and Theiss-Morse, *Congress as Public Enemy*, 19.

[62]Hibbing and Theiss-Morse, *Congress as Public Enemy*, 82.

[63]See Robert H. Durr, John B. Gilmour, and Christina Wolbrecht, "Explaining Congressional Approval," *American Journal of Political Science* 41 (1997): 175–207.

everyone could scorn the confrontational politics that were, in reality, the inevitable result of deeply rooted partisan differences on issues of fundamental national importance. Similarly, approval of Congress rose from an average of 19 percent in the last quarter of 2010 to 24 percent in the first quarter of 2011 after the Republicans took over the House, but that was the high point until late 2019 and briefly into early 2021 before it began decreasing again.

The data in figure 7.16 and other research suggest that Congress is most popular when the country is at peace, the economy is booming, and leaders cut successful legislative deals with the president, such as in the latter years of the Clinton administration. Congress shared in the huge rally in public support enjoyed by President Bush (and all other American institutions) in the aftermath of the terrorist attacks of September 11, 2001. It also shared in the falloff in presidential approval as the Iraq War dragged on and in the further drop in Bush's standing provoked by the economic crisis at the end of his term in 2008. Evaluations of Congress rise and fall with evaluations of presidents, for they are driven largely by the same considerations, although Congress is almost invariably rated lower than the president. Bill Clinton's approval ratings averaged eighteen percentage points higher than those of Congress; for George W. Bush, the gap was twelve points, but for Obama's presidency, it was thirty-one points, underlining the unusually dismal public evaluations of the most recent congresses. The gap for Trump averaged a smaller twenty-one points, reflecting Trump's generally lower approval ratings. For President Biden, the gap has averaged twenty-two points, reflecting a surge in approval at the outset of his presidency before settling into a gradual decline over time.

Does Congress's standing with the public have electoral consequences? David L. Jones and Monika McDermott provide evidence that House incumbents (particularly those in the majority) do a bit worse when Congress is unpopular, although their evidence also indicates that the effects of voters' evaluations of the candidates are about ten times as large as the effects of evaluations of Congress, so members have little incentive to polish their institution's collective reputation at any expense to their own.[64] As we saw in chapter 6, Congress's abysmal ratings were inconsequential in 2014, because even voters fed up with Congress were disinclined to punish its members if that meant defecting to the other party's candidate; in the 2018 midterms, voters took their anger out on Trump's party rather than Congress generally (every incumbent

[64]David R. Jones and Monika L. McDermott, *Americans, Congress, and Democratic Responsiveness: Public Evaluations of Congress and Electoral Consequences* (Ann Arbor: University of Michigan Press, 2009), chapter 5.

Democrat won reelection). In 2022, voters expressed their frustration with both parties as well as President Biden and former President Trump, but the effects were relatively modest in comparison to prior midterms.

REFORMING CONGRESS

By the early 1990s, Congress had become more widely distrusted and disdained than at any time to that date since the advent of scientific polling (but at rates now surpassed in the 2010s). Politicians by trade, members of Congress have never inspired much respect as a class, but the degree of suspicion and contempt expressed in polls and other venues in the early 1990s (call-in talk shows, focus groups, letters to editors) was extraordinary by any standard. Solid majorities of citizens told pollsters that most members were financially corrupt, misused office to enrich themselves, and lied when the truth would hurt them politically. Even larger majorities believed that the people they elected to Congress quickly lost touch and cared more about keeping power and serving themselves than about the welfare of the nation or their constituents.[65]

The public's image of members of Congress as indifferent and out of touch was deeply ironic to anyone aware of the enormous investment of effort most members put into keeping in touch with constituents, their devotion to casework, and their sensitivity to district opinion on policy issues. Yet individual responsiveness of this sort evidently failed to penetrate deeply enough to counteract the general image of members as a bunch of self-serving, pampered, overpaid, arrogant hacks. Republicans took advantage of this image in their 1994 campaigns, making internal reforms of Congress "aimed at restoring the faith and trust of the American people in their government" the first element in the Contract with America.[66] The proposed reforms included ending Congress's exemption from workplace laws, reducing the number of committees and committee staff, limiting terms of committee chairs, and banning the casting of proxy votes in committee, all of which were quickly adopted.

Term Limits
The most radical reform, limiting House and Senate terms, failed to win enough votes to move forward, however. Although the Contract with America promised only a vote on a constitutional amendment limiting terms, the idea had been an official part of the 1988 and 1992 Republican platforms, and many Republican candidates had campaigned in

---

[65]"A Public Hearing on Congress," *Public Perspective* 3 (November/December 1992): 82.
[66]Clyde Wilcox, *The Latest American Revolution? The 1994 Elections and Their Implications for Governance* (New York: St. Martin's Press, 1995), 69.

1994 as avid supporters of congressional term limits, so the distinction between "voting on" and "voting for" probably escaped most of the public. However, many senior House Republicans as well as a majority of Democrats opposed term limits, and the only option of the four voted upon to get even a simple majority of votes (twelve-year limits for both the House and Senate) still fell sixty-one votes short of the constitutionally required two-thirds.

There is no mystery as to why so many Republican candidates championed term limits in 1994. The public loved the idea then and still does. Opinion surveys typically find overwhelming majorities in favor of limiting legislative terms, and term-limit measures have passed in almost every state where they have been put to a popular vote. By 1995, when the Supreme Court struck down state-imposed term limits on federal officials as unconstitutional, twenty-two states had adopted them, and they remain highly popular.[67]

The logic behind the idea is curious. Its supporters claim that the high success rates of incumbent candidates has given us an ossified ruling clique, out of touch with voters and responsive only to the special interests whose money keeps them in office. The only way to ensure change is to limit tenure. But Congress was scarcely starved for new blood at the time; more than half of the representatives in the 104th Congress (1995–96) had served fewer than three terms, and more than half of the senators were in their first or second term; the same is true of the 118th Congress (2023–24), elected twenty-four years later.[68] Moreover, in 1992, 1994, 2006, 2010, and 2018, voters demonstrated that they could limit terms the old-fashioned way, by voting out incumbents or compelling them to retire in the face of almost certain defeat.

Beyond that, it seems strange to expect better representation from members who must give up their seats regardless of how well they perform; what quality of work should be expected from an employee who is sure to be fired on a certain date no matter how well he or she does the job? It also strains credulity to imagine that someone who will soon be looking for a new job, probably in the private sector, will be less solicitous of special interests than someone whose future the voters ultimately control. It seems equally doubtful that we would receive better representation from elected officials inferior in knowledge and experience to unelected bureaucrats, congressional staff, and professional lobbyists. Boosting

---

[67] *U.S. Term Limits v. Thornton*, 514 U.S. 779 (1995); in the Quinnipiac Poll's November 2016 survey, 82 percent of respondents said they supported term limits for senators and representatives.

[68] Sarah J. Eckman and Amber Hope Wilhelm, "Congressional Careers: Service Tenure and Patterns of Member Service, 1789–2023," *Congressional Research Service*, January 17, 2023, https://sgp.fas.org/crs/misc/R41545.pdf.

the number of open seats, which attract the most expensive campaigns, seems an odd way to reduce the electoral importance of money (and hence the political clout of donors). Finally, it seems unlikely that representatives would be more responsive to district sentiments when casting votes or taking positions in Washington if the political cost of ignoring constituents were reduced. Indeed, for some proponents, the chief virtue of term limits lies in freeing members to do the right thing regardless of what constituents want.[69] Members would, of course, become equally free to do the wrong thing.

Term limits would have their most profound effect on representation, however, by diminishing members' opportunities and incentives for developing strong ties with constituents. As Fenno has so vividly shown, it takes years of time and effort simply to learn who one's constituents are, what they want, and what they need. Even after this has been accomplished, keeping in touch is an endless, labor-intensive chore. Only the prospect of a lengthy series of future elections makes the effort worthwhile. Given the size (averaging more than 761,000 residents) and diversity of most present-day House districts, authentic "citizen legislators" would begin with little knowledge of the opinions, lives, and values of most of their constituents. With a limited electoral future in the district, they would have little reason to invest in learning more. The only "people" they would perhaps be closer to would be those in their own limited social or occupational circles. This hardly seems a recipe for better representation for everyone else.

Constituents, from their side, would know even less about their representatives than they do now, in part because the faces would change more often and in part because incumbents would put less effort into making themselves known. Voting decisions would thus be, on average, less informed than they are today. Jeffrey Mondak and Carl McCurley have shown that elections tend to filter out the more incompetent and corrupt incumbents over time; the average quality of members remaining in each electoral class increases with each election they survive. Truncating House careers would interrupt this filtering process, reducing the aggregate quality of House members significantly.[70] This hardly seems a recipe for better representation either.

These are mostly obvious points, but they do little to undermine support for term limits because it rests on emotion, not analysis. The idea

---

[69]George F. Will, *Restoration: Congress, Term Limits, and the Recovery of Deliberative Democracy* (New York: The Free Press, 1992).

[70]Jeffrey Mondak, "Competence, Integrity, and the Electoral Success of Congressional Incumbents," *Journal of Politics* 57 (1995): 1043–69; Jeffrey Mondak and Carl McCurley, "Inspected by #118406313: The Influence of Incumbents' Competence and Integrity in U.S. House Elections," *American Journal of Political Science* 39 (1995): 864–85.

provided a focus for public anger at members of Congress as a class and at the more general failure of the political establishment in Washington to solve major national problems. It is no accident that the movement arose at a time when divided government blurred responsibility. In an ironic inversion of the usual pattern, even people who continued to like and support their own representatives could still support a move to punish politicians wholesale by automatically firing them after a fixed period.

After 1995, the drive toward congressional term limits stalled. The Supreme Court declared state-level action imposing term limits on federal officials to be unconstitutional. Republicans' enthusiasm for term limits faded with their enjoyment of majority status, and a number from the class of 1994 who had promised to serve only three terms renounced their pledges and sought reelection in 2000. Term-limit advocacy groups vowed to campaign heavily against them,[71] but none were defeated; three members who had promised to leave in 2000 were still in office in 2004, and one lasted until 2007. Even if public support for term limits remains at the level of intensity of the early 1990s, however, amending the Constitution is never easy, particularly when the prime targets of the amendment would have to provide two-thirds majorities.

If term limits were ever imposed, it is doubtful that either their proponents or the public would like the consequences. Term limits would probably make the parties even more important in congressional elections and politics than they are today. The irony is, of course, that most term-limit advocates despise political parties as much as they despise career politicians. With less information about incumbents and with a larger number of open seats to contend with, voters would rely more heavily on cheap information shortcuts, the readiest of which is the party label, to sort out the candidates. With higher turnover, interest groups would see less advantage in cultivating individual members and more in cultivating parties and factions, redeploying their resources accordingly. With weaker ties to constituents, representatives would be freer to follow the party line, and with less time to develop their own sophisticated understanding of policy issues, they would be more open to party or ideological guidance. It would be a fine irony indeed if a populist movement inspired by fantasies of government by citizen legislators actually furthered something like the British-inspired "responsible two-party system" advocated by an earlier generation of political scientists.[72]

---

[71]Kristian Brainerd, "Several Term Limit Supporters Recant Vows to Leave the House, Saying Their Work Is Not Yet Done," *Congressional Quarterly Weekly Report*, June 19, 1999, 1444.

[72]Committee on Political Parties of the American Political Science Association, "Towards a More Responsible Two-Party System," *American Political Science Review* 44 (1950): pt. 2.

While failing on term limits, the Republicans of the class of 1994 did succeed in forcing votes on a rule banning all manner of gifts from lobbyists, tightening up their registration and reporting requirements, which then passed overwhelmingly. Like Republicans in 1994, Democrats in 2006 exploited public unhappiness with Congress by promising to reform the institution, enacting additional constraints on lobbying activities and ending secret legislative earmarking. The Republican House majority elected in 2010, as noted earlier, forswore legislative earmarks entirely. Obviously, none of these actions has restored the American public's faith in its national legislature (figure 7.16). The Democratic majority taking over in 2019 made a package of campaign finance, ethics, and voting rights reforms their first order of business (HR 1—For the People Act of 2019), although it was repeatedly blocked in the Senate when it came up for consideration over the next few years. Past experience suggests that even if these measures were to pass, they would do little to enhance Congress's public standing.

Other recently proposed reforms have focused on reducing partisan polarization in Congress and its unwelcome consequences.[73] Prominent on the list are changes in redistricting and election processes designed to produce more balanced districts, more moderate electorates, and thus more moderate members. None is particularly promising because none can reverse the long-term social, economic, cultural, and demographic trends driving partisan polarization in Congress and the electorate. Ultimately, it will be up to voters to decide when partisan warriors on the Hill have outstayed their welcome.

2024 AND BEYOND: GEOGRAPHY, DEMOGRAPHY, AND NATIONALIZED POLITICS

Elections since 2000 have revealed an electorate nearly evenly divided between the parties nationally, but with strong regional biases that reflect clearly defined differences in cultural and political values. Polling data from these elections show Republican voters are disproportionately white, male, fond of guns, religiously conservative, rural, married, older, and affluent. People with such characteristics are relatively more common in states of the South, Plains, and Mountain West. Democratic voters are disproportionately female, African American, Latino, secular, unmarried, unarmed, younger, and of modest means. People with these characteristics are more common in the states of the Northeast, Mid-Atlantic, and West Coast.[74]

---

[73]See the collection of essays in Nathaniel Perseley, ed., *Solutions to Political Polarization in America* (New York: Cambridge University Press, 2015).

[74]Jacobson, "Partisan Polarization in Presidential Support," 8–11.

Figure 7.17 Republicans' Share of House Seats, by Region, 1946–2022

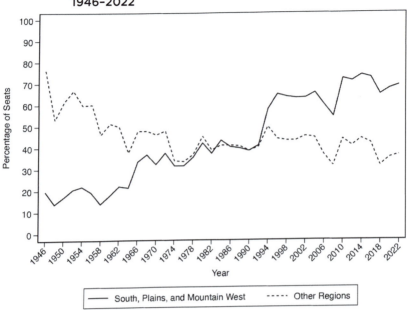

Source: Compiled by authors.

The strongly regional character of current alignments is the culmination of a decades-long shift in regional voting patterns in which the two parties have gradually exchanged areas of dominance. Figures 7.17 and 7.18 display these changes, showing the regional distribution of House and Senate seats since 1946. Republican gains in the South, Plains, and Mountain West put the party in control of Congress in 1994, and the party has dominated these regions ever since. The Democrats have become dominant in the Northeast, Mid-Atlantic, Midwest, and West Coast. After the 2022 election, Republicans held 69 percent of House seats and 79 percent of Senate seats in the South, Plains, and Mountain West, while Democrats held 63 percent of House seats and 78 percent of Senate seats outside these regions.[75]

---

[75]The South includes Alabama, Arkansas, Florida, Georgia, Kentucky, Louisiana, Mississippi, North Carolina, Oklahoma, South Carolina, Tennessee, Texas, and Virginia; the Plains include Kansas, Nebraska, North Dakota, and South Dakota; the Mountain West includes Alaska, Arizona, Colorado, Idaho, Montana, Nevada, New Mexico, Utah, and Wyoming. The Northeast includes Connecticut, Delaware, Maine, Maryland, Massachusetts, New Hampshire, New Jersey, New York, Pennsylvania, Rhode Island, and Vermont; the Midwest includes Illinois, Indiana, Iowa, Michigan, Minnesota, Missouri, Ohio, West Virginia, and Wisconsin; the West Coast includes California, Hawaii, Oregon, and Washington. We have placed Alaska in the Mountain West because it has far more in common—geographically, culturally, and politically—with the Mountain states than with the West Coast states.

Figure 7.18 Republicans' Share of Senate Seats, by Region, 1946–2022

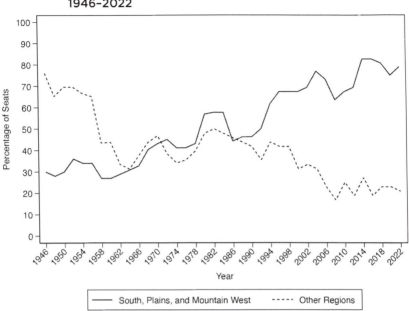

Source: Compiled by authors.

A closely divided electorate and the sharp cultural and ideological differences between the party coalitions make for high electoral stakes. The Republicans' structural advantage gives them a large head start in the battle to control the House (table 7.1). As noted in chapter 2, Democrats have to win a significant number of seats against the partisan grain in order to win majorities, a task that has become more difficult with the increase in party-line voting and consistency of presidential and congressional outcomes at the state and district levels (note the trends in at-risk seats in table 7.1). It is not an impossible task; with powerful pro-Democratic tides running in 2006 and 2008, they ended up with a larger share of Republican-leaning seats than in any election since 1992. But this left their majority at serious risk when conditions were not so favorable to their party, as became clear in 2010, when Republicans picked up thirty-eight of these seats, which alone would have been enough to give them a majority. In 2022, Republicans were again able to make modest inroads into Democratic-leaning districts (adding three), but all of their gains came in Republican-leaning districts (adding five). Their majority is thus quite precarious and they would still have to hold on to at least a few of the Democratic-leaning seats to maintain control in 2024.

Republicans also hold a structural advantage in Senate elections. As noted in chapter 2, equal representation of states in the Senate now favors Republicans because Democrats do relatively better in states with large

Table 7.1 At-Risk and Safe House Seats, by Party, 1992–2022

Electoral Risk as Determined by Presidential Vote	1992	1994	1996	1998	2000	2002	2004	2006	2008	2010	2012	2014	2016	2018	2020	2022	Change, 1992–2022
At-risk																	
Democrats	67	36	40	36	36	28	31	47	57	13	9	5	7	23	13	8	−59
Republicans	14	20	22	18	24	12	13	5	7	13	3	7	10	0	2	5	−9
Total	81	56	62	54	60	40	44	52	64	26	12	12	17	23	15	13	−68
Competitive																	
Democrats	49	32	27	31	26	19	14	21	24	10	15	10	13	26	26	23	−26
Republicans	23	40	29	27	27	19	20	16	16	30	14	19	18	4	8	8	−15
Total	72	72	56	58	53	38	34	37	40	40	29	29	31	30	34	31	−41
Safe																	
Democrats	143	137	141	145	151	151	158	165	176	170	177	173	174	186	182	182	39
Republicans	139	170	176	178	171	198	199	181	155	199	217	221	213	196	204	209	70
Total	282	307	317	323	322	357	357	346	331	369	394	394	387	382	386	391	109

Note: "At-risk" seats are those in which the winning party's presidential candidate received at least 2 percent less than his average across all districts; "Safe" seats are those in which the winning party's presidential candidate got at least 2 percent more than his or her average across all districts; "Competitive" seats fall in between these ranges. Midterm data are calculated from the previous presidential election; the district presidential vote has been adjusted where necessary for changes in district boundaries.

Source: Calculated by the authors.

populations, while Republicans do relatively better in states with small populations. In Senate as in House elections, the trend toward greater consistency in voting across federal offices compounds the Democrats' problem, exemplified by the Senate seats they lost in 2014 and 2018. But as 2022 also showed, Senate prospects depend heavily on the set of states holding contests. In 2024, Democrats will be defending twenty-three of the thirty-three contested seats; three are in states won by Trump in 2016 and 2020, whereas no Republican represents a Senate seat up for reelection in 2024 that was carried by Biden in 2020. Control of both chambers will be closely contested in 2024.

If recent history is any guide, much of what occurs in the 2024 elections will be determined by the final two years of the Biden presidency and Trump's quixotic desire for a second term in the White House. Even without Trump on the ballot in 2022, he made the midterms as much about himself as about Biden, which appears to have cost the Republicans seats in Congress, despite winning a narrow majority in the House.[76] Trump remains an extraordinarily polarizing figure after the events of the past few years, and with him again seeking the nomination for president, the congressional elections in 2024 will likely be about him too. This is even more true now that Trump has become the first current or former president to be indicted on criminal charges in light of allegations that he made cash payments to women who claimed they had extramarital affairs with him. With the criminal trial not set to start until early 2024, this will likely take center stage in the midst of the campaign for presidency. Additionally, Republican candidates will have an extremely difficult time trying to distance themselves from all of the media attention focused on Trump's criminal trial in a highly nationalized political climate.[77]

Even with recent events, the Republican Party remains Trump's party, posing a dilemma for Republican congressional candidates outside the reddest states and districts as we saw in 2022. Breaking with Trump could alienate their core partisan supporters but allying with Trump makes them unmarketable to the broader electorate in their attempt to win a national majority in 2024. Congressional candidates of a Republican Party that continues to be defined by Trump also face a demographic quandary. Their core voters continue to be overwhelmingly white as well as older, married, less educated, religiously observant, and socially conservative, all representing shrinking segments of the electorate. It is doubtful that Republicans can increase their support enough among older, less

[76]Gary C. Jacobson, "The 2022 Elections: A Test of Democracy's Resilience and the Referendum Theory of Midterms," *Political Science Quarterly* 138 (Spring 2023): 1–22.

[77]Kara Scannell, John Miller, Jeremy Herb, and Devan Cole, "Donald Trump Indicted by Manhattan Grand Jury on More than 30 Counts Related to Business Fraud," *CNN*, March 31, 2023, https://www.cnn.com/2023/03/30/politics/donald-trump-indictment/index.html.

educated whites to offset the demographic trends that increasingly favor the Democratic Party.

Democrats, for instance, enjoy disproportionate support from growing segments of the population: young people, singles (especially single women), college graduates, social liberals, seculars, and ethnic minorities—including Latinos—the fastest-growing category. The Democrats' demography makes their coalition harder to mobilize, however; its components turned out in force for Obama in 2008 and 2012, but not for Clinton in 2016. Reaction to Trump rekindled their enthusiasm for voting in 2018, and unusually high turnout was a crucial reason Democrats won the House that year. A similar degree of enthusiasm among Democratic voters appears to have mitigated their losses in the 2022 midterm elections coupled with high levels of frustration over abortion politics and continued threats to democracy. Whether this enthusiasm is sustained will be a major determinant of what happens in 2024; in an era of polarized partisanship, with little cross-party voting, mobilization is critical. Certainly both parties will go all out to maximize their vote up and down the ticket in 2024, not only to win the federal offices, but also because in many states the governors and state legislatures will be shaping the politics of abortion in light of the *Dobbs* decision.

With Biden's approval ratings remaining in the low to mid-40s after the midterms, he will face numerous challenges during the second half of his first term, not the least of which will be trying to negotiate with a conservative, but narrow majority in the House over issues such as the budget and raising the debt ceiling. The prospect of President Biden achieving major legislative accomplishments seems rather remote, so the best chance at lifting his approval ratings involves major economic improvements or significant reductions in inflation. With Biden announcing that he is running for a second term, there is now the real possibility that 2024 will feature the same two candidates for president as 2020.[78] Given concerns over Biden's age and Trump's ongoing legal and political troubles, many voters are probably less than enthusiastic about this scenario. Raising the stakes of this rematch, both candidates threaten to undermine the legacy and policy that the other has built, shaping up to be a historic grudge match with implications on a national scale. Needless to say, the 2024 elections will be momentous for many reasons, not the least for their effect on the electoral politics for the remainder of the decade.

---

[78]Zeke Miller, "Biden Announces 2024 Reelection Bid: 'Let's Finish This Job,'" *AP News*, April 25, 2023, https://apnews.com/article/joe-biden-election-2024-president-democrats-trump-9c72115656855da89a41cac3f79aa65b.

Bibliography

★ ★ ★

Abramowitz, Alan I. "Name Familiarity, Reputation, and the Incumbency Effect in a Congressional Election." *Western Political Quarterly* 28 (1975): 668–84.

———. "Partisan Redistricting and the 1982 Congressional Elections." *Journal of Politics* 45 (1983): 767–70.

———. "National Issues, Strategic Politicians, and Voting Behavior in the 1980 and 1982 Elections." *American Journal of Political Science* 28 (1984): 710–21.

———. "Economic Conditions, Presidential Popularity, and Voting Behavior in Midterm Congressional Elections." *Journal of Politics* 47 (1985): 31–43.

———. "Explaining Senate Election Outcomes." *American Political Science Review* 82 (1988): 385–403.

———. "The End of the Democratic Era? 1994 and the Future of Congressional Election Research." *Political Research Quarterly* 48 (1995): 873–89.

———. "It's Monica, Stupid: The Impeachment Controversy and the 1998 Midterm Election." *Legislative Studies Quarterly* 26 (May 2001): 211–26.

Abramowitz, Alan I., Brad Alexander, and Mathew Gunning. "Incumbency, Redistricting, and the Decline of Competition in U.S. House Elections." *Journal of Politics* 68 (2006): 75–88.

Abramowitz, Alan I., and Jeffrey A. Segal. "Determinants of the Outcomes of U.S. Senate Elections." *Journal of Politics* 48 (1986): 433–39.

Achen, Christopher H. "Measuring Representation." *American Journal of Political Science* 22 (1978): 475–510.

Ahuja, Sunil, Staci L. Beavers, Cynthia Berreau, Anthony Dodson, Patrick Hourigan, Steven Showalter, Jeff Waltz, and John R. Hibbing. "Modern Congressional Election Theory Meets the 1992 House Elections." *Political Research Quarterly* 47 (1994): 909–21.

Aldrich, John, Jamie Carson, Brad Gomez, and Jennifer Merolla. *Change and Continuity in the 2020 and 2022 Elections* (Lanham, MD: Rowman & Littlefield, 2023).

Alesina, Alberto, and Howard Rosenthal. "Partisan Cycles in Congressional Elections and the Macroeconomy." *American Political Science Review* 83 (1989): 373–98.

Ansolabehere, Stephen, and Alan Gerber. "The Mismeasure of Campaign Spending: Evidence from the 1990 U.S. House Elections." *Journal of Politics* 56 (1994): 1106–18.

————. "The Effects of Filing Fees and Petition Requirements on U.S. House Elections." *Legislative Studies Quarterly* 21 (1996): 249–64.

Ansolabehere, Stephen, and Philip Edward Jones. "Constituents' Responses to Congressional Roll-Call Voting." *American Journal of Political Science* 54 (2010): 583–97.

Ansolabehere, Stephen, Eric C. Snowberg, and James M. Snyder Jr. "Television and the Incumbency Advantage in U.S. Elections." *Legislative Studies Quarterly* 31 (2006): 469–90.

Ansolabehere, Stephen, James M. Snyder Jr., and Charles Steward III. "Old Voters, New Voters, and the Personal Vote: Using Redistricting to Measure the Incumbency Advantage." *American Journal of Political Science* 44 (2000): 17–34.

————. "Candidate Positioning in U.S. House Elections." *American Journal of Political Science* 45 (2001): 136–59.

Arcelus, Francisco, and Allan H. Meltzer. "The Effects of Aggregate Economic Variables on Congressional Elections." *American Political Science Review* 69 (1975): 1232–39.

Arceneaux, Kevin, Johanna Dunaway, Martin Johnson, and Ryan J. Vander Wielen. "Strategic Candidate Entry and Congressional Elections in the Era of *Fox News*." *American Journal of Political Science* 64 (2019): 398–415.

Arnold, R. Douglas. *The Logic of Congressional Action*. New Haven, CT: Yale University Press. 1990.

Banks, Jeffrey S., and D. Roderick Kiewiet. "Explaining Patterns of Candidate Competition in Congressional Elections." *American Journal of Political Science* 33 (1989): 997–1015.

Bauer, Monica, and John R. Hibbing. "Which Incumbents Lose in House Elections: A Reply to Jacobson's 'The Marginals Never Vanished.'" *American Journal of Political Science* 33 (1989): 262–71.

Berch, Neil. "The 'Year of the Woman' in Context." *American Politics Quarterly* 24 (1996): 169–93.

Berkman, Michael, and James Eisenstein. "State Legislators as Congressional Candidates: The Effects of Prior Experience on Legislative Recruitment and Fundraising." *Political Research Quarterly* 52 (1999): 481–98.

Bianco, William T. "Strategic Decisions on Candidacy in U.S. Congressional Districts." *Legislative Studies Quarterly* 9 (1984): 351–64.

Biersack, Robert, Paul S. Herrnson, and Clyde Wilcox. "Seeds for Success: Early Money in Congressional Elections." *Legislative Studies Quarterly* 18 (1993): 535–51.

Bloom, Howard S., and H. Douglas Price. "Voter Response to Short-Run Economic Conditions: The Asymmetric Effect of Prosperity and Recession." *American Political Science Review* 69 (1975): 1240–54.

Boatright, Robert G. *Expressive Politics: Issue Strategies of Congressional Challengers*. Columbus: Ohio State University Press. 2004.

———. *Getting Primaried: The Changing Politics of Congressional Primary Challengers*. Ann Arbor: University of Michigan Press. 2014.

Bond, Jon R. "The Influence of Constituency Diversity on Electoral Competition in Voting for Congress, 1974–1978." *Legislative Studies Quarterly* 8 (1983): 201–18.

Bond, Jon R., Cary Covington, and Richard Fleisher. "Explaining Challenger Quality in Congressional Elections." *Journal of Politics* 47 (1985): 510–29.

Bond, Jon R., and Richard H. Fleisher. *The President in the Legislative Arena*. Chicago: University of Chicago Press. 1990.

Bonica, Adam. "Ideology and Interests in the Political Marketplace." *American Journal of Political Science* 57 (2013): 294–311.

Born, Richard. "House Incumbents and Inter-election Vote Change." *Journal of Politics* 39 (1977): 1008–34.

———. "Reassessing the Decline of Presidential Coattails: U.S. House Elections, 1952–1980." *Journal of Politics* 46 (1984): 60–79.

———. "Partisan Intentions and Election Day Realities in the Congressional Redistricting Process." *American Political Science Review* 79 (1985): 305–19.

———. "Strategic Politicians and Unresponsive Voters." *American Political Science Review* 80 (1986): 599–612.

———. "Surge and Decline, Negative Voting, and the Midterm Loss Phenomenon: A Simultaneous Choice Model." *American Journal of Political Science* 34 (1990): 615–45.

———. "Assessing the Impact of Institutional and Election Forces on the Evaluations of Congressional Incumbents." *Journal of Politics* 53 (1991): 764–99.

———. "Congressional Incumbency and the Rise of Split Ticket Voting." *Legislative Studies Quarterly* 25 (2000): 365–87.

Bovitz, Gregory. "Electoral Consequences of Porkbusting in the U.S. House of Representatives." *Political Science Quarterly* 117 (Fall 2002): 455–77.

Box-Steffensmeier, Janet, Gary C. Jacobson, and J. Tobin Grant. "Question Wording and the House Vote Choice: Some Experimental Evidence." *Public Opinion Quarterly* 64 (Fall 2000): 257–70.

Box-Steffensmeier, Janet M., Peter M. Radcliffe, and Brandon L. Bartels. "The Incidence and Timing of PAC Contributions to Incumbent U.S. House Members." *Legislative Studies Quarterly* 30 (2005): 549–80.

Brady, David W. "A Reevaluation of Realignments in American Politics: Evidence from the House of Representatives." *American Political Science Review* 79 (1985): 28–49.

Brunell, Thomas L. "Partisan Bias in U.S. Congressional Elections: Why the Senate Is Usually More Republican than the House of Representatives." *American Politics Quarterly* 27 (1999): 316–37.

Bullock, Charles S. III. "Redistricting and Congressional Stability." *Journal of Politics* 37 (1975): 569–75.

———. "The Impact of Changing the Racial Composition of Congressional Districts on Legislators' Roll Call Behavior." *American Politics Quarterly* 23 (1995): 141–58.

Bullock, Charles S. IIII, and Karen L. Owen. *Special Elections: The Backdoor Entrance to Congress.* New York: Oxford University Press. 2021.

Burden, Barry C., and David C. Kimball. *Why Americans Split Their Tickets: Campaigns, Competition, and Divided Government.* Ann Arbor: University of Michigan Press. 2002.

Burnham, Walter Dean. "Insulation and Responsiveness in Congressional Elections." *Political Science Quarterly* 90 (1975): 411–35.

Busch, Andrew E. *Horses in Midstream: U.S. Midterm Elections and Their Consequences, 1894–1998.* Pittsburgh, PA: University of Pittsburgh Press. 1999.

Buttice, Matthew, and Walter Stone. "Candidates Matter: Policy and Quality Differences in Congressional Elections." *Journal of Politics* 74 (2012): 870–87.

Cain, Bruce E. *The Reapportionment Puzzle.* Berkeley: University of California Press. 1984.

———. "Assessing the Partisan Effects of Redistricting." *American Political Science Review* 79 (1985): 320–33.

Caldeira, Gregory A., Samuel C. Patterson, and Gregory A. Markko. "The Mobilization of Voters in Congressional Elections." *Journal of Politics* 47 (1985): 490–509.

Calvert, Randall L., and John A. Ferejohn. "Coattail Voting in Recent Presidential Elections." *American Political Science Review* 77 (1983): 407–19.

Campbell, Angus, Philip E. Converse, Warren E. Miller, and Donald E. Stokes. *Elections and the Political Order.* New York: John Wiley. 1966.

Campbell, James E. "Predicting Seat Gains from Presidential Coattails." *American Journal of Political Science* 30 (1986): 397–418.

———. "The Presidential Surge and Its Midterm Decline in Congressional Elections." *Journal of Politics* 53 (1991): 477–87.

———. *The Presidential Pulse of Congressional Elections.* Lexington: University of Kentucky Press. 1993.

———. "The Presidential Pulse and the 1994 Midterm Congressional Election." *Journal of Politics* 59 (1997): 830–57.

Campbell, James E., John R. Alford, and Keith Henry. "Television Markets and Congressional Elections." *Legislative Studies Quarterly* 9 (1984): 665–78.

Campbell, James E., and Joe A. Sumners. "Presidential Coattails in Senate Elections." *American Political Science Review* 84 (1990): 513–24.

Cann, Damon. *Sharing the Wealth: Member Contributions and the Exchange Theory of Party Influence in the U.S. House of Representatives.* Albany: State University of New York Press. 2008.

Canon, David T. *Actors, Athletes, and Astronauts: Political Amateurs in the United States Congress.* Chicago: University of Chicago Press. 1990.

———. "Sacrificial Lambs or Strategic Politicians? Political Amateurs in U.S. House Elections." *American Journal of Political Science* 37 (1993): 1119–41.

———. *Race, Redistricting, and Representation.* Chicago: University of Chicago Press. 1999.

Carson, Jamie, and Aaron Hitefield. "Donald Trump, Nationalization, and the 2018 Midterm Elections." *The Forum* 16 (2018): 495–513.

Carson, Jamie L., and Aaron A. Hitefield, "A Red Wave or a Ripple? Nationalized Politics and the 2022 Midterms," *The Forum* 21 (2023): 3–25.

Carson, Jamie L. "Strategy, Selection, and Candidate Competition in U.S. House Elections." *Journal of Politics* 67 (2005): 1–28.

Carson, Jamie L., Michael Crespin, Carrie Eaves, and Emily Wanless. "Constituency Congruency and Candidate Competition in U.S. House Elections." *Legislative Studies Quarterly* 36 (2011): 461–82.

———. "Constituency Congruency and Candidate Competition in Primary Elections for the U.S. House." *State Politics & Policy Quarterly* 12 (2012): 127–45.

Carson, Jamie L., Michael Crespin, and Ryan Williamson. "Re-evaluating the Effects of Redistricting on Electoral Competition, 1972–2012." *State Politics & Policy Quarterly* 14 (2014): 162–74.

Carson, Jamie L., Erik J. Engstrom, and Jason M. Roberts. "Redistricting, Candidate Entry, and the Politics of Nineteenth-Century U.S. House Elections." *American Journal of Political Science* 50 (2006): 283–93.

———. "Candidate Quality, the Personal Vote, and the Incumbency Advantage in Congress." *American Political Science Review* 101 (2007): 289–301.

Carson, Jamie L., Gregory Koger, Matthew J. Lebo, and Everett Young. "The Electoral Costs of Party Loyalty in Congress." *American Journal of Political Science* 54 (2010): 598–616.

Carson, Jamie L., and Jason M. Roberts. "Strategic Politicians and U.S. House Elections, 1874–1914." *Journal of Politics* 67 (2005): 474–96.

———. *Ambition, Competition, and Electoral Reform: The Politics of Congressional Elections across Time*. Ann Arbor: University of Michigan Press. 2013.

Carson, Jamie L., and Joel Sievert. "Electoral Reform and Changes in Legislative Behavior: Adoption of the Secret Ballot in Congressional Elections." *Legislative Studies Quarterly* 40 (2015): 83–110.

———. *Electoral Incentives in Congress*. Ann Arbor: University of Michigan Press. 2018.

Carson, Jamie L., Joel Sievert, and Ryan D. Williamson. *Nationalized Politics: Evaluating Electoral Politics Across Time*. New York: Oxford University Press. 2024.

Carson, Jamie L., and Ryan Williamson. "Candidate Ideology and Electoral Success in Congressional Elections." *Public Choice* 176 (2018): 175–92.

Clarke, Harold D., Frank B. Feigert, Barry J. Seldon, and Marianne C. Stewart. "More Time with My Money: Leaving the House and Going Home in 1992 and 1994." *Political Research Quarterly* 52 (1999): 67–85.

Clarke, Peter, and Susan Evans. *Covering Campaigns: Journalism in Congressional Elections*. Stanford, CA: Stanford University Press. 1983.

Clemens, Austin C., Michael H. Crespin, and Charles J. Finocchiaro. "The Political Geography of Distributive Politics." *Legislative Studies Quarterly* 40 (2015): 111–36.

Clinton, Joshua D. "Representation in Congress: Constituents and Roll Calls in the 106th House." *Journal of Politics* 68 (2006): 397–409.

Cnudde, Charles F., and Donald J. McCrone. "The Linkage between Constituency Attitudes and Congressional Voting Behavior: A Causal Model." *American Political Science Review* 60 (1966): 66–72.

Coleman, John J. "The Importance of Being Republican: Forecasting Party Fortunes in House Midterm Elections." *Journal of Politics* 59 (1997): 497–519.

Collie, Melissa P. "Incumbency, Electoral Safety, and Turnover in the House of Representatives, 1952–1976." *American Political Science Review* 75 (1981): 119–31.

Copeland, Gary. "Activating Voters in Congressional Elections." *Political Behavior* 5 (1983): 391–402.

Cottrell, David. "Using Computer Simulations to Measure the Effect of Gerrymandering on Electoral Competition in the U.S. Congress," *Legislative Studies Quarterly* 44 (2019): 487–514.

Cover, Albert D. "One Good Term Deserves Another: The Advantage of Incumbency in Congressional Elections." *American Journal of Political Science* 21 (1977): 523–42.

———. "Contacting Congressional Constituents: Some Patterns of Perquisite Use." *American Journal of Political Science* 24 (1980): 125–35.

Cover, Albert D., and Bruce S. Brumberg. "Baby Books and Ballots: The Impact of Congressional Mail on Constituency Opinion." *American Political Science Review* 76 (1982): 347–59.

Cover, Albert D., and David R. Mayhew. "Congressional Dynamics and the Decline of Competitive Congressional Elections." In *Congress Reconsidered*, edited by Lawrence C. Dodd and Bruce I. Oppenheimer. 2nd ed, 62–82. Washington, DC: Congressional Quarterly Press. 1981.

Cox, Gary, and Samuel Kernell, eds. *Divided Government*. Boulder, CO: Westview Press. 1991.

Cox, Gary W., and Jonathan Katz. "Why Did the Incumbency Advantage in U.S. House Elections Grow?" *American Journal of Political Science* 40 (1996): 478–97.

———. "The Reapportionment Revolution and Bias in U.S. Congressional Elections." *American Journal of Political Science* 43 (1999): 812–40.

———. *Elbridge Gerry's Salamander: The Electoral Consequences of the Reapportionment Revolution*. Cambridge: Cambridge University Press. 2002.

Cox, Gary W., and Eric Magar. "How Much Is Majority Status in the U.S. Congress Worth?" *American Political Science Review* 93 (1999): 299–309.

Cox, Gary W., and Mathew D. McCubbins. *Legislative Leviathan: Party Government in the House*. 2nd ed. Cambridge: Cambridge University Press. 2007.

Cummings, Milton C., Jr. *Congressmen and the Electorate*. New York: The Free Press. 1966.

Currinder, Marian. *Money in the House: Campaign Funds and Congressional Party Politics*. Boulder, CO: Westview Press. 2008.

Dabelko, Kristen la Cour, and Paul S. Herrnson. "Women's and Men's Campaigns for the U.S. House of Representatives." *Political Research Quarterly* 50 (1997): 121–35.

Damore, David F., and Thomas G. Hansford. "The Allocation of Party Controlled Campaign Resources in the House of Representatives, 1989–1996." *Political Research Quarterly* 52 (1999): 371–85.

De Boef, Suzanna, and James A. Stimson. "The Dynamic Structure of Congressional Elections." *Journal of Politics* 57 (1995): 630–48.

Desposato, Scott W., and John R. Petrocik. "The Variable Incumbency Advantage: New Voters, Redistricting, and the Personal Vote." *American Journal of Political Science* 47 (2003): 18–32.

Diana, Evans. "The Grateful Electorate: Casework and Congressional Elections." *American Journal of Political Science* 25 (1981): 568–80.

Dimock, Michael A., and Gary C. Jacobson. "Checks and Choices: The House Bank Scandal's Impact on Voters in 1992." *Journal of Politics* 57 (1995): 1143–59.

Druckman, James N., Martin J. Kifer, and Michael Parkin. "Campaign Communications in U.S. Congressional Elections." *American Political Science Review* 103 (2009): 343–66.

Dwyre, Diana. "Spinning Straw into Gold: Soft Money and U.S. House Elections." *Legislative Studies Quarterly* 21 (1996): 409–24.

Edwards, George C. III. *Presidential Influence in Congress.* San Francisco: W. H. Freeman. 1980.

Eismeier, Theodore J., and Philip H. Pollack, III. *Business, Money, and the Rise of Corporate PACs in American Elections.* New York: Quantum Books. 1988.

Engstrom, Erik J. "The Rise and Decline of Turnout in Congressional Elections: Electoral Institutions, Competition, and Strategic Mobilization." *American Journal of Political Science* 56 (2012): 373–86.

Engstrom, Erik J., and Samuel Kernell. *Party Ballots, Reform, and the Transformation of America's Electoral System.* New York: Cambridge University Press. 2014.

Engstrom, Erik J., and Jason M. Roberts. *The Politics of Ballot Design: How States Shape American Democracy.* New York: Cambridge University Press. 2020.

Engstrom, Richard N., and Christopher Kenny. "The Effects of Independent Expenditures in Senate Elections." *Political Research Quarterly* 55 (2002): 885–905.

Ensley, Michael J., Michael W. Tofias, and Scott De Marchi. "District Complexity as an Advantage in Congressional Elections." *American Journal of Political Science* 53 (2009): 990–1005.

Epstein, David, and Sharon O'Halloran. "Measuring the Electoral Impact of Majority-Minority Voting Districts." *American Journal of Political Science* 43 (1999): 367–95.

Erikson, Robert S. "The Advantage of Incumbency in Congressional Elections." *Polity* 3 (1971): 395–405.

———. "The Electoral Impact of Congressional Roll Call Voting." *American Political Science Review* 65 (1971): 1018–32.

———. "Malapportionment, Gerrymandering, and Party Fortunes in Congressional Elections." *American Political Science Review* 66 (1972): 1234–45.

———. "Is There Such a Thing as a Safe Seat?" *Polity* 9 (1976): 623–32.

———. "Constituency Opinion and Congressional Behavior: A Reexamination of the Miller-Stokes Representation Data." *American Journal of Political Science* 22 (1978): 511–35.

———. "Economic Conditions and the Congressional Vote: A Review of the Macrolevel Evidence." *American Journal of Political Science* 34 (1990): 373–99.

Erikson, Robert S., and Thomas R. Palfrey. "Campaign Spending and Incumbency: An Alternative Simultaneous Equations Approach." *Journal of Politics* 60 (1998): 355–73.

Erikson, Robert S., and Lee Sigelman. "Poll-Based Forecasts of the House Vote in Presidential Election Years, 1952–1992 and 1996." *American Politics Quarterly* 24 (1996): 520–31.

Erikson, Robert S., and Gerald F. Wright, Jr. "Policy Representation of Constituency Interests." *Political Behavior* 1 (1980): 91–106.

Esterling, Kevin M., David M. J. Lazer, and Michael A. Neblo. "Connecting to Constituents: The Diffusion of Representation Practices among Congressional Websites." *Political Research Quarterly* 66 (2013): 102–14.

Eulau, Heinz, and Paul D. Karps. "The Puzzle of Representation: Specifying Components of Responsiveness." *Legislative Studies Quarterly* 2 (1977): 233–54.

Feldman, Paul, and James Jondrow. "Congressional Elections and Local Federal Spending." *American Journal of Political Science* 28 (1984): 147–63.

Fenno, Richard F., Jr. *Home Style: House Members in Their Districts.* Boston: Little, Brown. 1978.

———. *The United States Senate: A Bicameral Perspective.* Washington, DC: American Enterprise Institute. 1982.

———. *Congress at the Grassroots: Representational Change in the South, 1970–1998.* Chapel Hill: University of North Carolina Press. 2000.

———. *The Challenge of Congressional Representation.* Cambridge, MA: Harvard University Press. 2013.

Ferejohn, John A. "On the Decline of Competition in Congressional Elections." *American Political Science Review* 71 (1977): 166–76.

Ferejohn, John A., and Randall L. Calvert. "Presidential Coattails in Historical Perspective." *American Journal of Political Science* 28 (1984): 127–46.

Ferejohn, John A., and Morris P. Fiorina. "Incumbency and Realignment in Congressional Elections." In *The New Direction in American Politics,* edited by John E. Chubb and Paul E. Peterson, 91–116. Washington, DC: Brookings Institution, 1985.

Fiorina, Morris P. *Representatives, Roll Calls, and Constituencies.* Lexington, MA: D. C. Heath. 1974.

———. "The Case of the Vanishing Marginals: The Bureaucracy Did It." *American Political Science Review* 71 (1977): 177–81.

———. "Economic Retrospective Voting in American National Elections: A Micro Analysis." *American Journal of Political Science* 22 (1978): 426–43.

———. *Retrospective Voting in American National Elections.* New Haven, CT: Yale University Press. 1981.

———. "Short and Long-Term Effects of Economic Conditions on Individual Voting Decisions." In *Contemporary Political Economy,* edited by D. A. Hibbs and H. Fassbender. 73–100. Amsterdam: North Holland, 1981.

———. "Some Problems in Studying the Effects of Resource Allocation in Congressional Elections." *American Journal of Political Science* 25 (1981): 543–67.

———. "Who Is Held Responsible? Further Evidence on the Hibbing-Alford Thesis." *American Journal of Political Science* 27 (1983): 158–64.

———. *Congress: Keystone of the Washington Establishment.* 2nd ed. New Haven, CT: Yale University Press. 1989.

———. *Divided Government.* 2nd ed. Boston: Allyn and Bacon. 1996.

Fiorina, Morris P., and David Rohde, eds. *Home Style and Washington Work: Studies of Congressional Politics.* Ann Arbor: University of Michigan Press. 1989.

Fishel, Jeff. *Party and Opposition: Congressional Challengers in American Politics.* New York: David McKay. 1973.

Flemming, Gregory H. "Presidential Coattails in Open-Seat Elections." *Legislative Studies Quarterly* 20 (1995): 197–211.

Fouirnaies, Alexander, and Andrew B. Hall. "The Financial Incumbency Advantage: Causes and Consequences." *Journal of Politics* 76 (2014): 711–24.

Fowler, Linda L. "Candidates' Perceptions of Electoral Coalitions." *American Politics Quarterly* 8 (1980): 483–94.

Fowler, Linda L., and Robert D. McClure. *Political Ambition: Who Decides to Run for Congress.* New Haven, CT: Yale University Press. 1989.

Fox, Richard Logan. *Gender Dynamics in Congressional Elections.* Thousand Oaks, CA: Sage Publications. 1997.

Franklin, Charles H. "Eschewing Obfuscation? Campaigns and the Perception of U.S. Senate Incumbents." *American Political Science Review* 85 (1991): 1193–214.

Frantzich, Stephen. "Opting Out: Retirement from the House of Representatives, 1966–1974." *American Politics Quarterly* 6 (1978): 251–73.

Freedman, Paul, and Ken Goldstein. "Measuring Media Exposure and the Effects of Negative Campaign Ads." *American Journal of Political Science* 43 (1999): 1189–208.

Froman, Lewis A., Jr. *Congressmen and Their Constituencies.* Chicago: Rand McNally. 1963.

Gaddie, Ronald Keith. "Congressional Seat Swings: Revisiting Exposure in House Elections." *Political Research Quarterly* 50 (1997): 699–710.

———. "Economic Interest Group Allocations in Open-Seat Senate Elections." *American Politics Quarterly* 25 (1997): 347–62.

———. *Born to Run: Origins of the Political Career.* Lanham, MD: Rowman & Littlefield. 2004.

Gaddie, Ronald Keith, and Charles S. Bullock, III. *Elections to Open Seats in the U.S. House: Where the Action Is.* Lanham, MD: Rowman & Littlefield. 2000.

Gaddie, Ronald Keith, Charles S. Bullock, III, and Scott E. Buchanan. "What Is So Special about Special Elections?" *Legislative Studies Quarterly* 24 (February 1999): 103–12.

Gelman, Andrew, and Gary King. "Estimating the Incumbency Advantage without Bias." *American Journal of Political Science* 34 (1990): 1142–64.

Gerber, Alan. "Estimating the Effects of Campaign Spending on Senate Election Outcomes Using Instrumental Variables." *American Political Science Review* 92 (1998): 401–11.

Gilliam, Franklin D., Jr. "Influences on Voter Turnout for U.S. House Elections in Non-presidential Years." *Legislative Studies Quarterly* 10 (1985): 339–52.

Gilmour, John B., and Paul Rothstein. "A Dynamic Model of Loss, Retirement, and Tenure in the U.S. House of Representatives." *Journal of Politics* 58 (1996): 54–68.

Gimpel, James G., Frances E. Lee, and Shanna Pearson-Merkowitz. "The Check Is in the Mail: Interdistrict Funding Flows in Congressional Elections." *American Journal of Political Science* 52 (2008): 373–94.

Glazer, Amihai, and Marc Robbins. "Voters and Roll Call Voting: The Effect on Congressional Elections." *Political Behavior* 4 (1983): 377–90.

———. "Congressional Responsiveness to Constituency Change." *American Journal of Political Science* 29 (1985): 259–73.

Goidel, Robert K., and Donald A. Gross. "A Systems Approach to Campaign Finance in U.S. House Elections." *American Politics Quarterly* 22 (1994): 125–53.

———. "Reconsidering the 'Myths and Realities' of Campaign Finance Reform." *Legislative Studies Quarterly* 21 (1996): 129–49.

Goldenberg, Edie N., and Michael W. Traugott. "Congressional Campaign Effects on Candidate Recognition and Evaluation." *Political Behavior* 1 (1980): 61–90.

———. *Campaigning for Congress*. Washington, DC: Congressional Quarterly Press. 1984.

Goldstein, Ken, and Paul Freedman. "New Evidence for New Arguments: Money and Advertising in the 1996 Senate Elections." *Journal of Politics* 62 (2000): 1087–108.

———. "Campaign Advertising and Voter Turnout: New Evidence for the Stimulation Effect." *Journal of Politics* 64 (2002): 721–40.

Goodliffe, Jay. "The Effect of War Chests on Challenger Entry in U.S. House Elections." *American Journal of Political Science* 45 (2001): 830–44.

Goodman, Saul, and Gerald H. Kramer. "Comment on Arcelus and Meltzer, The Effect of Aggregate Economic Conditions on Congressional Elections." *American Political Science Review* 69 (1975): 255–65.

Green, Donald P., and Jonathan S. Krasno. "Salvation for the Spendthrift Incumbent: Reestimating the Effects of Campaign Spending in House Elections." *American Journal of Political Science* 32 (1988): 844–907.

———. "Rebuttal to Jacobson's 'New Evidence for Old Arguments.'" *American Journal of Political Science* 34 (1990): 363–72.

Griffin, John D. "Senate Apportionment as a Source of Political Inequality." *Legislative Studies Quarterly* 31 (2006): 405–32.

Griffin, John D., and Brian Newman. "Are Voters Better Represented?" *Journal of Politics* 67 (2005): 1206–27.

Grimmer, Justin. "Appropriators Not Position Takers: The Distorting Effects of Electoral Incentives on Congressional Representation." *American Journal of Political Science* 57 (2013): 624–42.

Grimmer, Justin, Solomon Messing, and Sean J. Westwood. "How Words and Money Cultivate a Personal Vote: The Effect of Legislator Credit Claiming on Constituent Credit Allocation." *American Political Science Review* 106 (2012): 703–19.

Grofman, Bernard, Thomas L. Brunell, and William Koetzle. "Why Gain in the Senate but Midterm Loss in the House? Evidence from a Natural Experiment." *Legislative Studies Quarterly* 23 (1998): 79–89.

Gronke, Paul. *Settings, Institutions, Campaigns, and the Vote: A Unified Approach to House and Senate Elections*. Ann Arbor: University of Michigan Press. 2000.

Gronke, Paul, Jeffrey Koch, and J. Matthew Wilson. "Follow the Leader? Presidential Approval, Presidential Support, and Representatives' Electoral Fortunes." *Journal of Politics* 65 (2003): 785–808.

Groseclose, Timothy, and Keith Krehbiel. "Golden Parachutes, Rubber Checks, and Strategic Retirements from the 102nd House." *American Journal of Political Science* 38 (1994): 75–99.

Hajnal, Zoltan, Nazita Lajevardi, and Lindsay Nielson, "Voter Identification Laws and the Suppression of Minority Votes," *The Journal of Politics* 79 (2017): 363–79.

Hall, Andrew B. "What Happens When Extremists Win Primaries?" *American Political Science Review* 109 (2015): 18–42.

Hall, Andrew B., and Daniel M. Thompson. "Who Punishes Nominees? Candidates' Ideology and Turning Out the Base in U.S. Elections." *American Political Science Review* 112 (2018): 509–24.

Hassell, Hans J. *The Party's Primary: Control of Congressional Nominations.* New York: Cambridge University Press. 2018.

Heberlig, Eric S., and Bruce A. Larson. "Redistributing Campaign Funds by U.S. House Members: The Spiraling Costs of the Permanent Campaign." *Legislative Studies Quarterly* 30 (2005): 597–624.

Herndon, James F. "Access, Record, and Competition as Influences on Interest Group Contributions to Congressional Campaigns." *Journal of Politics* 44 (1982): 996–1019.

Herrick, Rebekah. "Is There a Gender Gap in the Value of Campaign Resources?" *American Politics Quarterly* 24 (1996): 68–80.

Herrnson, Paul S. "Do Parties Make a Difference? The Role of Party Organizations in Congressional Elections." *Journal of Politics* 48 (1986): 612–13.

———. *Party Campaigning in the 1980s.* Cambridge, MA: Harvard University Press. 1988.

———. "The Role of Party Organizations, Party-Connected Committees, and Party Allies in Elections." *Journal of Politics* 71 (2009): 1207–24.

———. *Congressional Elections: Campaigning at Home and in Washington.* 6th ed. Washington, DC: Congressional Quarterly Press. 2012.

Hershey, Marjorie Randon. "Incumbency and the Minimum Winning Coalition." *American Journal of Political Science* 17 (1973): 631–37.

———. *The Making of Campaign Strategy.* Lexington, MA: Lexington Books. 1974.

———. *Running for Office: The Political Education of Campaigners.* Chatham, NJ: Chatham House. 1984.

Hetherington, Marc J., Bruce Larson, and Suzanne Globetti. "The Redistricting Cycle and Strategic Candidate Decisions in U.S. House Races." *Journal of Politics* 65 (2003): 1221–34.

Hibbing, John R. "Voluntary Retirements from the House in the Twentieth Century." *Journal of Politics* 44 (1982): 1020–34.

———. "The Liberal Hour: Electoral Pressures and Transfer Payment Voting in the U.S. Congress." *Journal of Politics* 46 (1984): 846–65.

———. *Congressional Careers: Contours of Life in the U.S. House of Representatives.* Chapel Hill: University of North Carolina Press. 1991.

Hibbing, John R., and John R. Alford. "The Electoral Impact of Economic Conditions: Who Is Held Responsible?" *American Journal of Political Science* 25 (1981): 423–39.

———. "Constituency Population and Representation in the United States Senate." *Legislative Studies Quarterly* 15 (1990): 581–98.

Hibbing, John R., and Sara L. Brandes. "State Population and the Electoral Success of U.S. Senators." *American Journal of Political Science* 27 (1983): 808–19.

Hibbing, John R., and Elizabeth Theiss-Morse. *Congress as Public Enemy: Public Attitudes toward American Political Institutions.* Cambridge: Cambridge University Press. 1995.

Highton, Benjamin, Eric McGhee, and John Sides. "Constitutional Design and 2014 Senate Election Outcomes." *Forum* 12 (2014): 653–61.

Hill, Kevin A. "Does the Creation of Majority Black Districts Aid Republicans? An Analysis of the 1992 Congressional Elections in Eight Southern States." *Journal of Politics* 57 (1995): 384–401.

Hinckley, Barbara. "Incumbency and the Presidential Vote in Senate Elections: Defining Parameters of Subpresidential Voting." *American Political Science Review* 64 (1970): 836–42.

———. "The American Voter in Congressional Elections." *American Political Science Review* 74 (1980): 641–50.

———. "House Re-elections and Senate Defeats: The Role of the Challenger." *British Journal of Political Science* 10 (1980): 441–60.

———. *Congressional Elections.* Washington, DC: Congressional Quarterly Press. 1981.

Hinckley, Barbara, Richard Hofstetter, and John Kessel. "Information and the Vote: A Comparative Election Study." *American Politics Quarterly* 2 (1974): 131–58.

Hirano, Shigeo, and James M. Snyder, Jr. *Primary Elections in the United States.* New York: Cambridge University Press. 2019.

Hopkins, Dan. *The Increasingly United States: How and Why American Political Behavior Nationalized.* Chicago: University of Chicago Press. 2018

Huckshorn, Robert J., and Robert C. Spencer. *The Politics of Defeat.* Amherst: University of Massachusetts Press. 1971.

Hunt, Charles. *Home Field Advantage: Roots, Reelection, and Representation in the Modern Congress.* Ann Arbor: University of Michigan Press. 2022.

Hurley, Patricia A. "Electoral Change and Policy Consequences: Representation in the 97th Congress." *American Politics Quarterly* 12 (1984): 177–94.

———. "Partisan Representation, Realignment, and the Senate in the 1980s." *Journal of Politics* 53 (1991): 3–33.

Hurley, Patricia A., and Kim Quaile Hill. "The Prospects for Issue Voting in Contemporary Congressional Elections: An Assessment of Citizen Awareness and Representation." *American Politics Quarterly* 8 (1980): 425–49.

Hutcheson, Richard G. III. "The Inertial Effect of Incumbency and Two-Party Politics: Elections to the House of Representatives from the South, 1952–1974." *American Political Science Review* 69 (1975): 1399–401.

Jackson, Brooks. *Honest Graft: Big Money and the American Political Process.* Updated ed. Washington, DC: Farragut Publishing. 1990.

Jackson, Robert A. "The Mobilization of Congressional Electorates." *Legislative Studies Quarterly* 21 (1996): 425–45.

Jackson, Robert A., Jeffery J. Monday, and Robert Huckfeldt. "Examining the Possible Corrosive Impact of Negative Advertising on Citizens' Attitudes toward Politics." *Political Research Quarterly* 62 (2009): 55–69.

Jacobson, Gary C. "Presidential Coattails in 1972." *Public Opinion Quarterly* 40 (1976): 194–200.

———. "The Effects of Campaign Spending in Congressional Elections." *American Political Science Review* 72 (1978): 469–91.

———. *Money in Congressional Elections.* New Haven, CT: Yale University Press. 1980.

———. "Congress: Politics after a Landslide without Coattails." In *The Elections of 1984*, edited by Michael Nelson. 215–37. Washington, DC: Congressional Quarterly Press, 1985.

———. "Money and Votes Reconsidered: Congressional Elections, 1972–1982." *Public Choice* 47 (1985): 7–62.

———. "Party Organization and Distribution of Campaign Resources: Republicans and Democrats in 1982." *Political Science Quarterly* 100 (1985–1986): 603–25.

———. "Enough Is Too Much: Money and Competition in House Elections, 1972–1984." In *Elections in America*, edited by Kay L. Schlozman, 173–95. New York: Allen & Unwin, 1987.

———. "The Marginals Never Vanished: Incumbency and Competition in Elections to the U.S. House of Representatives, 1952–1982." *American Journal of Political Science* 31 (1987): 126–41.

———. "Running Scared: Elections and Congressional Politics in the 1980s." In *Congress: Structure and Policy*, edited by Mathew McCubbins and Terry Sullivan, 34–81. New York: Cambridge University Press. 1987.

———. "Congress: A Singular Continuity." In *The Elections of 1988*, edited by Michael Nelson. 127–52. Washington, DC: Congressional Quarterly Press, 1989.

———. "Parties and PACs in Congressional Elections." In *Congress Reconsidered*, edited by Lawrence C. Dodd and Bruce I. Oppenheimer. 117–52. 4th ed. Washington, DC: Congressional Quarterly Press, 1989.

———. "Strategic Politicians and the Dynamics of U.S. House Elections, 1946–1986." *American Political Science Review* 83 (1989): 773–93.

———. "The Effects of Campaign Spending in House Elections: New Evidence for Old Arguments." *American Journal of Political Science* 34, no. 2 (1990): 334–62.

———. *The Electoral Origins of Divided Government: Competition in U.S. House Elections, 1946–1988.* Boulder, CO: Westview Press. 1990.

———. "Congress: Unusual Year, Unusual Election." In *The Elections of 1992*, edited by Michael Nelson. 153–82. Washington, DC: Congressional Quarterly Press. 1993.

———. "Deficit Cutting Politics and Congressional Elections." *Political Science Quarterly* 108 (1993): 375–402.

———. "The 1994 House Elections in Perspective." *Political Science Quarterly* 111, no. 2 (Summer 1996): 203–23.

———. "The 105th Congress: Unprecedented and Unsurprising." In *The Elections of 1996*, edited by Michael Nelson. 143–67. Washington, DC: Congressional Quarterly Press. 1997.

———. "The Effect of the AFL-CIO's 'Voter Education' Campaigns on the 1996 House Elections." *Journal of Politics* 61 (1999): 185–94.

———. "Impeachment Politics in the 1998 Congressional Elections." *Political Science Quarterly* 114 (1999): 31–51.

———. "Party Polarization in National Politics: The Electoral Connection." In *Congress and the President in a Partisan Era*, edited by Jon R. Bond and Richard Fleisher. 9–30. Washington, DC: Congressional Quarterly Press. 2000.

———. "Reversal of Fortune: The Transformation of U.S. House Elections in the 1990s." In *Continuity and Change in Congressional Elections*, edited by David W. Brady, John Cogan, and Morris P. Fiorina. 10–38. Stanford, CA: Stanford University Press. 2000.

———. "Congress: Elections and Stalemate." In *The Elections of 2000*, edited by Michael Nelson. 185–209. Washington, DC: Congressional Quarterly Press. 2001.

———. "A House and Senate Divided: The Clinton Legacy and the Congressional Elections of 2000." *Political Science Quarterly* 116 (Spring 2001): 5–27.

———. "Partisan Polarization in Presidential Support: The Electoral Connection." *Congress and the Presidency* 30 (Spring 2003): 1–36.

———. "Terror, Terrain, and Turnout: Explaining the 2002 Midterm Elections." *Political Science Quarterly* 118 (Spring 2003): 1–22.

———. "All Quiet on the Western Front: Redistricting and Party Competition in California House Elections." In *Redistricting in the New Millennium*, edited by Peter Galderisi. 217–44. Lanham, MD: Lexington Books, 2005.

———. "The Congress: The Structural Basis of Republican Success." In *The Elections of 2004*, edited by Michael Nelson. 163–86. Washington, DC: Congressional Quarterly Press, 2005.

———. "Polarized Politics and the 2004 Congressional Elections." *Political Science Quarterly* 120 (2005): 199–218.

———. "Campaign Spending Effects in U.S. Senate Elections: Evidence from the National Annenberg Election Survey." *Electoral Studies* 25 (2006): 195–226.

———. "Competition in U.S. Congressional Elections." In *The Marketplace of Democracy: Electoral Competition and American Politics*, edited by Michael P. McDonald and John Samples. 26–52. Washington, DC: Brookings Institution, 2006.

———. "The First Congressional Elections after BCRA." In *One Election Later: 2004 Politics after the Bipartisan Campaign Reform Act*, edited by Michael Malbin. 185–203. Lanham, MD: Rowman & Littlefield, 2006.

———. "Measuring Campaign Spending Effects in U.S. House Elections." In *Capturing Campaign Effects*, edited by Henry E. Brady and Richard Johnston. 199–220. Ann Arbor: University of Michigan Press, 2006.

———. "Referendum: The 2006 Midterm Congressional Elections." *Political Science Quarterly* 122 (2007): 1–24.

———. "The 2008 Presidential and Congressional Elections: Anti-Bush Referendum and Prospects for the Democratic Majority." *Political Science Quarterly* 124 (Spring 2009): 1–30.

———. "Congress: The Second Wave." In *The Elections of 2008*, edited by Michael Nelson. 100–21. Washington, DC: Congressional Quarterly Press, 2009.

———. "A Collective Dilemma Solved: The Distribution of Party Campaign Resources in the 2006 and 2008 Congressional Elections." *Election Law Journal* 9 (2010): 381–97.

———. "The Republican Resurgence in 2010." *Political Science Quarterly* 126 (Spring 2011): 27–52.

———. "Barack Obama and the Nationalization of Electoral Politics in 2012." *Electoral Studies* 40 (2015): 471–81.

———. "It's Nothing Personal: The Decline of the Incumbency Advantage in U.S. House Elections." *Journal of Politics* 77, no. 3 (2015): 861–73.

———. "Obama and Nationalized Electoral Politics in the 2014 Midterm." *Political Science Quarterly* 130 (Spring 2015): 1–26.

———. "The Triumph of Polarized Partisanship in 2016: Donald Trump's Improbable Victory." *Political Science Quarterly* 132 (2017): 9–41.

———. "Extreme Referendum: Donald Trump and the 2018 Midterm Elections." *Political Science Quarterly* 134 (2019): 9–38.

———. "Explaining the Shortfall of Trump Voters in the 2020 Pre- and Post-Election Surveys," Paper presented at the Annual Meeting of the Midwest Political Science Association (2022).

———. "The 2022 Elections: A Test of Democracy's Resilience and the Referendum Theory of Midterms." *Political Science Quarterly* 138 (2023): 1–22.

Jacobson, Gary C., and Michael A. Dimock. "Checking Out: The Effects of Bank Overdrafts on the 1992 House Elections." *American Journal of Political Science* 38 (1994): 601–24.

Jacobson, Gary C., and Samuel Kernell. *Strategy and Choice in Congressional Elections.* 2nd ed. New Haven, CT: Yale University Press. 1983.

———. "National Forces in the 1986 U.S. House Elections." *Legislative Studies Quarterly* 15 (1990): 72–85.

Jacobson, Gary C., Samuel Kernell, and Jeffrey Lazarus. "Assessing the President's Role as Party Agent in Congressional Elections: The Case of Bill Clinton in 2000." *Legislative Studies Quarterly* 29 (2004): 159–84.

Jacobson, Gary C., and Raymond E. Wolfinger. "Information and Voting in California Senate Elections." *Legislative Studies Quarterly* 14 (1989): 509–24.

Johannes, John R. *To Serve the People: Congress and Constituency Service.* Lincoln: University of Nebraska Press. 1984.

Johannes, John R., and John C. McAdams. "The Congressional Incumbency Effect: Is It Casework, Policy Compatibility, or Something Else?" *American Journal of Political Science* 25 (1981): 512–42.

———. "Congressmen, Perquisites, and Elections." *Journal of Politics* 50 (1988): 412–39.

Jones, Charles O. "A Suggested Scheme for Classifying Congressional Campaigns." *Public Opinion Quarterly* 26 (1962): 126–32.

———. "Inter-party Competition for Congressional Seats." *Western Political Quarterly* 17 (1964): 461–76.

———. *Every Second Year. Washington*, DC: Brookings Institution. 1967.

Jones, David R., and Monika L. McDermott. *Americans, Congress, and Democratic Responsiveness: Public Evaluations of Congress and Electoral Consequences*. Ann Arbor: University of Michigan Press. 2009.

Kahn, Kim Fridkin. "Senate Elections in the News: Examining Campaign Coverage." *Legislative Studies Quarterly* 16 (1991): 349–74.

———. "Does Being Male Help? An Investigation of the Effects of Candidate Gender and Campaign Coverage on Evaluations of U.S. Senate Candidates." *Journal of Politics* 54 (1992): 497–517.

Kahn, Kim Fridkin, and Patrick J. Kenney. "A Model of Candidate Evaluations in Senate Elections: The Impact of Campaign Intensity." *Journal of Politics* 59 (1997): 1173–205.

———. *The Spectacle of U.S. Senate Campaigns*. Princeton, NJ: Princeton University Press. 1999.

———. "The Importance of Issues in Senate Campaigns: Citizens' Reception of Issue Messages." *Legislative Studies Quarterly* 26 (2001): 573–97.

———. *No Holds Barred: Negativity in U.S. Senate Campaigns*. Upper Saddle River, NJ: Prentice Hall. 2004.

Kazee, Thomas A., ed. *Who Runs for Congress? Ambition, Context, and Candidate Emergence*. Washington, DC: Congressional Quarterly Press. 1994.

Kazee, Thomas A., and Mary C. Thornberry. "Where's the Party? Congressional Candidate Recruitment and American Party Organization." *Western Political Quarterly* 43 (1990): 61–80.

Kenny, Christopher, and Michael McBurnett. "Up Close and Personal: Campaign Contact and Candidate Spending in U.S. House Elections." *Political Research Quarterly* 50 (1997): 75–96.

Kernell, Samuel. "Presidential Popularity and Negative Voting: An Alternative Explanation of the Midterm Congressional Decline of the President's Party." *American Political Science Review* 71 (1977): 44–66.

Kiewiet, D. Roderick, and Mathew D. McCubbins. "Congressional Appropriations and the Electoral Connection." *Journal of Politics* 47 (1985): 59–82.

Kiewiet, D. Roderick. "Policy-Oriented Voting in Response to Economic Issues." *American Political Science Review* 75 (1981): 448–59.

———. *Macroeconomics and Micropolitics*. Chicago: University of Chicago Press. 1983.

Kim, Henry, and Brad Leveck. "Money, Reputation, and Incumbency in U.S. House Elections, or Why Marginals Have Become More Expensive." *American Political Science Review* 57 (2013): 492–504.

Kim, Thomas P. "Clarence Thomas and the Politicization of Candidate Gender in the 1992 Senate Elections." *Legislative Studies Quarterly* 23 (1998): 399–418.

Kinder, Donald R., and D. Roderick Kiewiet. "Economic Discontent and Political Behavior: The Role of Personal Grievances and Collective Economic Judgments in Congressional Voting." *American Journal of Political Science* 23 (1979): 495–527.

King, Gary, and Robert X. Browning. "Democratic Representation and Partisan Bias in Congressional Elections." *American Political Science Review* 81 (1987): 1251–73.

Kingdon, John W. *Candidates for Office: Beliefs and Strategies.* New York: Random House. 1968.

Koetzle, William. "The Impact of Constituency Diversity upon the Competitiveness of U.S. House Elections, 1962–96." *Legislative Studies Quarterly* 23 (1998): 561–73.

Kolodny, Robin. *Pursuing Majorities: Congressional Campaign Committees in American Politics.* Norman: University of Oklahoma Press. 1998.

Kostroski, Warren Lee. "Party and Incumbency in Post-war Senate Elections: Trends, Patterns, and Models." *American Political Science Review* 67 (1973): 1213–34.

Kramer, Gerald H. "Short-Term Fluctuations in U.S. Voting Behavior, 1896–1964." *American Political Science Review* 65 (1971): 131–43.

Krasno, Jonathan S. *Challengers, Competition, and Reelection: Comparing Senate and House Elections.* New Haven, CT: Yale University Press. 1994.

Kritzer, Herbert M., and Robert B. Eubank. "Presidential Coattails Revisited: Partisanship and Incumbency Effects." *American Journal of Political Science* 23 (1979): 615–26.

Kujala, Jordan. "Donors, Primary Elections, and Polarization in the United States." *American Journal of Political Science* 64 (2020): 587–602.

Kuklinski, James H., and Donald J. McCrone. "Policy Salience and the Causal Structure of Representation." *American Politics Quarterly* 8 (1980): 139–64.

Kuklinski, James H., and Darrell M. West. "Economic Expectations and Mass Voting in United States House and Senate Elections." *American Political Science Review* 75 (1981): 436–47.

Larson, Bruce A. "Incumbent Contributions to the Congressional Campaign Committees, 1990–2000." *Political Research Quarterly* 57 (2004): 155–61.

Lau, Richard R., and Gerald M. Pomper. "Effects of Negative Campaigning on Turnout in U.S. Senate Elections, 1988–1998." *Journal of Politics* 63 (2001): 804–19.

———. "Effectiveness of Negative Campaigning in U.S. Senate Elections." *American Journal of Political Science* 46 (2002): 47–66.

———. *Negative Campaigning: An Analysis of Senate Elections.* Lanham, MD: Rowman & Littlefield. 2004.

Lau, Richard R., Lee Sigelman, and Ivy Brown Rovner. "The Effects of Negative Political Campaigns: A Meta-analytic Reassessment." *Journal of Politics* 69, no. 4 (2007): 1176–209.

Lawless, Jennifer L., and Richard L. Fox. *It Takes a Candidate: Why Women Don't Run for Office.* New York: Cambridge University Press. 2005.

Lazarus, Jeffrey. "Unintended Consequences: Anticipation of General Election Outcomes and Primary Election Divisiveness." *Legislative Studies Quarterly* 30 (2005): 435–61.

———. "Why Do Experienced Challengers Do Better than Amateurs?" *Political Behavior* 30 (2008): 185–98.

Lee, Frances E., and Bruce I. Oppenheimer. "Senate Apportionment: Competitiveness and Partisan Advantage." *Legislative Studies Quarterly* 22 (1997): 3–24.

Leveaux-Sharpe, Christine. "Congressional Responsiveness to Redistricting Induced Constituency Change: An Extension into the 1990s." *Legislative Studies Quarterly* 26 (2001): 275–86.

Levendusky, Matthew S. "Why Do Partisan Media Polarize Viewers?" *American Journal of Political Science* 57 (2013): 611–23.

Levy, Dena, and Peverill Squire. "Television Markets and the Competitiveness of U.S. House Elections." *Legislative Studies Quarterly* 25 (2000): 313–25.

Lewis-Beck, Michael, and Tom W. Rice. "Forecasting U.S. House Elections." *Legislative Studies Quarterly* 9 (1984): 475–86.

Lockerbie, Brad. "Prospective Economic Voting in U.S. House Elections." *Legislative Studies Quarterly* 16 (1991): 239–62.

Lublin, David. "Quality, Not Quantity: Strategic Politicians in U.S. Senate Elections, 1952–1990." *Journal of Politics* 56 (1994): 228–41.

———. "The Election of African Americans and Latinos to the U.S. House of Representatives, 1972–1994." *American Politics Quarterly* 25 (1997): 269–86.

Lyons, Michael, and Peter F. Galderisi. "Incumbency, Reapportionment, and U.S. House Redistricting." *Political Research Quarterly* 48 (1995): 857–71.

Maestas, Cherie D., Sarah Fulton, L. Sandy Maisel, and Walter J. Stone. "'When to Risk It': Institutions, Ambitions, and the Decision to Run for the U.S. House." *American Political Science Review* 100 (2006): 195–208.

Maestas, Cherie D., L. Sandy Maisel, and Walter J. Stone. "National Party Efforts to Recruit State Legislators to Run for the U.S. House." *Legislative Studies Quarterly* 30 (2005): 277–300.

Maestas, Cherie D., and Cynthia R. Rugeley. "Assessing the 'Experience Bonus' through Examining Strategic Entry, Candidate Quality, and Campaign Receipts in U.S. House Elections." *American Journal of Political Science* 53 (2008): 530–35.

Magleby, David B. *The Change Election: Money, Mobilization, and Persuasion in the 2008 Federal Elections.* Philadelphia: Temple University Press. 2011.

Magleby, David B., and J. Quin Monson, eds. *The Last Hurrah? Soft Money and Issue Advocacy in the 2002 Congressional Elections.* Washington, DC: Brookings Institution. 2004.

Magleby, David B., J. Quin Monson, and Kelly Patterson, eds. *Dancing without Partners: How Candidates, Parties and Interest Groups Interact in the New Campaign Finance Environment.* Provo, UT: Brigham Young University, Center for the Study of Elections and Democracy. 2005.

Magleby, David B., and Candice J. Nelson. *The Money Chase: Congressional Campaign Finance Reform*. Washington, DC: Brookings Institution. 1990.

Magleby David B., and Kelly Patterson, eds. *The Battle for Congress: Iraq, Scandal, and Campaign Finance in the 2006 Election*. Boulder, CO: Paradigm Publishers. 2008.

———. *War Games: Issues and Resources in the Battle for Control of Congress*. Provo, UT: Brigham Young University, Center for the Study of Elections and Democracy. 2007.

Maisel, Louis Sandy. "Congressional Elections in 1978: The Road to Nomination, the Road to Election." *American Politics Quarterly* 8 (1981): 23–48.

———. *From Obscurity to Oblivion: Running in the Congressional Primary*. Knoxville: University of Tennessee Press. 1982.

Maisel, Louis Sandy, and Joseph Cooper, eds. *Congressional Elections*. Beverly Hills, CA: Sage Publications. 1981.

Maisel, L. Sandy, and Walter P. Stone. "Determinants of Candidate Emergence in U.S. House Elections: An Exploratory Study." *Legislative Studies Quarterly* 22 (1997): 72–96.

Maisel, L. Sandy, and Darrell M. West. *Running on Empty? Political Discourse in Congressional Elections*. Lanham, MD: Rowman & Littlefield. 2004.

Malbin, Michael, ed. *Parties, Interest Groups, and Campaign Finance Laws*. Washington, DC: American Enterprise Institute. 1980.

———. *Money and Politics in the United States: Financing Elections in the 1980s*. Washington, DC: American Enterprise Institute. 1984.

———. *The Election after Reform*. Boulder, CO: Rowman & Littlefield. 2006.

Mann, Thomas E. *Unsafe at Any Margin: Interpreting Congressional Elections*. Washington, DC: American Enterprise Institute. 1977.

———. *The American Elections of 1982*. Washington, DC: American Enterprise Institute. 1983.

Mann, Thomas E., and Raymond E. Wolfinger. "Candidates and Parties in Congressional Elections." *American Political Science Review* 74 (1980): 617–32.

Martin, Gregory J., and Zachary Peskowitz. "Agency Problems in Political Campaigns: Media Buying and Consulting." *American Political Science Review* 112 (2018): 231–48.

Mattei, Franco. "Senate Apportionment and Partisan Advantage: A Second Look." *Legislative Studies Quarterly* 26 (2001): 391–409.

Mattei, Laura Winsky, and Franco Mattei. "If Men Stayed Home. The Gender Gap in Recent Congressional Elections." *Political Research Quarterly* 51 (1998): 411–36.

Mayhew, David R. *Congress: The Electoral Connection*. New Haven, CT: Yale University Press. 1974.

———. "Congressional Elections: The Case of the Vanishing Marginals." *Polity* 6 (1974): 295–317.

McAdams, John C., and John R. Johannes. "The 1980 House Elections: Reexamining Some Theories in a Republican Year." *Journal of Politics* 45 (1983): 143–62.

———. "The Voter in the 1982 House Elections." *American Journal of Political Science* 28 (1984): 778–81.

McDermott, Monika L., and David R. Jones. "Congressional Performance, Incumbent Behavior, and Voting in Senate Elections." *Legislative Studies Quarterly* 30 (2005): 235–57.

McGhee, Eric, Seth Masket, Boris Shor, Steven Rogers, and Nolan McCarty. "A Primary Cause of Partisanship? Nomination Systems and Legislator Ideology." *American Journal of Political Science* 58 (2014): 337–51.

McKee, Seth C. *The Republican Ascendancy in Southern U.S. House Elections.* Boulder, CO: Westview Press. 2010.

McLeod, Jack M., Jane D. Brown, and Lee B. Becker. "Watergate and the 1974 Congressional Elections." *Public Opinion Quarterly* 41 (1977): 181–95.

Miller, Warren E., and Donald E. Stokes. "Constituency Influence in Congress." *American Political Science Review* 57 (1963): 45–57.

Mondak, Jeffrey. "Presidential Coattails in Open Seats: The District-Level Impact of Heuristic Processing." *American Politics Quarterly* 21 (1993): 307–19.

Mondak, Jeffrey, and Carl McCurley. "Cognitive Efficiency and the Congressional Vote: The Psychology of Coattail Voting." *Political Research Quarterly* 47 (1994): 151–75.

Mondak, Jeffrey J., and Dona-Gene Mitchell. *Fault Lines: Why the Republicans Lost Congress.* New York: Routledge. 2008.

Nelson, Candice J. "The Effects of Incumbency on Voting in Congressional Elections, 1964–1974." *Political Science Quarterly* 93 (1978/1979): 665–78.

Nice, David. "Competitiveness in House and Senate Elections with Identical Constituencies." *Political Behavior* 6 (1984): 95–102.

Nicholson, Stephen P. *Voting the Agenda: Candidates, Elections, and Ballot Propositions.* Princeton: Princeton University Press. 2005.

Nicholson, Stephen P., and Ross A. Miller. "Prior Beliefs and Voter Turnout in the 1986 and 1988 Congressional Elections." *Political Research Quarterly* 50 (1997): 199–213.

Nicholson, Stephen P., and Gary M. Segura. "Midterm Elections and Divided Government: An Information-Driven Theory of Electoral Volatility." *Political Research Quarterly* 52 (1999): 609-629.

Niemi, Richard G., and Alan I. Abramowitz. "Partisan Redistricting and the 1992 Congressional Elections." *Journal of Politics* 56 (1994): 811–17.

Nokken, Timothy. "Ideological Congruence vs. Electoral Success: Distribution of Party Organization Contributions in Senate Elections, 1990–2000." *American Politics Research* 31 (2003): 3–26.

Oppenheimer, Bruce I., James A. Stimson, and Richard W. Waterman. "Interpreting U.S. Congressional Elections: The Exposure Thesis." *Legislative Studies Quarterly* 11 (1986): 227–47.

Ornstein, Norman J., Thomas E. Mann, and Michael J. Malbin. *Vital Statistics on Congress, 2001–2002.* Washington, DC: American Enterprise Institute. 2002.

Owens, John R. "Economic Influences on Elections to the U.S. Congress." *Legislative Studies Quarterly* 9 (1984): 123–50.

Paletz, David. "The Neglected Context of Congressional Campaigns." *Polity* 3 (1971): 195–218.

Panagopoulos, Costas. *Congressional Challengers: Candidate Quality in U.S. Elections to Congress.* Philadelphia: Routledge. 2021.

Paolini, Philip. "Group-Salient Issues and Group Representation: Support for Women Candidates in the 1992 Senate Elections." *American Journal of Political Science* 39 (1995): 294–313.

Parker, Glenn R. "The Advantage of Incumbency in House Elections." *American Politics Quarterly* 8 (1980): 449–64.

———. "Interpreting Candidate Awareness in U.S. Congressional Elections." *Legislative Studies Quarterly* 6 (1981): 219–34.

———. *Homeward Bound: Explaining Changes in Congressional Behavior.* Pittsburgh, PA: University of Pittsburgh Press. 1986.

Parker, Glenn R., and Roger H. Davidson. "Why Do Americans Love Their Congressmen So Much More than Their Congress?" *Legislative Studies Quarterly* 4 (1979): 53–61.

Parker, Glenn R., and Suzanne L. Parker. "Correlates and Effects of Attention to District by U.S. House Members." *Legislative Studies Quarterly* 10 (1985): 223–42.

Payne, James L. "The Personal Electoral Advantage of House Incumbents, 1936–1976." *American Politics Quarterly* 8 (1980): 465–82.

Peters, John G., and Susan Welch. "The Effects of Charges of Corruption on Voting Behavior in Congressional Elections." *American Political Science Review* 74 (1980): 697–708.

Petrocik, John R., and Scott W. Desposato. "The Partisan Consequences of Majority-Minority Redistricting in the South, 1992 and 1994." *Journal of Politics* 60 (1998): 613–33.

———. "Incumbency and Short-Term Influences on Voters." *Political Research Quarterly* 57 (2004): 363–73.

Piereson, James E. "Presidential Popularity and Midterm Voting at Different Electoral Levels." *American Journal of Political Science* 19 (1975): 683–93.

Porter, Rachel, and Tyler S. Steelman. "No Experience Required: Early Donations and Amateur Candidate Success in Primary Elections." *Legislative Studies Quarterly* 47 (2022): https://doi.org/10.1111/lsq.12396

Powell, Lynda W. "Issue Representation in Congress." *Journal of Politics* 44 (1982): 658–78.

Prior, Marcus. "The Incumbent in the Living Room: The Rise of Television and the Incumbency Advantage in U.S. House Elections." *Journal of Politics* 68 (2006): 657–73.

Ragsdale, Lyn. "The Fiction of Congressional Elections as Presidential Events." *American Politics Quarterly* 8 (1980): 375–98.

———. "Incumbent Popularity, Challenger Invisibility, and Congressional Voters." *Legislative Studies Quarterly* 6 (1981): 201–18.

Ridout, Travis N., and Glen R. Smith. "Free Advertising: How the Media Amplify Campaign Messages." *Political Research Quarterly* 61 (2008): 598–608.

Robeck, Bruce W. "State Legislator Candidates for the U.S. House: Prospects for Success." *Legislative Studies Quarterly* 7 (1982): 507–14.

Robertson, Andrew W. "American Redistricting in the 1980s: The Effect on Midterm Elections." *Electoral Studies* 2 (1983): 113–29.

Romero, David W. "The Case of the Missing Reciprocal Influence: Incumbent Reputation and the Vote." *Journal of Politics* 58 (1996): 1198–207.

———. "Divisive Primaries and the House District Vote: A Pooled Analysis." *American Politics Research* 31 (2003): 178–90.

———. "The Prospects-Based Dynamics of the House Candidacy Decision." *American Politics Research* 32 (2004): 119–41.

Romero, David W., and Francine Sanders. "Loosened Partisan Attachments and Receptivity to Incumbent Behaviors: A Panel Analysis, 1972–1976." *Political Research Quarterly* 47 (1994): 177–92.

Romero, David W., and Stephen J. Stambough. "Personal Economic Well-Being and the Individual Vote for Congress: A Pooled Analysis, 1980–1990." *Political Research Quarterly* 49 (1996): 607–16.

Schantz, Harvey L. "Contested and Uncontested Primaries for the U.S. House." *Legislative Studies Quarterly* 5 (1980): 545–62.

Scheve, Kenneth, and Michael Tomz. "Electoral Surprise and the Midterm Loss in U.S. Congressional Elections." *British Journal of Political Science* 29 (1999): 507–21.

Schiller, Wendy J., and Charles Stewart III. *Electing the Senate: Indirect Democracy before the Seventeenth Amendment.* Princeton, NJ: Princeton University Press. 2014.

Schoenberger, Robert A. "Campaign Strategy and Party Loyalty: The Electoral Relevance of Candidate Decision Making in the 1964 Congressional Elections." *American Political Science Review* 63 (1969): 515–20.

Schuster, Steven Sprick. "Does Campaign Spending Affect Election Outcomes? New Evidence from Transaction-82(4) Level Disbursement Data." *The Journal of Politics* 82 (2020): 1502–15.

Segura, Gary M., and Stephen P. Nicholson. "Sequential Choices and Partisan Transitions in U.S. Senate Delegations, 1972–1988." *Journal of Politics* 57 (1995): 86–100.

Serra, George. "What's in It for Me? The Impact of Congressional Casework on Incumbent Evaluation." *American Politics Quarterly* 22 (1994): 403–20.

Serra, George, and Albert D. Cover. "The Electoral Consequences of Perquisite Use: The Casework Case." *Legislative Studies Quarterly* 17 (1992): 233–46.

Shields, Todd G., Robert K. Goidel, and Barry Tadlock. "The Net Impact of Media Exposure on Individual Voting Decisions in U.S. Senate and House Elections." *Legislative Studies Quarterly* 20 (1995): 415–30.

Simon, Dennis M., Charles W. Ostrom Jr., and Robin F. Marra. "The President, Referendum Voting, and Subnational Elections in the United States." *American Political Science Review* 85 (1991): 1177–92.

Sinclair, Barbara. "Agenda Control and Policy Success: Ronald Reagan and the 97th House." *Legislative Studies Quarterly* 10 (1985): 291–314.

———. "Washington Behavior and Home-State Reputation: The Impact of National Prominence on Senators' Visibility and Likability." *Legislative Studies Quarterly* 15 (1990): 475–94.

Sorauf, Frank J. *Money in American Elections.* Glenview, IL: Scott, Foresman. 1988.

Squire, Peverill. "Challengers in Senate Elections." *Legislative Studies Quarterly* 14 (1989): 531–47.

———. "Preemptive Fund-Raising and Challenger Profile in Senate Elections." *Journal of Politics* 53 (1991): 1150–64.

———. "Challenger Quality and Voting Behavior in U.S. Senate Elections." *Legislative Studies Quarterly* 17 (1992): 247–64.

Squire, Peverill, and Eric R. A. N. Smith. "Repeat Challengers in Congressional Elections." *American Politics Quarterly* 12 (1984): 51–70.

Steen, Jennifer A. *Self-Financed Candidates in Congressional Elections.* Ann Arbor: University of Michigan Press. 2006.

Stein, Robert, and Kenneth N. Bickers. "Congressional Elections and the Pork Barrel." *Journal of Politics* 56 (1994): 349–76.

Stewart, Charles III, and Mark Reynolds. "Television Markets and U.S. Senate Elections." *Legislative Studies Quarterly* 15 (1990): 495–524.

Stimson, James A., Michael B. MacKuen, and Robert S. Erikson. "Dynamic Representation." *American Political Science Review* 89 (1995): 543–65.

Stone, Walter J. "Measuring Constituency-Representative Linkages: Problems and Prospects." *Legislative Studies Quarterly* 4 (1979): 623–39.

———. "The Dynamics of Constituency: Electoral Control in the House." *American Politics Quarterly* 8 (1980): 399–424.

Stone, Walter J., Sarah A. Fulton, Cherie D. Maestas, and L. Sandy Maisel. "Incumbency Reconsidered: Prospects, Strategic Retirement, and Incumbent Quality in U.S. House Elections." *Journal of Politics* 72 (2010): 178–90.

Stone, Walter J., and L. Sandy Maisel. "The Not-So-Simple Calculus of Winning: Potential U.S. House Candidates' Nomination and General Election Prospects." *Journal of Politics* 65 (2003): 951–77.

Stone, Walter J., and Elizabeth N. Simas. "Candidate Valence and Ideological Positions in U.S. House Elections." *American Journal of Political Science* 54 (2010): 371–88.

Sulkin, Tracy. "Explaining Campaign Intensity." *American Politics Research* 29 (2001): 608–24.

———. *The Legislative Legacy of Congressional Campaigns.* New York: Cambridge University Press 2011.

Sulkin, Tracy, and Nathaniel Swigger. "Is There Truth in Advertising? Campaign Ad Images as Signals about Legislative Behavior." *Journal of Politics* 70 (2008): 232–44.

Sullivan, John L., and Eric M. Uslaner. "Congressional Behavior and Electoral Marginality." *American Journal of Political Science* 22 (1978): 536–53.

Swain, John W., Stephen A. Borrelli, and Brian C. Reed. "Partisan Consequences of the Post-1990 Redistricting for the U.S. House of Representatives." *Political Research Quarterly* 51 (1998): 945–67.

Tausanovitch, Chris, and Christopher Warshaw. "Does the Ideological Proximity between Congressional Candidates and Voters Affect Voting Decisions in Recent U.S. House Elections?" *Political Behavior* 40 (2018): 223–45.

Taylor, Andrew J., and Lowell W. Barrington. "The Personal and the Political in Repeat Congressional Candidacies." *Political Research Quarterly* 58 (2005): 599–605.

Thomas, Martin. "Election Proximity and Senatorial Roll Call Voting." *American Journal of Political Science* 29 (1985): 96–111.

Thomsen, Danielle, M. *Opting Out of Congress: Partisan Polarization and the Decline of Moderate Candidates.* New York: Cambridge University Press. 2017.

Thomsen, Danielle, and Aaron King. "Women's Representation and the Gendered Pipeline to Power." *American Political Science Review* 114 (2020): 989–1000.

Tufte, Edward R. "The Relationship between Seats and Votes in Two-Party Systems." *American Political Science Review* 67 (1973): 540–54.

———. "Determinants of the Outcomes of Midterm Congressional Elections." *American Political Science Review* 69 (1975): 812–26.

———. *Political Control of the Economy*. Princeton, NJ: Princeton University Press. 1978.

Uslaner, Eric. "Ain't Misbehavin': The Logic of Defensive Issue Strategies in Congressional Elections." *American Politics Quarterly* 9 (1981): 3–22.

Uslaner, Eric M., and M. Margaret Conway. "The Responsible Electorate: Watergate, the Economy, and Vote Choice in 1974." *American Political Science Review* 79 (1985): 788–803.

Utych, Stephen M. "Man Bites Blue Dog: Are Moderates Really More Electable than Ideologues?" *The Journal of Politics* 82 (2020): 392–96.

Waterman, Richard. "Comparing Senate and House Electoral Outcomes: The Exposure Thesis." *Legislative Studies Quarterly* 15 (1990): 99–114.

Weatherford, M. Stephen. "Economic Conditions and Electoral Outcomes: Class Differences in the Political Response to Recession." *American Journal of Political Science* 22 (1978): 917–38.

Welch, Susan, and John R. Hibbing. "The Effects of Charges of Corruption on Voting Behavior in Congressional Elections, 1982–1990." *Journal of Politics* 59 (1997): 226–39.

Westlye, Mark C. "Competitiveness of Senate Seats and Voting Behavior in Senate Elections." *American Journal of Political Science* 27 (1983): 253–83.

———. *Senate Elections and Campaign Intensity*. Baltimore: Johns Hopkins University Press. 1991.

Wilkins, Arjun. "Electoral Security of Members of the U.S. House, 1900–2006." *Legislative Studies Quarterly* 37 (2012): 277–304.

Wolfinger, Raymond E., and Steven J. Rosenstone. *Who Votes?* New Haven, CT: Yale University Press. 1980.

Wolfinger, Raymond E., Steven J. Rosenstone, and Richard A. McIntosh. "Presidential and Congressional Voters Compared." *American Politics Quarterly* 9 (1981): 245–55.

Wolpert, Robin M., and James G. Gimpel. "Information, Recall, and Accountability: The Electorate's Response to the Clarence Thomas Nomination." *Legislative Studies Quarterly* 22 (1997): 535–50.

Wright, Gerald C. Jr. *Electoral Choice in America*. Chapel Hill, NC: Institute for Research in Social Science. 1974.

———. "Constituency Response to Congressional Behavior: The Impact of the House Judiciary Committee Impeachment Votes." *Western Political Quarterly* 30 (1977): 401–10.

———. "Candidates' Policy Positions and Voting in U.S. Congressional Elections." *Legislative Studies Quarterly* 3 (1978): 445–64.

Wright, Gerald C., and Michael B. Berkman. "Candidates and Policy in U.S. Senate Elections." *American Political Science Review* 80 (1986): 567–88.

Index

★ ★ ★

About the Authors

★ ★ ★

JAMIE L. CARSON is the UGA Athletic Association Professor of Public and International Affairs II in the Department of Political Science at the University of Georgia. He received his PhD from Michigan State University in 2003, where he was a fellow in the Political Institutions and Public Choice Program. Carson's research interests include American politics with a specific emphasis on the US Congress, congressional elections, separation of powers, and American political development. His most recent books include *Nationalized Politics: Evaluating Electoral Politics Across Time* (with Joel Sievert and Ryan Williamson) and *Change and Continuity in the 2020 and 2022 Elections* (with John Aldrich, Brad Gomez, and Jennifer Merolla).

GARY C. JACOBSON is Distinguished Emeritus Professor of Political Science at the University of California San Diego. He received his PhD from Yale University in 1972 and has served on the Council of the American Political Science Association and on the Board of Overseers of National Election Studies. Jacobson's field of interest is American national politics, with a subfield focus on Congress and congressional elections, and his current research is on the electoral basis of partisan polarization in Congress. Among books he has authored or coauthored are *Money in Congressional Elections*, *The Electoral Origins of Divided Government*, and *The Logic of American Politics*.